Islam and Law in Lebanon

The modern state of Lebanon, created after the fall of the Ottoman Empire, is home to eighteen different officially recognised religious communities (or sects). Crucially, political office and representation came to be formally shared along confessional lines, and the privileges of power are distributed accordingly. One key prerogative is exclusivity when it comes to personal status laws: the family legal affairs of each community. In this book, Morgan Clarke offers an authoritative and dynamic account of how the sharia is invoked both within Lebanon's state legal system, as Muslim family law, and outside of it, as a framework for an Islamic life and society. By bringing together an in-depth analysis of Lebanon's state-sponsored sharia courts with a look at the wider world of religious instruction, this book highlights the breadth of the sharia and the complexity of the contexts within which it is embedded.

MORGAN CLARKE is Associate Professor of Social Anthropology at the University of Oxford and a fellow of Keble College. He previously held a Simon Fellowship at the University of Manchester and a British Academy Postdoctoral Fellowship at the University of Cambridge. He is the author of *Islam and New Kinship: Reproductive Technology and the Shariah in Lebanon* (2009) and many articles on the anthropology of Islam and the Middle East.

Islam and Law in Lebanon

Sharia within and without the State

Morgan Clarke
University of Oxford

CAMBRIDGE
UNIVERSITY PRESS

CAMBRIDGE
UNIVERSITY PRESS

University Printing House, Cambridge CB2 8BS, United Kingdom

One Liberty Plaza, 20th Floor, New York, NY 10006, USA

477 Williamstown Road, Port Melbourne, VIC 3207, Australia

314–321, 3rd Floor, Plot 3, Splendor Forum, Jasola District Centre, New Delhi – 110025, India

79 Anson Road, #06–04/06, Singapore 079906

Cambridge University Press is part of the University of Cambridge.

It furthers the University's mission by disseminating knowledge in the pursuit of education, learning, and research at the highest international levels of excellence.

www.cambridge.org
Information on this title: www.cambridge.org/9781107186316
DOI: 10.1017/9781316888957

First published 2018

Printed in the United Kingdom by Clays, St Ives plc

A catalogue record for this publication is available from the British Library.

Library of Congress Cataloging-in-Publication Data
Names: Clarke, Morgan, 1972– author.
Title: Islam and law in Lebanon : Sharia within and without the state / Morgan Clarke, University of Oxford.
Description: Cambridge, United Kingdom ; New York, NY, USA : Cambridge University Press, 2018. | Includes bibliographical references and index.
Identifiers: LCCN 2018012808| ISBN 9781107186316 (hardback) | ISBN 9781316637142 (paperback)
Subjects: LCSH: Law–Lebanon–Islamic influences. | Islamic law–Lebanon | BISAC: POLITICAL SCIENCE / Government / International.
Classification: LCC KMP46.7 .C58 2018 | DDC 349.5692–dc23
LC record available at https://lccn.loc.gov/2018012808

ISBN 978-1-107-18631-6 Hardback

To all those in Lebanon who helped make this book possible

Contents

Tables

Acknowledgements

I could not have written this book without the help of a great many people in Lebanon. The fieldwork I draw on took place mostly in 2007–2008, but I also depended upon enduring relationships made during my doctoral fieldwork in 2003–2004. It is a profound pleasure to be able finally to acknowledge these debts here.

Shaykh Muhammad Kana'an, the then president of the Sunni *mahakim shar'iyya*, gave me my first opportunity in 2003 to enter the world of the courts, and gave generously of his time subsequently. I owe him a great deal. In 2007–2008, my work in the Sunni courts took place during the presidency of Shaykh 'Abd al-Latif Daryan, and I am grateful to him for allowing me to conduct my research there. I am grateful for the same reason to Shaykh Hasan 'Awwad, president of the Ja'fari courts, who also kindly met with me. A number of judges granted me repeated access to their courts, in some cases over many years, and this book is owed in very large part to their great patience and generosity. Shaykh Hasan Marmar has been an exceptionally open and patient interlocutor since the very beginning and has taught me an incalculable amount. So too Shaykh Ahmad al-Kurdi, who welcomed me not only into his court, but also showed me other paths to understanding Islam. If I have not followed those paths to their ends, the fault is not his. Shaykh Zakaria Ghandour, Shaykh 'Ali Haydar, Shaykh 'Ali Mawla and Shaykh 'Abd al-Rahman al-Mughrabi all allowed me to sit in their courts for months on end in 2007–2008. Thank you to you all. Without your continued help and openness, I could not have written this book. Shaykh Humam al-Sha'ar was very generous with his insights and other materials. I sat with Shaykh Muhammad Dali-Baltah many times in 2003–2004; these experiences were formative. Civil court judge John al-Qazzi also allowed me to sit in his court and met with me several times. I am very grateful to them all. I must also thank Shaykh Muhammad Hasan al-Amin, Shaykh Muhammad 'Assaf, Shaykh Muhammad Kana'an (the Ja'fari consultant judge) and Shaykh 'Abd al- Halim Sharara for their time and insights, as well as Dr Ahmad Fawzi, inspector of the sharia courts. Aside from the judges,

I am also very grateful to the other sharia court personnel, the judges' assistants, scribes and others, in both the Sunni and Ja'fari courts. There are too many to name individually here, but I note my especial thanks to Shaykh Mustafa al-Ja'fari for also welcoming me into his Islamic Centre. And beyond the courts but within their ambit I must thank Dr Ahmad al-Faris and Shaykh Muhy al-Din Ba'yun.

Many lawyers also helped me. I cannot thank them all, but, for granting me their time and many other kindnesses, I am very grateful to Ustaz Ramiz al-Atat, Ustaz Basim Ghzayl, Dr 'Ali al-Homsi, Ustaz Muhammad al-Jawhari, Ustaz Musa Mnaymne and Professor Ibrahim Traboulsi. Most of all, I must record my overwhelming debt of gratitude to the late Professor Talal Khodari. His patience with my endless questions and his bottomless fund of legal knowledge were simply invaluable. It is of enormous regret to me that he passed away before he could see the realisation of the book that I promised for so long. I can only hope that in some small way it is worthy of what he might have expected. Thank you, Dr Talal. I miss you.

The courts are only half of my story, and I depended on the help of many others for understanding Islam in Lebanon beyond them. Ayatollah Fadlallah's offices have been exceptionally helpful throughout my researches and I must thank Sayyid 'Ali Fadlallah and Sayyid Ja'far Fadlallah, as well as Shaykh Husayn al-Khishn, for their time, patience and knowledge. Shaykh Muhsin 'Atwi, head of Ayatollah Fadlallah's *maktab shar'i*, was perhaps the first shaykh I ever met. His generosity to a bewildered doctoral student was exceptional, and crucial to all I have learned since: I have lost track of the number of hours of his time he has given subsequently. His door was always open to me. But he also opened a great many other doors to me besides, socially and intellectually. I will always be profoundly grateful to him for doing so. Thank you so much, Shaykh Muhsin. Hajj 'Ali Sammour was also unendingly patient in facilitating my access to the Ayatollah's world. Thank you, Hajj 'Ali. I would also like to thank Shaykh 'Ali Mir'i, Shafiq al-Musawi, Hani 'Abdallah, and all the other staff at the Ayatollah's offices. Mona Sukkariyya helped me in understanding Sayyid Fadlallah's impact beyond the Shi'i community. I also benefited from being able to visit the offices of Ayatollahs Sistani and Khamenei and must thank Hajj Hamid al-Khaffaf and Shaykh Muhammad Tawfiq al-Muqdad, respectively.

Shaykh 'Umar Jalloul has been an exceptionally engaging and generous interlocutor. I learned a huge amount from him and will always be grateful to him for that. Thank you, Shaykh 'Umar. I must also thank Shaykh Mahmud Khatib for his generosity and his time, as well as Shaykh Husam al-Ghali, Shaykh Amin al-Kurdi and Shaykh Maher Hammoud.

Last, but by no means least, I would also like to thank all those at the 'A'isha Bekkar mosque and the Naqshbandi-Qadari Centre, as well as Shaykh Muhammad al-Azhari and Shaykh Ahmad, and, with especial affection, Mustafa, his brother 'Ali and Shaykh Khalid al-Rifa'i and all his circle.

Finally, I also owe very special thanks to Laila Bassam and Nadim Ladki. Without their trust and help in need, I could not have seen this project through. Thank you so much to you both. And I owe the very greatest debt of all to Tom Perry, without whom much of this would have been impossible – and certainly much less fun. You have been the truest of friends.

The support of these people was simply invaluable. Without it, I could not have written this book. It is a great pleasure to acknowledge that here. No doubt they would not all agree with everything I have written. This is my account, not theirs. But I do hope that they will find it a respectful and rewarding one. I owe them everything, and it is thus to them that I dedicate this book.

I also depended on the support of many academic colleagues and institutions. The initial research and early stages of writing were conducted during a British Academy Postdoctoral Fellowship at the University of Cambridge, mentored by James Laidlaw, and a Simon Fellowship at the University of Manchester and I am very grateful to all concerned. Paul Dresch taught me anthropology and a lot more besides – I will be forever in his debt. I am also profoundly grateful to Michael Gilsenan for his peerless hospitality and for inviting me on numerous occasions to the Islamic Law and Society workshops that he convened at New York University, where I presented parts of this book. I owe a great many insights to the circle of scholars that Michael brought together there, too many to name all individually here, although I should acknowledge in particular the sustained encouragement of Jonathan Brown, Guy Burak, Brinkley Messick and Michael Peletz. Getting to know the work of James Baldwin was important at a crucial stage. The sections of this book bearing on Shi'i studies benefited hugely from discussions with colleagues met through the Hawza Project convened by Robert Gleave and later enabled by a Princeton–Oxford collaborative grant with Mirjam Künkler. Again, there are just too many people to name them all here, but thank you all so much for so many stimulating meetings and conversations. I presented portions of this work at various venues in Oxford and would like to thank Fernanda Pirie, Matthew Erie, Michael Feener and Talal al-'Azm especially. A sabbatical term was crucial: many thanks to my colleagues for that and especially Lambros Malafouris. Emanuel Schaeublin and Alex Henley both read several chapters and provided invaluable comments on them: I am very grateful indeed to them both for doing so. Samer El-Karanshawy was with me at the very beginnings of my research in Lebanon, invited me to fertile meetings in Doha, and went on to read and comment on the entirety of the book. Thank you so much Samer – it is very much appreciated. Thanks are also due to Samer Ghamroun and Moussa Abou Ramadan for helping fill some important gaps in my knowledge late in the day. Portions of Chapter 9 were previously published in *American Ethnologist*, as I gratefully acknowledge here. I would also like to thank Maria Marsh and all at Cambridge University Press.

In academia today, some speak (disparagingly) of the 'lone scholar' model. I hope the preceding acknowledgements go some way to showing that there is no such thing. But beyond those named above, I have – thankfully – not had to work alone. I have been able to count on the support of my wonderful wife Alex and the shared joys of our young son Louis and now, as I write these words, our daughter Lily, freshly arrived into this world. Thank you Alex. I must also thank my mother Joan for countless years of support. Some portions of the book were written while enjoying the hospitality of Alex's parents and I thank them too. I only wish that my father Michael and my brother Parry were alive to see it.

Note on Transliteration

I have used a standard, if much simplified, system for transliterating Arabic words in English. I have not used any diacritical marks, although I have marked *'ayn* and *hamza* using apostrophes and I have italicised all words coming from languages other than English. Where an English spelling has become commonplace, or accepted, then I use that without italics: for example, sharia. Non-specialists will hopefully thereby find the text more approachable; specialists should be able to work out the Arabic without too much difficulty. As for names of people and places, where there are commonly accepted English spellings, or where the people themselves have adopted a particular spelling, then I use that. Sometimes one has to make choices: I have preferred 'Quran' to 'Koran' or 'Qur'an', and 'Hizballah' to 'Hezbollah', for instance. I also use 'shaykh' rather than 'sheikh', as well as a derived adjective, 'shaykhly', a neologism meaning 'associated with shaykhs' on the lines of 'priestly'. Where I have referred to articles from the *Encyclopaedia of Islam*, I have done so explicitly in the footnotes rather than as a separate entry in the bibliography and I have used the conventional abbreviations: EI^2 for the second edition of the *Encyclopaedia of Islam* and EI^3 for the third edition.

Introduction

This book is an account of the social life of the sharia in Lebanon at the beginning of the twenty-first century. It draws on extensive and in-depth anthropological fieldwork in both Sunni and Shi'i Muslim settings, and seeks to describe and analyse the diverse modes and contexts in which different actors invoke the sharia, God's right path through life, as legalistically conceived within the Islamic tradition.[1] I turn from lessons in the mosque, to sessions in Lebanon's state-sponsored sharia (family law) courts, and on to the projects and institutions of one of the country's then most famous Islamic personalities, Ayatollah Muhammad Husayn Fadlallah (d. 2010). This breadth of scope seeks to capture something of the breadth of the sharia itself. It has been said that the sharia is a 'total' discourse, potentially addressing every aspect of life, even if, importantly, the sharia does not comprise the totality of Islam.[2] This book thus provides a sustained examination of what it means to take seriously a transcendent normative ideal, as a model for one's own life and as a model for the lives of others.

While often glossed as 'Islamic law', the sharia can be seen as providing not just legal, but also ethical precepts, as well as defining correct worship. Given that the content of those precepts is a matter of interpretation and debate, I thus prefer to talk of 'sharia discourse':[3] the mass of texts, conversations and institutions focused on the divine sharia. There are many excellent academic studies of the employment of such sharia discourse as law for the settlement of disputes in a wide range of historical contexts, very often based on court records. An important strand of this work has been interested in comparing the classical Islamic legal tradition with law in the West. Contemporary instances of sharia as state

[1] This is my own attempt at glossing the sharia, hopefully not too far from either Muslim or current academic understanding.

[2] Messick 1993: 3; Reinhart 1994: 8 and Hallaq 2009: 1–6. For trenchant comments on the dangers of a 'legal supremacist' view that takes sharia discourse as central to and definitive of Islam more generally, see Ahmed 2015.

[3] A term I derive from Messick (1993: 3).

law have, however, an ambivalent status. Sometimes taken as representative of the tradition, they are also often seen as distinct due to the ruptures of colonial and indigenous modernity. These contemporary instances generally take the form of the use of sharia discourse as family law within a larger, more or less secular legal system, as is the case in Lebanon. There is thus a rich literature on Muslim family law, which understandably focuses on issues of gender and reform and has more obviously pragmatic implications. For reasons I come to, Lebanon has not been so thoroughly studied as other countries in this regard, and it is one aim of this book to help address that. Among other things, I give an account of how marriage, divorce and other family legal issues are treated in the Lebanese Sunni and Shiʿi sharia courts.[4] Another equally fascinating body of work, much of it by anthropologists, has examined Muslim piety and ethical practice in what is sometimes styled as 'everyday life' beyond the courts. This literature is not always interested in sharia per se, but the sharia provides a hugely important resource for Muslims seeking to lead a virtuous life and it is this aspect of sharia-minded practice that I am thinking of here as ethical.

These literatures are to a large extent separate. In this book, by contrast, I have tried to consider sharia as both ethics and law, and further, the relations between the two.[5] While a study of Lebanon's sharia courts lies at the centre of the book, I also explore the ways in which the sharia is invoked outside the courts, in the mosque and in the offices of religious authorities whose legalistic ethical interventions shape virtuous Muslim practice. I thus bring together different sorts of ethnographic material as well as different sets of theoretical concerns. My overall aim in doing so is both to make a substantial and novel contribution to the study of Islam, family law and the communitarian state in Lebanon and, more ambitiously, to address larger themes about the nature of the sharia more generally. More than that, as an anthropologist, I think my findings and ideas relevant to still more general conversations about the human condition, in particular the relationship between transcendental values – 'religious' or otherwise – and social practice.

Academic understanding of Islam has made genuine advances over the last century and more. Recent work, sensitive to the possible pernicious effects of Western depictions of Islam, has stressed the flexibility and

[4] For those who do look to this book for a guide to Muslim family law in Lebanon, I should stress, as I explain later in this Introduction, that my fieldwork mainly took place in 2007–2008 and there have been some important developments since.

[5] I am not the only person to do so. See e.g. Asad 2003: 202–256 and Agrama 2012, as well as Hallaq 2013.

progressive nature of Islamic discourse, in contrast with an alleged previous caricature of the Islamic tradition as static and conservative. This is important. But it is obvious that Islamic actors and discourse can in fact be both, sometimes rigid and unsympathetic, sometimes open-minded and flexible. How that can be so – a question not so often asked – is a key concern of this book. Instead of the sharia's flexibility, I thus like to think (loosely) in terms of what biologists call plasticity. Characteristics will be expressed differently in different environments. Some environments tend to express the sharia's flexibility, while others tend to harden it. In Lebanon, non-state, 'ethical' uses of the sharia are more likely to favour the former, I contend, and state legal ones the latter. This is therefore an ecological approach to the sharia, one with which an anthropologist, used to field study, can be happy.

However, I do correspondingly still hold that environment is not all: the sharia does have its own distinctive qualities which favour characteristic forms of expression. That is, there are some things that are crucial to it, without which it would surely be implausible to claim of something that it is genuinely of the sharia.[6] One such necessary characteristic, to my mind, is the divinity of the sharia's ultimate source: it is God's law, and thus in theory perfect. However, human attempts to understand and apply this perfect law are necessarily flawed, to a greater and lesser extent. The human science of Islamic legal studies, *fiqh*, is thereby often distinguished from its object, the divine sharia. And consequently there is an intrinsic tension between the divine ideal and its mundane instantiation whose consequences I trace through this book.[7]

This tension can be expressed in many forms and leads to others. My central organising theme is the contrast between the employment of sharia discourse within the state and outside it. This comes to me from my fieldwork: only certain portions of the sharia are applied as family law in Lebanon with the backing of the executive arms of the state; only a limited set of Lebanon's Islamic religious professionals are employed to do so. There are many who invoke the sharia in contexts outside those sanctioned by the state, and the contrast between working for the state or the state-backed official religious establishment and working independently of it is one that I found frequently discussed. Whether or not to work for the potentially unjust ruler is a long-standing dilemma in the

[6] To say so, I would argue, is not the same as to identify one particular instance of sharia practice as its essence – to essentialise it, in other words.

[7] This is what Johansen (1999) refers to as the 'contingency' of *fiqh*. On the distinction between *fiqh* and sharia see also Vikør 2005: 2–3. Some might see any claim as to something intrinsic to sharia-ness as challengeable, but I think this one relatively uncontroversial.

Islamic tradition; our contemporary environment of nation states poses the question in its own way.[8] It also provides a characteristically modern way of imagining an alternative, a putative 'Islamic state' that would in some way instead form an integrated and legitimate whole.

The tension between state and non-state does not, however, map simply onto the distinction between 'law' and 'ethics' that I have just invoked and that now needs further comment. In the modern Western tradition, now globalised in the form of the nation state, one does indeed think broadly of law as the domain of actionable norms subject to the tribunals and sanctions of the state, and ethics as the domain of personal and inter-personal norms beyond. These are the senses in which I rather loosely employ the terms in this book, and which do make sense in the context of modern Lebanon. But while this monopolisation of law by the state may be axiomatic for Western 'bourgeois legality', it is not necessarily so for other traditions, including the sharia, which gives ultimate legal sovereignty instead to God.[9] One can, for example, marry and divorce to God's satisfaction independently of the state. A key and related distinction made by the Muslim actors I worked with is thus between 'sharia' (*al-shar'*) and 'law' (*qanun*), by which they mean human-made state law. A form of law other than that of the state is not only imaginable, but readily available in sharia discourse. It can be acted upon without, even contrary to, the sanction of the state, as we will see.[10] This does not preclude the possibility that sharia discourse might itself be employed as state law, nor indeed that the sharia itself contains distinctions between different sorts of norms, ones that could be glossed as 'legal' and 'ethical' in meaningful ways. But such differentiation does not turn on the notion of the state in the same manner.[11] When I talk of law and ethics here, then, I do so in a correspondingly open-ended way, as a

8 See e.g. Vikør 2005: v and passim.

9 On 'bourgeois legality' see Fitzpatrick 1984, a reference I owe to Strathern 1985. On the broader point see Dresch 2012.

10 We can thus think in terms of 'legal pluralism', both in colonial and postcolonial Lebanon and related contemporary contexts, but also in the pre-modern Muslim world. The notion of legal pluralism has generated a considerable literature, and some working on Islam and the Middle East find it helpful (see e.g. Dupret et al. 1999; Shahar 2008, 2015; Tillier 2015 and Baldwin 2017). Having noted the plurality, however, I have largely gone my own way in analysing it.

11 Putting aside the broad distinction between matters of worship (*'ibadat*) and social transactions (*mu'amalat*), the Islamic legal tradition also differentiates between matters of inner conscience, which only God can judge, and those of outward behaviour, which are available to human judgement. See Johansen 1999; Peters and Bearman 2014 and Chapter 10 of this book.

means to expand the scope of my research into the uses of sharia discourse, rather than in a rigid or doctrinaire fashion.[12]

The distinction I heard drawn between divine sharia and human law also has its echoes in others. Through the book, I trace a ramifying series of other such binaries, many valorisations of different approaches to legal practice: flexible versus wooden; easy versus strict; humanity versus bureaucracy. In putting such contrasts and tensions at the centre of my account, I not only follow the lead of my informants, but I also foreground the dynamism that ensues. Dissatisfaction at imperfect practice of the sharia leads to attempts (not always successful) to do otherwise, which are in their turn subject to critique, in what one could see as a dialectical process.[13] I thereby seek to avoid a static depiction of sharia discourse, seen by recent academic scholarship as pejorative. However, I do so not merely by privileging examples of the sort of change and flexibility that appears attractive to a Western liberal audience. In short, I aim to provide an analysis of sharia discourse that is realistic as well as genuinely dynamic, one that I hope will resonate with similar such studies in other contexts. In the rest of this introduction, I start by expanding on these themes, before explaining more of the distinctively Lebanese context of my project and the nature of my sources.

Understanding the Sharia

To the best of my knowledge, no comparable study exists for the case of Lebanon, although there is obviously no shortage of discussion of the sharia more generally. Even restricting oneself to academic works in English – and there is no good reason why one should – one is faced with a vast literature. That literature, in one way or another, explicitly or implicitly, is written in response to a wider, non-Muslim, mostly 'Western' preoccupation with Islam and the sharia. Translated into academic terms, that amounts to a set of stock concerns, largely negative in polarity. Is religion, and *a fortiori* Islam, fundamentally non-modern? If so, how does one explain its enduring and currently highly visible power and popularity? Otherwise put, are Islam and the sharia distinctively 'other', essentially and irreconcilably different from the modern liberal

12 I take this to be the most problematic aspect of the analytical lens of 'legal pluralism': the seemingly irresolvable debates about what makes something 'legal' or otherwise. See e.g. Roberts 1998.

13 More in the spirit of Weber, or a micro-historical version of Marshall Hodgson's (1974: 79ff.) notion of Islamic history as a dialogical process perhaps, than Ernest Gellner's (1981) rather different dialectical account of 'Muslim society' after Ibn Khaldun. Again, see also Vikør 2005: v.

tradition (or, in vulgar terms, 'Western values')? Is Islam intrinsically and irredeemably patriarchal, for instance?[14] Can we see the sharia – so often glossed as 'Islamic law' – as law proper? If so, what might 'sharia law' look like? As 'religious law', is it based on fundamentally irrational principles? Is its (Western) reputation for harshness and arbitrariness deserved? Further, is there indeed, as the cliché goes, no distinction between religion and politics in Islam? Does the sharia amount to a totalising vision that seeks to govern every domain of life and allows no rival? And is that vision one trapped in an idealised past of religious nostalgia?

In keeping with the spirit of postcolonial times generally, and in response to the prejudice and indeed organised violence meted out to Muslims by Western liberal democracies more particularly, much of this literature takes an apologetic stance towards such suspicious interrogations. Islam and the sharia are fundamentally misunderstood. For one thing, one would want to emphasise the diversity of positions and practices across the world's more than one billion Muslims. Further, the pragmatism, openness and flexibility of sharia discourse are stressed. Despite the uncommon, horrific exceptions, one can put aside largely unrealistic fantasies of judicial stonings and amputations, which actually require improbably demanding burdens of proof.[15] And while much of the prolific field of studies of gender in Islamic contexts is critical in tone – and for good reasons – much also highlights the possibilities within the tradition for women to further their interests, and indeed also the receptivity of the largely male body of Islamic legal scholars to such projects and their ability to respond to the challenges of mundane life and its changing circumstances more generally.[16]

Again, recent scholarship on these and other issues often seeks to distance itself from an earlier 'Orientalist' literature that allegedly thought of the Islamic tradition as, on the contrary, static, rigid, hidebound and stuck in the past.[17] Rather, the sharia can 'keep up with the times', as I heard it put in Lebanon. This keeping pace with change is, in the academic literature, largely thought of as taking place through the exertions of the mufti, the Islamic legal scholar who produces fatwas, or

[14] It has of course been extensively argued that liberal modernity is itself intrinsically patriarchal.

[15] See e.g. Peters 2005.

[16] The field of Islam and gender is too vast to cite comprehensively here. But on both counts one could cite the work of Ziba Mir-Hosseini (1993, 2000), for instance. For a historical account in such a vein, see Tucker 1998.

[17] Whether fairly or unfairly, the scholars most frequently cited here are Snouck Hurgronje, Joseph Schacht and Noel Coulson.

ethical-legal opinions, in response to the questions and dilemmas of the Muslims of his (or, rarely, her) time. Such deliberations extend even to the most super-modern of ethical challenges such as cloning, in vitro fertilisation or sex-change operations, on which the 'open-mindedness' of such scholars often surprises, but are also less sensationally seen as underpinning the historical evolution of the corpus of Islamic law more broadly.[18]

In parallel with this emphasis on the flexibility of the sharia, there has also developed another, seemingly opposing theme that is rooted more in the study of 'sharia courts' and responds to a different strand of criticism of the sharia; its 'irrationality' in legal terms. Here one is faced with an almost proverbial trope of the Islamic judge's arbitrary and unfettered discretion: 'Qadi-justice', in the phrase now rather unfortunately associated with Max Weber's wide-ranging comparative investigations. A considerable literature has arisen in response to this accusation of excessive flexibility.[19] On the contrary, it is argued, sharia discourse forms (or at least formed) a coherent and predictable legal system where the judge rules according to a settled array of principles and standards and within a set of firmly established institutions that can be seen to include judicial review and courts of equity.[20] In response to the nominal 'totality' of the sharia, which overflows the bounds of what the liberal tradition denotes as law, one strand of writing thus wishes to recuperate and recognise its strictly legal part.[21]

It is important to see, then, that the sharia could and no doubt has underpinned a workable, organic legal system, worthy of respect as such. But another body of work wants to remind us that this is still not the same sort of legal system as that of the modern nation state – and indeed, some would say, all the better for it. One thinks here especially of the work of Wael Hallaq, perhaps the most prominent of contemporary academic scholars of the sharia. For Hallaq, modern nation-state rule comes from above and can thus only be realized through surveillance, discipline and punishment, not to say violence. The nation state is the creature of the post-Enlightenment tradition, a ruinous power-knowledge complex oriented towards domination and destruction, of the natural world and

[18] On the work of the mufti see Masud et al. 1996. For the super-modern examples see e.g. Clarke 2009. For the centrality of the mufti to the evolution of the Islamic legal tradition in response to changing times more generally, see Hallaq 1994 and Gerber 1998, among many others. For a critical response to this strand of literature see Calder 2010 (and Gleave's (2010) introduction to it).

[19] I discuss 'qadi-justice' at greater length below, but key references here would include Rosen 1989; Gerber 1994 and Powers 1994.

[20] On the latter points see Powers 1992.

[21] See Johansen 1999.

the human world, as in the horrors of European colonialism. Historical societies subject to Islamic law, by contrast, were largely self-governing, because the sharia constituted a non-state legal system rooted in the morality and concerns of the communities from which it sprang. Sharia was independently formulated by Islamic legal scholars and practitioners in response to popular need, and not codified and imposed by a state legislature and executive until the onset of 'modernization'. The institutions that animated this admirable grass roots, morally infused legal system were then systematically destroyed under colonial rule.[22]

Hallaq's particular, polemical expression of this position aside, the notion that the advent of modernity constitutes a historical rupture for Muslim societies and their sharia-oriented institutions is a well-established one. In Brinkley Messick's characterisation, the 'calligraphic' mode of textual domination typical of sharia-oriented society stands for the personal and open nature of sharia authority: given its transcendental, divine source, the sharia is in theory available for continuous reinterpretation by any qualified scholar and fully knowable only by God. In the resonant phrase of the Ottoman modernisers who sought to fashion a European-style code out of Islamic legal materials, sharia discourse has thus become a vast 'ocean without shores'. Contrast, however, the impersonality of the printed text of the modes of bureaucratic domination typical of modernity: set at the centre by the state, law is restricted, standardised and reproducible.[23]

And yet the notion of rupture would seem to entail the inevitable consequence that 'sharia proper' has to be regarded as something pre-, or at least non-, modern. At the present juncture, subsequent to modernization and secularization, with the educational and other institutional and moral structures that nourished the Islamic legal tradition destroyed, there can be no return to the sharia. In Hallaq's words, it is left 'in tatters'. And thus, he argues, despite the delusions of modern Islamists, current claims to Islamic Republics and Islamic States are anachronistic and doomed to failure.[24] 'The Islamic [nation] state' (*al-dawla al-islamiyya*) is a modernist fantasy.[25] By extension, those institutions that currently claim some connection to the sharia, not least the 'sharia courts' that are effectively restricted to family law across much of the Middle East, would be 'sharia' in name only.

[22] Hallaq 2004, 2009: 357–550, 2013. [23] Messick 1993: 54 and passim.
[24] Hallaq 2009: 429, 500, 549–550, 2013. On the Iranian Islamic Republic see e.g. Zubaida 1993.
[25] On the modernity of the use of the Arabic term *dawla* for 'the state', let alone the construction *dawla islamiyya* ('Islamic state'), see Hallaq 2013: 62–63, 190nn145–146.

To take up my own particular example, Lebanon's contemporary sharia courts would seem a case in point, taking their place as they do alongside other religious personal status tribunals within a civil republic founded in the twentieth century, one of the many nation states carved out of the ruins of the Ottoman Empire by the 'Great Powers'. The actual systematicity of pre-modern sharia discourse and sharia-minded polities might be worth debating.[26] But I certainly agree that one does not find much structural coherence in the social life of the sharia in present-day Lebanon: the activities of scholars generating Islamic legal discourse outside the courts seem largely disconnected from the activities within them, for example. Where I perhaps differ is in thinking that this does not render contemporary sharia discourse and the personalities who employ it necessarily inauthentic to a true, now deceased tradition, even if many of the religious professionals I worked with had an equally bleak view of Islam's current predicament.[27] As an anthropologist, working with people in person, one is in an immediate sense obliged to take one's subjects seriously, to assume the sincerity of those who seek today to live a life oriented towards the sharia, even if in doing so they move through a fragmented landscape of authority. In any case, even if a tradition has been fragmented, it does not make it any the less worth studying.[28] But I also wonder whether some sort of incoherence, between ideal and practice at least, is not inevitable for any transcendental tradition.[29]

There are good reasons to think that mass literacy, education and media have transformed the relationship between individual believer and their religion.[30] Another approach thus talks instead of Muslim modernities – different visions of what it is to be modern from the hegemonic Western version.[31] Some of the impulse to do so stems no doubt from the normative character of modernity. To be non-modern is, for moderns, to be in some sense inadequate. A sympathetic account thus insists on the recognition of co-evalness. But one should nevertheless remember that the critique of modernity has an eminently respectable genealogy in the hegemonic West too. It should not be inconceivable to sympathetic analysts that part of the appeal of sharia discourse might in fact lie in its non-, or anti-modernity, even if the theme needs careful handling.

[26] See e.g. Calder 2010. [27] Contra Hallaq, see also e.g. March 2015.

[28] As Anand Pandian (2008) has argued, with reference to India but in conversation with MacIntyre's (1981) notion of the fragmentation of the Western moral tradition in the wake of the Enlightenment.

[29] See also Laidlaw 2014: 126–137, 154.

[30] See e.g. Eickelman 1992 and Starrett 1998.

[31] See especially Deeb 2006, but also e.g. Bernal 1994 and Brenner 1996.

A different response might be to abandon particularism altogether. The focus on sharia in the legal history of the Middle East has arguably led not only to a relative lack of interest in much else of obvious importance – Ottoman Sultanic law (*qanun*), for instance, or 'custom' (*'urf*) – but has also hindered a proper comparative discussion that can place historical Muslim contexts alongside those of Europe, say, rather than seeing them as radically other.[32] To take this approach would also be to argue against the Orientalist tradition, but not through an 'Orientalism in reverse' that preserves an Occident/Orient dichotomy while reversing the moral judgements associated with it.[33] So too the particularism that the discourse of modernity and its ruptures implies. While I do find modernity more than a term of normative judgement and imagine that no one would dispute that there have been dramatic changes in Middle Eastern cultures and societies in the last few hundred years, I also agree that we need to keep continuities in mind, in time and space.[34] Tension and disconnection between sharia-minded institutions is not, I would imagine, a function of modernity per se; it surely could be found before. But there is in any case no necessity (in academic discussion at least) for any particular historical instance of the sharia tradition to stand for the paradigmatic version of it, nor any compulsion to take up such an essentialised version as a model of difference from other essentialised legal, ethical and political traditions. In sum, I accept the particularities of the contemporary Lebanese context, but would find it harder to accept that they render my findings irrelevant to broader discussions about Islamic and other legal history.

Anthropological Approaches

To turn to my own discipline, the anthropological contribution to the study of Islam has largely been seen as a matter of capturing real-life practice as opposed to mere theory and doctrine. We thus now have a set of excellent ethnographies of sharia courts to set alongside the burgeoning historical literature.[35] It has nevertheless become commonplace after Talal Asad's hugely influential proposition that Islam be seen as a

[32] See e.g. Shalakany 2008. Mallat (2007) develops instead the more capacious notion of 'Middle Eastern law'.

[33] Al-Azm 1981.

[34] For the same point in deeper historical perspective, see Baldwin 2017: 55–56.

[35] Many are referred to below, but for the ethnographies see e.g. Rosen 1989; Messick 1993; Mir-Hosseini 1993; Hirsch 1998; Peletz 2002; Bowen 2003 and Stiles 2009. For the historical accounts see e.g. the references made in Masud et al. 2006: 3–4 and Agmon and Shahar 2008 – more have of course followed since.

'discursive tradition', one constituted around – if not reducible to – a set of debated texts, that anthropologists pay attention to the ways in which practice and discourse are related, in different ways in different places of course.[36] And since the pioneering work of Brinkley Messick, close attention to the production and consumption of Islamic legal texts has become indispensable for those with pretensions to produce 'sharia ethnography'.[37]

More recently there has been a flow of ideas from anthropology that have concentrated more on the personal ethical dimensions of the Islamic tradition, also stemming in part from the work of Talal Asad and those influenced by him, most prominently Saba Mahmood.[38] This work can be seen as part of an emergent new anthropology of ethics, inspired on the one hand by the virtue ethics of Alasdair MacIntyre (whose notion of tradition underpins Asad's notion of Islam as a discursive tradition) and on the other by the later writings of Michel Foucault on what he called 'the care of the self'.[39] From this perspective, the ethical field is not reducible to a set of norms: it includes the broader projects of the self to which those norms are related, the development of one's capacities for virtue and excellence. Thus, Mahmood rethinks the rise of highly visible, public Islamic commitment, symbolised above all by mass adoption by Muslim women of 'the veil' (i.e. modest dress, *hijab*), not in terms of oppression, false-consciousness, resistance to Western domination or expediency, but by taking seriously the reasons given by the Egyptian Muslim women with whom she works – their desire to become good Muslims.[40] Students of the sharia also need to take this anthropological work seriously. It is arguable that, consequent to the rupture of modernisation and legal and other institutional secularisation, the sharia has come to have greater vitality in the form of such personal ethics than as state law.[41]

There is a tension here. Ethical visions of personal virtue can in some ways remain more idealistic, and thus 'purer', than legal ones applied in state bureaucratic settings. They can also more easily preserve plurality. The institutionalisation of sharia discourse tends to restrict the

36 Asad 1986. See also Bowen 2012.

37 Messick 1993, 2008. Messick's new book (2017) will no doubt prove equally formational, although I have not had time to take it into account here.

38 Asad 1993, 2003; Mahmood 2005. See also Hirschkind 2006 and Agrama 2010a.

39 See Laidlaw 2014 for a helpful overview of this body of work.

40 Mahmood 2005.

41 Messick 1996. In such ethical contexts, the sharia thus serves as what Foucault called a 'technology of the self', one of the prime resources Muslims have to shape virtuous selves. While I agree that we need to understand ethics in general as more than just a 'code of conduct', I have also argued that the fact that the sharia does indeed take legalistic form has consequences for such uses (Clarke 2015).

possibilities for conversation as to its contents, a situation which can seem unsatisfactory by contrast. In an attempt to capture something of the compulsion of this tension and others, and in keeping with this recent anthropological focus on projects of the virtuous self, in this book I look not just at the different discourses on the sharia produced in different domains, but also at the people who generate, impart and apply them. My main interlocutors in this research were Islamic religious professionals, or shaykhs. As an organisational motif, my account of sharia discourse in Lebanon is framed in part as one of the sharia as a vocation – a story of those who live for the sharia, as well as off it, as Max Weber might have put it.[42] Cross-cutting the book's broader division between uses of the sharia within the state and outside it, I also present a narrative of the sharia as career. I move from a depiction at the beginning of the book of a young shaykh who serves as a mosque imam and judge's assistant before moving in the central chapters to the post to which he aspires, that of judge in the sharia courts, and finally ending with a figure at the summit of a scholarly career, an independent religious-legal authority who has his own network of offices, charitable institutions and staff. In each case, I argue, an understanding of the ethos expected of an Islamic religious professional helps us better to understand the dynamics of the different settings within which they find themselves working.

This focus on Islamic professionals admittedly privileges a particular perspective on my subject, that of a specialist group of 'religious virtuosi' who have put Islam and the sharia at the centre of their lives.[43] There has been some criticism of recent anthropological work on Islam on precisely these grounds: such total ethical projects are at odds with the great majority of Muslim experience, which, it is argued, is by contrast incoherent, messy and fallible.[44] Put another way, my research is devoted to an elite view, to the neglect of that of the ordinary person. While one might question the privileged nature of the status of many religious professionals in Lebanon, I have absolutely no doubt that my work would have been much enhanced by a closer attention to the paths 'ordinary Muslims' take through the institutions I describe. That point taken, one might also say that one would not want to ignore the fallibility of the virtuoso either. A theme that came through repeatedly in my research was an interest in the extent to which a religious professional was committed to their role, actually inhabiting it totally as a vocation, as opposed

42 Weber 2004 [1919]: 40, on the political life.

43 Of course, one scholar's 'religious virtuoso' is another's 'popular preacher'. Cf. Berkey 2001: 7.

44 Schielke 2009, 2010.

to viewing it just 'as a job'. Maintaining the coherence of one's actions and commitments – in short, one's integrity – is a challenge even, perhaps especially, for the religious virtuoso. That one might take different paths in response to such challenges is a major proposition of this book.

In invoking the term 'vocation' I do not mean anything too specific, and certainly not to draw any precise analogy with the distinctive history of the Calvinist notions of vocation that so fascinated Weber.[45] The term is not intended to bear too much theoretical weight. But the notion of a calling, from God, is clearly apt, and suggests something of the compulsion to these ethical commitments.[46] It entails the 'spiritual discipline' and virtuous self-formation that have been a central focus in much recent scholarship in the anthropology of Islam and of ethics more generally, as I have just described. But it also responds to a criticism of that scholarship, in that it invokes the world of work, and thus allows me to reconnect these individual projects to broader social dynamics in a way that previous literature has been thought not to.

Weber found what he saw as the peculiar tensions of the Puritan ethic as generative of a distinctive energy, an energy that led to Western capitalism and modernity. He also put tension and dilemma at the centre of his two late, great essays on vocation under modernity. Setting aside Weber's incomplete understanding of the Islamic tradition, again, I too see a dynamism resulting from the tensions of taking the ideal sharia as one's vocation.[47] To take the ideal vision seriously is to try to realise it, as embodied virtue or as legal order. But to try to implement an ideal is in some sense inevitably to fail and create the impetus for further action. These tensions, in my argument, thus drive a dialectical unfolding of biography, as well as history. Some judges in the sharia courts, for instance, dissatisfied with the version of sharia applied there, feel impelled to attempt reform; others associated with the courts leave them for a life of contemplative scholarship; some even set up independent tribunals. By working in the mosque as well as the court, I try to bring the anthropological study of law and ethics closer together. By thinking in

45 One can argue that 'vocation' is an innovation of the Reformation, and, in the sense Weber is interested in, most notably in *The Protestant Ethic* (Weber 2001 [1904–1905]), of Calvinism in particular. Nevertheless, the notions of ascetic 'domination of self' in the pursuit of integrated ethical activity that this idea of vocation depends on were prefigured in Catholic monasticism and can also be discerned in other traditions, including Islam (Goldman 1988: 13, 19, 35–49 and Schluchter 1999: 68–85; see also Peters 1999).

46 See Owen and Strong 2004: xiii, and also Mittermaier 2012.

47 Goldman 1988: 3–4, 27–35, 49 and Weber 2004 [1917, 1919]; on Weber on Islam, Turner 1974 and Huff and Schluchter 1999; on Islam, ethical tension and dynamism, Peters 1999: 212–213 and Schluchter 1999: 72–81.

terms of vocation and career, I resituate interest in the virtuous self within wider society and historical process.

The Lebanese Context

Lebanon of course constitutes a particular context for such a study. Despite its Middle Eastern setting, it can hardly be thought of as a 'Muslim society'. A civil republic, it is home to eighteen officially recognised different religious communities, or 'sects' (*tawa'if*, sing. *ta'ifa*), Christian, Jewish and Muslim. Under late Ottoman rule, Mount Lebanon had already acquired a distinctive mode of political accommodation constituted around what were in some senses new and modern notions of religious identity.[48] This privileging of religious identity in the political sphere was entrenched in the new state of Lebanon under French Mandate rule and after independence, despite – in some ways because of – the subsequent, widely acknowledged and frequently realised danger of political conflict taking sectarian form, most notoriously during the 1975–1990 civil war. Crucially, political office and representation came to be formally shared along confessional lines; and each official religious community was granted extensive legal prerogatives and autonomies vis-à-vis the state. Religious communities can thus be seen as 'established' in a distinctive way in Lebanon.

One key such prerogative is more or less exclusive jurisdiction over the personal status, that is, family legal affairs of the community's members. Such is the centrality of this mode of community organisation that one can think in terms of a set of 'legally imagined communities'.[49] As one of a number of institutional instantiations of official community, there is thus a multiplicity of different 'religious courts' (*mahakim diniyya*), including provision for members of Lebanon's five official Muslim communities: Sunni, Twelver Shi'i, Druze, Isma'ili and 'Alawi. Here I focus on the 'sharia courts' (*mahakim shar'iyya*), which have their roots in Ottoman antecedent institutions, now subdivided into Sunni and Ja'fari (i.e. Twelver Shi'i) court systems. Lebanon's Druze and 'Alawi communities have their own independent, smaller *madhhab* court systems, which I did not study (Isma'ilis are to have recourse to the Ja'fari courts). Parts of the sharia, variously interpreted, are thus applied as state law in Lebanon, as in these (Hanafi) Sunni and Ja'fari sharia courts; and Muslim religious professionals, shaykhs, serve as judges in them.

48 Makdisi 2000.

49 An obvious play on Benedict Anderson's (1983) account of nationalism as 'imagined community'.

While there are ongoing attempts, individual and organised, to make it otherwise, broadly speaking one still cannot opt out of the religious family law court system, and Lebanese citizens are in this respect defined as members of a religious tradition regardless of their commitment to it. There is, as yet (at the time of writing), no civil Lebanese law of personal status, despite several attempts to introduce one. The religious courts are thus a special focus for critique of Lebanon's communitarian political settlement on the part of secularists and civil society activists (and some religious actors too, let it be said).

While one does not wish to exaggerate the place of religion within Lebanese public and private life, consonant with the sharia's comprehensive address and transcendent status, the Islamic tradition also of course has an important social life outside the state-sponsored sharia courts – within the country's mosques and pious Muslim communities, in Islamic scholarly intellectual life, and in the discourse of political figures with Islamic repertoires, styles and resources. Islamic religious specialists, alongside the religious professionals of Lebanon's other religious communities, play a notable role in the public and political life of the country, whether as representatives and functionaries of the official religious communities bound in to the country's political and legal system, or as oppositional figures. 'Political Islam' has been a prominent phenomenon in the nation's modern political life, most importantly in recent times in the form of the Lebanese Hizballah. In the context of a notoriously weak state, such non-state actors may themselves take on some of the functions it claims, as in the adjudication of family and marital disputes, as we will see.

In investigating these complex relations between state and non-state actors and institutions, I also probe the relationship between sharia discourse and various notions of civility. Civility has come to be associated with the secular.[50] But the still current Lebanese political accommodation rests on a different vision of civility, one constituted by a respectful acknowledgement of 'the Other' as adherent of a different religious tradition. Such respect – not always maintained, to be sure – is a convention of public and political discourse; separate religious jurisdictions over family law, and the absence to date of a common civil law of personal status, are crucial to its institutionalisation, as are the autonomous institutions of 'official' religious community that might elsewhere be considered as an important part of 'civil society'. Civilised life,

[50] Although civility's genealogy includes distinctions between religion and irreligion (Fitzgerald 2007).

according to this vision, requires the moral substance of religious tradition rather than the free-for-all of amoral Western atheism.

It is often said of Lebanon that it is 'complicated', more so, it is implied, than other places. It is on the contrary no more complicated than Britain, say. It has 'remarkable religious diversity': but so does Manhattan. The difference is that this vision of Lebanese civility, and by extension due academic diligence, demands respectful acknowledgement of all. Lebanon is small enough to allow the ambition of a comprehensive study. It is also contested enough to make a study that denies that ambition in some sense politically incorrect. Just to focus on Islam (and just two of the five Muslim communities!) is to raise hackles. I should thus stress that my presentation, while hopefully illuminating for students of Lebanon, is not to be understood as standing for the country as a whole. In terms of Lebanese politics and society, this is a partial analysis, which pertains in limited ways to only two of Lebanon's eighteen official religious communities and their relationships with the wider Lebanese polity. I am certainly not claiming that an understanding of 'Islam' is sufficient, nor even perhaps necessary, for an understanding of family law in Lebanon, let alone the rest of life. But my care to cover both Sunni and Shi'i visions within my treatment of Islamic discourse – surprisingly rare I find – is of a piece with this impulse towards inclusivity.

This vision of civility as mutual respect between religiously defined communities is, while dominant, heavily contested in Lebanon, and rivalled by that of the modern nation of formally identical citizens equal before one common law upheld by a strong secular state. (And so my project of describing Islam in Lebanon again looks potentially dubious, if from a different angle.) In this context, 'civil' (*madani*) is clearly opposed to 'religious' (*dini*), as it is in the official classification of different legal jurisdictions. My use of the term civility thus does not map onto the current use of the term 'civil' (*madani*) in Lebanon.[51] It is a broader term of comparative analysis, one that can be stretched to include relations between men and women as well as between members of different religious and ideological communities.[52] We should also bear in mind

[51] On which see Abisaab and Abisaab 2014: xxxi–xxxii.

[52] The notion that different models and modes of civility and civil society may apply in different contexts is an established one (see e.g. Hann and Dunn 1996; Pye 1999), even though prevailing conceptions clearly centre on liberal democratic notions. Ernest Gellner, for instance, thought the Muslim Middle East profoundly uncivil (1991; 1994: 14). Against that, see e.g. Antoun 2000 and the papers collected in Norton 1995 and 1996. Edward Shils, doyen of civility studies, wrote an early essay on 'the prospect for Lebanese civility' (1966). Of course, as we know, things did not turn out well. My use of civility here is not blind to its fragile nature in Lebanon. See Khalaf 2002.

a further rival ideal of polity, that of the 'Islamic state' (*al-dawla al-islamiyya*). Not always clearly defined, this notion has much rhetorical currency in contemporary Muslim circles, but little prospect of realisation in multi-confessional Lebanon, notwithstanding the fears occasioned in many quarters by Hizballah's rise and ties to the Islamic Republic of Iran. I heard it frequently invoked by the Islamic actors I studied, Sunni and Shi'i, but in what I took to be more a vague and utopian sense than in reference to a definite political project.[53]

In keeping with my interest in bridging the personal ethical and the social political, I note in passing that civility can be seen as a virtue.[54] One's reflexes when faced with others are conditioned by such learned dispositions. 'Political correctness' in Lebanon first and foremost entails erasing confessional signifiers as much as possible from public speech. To ask someone straight out, 'are you Sunni or Shi'i?' for instance, would be in poor taste, even if those in the know can quickly find out with a few well-judged indirect questions. And when one does refer to religious community in public discourse, one should do so in idealised mode: 'our brothers the Christians ...' Such delicacy is demanded in public life, even if sometimes violated for political effect, but comes easily to most. Having been imbued with such sensibilities, I was shocked by the casually and repellently sectarian discourse of a religious specialist in another country in the region. Of course, one does not wish to seem naïve. Lebanon's 1975–1990 civil war is a paradigmatic case of civility's tragic failure. And at the time of writing, the tensions continue, amid the almost unbearable pressures of the disastrous situation in the region. But one can only hope that there are resources here for resilience too.

The Fieldwork

I started research in Lebanon in 2003 and 2004, working towards my first book, on Islamic medical ethics. I met then many of those who would become enduring and much-appreciated colleagues and had the opportunity to attend a number of sharia court sessions as part of an effort to gain a clearer picture of Islamic law in action. After a brief visit in 2006, I returned to Lebanon in 2007 (three months) and 2008 (a particularly rich six months) to work towards a new project, this time focusing on the courts. This latter fieldwork provided the bulk of the

[53] And certainly not in reference to the Islamic State of Iraq and the Levant that emerged subsequent to my fieldwork and constitutes the West's current quintessential image of Muslim incivility.

[54] See e.g. Calhoun 2000.

material I present here, and so, when I use the present tense, 2007–2008 is the context I have in mind. I also visited Lebanon briefly subsequently in 2009 and have kept abreast with events since by other means. There was a major reform in 2011 to the law applied in the Sunni sharia courts which, formally at least, constitutes a substantial change to the situation that I describe. I have not been able fully to assess its effects, although I do make reference to it at the appropriate junctures. But my account is thus already in this sense a historical one, and that should be kept in mind by those readers most interested in the current legal situation

One key fieldsite was the Sunni court complex at Jami' Imam 'Ali in West Beirut, home to the supreme appeals court and several initial courts. I had attended a number of sessions at the appeals court in 2004; in 2007–2008 I focused on the initial courts, regularly attending sessions with three judges. I continued work from 2004 with a Shi'i initial court judge in the suburbs of Beirut and forged new ties with two more Shi'i initial court judges with whom I regularly attended sessions, one in the suburb of Harat Hrayk, the other in the Ja'fari court complex in Ra's Beirut, home to the supreme Ja'fari appeals court, which I also attended occasionally. In 2004 I had spent many days at the Sunni courts in Sidon; in 2007–2008 I restricted my research to Beirut. Besides attending formal sessions, at all these locations I had opportunities to gain a grasp of the wider operations of the courts, and to interview a number of other key figures as well as court functionaries. In total, in 2007–2008, I was in court 80 days over 8 months attending something in the order of 500 case sessions (*jalsat*), including marriage contracts. In my accounts of those legal proceedings, I do not name the particular judges with whom I was sitting, as part of a wider anonymisation of my sources throughout, except in the few cases of truly public figures.

In terms of the formalities of my access to the courts, the law that governs sharia court procedure stipulates that court proceedings are public, despite the intimate nature of the matters discussed.[55] The judges I worked with thus felt that it was entirely proper that I be allowed to attend – indeed they would, they said (not wholly seriously, I imagine), be powerless to prevent me. I could also take notes, with the proviso that I preserve the anonymity of the parties involved, which I have done, as I also have with the unpublished and published discussions of cases on the part of lawyers and jurists that I have had access to. So too the archives remained closed to me, 'to protect the secrets of the people'.

[55] Section 171 of the Law of Sharia Courts (Zayn 2003a: 68). Cf. Agrama 2012: 99–100, 131–132, 137 on the different way this was constructed for his similar fieldwork in Egyptian courts.

It would not have been feasible to obtain informed consent from the continuous stream of people moving through the court offices, but I trust that my anonymisation of all parties mitigates any concerns in this regard, and I should stress again that I was attending with the judges' permission and under their supervision.

I would usually position myself in one of the black, leather-look easy chairs that line judges' offices in a discreet corner with a good view of proceedings, near enough to catch all that was said, taking notes almost continuously. I would, I suppose, generally be taken for a lawyer or court functionary, although a judge would never hesitate to clarify my position where necessary, and I was well known to court regulars. Very rarely I might get roped into things, appealed to mistakenly by a petitioner, or perhaps some English might need translating, or a point of information clarified, although this was never more than on the most informal basis. When the court's official business was over, or slack, my presence might offer an occasion for some sport, political or theological debate with the shaykhs that could be watched with amusement by the court staff. And at the end of the day's sessions I could usually sit and chat to the judge for a while, discussing the cases and clarifying points as required. Besides sitting with the judges themselves, I also sat with their assistants and other more or less junior shaykhs manning the desks in the outer offices, the first line of approach for parties seeking to bring cases, which gave me ample opportunity to see the more prosaic aspects of the court's proceedings, the bureaucratic hurdles that have to be overcome, as well as the more personal contact with the parties and their problems on the part of judges and functionaries that meetings outside the formal sessions allow.

Although Islamic discourse and practice were my focus, my research in the courts included another very important constituency, the lawyers who practise in them, who are trained in the civil legal tradition. I worked closely with several, as well as interviewing and sitting with a prominent civil court judge. This gave me a very different outlook from that of the religious specialists. However, as already noted, I struggled to incorporate the perspectives of the parties to the cases themselves, whose affairs both the judges and the lawyers deemed private and thus out of bounds. I also found it very difficult to follow individual legal cases throughout their development, as the sessions in which they were heard could be months apart and frequently rescheduled.[56] And a large

[56] That has a bearing also on the perspective I present here on Lebanon's 'legal pluralism'. What from the religious professionals' point of view look like questions of ontology (God's law versus human law) might, from that of parties to cases, look more like questions of utility ('forum shopping').

proportion involved residents of different countries – an estimated more than ten million Lebanese live outside the country, as to some four and a half million within.[57]

As I have explained, however, I did not work in the courts alone. I followed judges and other court workers outside the courts, when invited to their homes or the mosques where they served as imam, for instance. One of the Sunni judges I sat with regularly was head of a Sufi circle and he invited me to their sessions, which led to invitations to others. I have described that material more fully elsewhere.[58] I also became involved in the religious life of Sunni Beirut more widely, regularly attending celebrations (*mawlid*s), Friday sermons and religious lessons in various mosques, and even receiving limited instruction in Quranic recitation. Most especially, I was a regular attendee at the lessons given by a young shaykh and mosque imam to whom I became particularly close, very often visiting him at the family home as well as at the mosque and at the courts, where he also worked as assistant to an important judge.

Although I enjoyed good relations with the Ja'fari court judges I worked with, and indeed their hospitality in several cases, I did not manage to establish a similar continuity with everyday religious practice within the Shi'i community. But my interest in Islamic law took me to the offices of major Shi'i religious authorities, the 'sources of emulation' (*maraji'* [sing. *marja'*] *al-taqlid*) or 'Grand Ayatollahs' – in this case Ayatollahs 'Ali al-Sistani of Iraq, 'Ali al-Khamenei of Iran and Lebanon's own Ayatollah Muhammad Husayn Fadlallah. The former are all represented in these branch offices by 'agents' or 'representatives' (*wukala'*, sing. *wakil*). Ayatollah Fadlallah, however, resided in Beirut. I had interviewed him and members of his staff in 2004 for my work on Islamic bioethics and formed enduring contacts. In 2007–2008, I had the opportunity of frequent visits to his offices, especially his fatwa or consultation office (*maktab al-istifta'at*), but also his 'court' (*maktab al-qada'*), radio station, library and other institutions in Beirut's southern suburbs. I also interviewed a number of other religious personalities close to him, in particular two of his sons, Sayyid 'Ali and Sayyid Ja'far, and one of his leading students Shaykh Husayn al-Khishn. I was a frequent attendee of

57 Demography in Lebanon is a notoriously sensitive subject. I draw on a range of widely available sources, but clearly such figures are highly approximate. See e.g. Faour 2007. Lebanon now also hosts more than a million refugees from the turmoil in Syria. I have seen lower estimates for the diaspora; much depends no doubt on how one defines it, but we can surely safely reckon on millions. On Lebanon's own history of migration see e.g. Hourani and Shehadi 1992 and Khater 2001.

58 Clarke 2014.

his Friday sermons and prayers in the grand mosque of the Two Right Imams (*Jami' al-Imamayn al-Hasanayn*). Given the political situation, these were exceptionally generous opportunities to understand more of Shi'i religious life, albeit particular ones and ones not necessarily comparable with those I had in Sunni circles.

I worked mainly in Arabic, but also in English with a handful of sources. I took notes by hand in the field and wrote up more comprehensive accounts at the end of the day. I tape-recorded one interview with a controversial shaykh (who insisted on taking my photo with his mobile phone, clearly for 'security' purposes), but otherwise found it more discreet not to do so. Following proceedings in court was more demanding, given the volume and intensity of conversations being conducted, and the different registers and dialects spoken. But I could check with the judges and other functionaries that I had got things more or less right. I stand by the accuracy of my material, although I am not complacent about the difficulties here.

I also gathered large quantities of written and audiovisual material: religious broadcasts, published monographs, journals, newspapers, fliers, legal case notes and judgements given to me by lawyers and by judges. Despite the breadth of this data, this is far from a comprehensive account. Fieldwork felt fractured, on the one hand by the tense political situation (see below), and on the other by the nature of working with urban professionals. Beirut is not London or Cairo, but it must be home to well over a million people and suffers from often appalling traffic congestion. My fieldsites were scattered across a large area, mainly split between West Beirut and the southern suburbs, and I spent a good proportion of most days travelling. The people I worked with have offices, with office hours and busy schedules. An independent authority might be generous enough to grant me an hour of his time, even once a week every week, but to ask for more would be to impose. The law courts, on the other hand, provide an excellent opportunity to sit and watch over a prolonged and extended period, although judges do not hold sessions every day. So I cultivated as many relationships as I could, and built up a weekly routine that maximized my contact time without (I hope) being unduly irritating. There is, however, no doubt an element of serendipity to the array of encounters that I ended up with and they certainly do not form a coherent whole.

The most important line of division within this mass of contacts was between Sunni and Shi'i religious specialists. This is not necessarily a matter of communitarianism. The two have largely different educational trajectories oriented towards different centres of prestige: Egypt or Syria versus Iraq or Iran, for instance. Even in professional life, opportunities for them to meet are not as many as one might imagine. Lawyers of different communities do know each other, having trained together, and frequently collaborate in inter-jurisdictional cases. But with regard to the religious courts, they also each have their own distinct circuits: Sunni lawyers practise in Sunni courts; Shi'i lawyers in the Ja'fari ones. My work in Sunni and Shi'i contexts was thus in many ways largely distinct. More problematically, the sort of work I was able to undertake in each differed. I give a great deal of room to Sayyid Fadlallah as an example of a legal thinker, for instance, with no Sunni equivalent. I have quite intimate portraits of Sunni shaykhs, especially younger ones, with no Shi'i equivalent. Given the current, poisonous nature of sectarianism in the region, I had and have no wish to make artificial divisions between the two traditions, but prefer rather to take them together, making sure of course to clarify any substantive particularities. But, all in all, I did not find the underlying issues in the two sets of contexts so very different. That might be seen as one key finding of my research.

The Political Situation

Some comment is required on the political circumstances in which this fieldwork was undertaken. 2007 and 2008 were times of particular tension, as well as economic hardship, subsequent to the disastrous war with Israel in 2006 precipitated by the kidnapping of two Israeli soldiers by Hizballah personnel. The consequences of Rafiq Hariri's assassination in 2005 and the subsequent 'Cedar Revolution' and Syrian withdrawal were still working themselves out, with the two opposing political blocs of that time (named after landmark political rallies) remaining at loggerheads: March 8 – the pro-Syrian bloc headed by Hizballah, then the opposition (*al-mu'arada*); and March 14 – the anti-Syrian bloc led by Hariri's son Sa'd, now leader of his 'Future Movement' (*Tayyar al-mustaqbal*), in government.[59]

This was not a starkly sectarian divide, although Sunni-Shi'i tensions were a regrettably prominent feature of it. The lines of division had political substance, bound up with questions as to the direction Lebanon should take: between a free-market, 'independent' (from Syrian and Iranian interference) orientation, allied to Saudi Arabia and other Western-allied Arab governments, versus a more socially redistributive economic vision, seeing independence as from Western interference and Israeli rather than Syrian aggression, and as best guaranteed by the

[59] See e.g. Blanford 2006; Mermier and Picard 2007 and Young 2010.

continued military strength of the 'national resistance movement' – that is, Hizballah. Lebanon's dire economic situation and class tensions, with food and petrol prices skyrocketing and frequent power shortages, were thus also at stake.

A series of car-bomb assassinations of leading anti-Syrian figures from 2005 to 2008 seemed most obviously linked to the burning issue of Lebanese co-operation with the United Nations investigation into the killing of Hariri. Government was paralysed, downtown Beirut occupied by March 8 demonstrators in a sit-in that crippled the capital's traffic and luxury commerce. Tensions between opposition and government supporters erupted into sporadic violence. Scenes of public disorder, tires set on fire to block traffic and cars vandalized, became common. The army was now routinely stationed on the streets to preserve order. And then, in May and June 2007, a series of car bombs in areas associated with tourism coincided with a bloody battle between the Lebanese army and the 'al-Qaeda linked' Fatah al-Islam group in Tripoli's Nahr al-Barid Palestinian refugee camp to add to Lebanon's woes and destroy the prospects for the lucrative summer tourist season.[60]

The end of pro-Syrian president Emile Lahoud's term in December 2007 left the presidency empty as the two factions could not agree on a successor. Talk of 'civil war' was in the air, and many people living in mixed areas felt under pressure to move. The anniversary of Hariri's assassination in February 2008, to be marked by a rally in Beirut's central Martyrs' Square, became a potential flash-point, intensified by the assassination in Damascus the day before of Hizballah's military commander, 'Imad Mughniyya, commonly attributed to Israeli secret services. In a piece of gunboat diplomacy reminiscent of the worst days of the 1975–1990 civil war, the American destroyer USS *Cole* was stationed off the coast, 'to safeguard the stability of Lebanon'.

In May 2008, in an inexplicably aggressive move, the government called for the dissolution of Hizballah's security infrastructure, in particular its private, self-contained telephone network. This was a red line for Hizballah, worried that the US was trying to cut their lines of communication, and heavy fighting started across Beirut. Rocket-propelled grenades were being deployed in the streets as well as automatic assault weapons, and the events were of a scale to attract global media attention. By the next day, however, it appeared that Hizballah's victory was complete, Beirut under their control, and the government's decision was revoked. The country's political leaders flew to Qatar for talks and a

[60] Rougier 2015: 124–170.

deal, the Doha agreement, was eventually stuck. The way was clear to elect an agreed presidential candidate and then a national unity government. A free party in downtown Beirut with performances by famous Lebanese pop stars was held to celebrate. This marked the end of this particular cycle of conflict, although the structural problems, political tensions and sporadic violence would continue, exacerbated by the revelation of Hizballah's alleged involvement in Hariri's assassination, and the truly catastrophic tragedy of civil war in Syria, its overwhelming refugee crisis and the spilling over of sectarian jihadism from across its borders.

These, then, were the events of the period of the main fieldwork on which this book was based. Clearly, it was a very tense, and occasionally very violent, time. At the trivial level of my research, this of course had an impact. Movement around and outside Beirut was occasionally severely curtailed, and frequently delayed. Sometimes one could hardly discuss anything else. However, it would not do to exaggerate these problems. Lebanese people are, sadly, well used to such tensions and normal life continued for the vast majority of the period.[61] The machinations of the political classes were treated with much cynicism by almost all I had contact with. One does not wish to dwell on violence, sectarian tension and political failure, and they are not the concern of this book. But if I concentrate instead on other matters, it is not through a wilful ignoring of the political realities. It is in keeping with the impressive resilience of Lebanese society, to that point at least. Very much pertinent to my focus on family law, however, was the uniformly grim economic situation. In addition to the consequences of the 2006 war and the ruin of the tourist industry, global economic trends had also led to painful inflation in fuel and food prices. Power cuts were a daily occurrence. The consequences for family life were sadly clear to see in the courts.

The Structure of This Book

The book is divided into three parts, the first setting the scene in terms of Lebanon's communitarian legal structure and what it means to be an Islamic religious professional working within it. Chapter 1 sketches the history of Lebanon's sharia courts and presents the tissue of laws that currently govern them. Here I take a broadly formalist approach, largely confining myself to a review of the relevant legislation. Much of the material will be familiar to specialists, although I hope that its

[61] See Hermez 2012.

compilation here is useful. Chapter 2 considers the often uncomfortable implications of this legal structure for what I am broadly calling 'civility', the ways in which people with different commitments can live together in one polity. Chapter 3 then introduces my depiction of the sharia as vocation by examining the career path of a young Sunni shaykh and his work as a mosque imam. We learn something of what it means to be considered a 'real shaykh' who lives for the role rather than just occupying it 'as a job'. One important requirement is to share one's learning with others, and Chapter 4 examines the weekly lessons that he gives in the mosque and the place of sharia discourse within them.

Part II of the book is devoted to the sharia courts and thus sharia discourse within the ambit of the state. Chapter 5 introduces the courts and the tensions they present as a hybrid institution: a domain of the sharia, staffed in part by religious professionals; but also part of the state bureaucracy, bound by civil law. This tension between sharia and law takes substantive form in the difference between what I call the 'God's eye view' of the sharia, concerned with good conscience and the afterlife, and the state perspective on the law, which pursues accountability in this world through bureaucratic governmentality. These points are illustrated in Chapter 6 through an examination of marriage contracts performed in the Shi'i courts. Formally speaking, in Islamic thought marriage need not concern the state at all, nor does it require a shaykh to preside. But in Lebanon marriages must be registered with the state, and can only be performed by an authorised religious professional. The sharia courts thus attempt to monopolise both the God's eye and state's perspective on marriage, in a knot of religious and state legal authority that sometimes seems in danger of unravelling.

Chapters 7 and 8 explore in more detail this tension between the idealised sharia and bureaucratic law by examining the processes and dynamics of the cases before the courts. The necessity of organised procedure for the running of a bureaucracy entails its own rhythm and frustrations. While noting that these dynamics are largely shared between both Sunni and Shi'i court systems, in Chapter 8 I exemplify them through the contentious topic of judicial divorce (*tafriq*) in the Sunni courts. Where most previous studies of sharia courts have concentrated on 'interesting' cases, here I show how the vast majority are 'boring', ground out over months of sessions and reams of paperwork. Most end in an agreed settlement (*sulh*) rather than a ruling (*hukm*). While one might expect that it would be in the latter, the intellectual construction of a legal argument, that a judge would display their prowess, it is in fact in the former, in personal engagement with the people before them, that the shaykhly judge can more often show their craft. Sharia-mindedness is here exemplified through an ethical stance rather than discursive citation practices.

In Chapter 9, I turn to what thus emerges as a dilemma for the shaykhs who work as judges in the courts: the need to obey the rules, mostly of procedure, can frustrate the virtuous impulse to manifest justice and pedagogical engagement. This bears on the well-worn theme of *qadi*-justice, the alleged excessive discretion of the Islamic judge. I see the temptation to exercise discretion as common to other legal systems, and the ability to do so as dependent on variable historical circumstance rather than Islamic particularity. The judges see these tensions as a function of the hybrid system within which they work, a compromise between the sharia and the civil law. 'If only there were an Islamic state', some say, then things would be different. I differ, again by resituating the discussion away from Islamic particularism. Procedure is a requirement of any legal system in practice, just like the tension between general rules and the impulse to justice in individual cases. Given the divine sharia's heavily idealised status, however, where court practice seems unsatisfactory, it is either civil law or the fallible human judge that tends to receive the blame.

In Chapter 10, I further develop the point by considering the example of certain forms of divorce within the Sunni courts (notably, divorce in anger and 'triple divorce'), where a mufti can be consulted as an out of court source of non-binding guidance for the conscience. Given the plurality of sharia discourse, as well as this non-adversarial and less bureaucratic setting, the opinions available may be 'easier' and the interaction more satisfying than in the courts, unattractive in comparison. In Chapter 11, I go on to examine some of the directions in which those associated with the courts can be impelled by these pressures. I take up first the example of a 'reformist' Sunni judge, whose progressive but unorthodox rulings are continuously overturned by the Supreme Court, and then that of a rebel Sunni shaykh who marries and divorces people on an independent and 'easier' basis.

That leads into Part III, devoted to the work of the autonomous author-jurist,[62] free to forge his own, independent vision of the sharia outside the state. Having begun with a young mosque imam and then considered the role of judge, in Chapter 12 I sketch the career of someone who reached the pinnacle of the shaykhly profession, Muhammad Husayn Fadlallah, one of the few claimants outside the traditional scholarly centres of Iran and Iraq to the distinctively Shi'i status of *marja'*, or

[62] To invoke a typology employed by Wael Hallaq (2001).

authoritative 'source' of sharia discourse. In an echo of the themes of Chapter 3 but on a grander scale, I show the importance for his reputation of committed social and political engagement, as well as scholarly credentials built with the aid of a circle of dedicated students. Due to his political prominence, Fadallah has been much studied and not all of this material will be new to specialists, but I rehearse it here in service of the larger argument.

In Chapter 13, I go on to examine in more detail how Fadlallah and his staff developed a 'contemporary' form of sharia discourse in a bottom-up response to popular need. Individual instances of ethical guidance led to more generalised formulations of opinion, assembled into comprehensive handbooks and disseminated through an array of institutions, including a fatwa office and sophisticated website. In Chapter 14, I end by considering the impact that this vision of the sharia had on the world of the courts, focusing in particular on the example of judicial divorce without the husband's consent. This is an exceptionally difficult case to win in the official tribunals, but Fadlallah had his own 'judicial office', where he ruled according to his own standards, arguably more favourable to wives. But his rulings had no official consequence, spurned by the state-sponsored Shi'i tribunals, which rejected his scholarly credentials. Fadlallah's sharia-legal project thus remained one of conscience rather than law, autonomous but not self-sufficient. We see the weight and gravitational pull that, despite its frustrations, implication with the state provides by contrast.

Finally, a brief conclusion sums up the overall argument of the book and links it to the wider debates over the relationship between Islam, the sharia and the modern state. The sharia's idealised status and legalistic form has made it an icon of what an authentic Islamic state practice might look like. But everday legal practice is rarely so satisfying. Lebanon is not an Islamic state. But it does have sharia courts where sharia precepts are employed as family law. Here, where the legal process seems unsatisfactory, the civil laws of court procedure can take the blame. In a putative, utopian 'Islamic state', things would be better, it is said. Some commentators think such an Islamic state an impossibility; some governments claim it as a reality. But whatever the case, the sharia's transcendental source means that there will always be multiple human interpretations of what the divine law should be, and thus always the possibility (however slim) of principled critique of any given instantiation of it. In the face of the reality of administration, the perfection of any state cannot but be up for review. Sharia discourse can thus work both for the state and against it.

Part I

Contextualising Sharia Discourse in Lebanon

1 Court, Community and State

A Legal Genealogy

This book is concerned with the relationship between Islam and law in Lebanon. As in many other Middle Eastern and postcolonial Islamic contexts, the primary domain within which Islam is directly involved in the law of the land is that of family law. In Lebanon this involvement takes a particular form, whereby jurisdiction over family, or 'personal status' law is delegated by the state to a defined set of eighteen different officially recognised Muslim and Christian religious communities or 'sects' (*tawa'if*, sing. *ta'ifa*), known indeed in Lebanese law as 'communities of personal status' (and also including the now insignificant Jewish community).[1] These powers over personal status law are thus fundamental to the very identity of these communities, although the latter have a far wider political significance, being bound up with the allocation of parliamentary seats and state offices, high and low.

At the level of public discourse, this political confessionalism that links religious and political identities and roles is well established, but intensely controversial, as undermining national unity and promoting sectarian tension. At the individual level, the undoubted fact that far from everyone wants to be defined as a member of a religious community, let alone be legally subject to their powers in matters of the family,

[1] The ubiquitous use of the no doubt originally French term 'personal status' (*statut personnel*) to describe family law here and in the wider region, generally rendered in Arabic in the plural form *ahwal shakhsiyya* ('personal statuses'), deserves some comment in passing. It has been commonly remarked that this usage is recent, stemming from colonial involvement. As a way of marking a distinct domain of law within the sharia it is foreign to the classical tradition, where the contract of marriage and family rights and duties find their place within the larger domain of 'transactions' (*mu'amalat*, as opposed to *'ibadat*, 'acts of worship'). But also, matters of 'personal statuses' are here often construed in a manner far broader than the personal status of individuals strictly defined, which is to say as single, married, divorced or widowed. This usage thus looks peculiar from a European perspective as well. See e.g. Nasir 2002: 34; Asad 2003: 230–231; Weiss 2010: 31, 123 and White 2011: 163–166; Mahmood 2016: 117. It would seem that there is perhaps also in operation some conflation, not to say confusion, with the notion of personal, as opposed to territorial, law (Mahmood 2016: 121).

also makes these legal and institutional arrangements fundamentally contested. Importantly, however, these religious affiliations are not the only legally imagined forms of community in Lebanon. Over and above religious community, Lebanon itself is legally conceived as a unified nation state and civil republic. These religious communitarian and nationalist civil republican visions are, while formally integrated, in perpetual tension. And these official visions hardly exhaust the possibilities. The sharia itself, for example, provides ways of imagining other polities, not least the notion of an 'Islamic state', a threatening if unlikely prospect in Lebanon's fragile plural context.

The identification of family law with religious tradition, notwithstanding far-reaching secularisation elsewhere in a legal system, is far from unique to Lebanon. It is common to much of the Middle East and the wider Muslim world, hence the considerable comparative literature on 'Muslim family law'. An older body of work assumed that the continuing legal applicability of the sharia to the domestic domain, but little else, could be seen as a survival from a bygone era. The sharia's tenacity in this last remaining field had then to be attributed to some sort of core status for family legal precepts within the Islamic tradition, as the most essential and sacrosanct part of the religious law.[2] This is implausible: Talal Asad has influentially argued that, on the contrary, this nominal core status for family law is in fact a function of modernity and the secularising process, colonial and indigenous. Secularisation entails a separation between domains of public concern, subject to state secular law, and those of private concern, domains of morality and religion. Indeed, the very notion of 'religion' as a distinct sphere of life is arguably modern, a necessary feature of the secularity defined in opposition to it. Under this schema, the family is the quintessential private domain; its moral and legal regulation is thus delegated to the patriarchal male and religious authority.[3]

Asad's chief example is Egypt. Given its distinctive confessional political accommodation, Lebanon is often seen as different. Certainly, the lines between state authority, religious authority and patriarchal authority are not drawn there in the same places as in Egypt. But here too it is the drawing up of those lines that could be seen as most clearly at stake, rather than the careful tending of some flickering spiritual flame. This would be to follow an important strand of revisionist historiography of Lebanon, which argues that Lebanon's 'culture of sectarianism' is a

[2] For examples, see Mahmood 2016: 116.
[3] Asad 2003: 205–256. See also Agrama 2012 and Mahmood 2016.

feature of its modern history rather than an atavistic hangover from its past.[4] The consequence is to acknowledge that Lebanon too is a product of the secular age, its political form based on a separation between state law and religious autonomy, to which jurisdiction over the family is crucial. That is the case even if that separation is constituted in particular, 'confessional' ways that make calling Lebanon in its current form a 'secular' polity implausible.

Amid the burgeoning literature on contemporary Muslim family law, however, Lebanon's sharia courts and personal status laws have received relatively little attention. Lebanon is treated in a number of the standard surveys, but such treatments are in certain important respects incomplete.[5] This relative lack of attention may be due in part to the complexity, which is to say plurality, of Lebanon's family legal system, or perhaps a perception that Lebanon, with its important Christian communities and cosmopolitan image, is not the right place to look for Muslim law or sharia courts. For another thing, in large part due to the autonomy given to Lebanon's religious communities under its communitarian legal and political system and the sensitivities involved in any adjustments to it, the codification and reform of Muslim family law found across most of the Islamic world has until recently been comparatively limited with regard to Lebanon's Sunni and Twelver Shi'i sharia courts (but not to the same extent in the case of the Druze and Christian courts).[6] This has long made it relatively hard to identify what the applied law is from a textual survey alone. We are thus faced with a rather different situation from that in much of the rest of the region, where more comprehensive and progressive modern codifications of the sharia are firmly in place, in many cases now into their 'third phase' of reform according to leading scholar Lynn Welchman, who observes that academic commentary 'can scarcely keep pace with events'.[7] Lebanon's Muslim family law has perhaps long seemed uneventful in comparison. More recently (2011–2012), there have been some important developments with regard to the Sunni courts, which I discuss below. These, however, came after the period of my fieldwork.

[4] See especially Makdisi 2000, but also e.g. Weiss 2010 and Henley 2013.

[5] See e.g. Mahmood 1972, 1987; El-Alami and Hinchliffe 1996; An-Na'im 2002 and Nasir 2002. Lebanon finds no mention in two relatively recent review articles of the field (Hirsch 2006; Agmon and Shahar 2008), and only passing mention in Welchman (2007) and Tucker's (2008b) synthetic works, for instance. But note the important exception constituted by Tarabey's (2013) account of the Druze courts.

[6] An-Na'im (2002: 128) refers to areas governed by 'classical law'.

[7] Welchman 2007: 40, 42–43 and passim. In Welchman's list of recent legislative initiatives around the region, none are associated with Lebanon.

Of course this is not to suggest that Lebanon's is (or was, until 2011) in any sense a 'pure', 'traditional' or 'unreformed' sharia system, should such a thing ever have existed. And the comparatively unreformed situation with regard to the legislation applied is certainly the subject of critique, from activists, lawyers and a good number of religious specialists too, including many judges. As Rania Maktabi has said, it is ironic – not to say outrageous – that while 'Lebanese women enjoy the most extensive forms of freedom of expression in the Middle East ... [they] are among those Arab women who have weakest independent legal subjecthood.' A more than 100-page report from Human Rights Watch in 2015 gave a scathing assessment of the way in which women are treated under the country's religious family legal system.[8] There have been a series of important attempts to reform family law in Lebanon. But, as we will see in the next chapter, these have almost all taken the form of proposals for a unitary civil law for all the communities, and have thus been most immediately bound up with highly political debates over the secularization of Lebanon's entire confessional political and legal system, rather than family law reform alone.

Lebanon's sharia courts and their associated religious community institutions depend for their existence on a tissue of legislation woven over the century of the country's existence. A proper understanding of the legal processes that are the subject of much of this book will depend in part on knowing something of the laws in effect. In presenting them in this chapter, I take a broadly genealogical approach, trying to give a sense of the contingent history through which this inevitably somewhat tangled body of law has developed.

From Ottoman Origins to the French Mandate

The law that, at the time of my fieldwork and now still (as far as I know) most directly governs Lebanon's sharia courts and is thus the most often cited in their rulings is the 1962 Law of Sharia Courts (*Qanun al-mahakim al-shar'iyya*, hereafter 'LSC', of 16 July of that year).[9] This situates the courts within the wider framework of the laws of the Republic and defines their institutions, jurisdiction and prerogatives. Two parallel systems of Sunni and Shi'i (or 'Ja'fari'[10]) initial courts are described, with a supreme appeals court for both. According to a previous president of

[8] Maktabi 2013: 304; Human Rights Watch 2015.
[9] For the text of the law see Zayn 2003a: 49–105.
[10] After the sixth of the Twelver Shi'a's twelve Imams, Imam Ja'far al-Sadiq (d. 765), a renowned jurist who gives his name to the Shi'i, or Ja'fari school of law.

the Sunni courts, in a forward-thinking move, his predecessor of that time had adopted much of the text of a draft revised law of civil court procedure.[11] The law can thus be seen as sophisticated and progressive in procedural terms, and is indeed largely a procedural law, dealing across its 492 clauses with, for instance, the proper presentation of cases, the modes by which evidence can be submitted and judgement made, and the recruitment and payment of court officials.[12]

Section 1 of the LSC affirms directly that 'The Sunni and Ja'fari sharia judiciary forms part of the judicial institutions of the state', under the authority of the Prime Minister's office as it later stipulates (in section 447, as the highest Muslim official in the land). One might observe that the Christian courts, by contrast, are not part of the state in the same way.[13] That points to the varied legal landscape and thus also to the differing genealogies of the different parts of Lebanon's religious legal system. One would not want to exaggerate thereby the effective differences in the resulting reach of the different court systems, nor suggest that the sharia courts are in any sense more official than the Christian ones. But the fact that the sharia courts are part of the state, and that those who work in them are thus state employees and civil servants, has consequences for the way in which a career within the sharia court system is imagined, as we will see in subsequent chapters.

This location within the state (and the Christian tribunals' default position outside of it) derives from the sharia courts' Ottoman past. The territories now called Lebanon were formerly part of the Syrian provinces of the Ottoman Empire. The Ottoman Empire's ideal of law was the sharia, and its courts applied it in the form of Hanafi Sunni precepts, along with imperial legislation, or *qanun*. Christians and Jews suffered various burdens as 'protected' peoples, but also enjoyed some forms of autonomy for their religious institutions and recourse to their own tribunals in certain legal matters – the so-called '*millet* system'. Non-Sunni forms of Islam suffered the vicissitudes of official disdain

[11] Interview with Shaykh Muhammad Kana'an, Beirut, 1 April 2008.

[12] It is thus not the codification of Muslim family law that some academic commentary implies (El-Alami and Hinchcliffe 1996: 147; Shehadeh 1998: 502). It superseded the existing law regulating the sharia courts of 4 November 1942 (Jalal al-Din 2002: 134).

[13] On these points see also Rondot 1947: 69; Rabbath 1986: 137 and Traboulsi 2000: 30–32 cited and discussed by Weiss 2010: 132. Both Rabbath and Traboulsi mention attempts to have the Christian courts also considered part of the state (and thus paid by it), the biggest obstacle to which, according to Traboulsi, was the availability of qualified judges. Prior to the 1962 LSC the sharia courts were apparently tied to the Ministry of Justice (Jalal al-Din 2002: 134).

and oppression, but also occasional recognition.[14] Under nineteenth-century reform, however, new courts and bodies of law were instituted in response to European civil and codified models, and the jurisdiction of the existing courts, which we can thus now think of as distinctively 'sharia courts', by contrast steadily shrank. So too did the prestige of what was, under the Ottomans, a distinct Islamic scholarly profession, class and career.[15]

In some of the new nation states that emerged after the demise of the empire, separate sharia courts would eventually be abolished altogether, as in Turkey in 1924 and Egypt in 1955, for instance. That was not the case in Lebanon, although that was not because it had been left out of the drive for modernisation. Beirut had been the exemplary capital of a newly created province, one of the centres of the Arab Renaissance (*al-Nahda*), and, subsequent to sectarian violence and European involvement in the nineteenth century, Mount Lebanon had been granted its own distinctive form of government, the *Mutasarrifiyya*, based on equal representation on religious lines.[16] Again, what has come to be viewed retrospectively as an essentially Lebanese 'culture of sectarianism' must be seen as something distinctively modern, a fusion of European Orientalist notions of Middle Eastern religious atavism and wider Ottoman programmes of modernisation that brought greater rights to the empire's non-Muslim subjects.[17]

The place of today's sharia courts within the state thus reflects their continued existence after this complex Ottoman past. One piece of late Ottoman legislation also remains in effect and is still cited, the Ottoman Law of Family Rights (OLFR) of 1917.[18] In its day, this was a significant piece of legal reform, making provision for Christians and Jews as well as Muslims.[19] For the latter, it drew on the legal tool of *talfiq*, that is, the

[14] The literature here is vast. I have drawn on Imber 2002, amongst others. Before the nineteenth century, forms of law on Mount Lebanon seem to have reflected this plurality of authority and combined local tradition and sharia. See Harik 1968: 26, 51, 62–63, 65n65; Makdisi 2000: 35, 45, 187n43, 189n82; Henley 2013: 80–82. On the 'millet system', see e.g. Masters 2001; on the place of Shi'i Islam within the Ottoman Empire, see Winter 2010.

[15] Again, there is a very considerable literature on Ottoman reform and modernisation. See e.g. Berkes 1964 and for the impact on the Syrian provinces Ma'oz 1968. Commins (1990) describes the subsequent changes in the class profile of religious professionals in Syria. For an insight into the complex and locally inflected processes of the nineteenth century court of Beirut, see Ghazzal 2007.

[16] See Hanssen 2005 on the former point and Akarli 1993 on the latter.

[17] Makdisi 2000.

[18] For a translation into English see Mahmood 1972: 40–47 and (less complete) Mahmood 1987: 97–106.

[19] See Tucker 1996.

'piecing together' of the rulings of the different Islamic legal schools (*madhhabs*) most conducive to the preferences of modernist reform. The law was unpopular with religious leaders and, under the French Mandate rule (1923–1946) that succeeded Ottoman government, Jews and Christians gained exemption from it; but it remained and remains still theoretically applied to Lebanon's Muslims.[20]

Section 242 of the crucial 1962 Law of Sharia Courts defines the laws to be applied in both the Sunni and Ja'fari court systems and, at the time of my fieldwork in 2007–2008, it read:

> The Sunni judge issues his ruling according to the preponderant statements of the school of Abu Hanifa, except in those cases where the [Ottoman] Law of Family Rights of 8 Muharram 1336/25 October 1917 speaks, whereupon the Sunni judge applies the rulings of that law. And the Ja'fari judge issues his ruling according to the Ja'fari *madhhab* and, where it is in harmony with this school, from among the rulings of the Law of the Family[21]

Beyond the far from comprehensive stipulations of the OLFR, however, which does not, for instance, discuss child custody or indeed inheritance, at this time section 242 pointed Sunnis back to the Hanafi school, a very much larger field of classical Islamic legal discourse. This fallback upon Hanafi *fiqh* applies too in Egypt, Syria and Jordan, for example; but, unlike Lebanon, those countries have in place in the first instance more substantial and recently codified laws of personal status, inspired by the sharia but enacted in modern form. Despite several attempts, that had not at this point happened for Lebanon's Sunni courts. In 2011, however, women's rights activists succeeded in a campaign to bring about reform in the area of custody, which resulted in a change to section 242. This was effected by Law 277 of 29 August 2011, which directed the Sunni judge to follow instead in the first instance the decrees of the Sunni community's Supreme Islamic Sharia Council (described later in this chapter) and only then, if no relevant decree has been issued, the OLFR and Hanafi *fiqh*. I discuss this in more detail in the next chapter.

As for the Shi'i courts (unaffected by the 2011 reform), the 'Ja'fari *madhhab*', which is to say Twelver Shi'i legal discourse, argued to disagree with the OLFR on almost every point. Under the terms of section 242 the

20 This despite the attempts of some Sunnis also to abolish it during the Mandate (Thompson 2000: 150–151). Lebanon is thus one of the very few places where the OLFR is still pertinent, if in qualified fashion (the other being Israel; see Abou Ramadan 2015). Indeed, one might take the (erroneous) impression from some of the standard surveys of Muslim family law that the text of the OLFR was largely sufficient for understanding the law applied in Lebanon (e.g. Mahmood 1972: 35–47, 1987: 93–106 and El-Alami and Hinchcliffe 1996: 147–180).

21 Zayn 2003a: 75.

Ja'fari courts are largely free to follow their own path, making it harder to identify what the 'Ja'fari law' applied in the courts is than some standard academic surveys might suggest. The vision of the sharia applied in Lebanon is thus, in both cases (at least up to 2011), potentially more open and certainly less readily apparent than in parallel jurisdictions.

Having considered the salience of Lebanon's Ottoman past to its legal present, we should also note that of the subsequent period of French Mandate rule (1923–1943) that effectively consolidated Lebanon's confessional political settlement, not least in the form of the Lebanese constitution of 1926, drafted under French tutelage[22] but still applicable, albeit with subsequent modifications. Article 7 stipulates that: 'All Lebanese are equal before the law. They enjoy equally civil and political rights and are equally subject to public responsibilities and duties without any distinction.' One is here in the domain of republican nationalist state civility.[23] But article 9 effectively undercuts this in its promise that:

> Freedom of conscience is absolute. In fulfilling its duty to venerate God the Sublime, the State respects all religions and creeds [*jami' al-adyan wa-l-madhahib*] and guarantees the freedom of religious practice under its protection, on condition that there be no breach thereby in the public order. And it guarantees also for the population, in their different confessions [*milal-hum*], respect for their regime of personal status [*nizam al-ahwal al-shakhsiyya*] and religious interests.[24]

We can agree with a leading contemporary expert, Ibrahim Traboulsi, that personal status law in Lebanon is something 'constitutional'. Indeed, according to him, despite all the subsequent modifications to the constitution, article 9 still stands as the 'cornerstone' of the Lebanese regime of personal status.[25] Respect for the family law particular to each community has become one of the central modes of imagining the sovereignty of that community.[26]

22 The degree of French direction is controversial. See Zamir 1985: 199.

23 Rabbath (1982: 88ff.) traces inspiration to the Egyptian constitution of 1923 and before then to the French declaration of 1789.

24 Here I translate the Arabic text (see Zayn 2003a: 5), with an eye also to the French version, cited with commentary by Rabbath (1982: 96ff). The ambivalence here is obviously characteristic of the liberal ideals dominant at the time; see White 2011 and Mahmood 2016.

25 Traboulsi 2000: 19–21. Ghamroun (2014: 63) points to the lack of challenge to the prevailing reading of article 9, which gives communitarian actors a monopoly over family legal matters and forbids the state to intervene.

26 Zayn (2003a: 5) also cites in this context article 19, subsequent to its modification by the 1990 constitutional law, which instituted a constitutional council. Among those with the right to have recourse to that council are 'the heads of the legally recognised

Given this weight accorded to religious community (*ta'ifa*), the corresponding interest in securing recognition for one's own community, as religiously imagined, and further, the importance of legal autonomy for that notion of recognition, it is no doubt unsurprising that it was also at this time that the legislation came to be passed that brought a separate Ja'fari, that is, Twelver Shi'i, court system into existence alongside the Sunni courts.[27] Law 3503 of 27 January 1926, 'Regarding the Ja'fari *madhhab*', which also still applies, determinedly states in its first article that, 'The Shi'i Muslims of Greater Lebanon form an independent religious community [*ta'ifa diniyya mustaqilla*], and will judge personal status matters according to the rulings of the *madhhab* known as the Ja'fari *madhhab*.'[28] As we have already seen, these terms run through into the legislation and practice of today, as in the reference to 'the Ja'fari *madhhab*' in clause 242 of the 1962 Law of Sharia Courts defining the law to be applied in the sharia courts.[29]

The French could be seen to have had an ambivalent mission, a function of the tensions in the prevailing liberal discourse of the time and reflected in the Lebanese constitution as we have seen. On the one hand they would seek to consolidate the new nation states of Lebanon and Syria over which they had been entrusted with their mandate, one requirement of which, in the modern view, was a single judicial system operating evenly throughout their territories. On the other hand, they would, as part of a guarantee to safeguard all the inhabitants' various rights and interests, simultaneously grant (restricted) legal autonomy

communities in what pertains strictly to personal status, freedom of belief, religious practice and freedom of religious education', thus effectively giving those communities the constitutional right to scrutinise family law. In a resolution on a question concerning the Druze community in 2000, for example, the constitutional council confirmed again that article 9 gives the religious communities 'independence' (Traboulsi 2000: 20).

27 Abisaab and Abisaab (2014: 10–11, 13, 18) find that this was not the fundamental change that the French advertised and that the academic literature has generally accepted, but rather merely a reinforcement of an earlier Ottoman move.

28 Zayn 2003a: 215. The law goes on to set out further details of the new Shi'i judiciary, including a supreme court. For a full discussion see Weiss 2010. The emergence of the notion of a 'Ja'fari *madhhab*', which could stand as equivalent to the various Sunni schools of law, and here to the Hanafi school in particular, would be an interesting story in itself, although not one to be told here. It perhaps has a correspondingly ecumenical flavour, on which see e.g. Brunner 2004.

29 Mikdashi (2014: 282) wants us to see that *madhhab* is also a core concept for the articulation of Lebanon's communal regime, constitutive of identity in many bureaucratic contexts, such as passports and ID cards, and not co-extensive with the notion of 'sect' or 'community' (*ta'ifa*). Not every official community has its own distinctive recognised legal tradition. Isma'ilis and 'Alawis are thus also considered as of the 'Ja'fari *madhhab*', even if the latter now have their own courts.

to a plurality of religious communities, resulting in what Elizabeth Thompson has called a 'dual legal system' and a certain measure of resulting confusion.[30] Several attempts would be made by the French and the Lebanese governments of the time to rationalise the situation; for them that meant bringing the religious courts further under state control and limiting their powers. The French also had an ongoing project to institute civil laws of personal status that would bring much of the religious courts' previous purview under the jurisdiction of the civil court system instead. That gave their opponents frequent opportunity to use religious opposition to such changes as a means to mobilise mass opposition to the Mandate itself. Religious leaders, who were in a position to mobilise such opposition, were also acutely sensitive to any attempt to limit their powers and were easily provoked into action.[31] As we will see, this dynamic whereby political unrest is readily roused by calling into question religious interests continues today, albeit mobilised against different opponents.

The most important such project was law 60LR of 1936, which, despite attempts to lay the ground beforehand, aroused immediate and intense hostility, and was thus modified, after further consultation, by law 146LR of 18 November 1938. That fared no better, meeting with a series of angry demonstrations disturbing enough for the French to institute direct rule. The then High Commissioner had in the end to rule, in decree 53LR of 30 March 1939, that the law would not be applied to Muslims.[32] Nevertheless, the vision it laid out has had fundamental effects on the way that Lebanese confessionalism has become instituted, and we should thus consider it briefly here.

Entitled, 'The arrangement of the religious communities' (*Nizam al-tawa'if al-diniyya*), 60LR defines in its first article what constitutes those communities, stating that it is a law, 'On communities having a personal regime' (*Fi al-tawa'if dhat al-nizam al-shakhsi*).[33] If the reference to a 'personal' organisation is not immediately transparent,[34] the law goes on to clarify it: 'The communities known in law as communities having personal status are the historical communities whose administration and courts and laws are defined in a legislative document.' Section 10, modified by 146LR, stipulates that 'Syrians and Lebanese belonging to

30 Thompson 2000. See also Méouchy 2006 and White 2011 passim.

31 On the attempts in the 1920s at such a project and the opposition to it, see Longrigg 1958: 175; Rabbath 1986: 101–103; Méouchy 2006: 363–365 and White 2011: 168.

32 White 2011: 171–177; Thompson 2000: 152–153.

33 For the Arabic text see Zayn 2003b: 15ff.

34 Zayn feels the need to add a French gloss, '*Statut personnel*', to his Arabic text.

the communities recognised as having personal statuses [now in the plural] are subject to the legal regime of their communities in matters related to personal status[es] and to the rulings of the civil law in matters not subject to this regime.'

The 'legislative document[s]' defining each community did not exist at that point – and the law goes on to set out the process through which they were to come into being[35] – but a prospective list of the communities envisaged is provided in the law's appendix: nine, later twelve, different Christian communities and the Jewish community as constituted by the three synagogues of Aleppo, Damascus and Beirut; and five Muslim communities, being the Sunni, Twelver Shi'i, 'Alawi, Isma'ili and Druze. Of what would become eighteen official religious communities, then, all in theory would have their own personal status laws and tribunals, although the actual number by now in effect is probably rather less.[36] The Christian and Jewish minorities were to be put on the same level as the Muslims; but further, the Sunni Muslim community was envisaged as just one minority community like all the others, instead of the unmarked majority whose law was the law of the state. And various provisions in the law, including those allowing a change in one's official community, seen as tantamount to conversion, were unacceptable to all. Hence the general uproar.[37]

This restricted list was not, however, foreseen as exhaustive of the possibilities. The law goes on (in section 10, as modified by 146LR) to distinguish these 'historical ... communities of personal status' from 'communit[ies] following common law' (*droit commun / al-haqq al-'adi*), which would instead be subject to civil law in personal status matters. This reference to communities of common law now seems obscure (and not a reference to the Anglo-Saxon common legal tradition), but demonstrates that there was at this point an

[35] The document was to include a description of the hierarchy and powers of the community's religious authorities, the law of personal status applied in their courts and their rules of procedure, and even their religious doctrine. Not surprisingly, this proved a dead letter, with the Muslim communities at least. Leaving aside the heresy of submitting the sharia for approval by French colonial authorities, it was clearly something of a category confusion to ask the esoteric Druze and 'Alawi traditions to provide an account of their theological doctrines for government scrutiny (Rabbath 1986: 102–104).

[36] Mikdashi (2014: 282) thinks fifteen are current; Maktabi (2013: 287) has fourteen; Ghamroun (2014: 62) 'less than a dozen'.

[37] Longrigg 1958: 220; Rabbath 1986: 105–106; Thompson 2000: 152–153 and White 2011: 172–173.

openness to the regime envisaged.[38] And these were not the only exceptions to the confessional regime of personal status foreseen at this point. Section 10 also stipulates that 'Syrians and Lebanese who do not belong to any community are subject to the civil law in matters related to personal status.' But, as things developed, nobody was in fact considered to be without a community. There was never to be any such ability to drop out of the religious system, as officially defined, and the official communities completely filled in the landscape of state-recognised citizenship. The openness here envisaged was foreclosed. But Section 10 of 60LR remains a touchstone for those who wish things were otherwise.

There were nevertheless other exceptions allowed. 'As for foreigners, even if they belong to a community recognised as having a regime for personal status, they are subject in their personal status affairs to the rulings of their national law.'[39] And, most significantly,

> If a marriage between Syrians, Lebanese, and including with a foreigner, is performed in a foreign country then it is sound if done according to that country's laws. If those laws are not fitting with those of the husband's community then the marriage is subject to civil law.[40]

This loophole, meaning that a marriage abroad will in many cases be subject to civil law rather than that of the couple's religious communities, has since been much exploited, as we will see. The 'dual legal regime' thus extends to within the domain of personal status itself. Notwithstanding the privileges of the religious tribunals, civil courts still have powers over the personal status affairs of some.

Post-Independence Consolidation

Traboulsi comments that while 60LR is considered the most important element of the legislation covering personal status in Lebanon, the

[38] Rabbath (1986: 104n32) finds only a single example of a subsequent attempt (in 1944) officially to register one such, 'The Orthodox community for the support of Russian émigrés in Beirut' (!). White (2011: 165) maintains that, at the time, the category covered the unrecognised Muslim communities and some Christian ones.

[39] Section 10, again, to which we should add section 1 of 109LR, 14 May 1935: 'The civil courts alone have competence to examine personal status cases pertaining to a foreigner or a number of foreigners if at least one of them belonged to a country in which personal status is subject to civil law, according to the prevailing laws' (Zayn 2003a: 16; see also Qazzi 2007: 13).

[40] Section 25, 60/146LR, to which we should add section 79 of the Law of Civil Courts (cited below; see Qazzi 2007: 25).

legislative process that it foresaw, whereby the religious communities would produce legislation defining themselves, did not take place until after independence in 1943. Indeed, for the prominent nationalist jurist Edmond Rabbath, this is the great irony: despite the many voices at that time that called for an end to confessionalism, including that of Riyad al-Sulh, the first Prime Minister of independent Lebanon, who called it a 'poison', it was under independence that the processes that had been started under the French Mandate reached their logical conclusion.[41]

The law of 2 April 1951, 'Defining the competencies of the confessional authorities [*al-maraji' al-madhhabiyya*] for the Christian communities and the Jewish community', which included family law as well as a host of other issues, was one important milestone.[42] As Traboulsi notes, the jurisdiction of these '*madhhab* courts' (now more commonly called 'spiritual courts', *mahakim ruhiyya*) is here stipulated as exceptional: it is to include only those matters specifically listed as under their purview; where they overstep those, their verdicts are null and void. Further, the law gives the Court of Cassation (*Mahkamat al-tamyiz*) the right to overrule their verdicts. The Court of Cassation is a higher, civil court with the power to adjudicate disputes over jurisdiction between the different religious courts or between them and the civil courts. One could thus see the 1951 law as in a sense limiting the powers of these religious tribunals. The law correspondingly met with opposition from the religious establishment. On the other hand, it expanded the powers of religious courts overall by giving the Christian courts the same powers as the sharia courts had. And there was thus also strenuous opposition to it from secularists, ending

[41] Rabbath 1986: 108–109. And of course al-Sulh was instrumental in the unwritten National Pact guaranteeing equitable power-sharing between Muslims and Christians post-independence.

[42] See Rabbath 1986: 111–113 and Traboulsi 2000: 25–32. For the text of the law see Zayn 2003b: 70–75. This superseded Decree 6, 3 Feb 1930, which had set important such precedents (Rabbath 1986: 122; Thompson 2000: 150 and White 2011: 201n27). Section 33 of the 1951 law enjoins the communities to submit their legislative texts for consideration and ratification, as also envisaged in 60LR. The laws, thus comprising various visions of Catholic, Orthodox and other Christian family law, were submitted but have never been ratified. They therefore remain essentially legal projects, although the Court of Cassation, the highest court in the land, has deemed them effective and to all intents and purposes they are (for their texts see Zayn 2003b). There is, according to Traboulsi, no clear answer as to why they have not yet been ratified, although that lack of ratification is clearly problematic. See also Ghamroun 2014: 62.

in a strike – ultimately unsuccessful – on the part of the lawyers' association.[43] Rabbath's comment is trenchant:

> There is no need to raise the character, wholly discordant with the very notion of the modern state, that these immunities present. The law of 1951 has had the effect of accentuating still more strongly the communitarian regime, in erecting the Christian communities and the Jewish community into political entities, enjoying their autonomy under the empire of their internal laws.[44]

But as Rabbath also goes on to say, 'the most remarkable phenomenon which has marked the era of independence is without contest the extension of the communitarian regime to Lebanese Muslims' in response.[45] With the abrogation of 60LR in 1939 for the Muslims, their status had remained undefined. But in 1955 a law was instituted regulating the workings of the Sunni community and guaranteeing its own autonomy: legislative decree 18 of 13 January 1955 (modified 5 March 1967).[46] Article 1 affirms that, 'Sunni Muslims are independent, of a complete independence, in their religious affairs.' An amendment was made in a law of 28 May 1956 which gave the community the right to alter the law governing it as it saw fit, providing this was not incompatible with the laws governing public order, and a number of such amendments have since been made and published in the official gazette.[47] 'Exorbitant', 'a veritable legislative sovereignty', as Rabbath puts it, which has 'erected their community into a political entity, become practically independent'.[48]

Much of the 1955 law is occupied with the election and competencies of the community's leader, the Mufti of the Lebanese Republic, 'The religious head [*ra'is*] for Muslims and their representative in this capacity before the public powers'. He is to have 'the dignity and the rights and the distinctions enjoyed by the highest religious leaders without restriction or exception' (section 2). As Alexander Henley describes, this was the culmination of a longer historical process, one that saw the evolution of the role of the Ottoman Mufti of Beirut from religious legal scholar to

43 Traboulsi 2000: 25ff.

44 Rabbath 1986: 113. But, as Rabbath notes, the 'Christian woman' revolted against the inequality thus enshrined in the area of inheritance, as the 'protected peoples' (*dhimmis*) had, as he has it, always applied the sharia for inheritance law, which grants women greater rights. A law was thus passed on 23 June 1959, the 'Law of succession for non-Muhammadans [*ghayr al-muhammadiin*]', i.e. Jews and Christians, directly inspired by Western models of inheritance (ibid.: 120–121; and see Zayn 2003b: 103ff.).

45 Rabbath 1986: 121.

46 Entitled, 'The issuing of fatwas [*ifta'*] and religious endowments [*awqaf*]'. See Zayn 2003a: 156–177.

47 See Zayn 2003a: 178–189.

48 Rabbath 1986: 126.

communitarian leader.[49] The French had wanted a Muslim equivalent to stand alongside the Maronite Catholic Patriarch, their close ally and archetype of 'religious leader' and colonial interlocutor, to represent the plural Lebanon they hoped to consolidate. The incumbent Mufti of Beirut, Mustafa Naja (d. 1932), refused to play the role, rejecting the title of State Mufti (*mufti al-dawla*). His successor Muhammad Tawfiq Khalid (d. 1951), however, embraced the possibility as well as the new title of Mufti of the Republic; and, with the support of powerful patrons, the role gradually assumed more and more importance and political attention.[50]

From his grand headquarters in West Beirut, the Dar al-Fatwa, the Mufti (Muhammad Rashid Qabbani at the time of my fieldwork[51]) appoints and directs a further hierarchy of Sunni institutions, functionaries and religious professionals (*'ulama'*), such as mosque imams, sermon-givers, muezzins and Quran-reciters. His work as leader of the community is channelled through his role as chair of the Supreme Sharia Council, the executive body of the community, made up of a number of *ex officio*, elected and appointed (by the Mufti) members, drawn from the clerical and political classes as well as the judiciary and wider society.[52] Below the Mufti stands a set of regional muftis with local such responsibilities, one for every governorate (*muhafaza*) and caza (*qada'*) with a sizeable Muslim population, thus mirroring the administrative categories of the Lebanese state. Another hierarchy of committees oversees the management of the community's endowments (*awqaf*), from which the salaries of these religious professionals are in part paid.[53] These professionals have to be certified by a qualification (*shahada*) in higher religious learning. An earlier ideal was certification by Egypt's prestigious al-Azhar University, which is specifically – but not exclusively – mentioned in the law. But to

[49] Henley 2013: 32–65 and passim. See also Skovgaard-Petersen 2004, 2005. Muftis had acted as community leaders and representatives in the past, but in a far more ad hoc manner.

[50] Skovgaard-Petersen (2004: 90–91; see also 1996: 340, 1998: 70–71) tracks this increase in perceived importance through changes in the process of the Mufti's election, which brought it more under the control of the political class.

[51] Succeeded, in 2014, by Shaykh 'Abd al-Latif al-Daryan, who had previously been head of the Sunni sharia courts.

[52] This body had already been established as far back as 1931, in decree 157/1 (Henley 2013: 52).

[53] On these points see sections 2, 28, 88 and 166–168 of the 1955 law and Henley 2013: 56. Henley (ibid.: 185) notes that the Mufti of the Republic receives a state salary and has it that other religious functionaries do too. There were persistent rumours at the time of my fieldwork that funds from Saudi Arabia, channelled through the Hariri network of patronage, were supplementing such sources in an attempt to maintain parity with the income that their Shi'i equivalents enjoyed.

serve the burgeoning needs of this new establishment Beirut's own Sharia College was created, situated within the Dar al-Fatwa complex.

Within this official salaried establishment, religious authority is thus, Henley argues, effectively routinized, more a bureaucratic office than a scholarly or charismatic achievement. In this modern instantiation, the Mufti himself no longer issues fatwas, expert opinions as to the sharia: officially that task is now dedicated to a 'fatwa secretary' (*Amin al-fatwa*); unofficially, people may prefer to have recourse to non-salaried jurists of especial reputation. The Mufti-ship is rather now more a matter of the political representation of the religious community, bound up with wider networks of politics, patronage and community-oriented educational and other charitable institutions, and in competition with a range of rivals claiming their own brands of religious legitimacy.[54]

As Henley explains, the Mufti-ship was clearly elaborated through a process of 'mirroring' of the existing institution of the Maronite Patriarchy, and the other communities had to follow suit. Henley talks of the formation of a 'national clerical elite'.[55] The Sunni precedent was thus followed by the Twelver Shi'a, despite the pretensions of the (Sunni) Mufti of the Republic to represent all the nation's Muslims (just as the Maronite Patriarch supposedly represented all Christians). The project was potentially a sensitive one: if Sunni communitarian institutionalisation was in itself controversial for rendering Sunnis a minority rather than 'living the life of the state' as they had,[56] Shi'i equivalence would rub it in. But with the impetus afforded by the arrival in Lebanon and spectacular success of the cosmopolitan Shi'i cleric and leader Musa al-Sadr, Law 72 of 19 December 1967 did indeed make the Twelver Shi'a also 'independent in their religious affairs' (section 1), in much the same terms as the Sunni law.[57]

With somewhat different emphasis from the Sunni version, but effectively reproducing the same structure, the Shi'i law (expanded upon in a 1969 decree) gives direction of the community to a council, the Supreme

[54] Khuri 1987; Skovgaard-Petersen 1996: 340–341 and Henley 2013:57, 59–60, 105–106, 221–226. On the wider politics of the Sunni community see especially Johnson 1986; for more recent developments see Rougier 2007.

[55] Henley 2013: 17f., 55, 83ff., 87, 114. And so we cannot see Shi'i communal politics, for instance, as essentially Shi'i, defined by Shi'i 'religious history' and Iranian direction; rather, it is a function of Lebanese communal politics and structures.

[56] Rabbath's (1986: 121) phrase, cited by Henley (2013: 63).

[57] Entitled 'The law of the management of the Shi'i Islamic community in Lebanon'. See Zayn 2003a: 216–236. On Sadr and the SSIC see Ajami 1986 and Norton 1987. Henley (2013: 84ff.), follows Weiss (2010) and Shaery-Eisenlohr (2008) in thinking Sadr's importance for the institutionalisation of the Shi'i community overdrawn in much of the literature.

Shi'i Islamic Council (SSIC), whose President (*ra'is*) enjoys wide-ranging powers, and who is, again, to be granted the same rights and immunities as the heads of the other religious communities. The 1967 law, with later modification, explicitly mentions (in section 12) Musa al-Sadr as 'founding president'; subsequent to his disappearance in Libya in 1978, two 'deputies', effectively presidents proper, have served as chair. The current incumbent, 'Abd al-Amir Qabalan, is also known as Distinguished Ja'fari Mufti (*al-Mufti al-Ja'fari al-Mumtaz*), which, even if his title predates his presidency of the SSIC, makes for an obvious parallel with the Mufti of the Republic.[58] Section 24 of the 1969 explicatory decree explicitly notes that the President of the SSIC should receive the same salary and benefits as the Mufti of the Republic.[59] A panoply of functionaries, local muftis and religious institutions is envisaged under the Council's direction. With the Council's control of endowments and spending, and the proposed formation of a Shi'i Islamic University, we see here too the emergence of a Shi'i national religious establishment to stand alongside its Sunni equivalent.[60]

Where the Sunni law of 1955 talks of running the community 'in accordance with the noble sharia', the 1967 Shi'i law talks (in section 1) of 'conforming to the rules of the noble sharia and the *fiqh* of the Ja'fari school', terms familiar from the earlier law of 1926 that gave official existence to the Shi'i courts, as well as the 1962 Law of Sharia Courts. Here, however, this is qualified as, 'within the limits of the fatwas emanating from the common authority [*marja' 'amm*] of the community in the world'. That is interesting, not just because it cites a jurisdiction outside of the Lebanese borders,[61] but also because it is far from clear who that common authority might be: the highest echelons of the Shi'i religious

[58] That is, this title of Mufti and the Presidency of the SSIC do not seem to be envisaged as co-extensive. Qabalan's title as Distinguished Ja'fari Mufti was apparently awarded in 1970 by Sadr, after Qabalan's recognition by 'the leaders of the community' as worthy successor to the previous 'Mufti' Husayn al-Husayni. See the relevant page of the SSIC website, www.shiitecouncil.com/edara/index.php?id=17, accessed 21 March 2016 (and see Norton 1987: 45–46).

[59] Parity in the salaries of the Sunni and Ja'fari court officials had been a bone of contention from the very beginning under the French Mandate (Weiss 2010: 115–117).

[60] The 1967 law makes the funding for the SSIC itself – its staff, its premises and their furnishing – payable from the state funding allocated to the Ja'fari sharia court system, while also envisaging a Council treasury to receive gifts and other income (see sections 26–28). There are also of course Shi'i religious endowments (*awqaf*; see Weiss 2010: 129ff.). As far as the wider wealth of the community is concerned, we should note the massive influx of money in the later twentieth century through remittances from the Gulf and the Shi'i migrant communities of West Africa and through the support of the Iranian Islamic Republic.

[61] Rabbath notes this along with the parallel of the Christian communities, with supreme authorities in Rome, Damascus, Baghdad or America (1986: 128). Ajami (1986: 116)

hierarchy, normally resident in the great seminary cities of Iraq and Iran, are and have been highly contested.[62]

This does point, however, to the potential tension between 'official', state-recognised and constituted religious authority and the hierarchy of non-state–sanctioned authority based on scholarly achievement within the circles of traditional learning – or what Sabrina Mervin calls a 'double religious hierarchy', further complicating the already 'dual' legal system. This duality predates the modern era: the Ottoman state did occasionally recognise Twelver Shi'i religious authorities, although it more generally ignored them, where it did not do worse; but the Shi'i communities had always had their own independent religious life, dependent on circles of clerical authority radiating from Iraq and Iran. This older division between 'official' but scorned authority and the real legitimacy of the jurists independent of it, which has resonances beyond Shi'i circles of course, continued under the institutionalisation of the community under the French Mandate. Lebanon's most prestigious Shi'i scholars eschewed the career opportunities that the new Ja'fari court system offered, just as the Sunni Mustafa Naja had refused the new post of State Mufti.[63]

The 1967 law envisages a president of the SSIC who is, ideally, an 'absolute *mujtahid*', the highest scholarly rank.[64] This is, as we will see later, a very demanding and eminently contestable condition. But in any case, under this latest round of official institutionalisation, many leading figures stayed away from the new SSIC, including Muhammad Husayn Fadlallah, who I discuss in detail later in the book. Just as in the case of the Sunni Muftis, then, but perhaps still more so, true expertise in the sharia is widely perceived to lie elsewhere than the official establishment. And so too in the case of the Shi'i community are there important networks of mosques, charitable foundations, schools and seminaries effectively outside of the SSIC's control, not least those linked to Hizballah.[65]

thinks this 'vintage Lebanon', in its appeal to a prestigious world outside to justify local claims.

62 See e.g. Walbridge 2001. In 1967, however, this would have been clearer. Muhsin al-Hakim (d. 1970) was the leading scholar of Najaf and pre-eminent authority for Arab Shi'a, and probably for Shi'a globally after the death of the Iranian Borujerdi in 1961.

63 Mervin 2000: 88–98 and 392–398, 405–408. See also Weiss 2010: 99–102, 107.

64 In section 11, which continues, 'or, in the event of this condition not obtaining, then [the president] is elected from among those scholars of religion known for their merit and piety [*al-fadl wa-l-war'*]'.

65 On the latter see e.g. Abisaab 2006 and Harik 2006. There is a rich literature on the wider world of the Shi'i community, its politics and varied institutions. For a recent account see Abisaab and Abisaab 2014.

For the sake of completeness, we should note that the Druze also gained their own law (two laws in fact) of community in 1962. Uniquely among the Muslim communities, the Druze also have a codified law of personal status, as applied in their courts, issued 24 February 1948. A separate decree no. 3473 of 5 March 1960 on the 'Arrangement [*tanzim*] of Druze *madhhabi* judging' speaks of 'Druze *madhhab* courts' – and thus not 'sharia courts', but also notes (in section 2) that, like the Sunni and Ja'fari sharia courts, these '*madhhab* courts' are considered a part of the state.[66] The 'Alawi courts, on the other hand, were only instituted by relatively recent (1995) legislation. The 'Alawis also now have their own community law as well, on the lines of the Sunni and Shi'i ones, Law no. 449 of 17 August 1995.[67]

Finally, however, we should not forget the embedding of these various religious tribunals in a wider civil legal apparatus. Some religious court rulings are final and have executive power, as stipulated by the law that governs the organisation of the state records of personal status (7 December 1951, sections 27–28). If one receives a ruling of divorce, for instance, then one must communicate that to the offices of personal status where it will automatically be recorded. The religious courts are thus only effective because they are part of a wider state legal-bureaucratic assemblage. Other rulings of the religious courts are still more dependent, in that they have to be taken to the civil court circuit of implementation (*da'irat al-tanfidh*) to be given executive power. Section 828 of the Law of Civil Courts (16 September 1983) gives this office the power to execute the rulings of all the communities, but also not to implement a ruling if it is faulty, if issued by an authority without the appropriate power for instance. Those in charge thus effectively have powers of supervision over the religious courts, as Traboulsi notes.[68]

And above all stands the Court of Cassation, with the power of decision over conflicts between the jurisdiction of different courts, religious

[66] Zayn 2003a: 267ff., 283. The 1948 Druze law is described by Layish (1982: 10) as 'the most impressive family law so far enacted in any Middle Eastern Arab state' for its 'far-reaching reforms'. On the Druze courts see Tarabey 2013.

[67] Zayn 2003a: 307ff., 315. Article 1 gives the usual independence – interestingly, according to the sharia and the *fiqh* of the Ja'fari school. The law of 'Alawi courts is no. 450 of 17 August 1995; article 1 makes the courts part of the state; article 5 commits them to apply the LSC although does not stipulate the substantive law to be applied. Zayn (2003a: 6) tells us, however, that they are to apply the Ja'fari *madhhab*. That echoes the use of Lebanese Ja'fari judges by the short-lived 'Alawi state under the French Mandate (Kramer 1987). I should say that whereas I have visited civil courts, Sunni courts, Ja'fari courts, Maronite courts and Druze courts, I have no first-hand experience of these legally recognized 'Alawi courts. Zayn also finds that, according to the best of his knowledge, the Isma'ilis do not have their own such law (ibid.: 9n3).

[68] Traboulsi 2000: 211, 214–215.

and civil, as well as over issues deemed to touch upon public order (*al-nizam al-'amm*).[69] The court's remit was substantially increased by the 1983 Law of Civil Courts (in sections 95 and 738), which extended the range of what could be appealed before the Court of Cassation beyond the sphere of final rulings to include express rulings (for instance, travel bans and requests for immediate maintenance and custody). Strong opposition to this increase in its powers was made by the sharia and Druze courts. This, combined with the problematic effects of the law – an appeal to the Court of Cassation became in effect a way arresting the effects of an immediate ruling for a year or so – led to its being rescinded.[70] It is clear, comments Traboulsi, that the Court of Cassation sees the civil courts as the source or foundation (*asl*) of the legal system and the religious courts as exceptional to it. But, he notes, we should not see it as overly interventionist: it rejects many of the appeals to it, and is clear that its function is not as a final court of appeal against rulings within the religious court system, except within its narrowly defined remit. And this generally non-interventionist policy is broadly acceptable to the religious courts.[71]

Conclusion

What we now call Lebanon's sharia courts have shifted from a provincial locus of imperial state rule under the Hanafi Sunni Ottoman Empire to a locus of confessional institutionalisation under the French Mandate and, still more so, the Lebanese republic. They have remained part of the state throughout, but where they were essentially officially Sunni and Hanafi, they are now formally recognised as having two separate streams, Sunni and Ja'fari. Druze and 'Alawi courts have official recognition too, and are

[69] Traboulsi (2000: 217ff.) sketches the history of this court from its origins in the Mandate. Its current status depends on section 24 of the law of 2 April 1951, modified by decree 121 of 12 June 1959, and the law of judicial arrangements of 16 October 1961. From the register of the court's cases from 1985 to 2000, Traboulsi estimates it receives 25–30 appeals a year. He gives a series of excerpts from its rulings from the archives to give a flavour of the court's deliberations and policy (2000: 223ff.; see also Mikdashi 2014). One ruling, for instance, notes that they do not consider as against public order (implying that this has been argued) that religious courts' rulings are made not 'In the Name of the Lebanese People', as civil court rulings are, but in the name of God (Traboulsi 2000: 239). For a discussion of the notion of 'public order' (in Egypt) see Agrama 2012.

[70] Although no such formal objection came from the Christian courts, Traboulsi notes their oral objections and also the criticisms some judges placed in 'political rulings'.

[71] Traboulsi 2000: 229, 231, 234, 239–242. Ghamroun (2014: 59, 63) sees the court as toothless, talking of its 'incapacity ... to impose on the communitarian courts a substantial definition of public order'.

Table 1.1 *The Most Relevant Lebanese Legislation*

Foundational laws		
1917	Ottoman Law of Family Rights (OLFR)	An early and important attempt at a codified law of personal status for Muslim, Christians and Jews. Its (limited) application is now effectively restricted to the Sunni courts.
1926 (with subsequent modifications)	Lebanese Constitution	Especially relevant is article 9, which guarantees religious freedoms and respect for the personal status law of the nation's various confessions.
1936 (modified in 1938)	60LR (modified by 146LR), 'Arrangement of the religious communities'	Defines the nation's 'historic/religious communities' or 'sects'. Article 10 sets out the consequences for personal status law: it is to be governed by these sects except in certain cases, including marriages contracted abroad. Does not formally apply to Lebanon's Muslims (following 53LR of 1939), but remains an important milestone and reference.
Community-specific laws		
1926	Resolution 3503 of 27 January 1926, 'Regarding the Ja'fari *madhhab* '	Established the existence of the Ja'fari courts within the sharia court system. They are to follow 'Ja'fari', i.e. Twelver Shi'i law.
1948	Law of 24 February 1948, 'Law of personal status for the Druze community'	A comprehensive and progressive codification of Druze personal status law.
1951	Law of 2 April 1951, 'Defining the competencies of the confessional authorities for the Christian communities and the Jewish community'	Gave the Christian courts equivalent powers to the sharia courts, but also limits them by giving the Court of Cassation the power to overrule them, with implications for the sharia court system as well.
1955	Decree 18 of 13 January 1955, 'The issuing of fatwas and religious endowments'	Officially established the Sunni community and gave it extensive legal autonomy. Governs the workings of the community and its head, the Mufti of the Republic.
1960	Decree 3473 of 5 March 1960, 'Regulation of the Druze confessional judiciary'	Procedural law regulating the Druze courts.

Table 1.1 (*cont.*)

Community-specific laws		
1962	Law of 13 July 1962, 'Establishment of the community council of the Druze sect'	Officially established the Druze community and its internal regulation
1967	Law 72 of 19 December 1967, 'The law of the management of the Shi'i Islamic community in Lebanon'	Officially established the Twelver Shi'i community and its governing body the Supreme Shi'i Islamic Council (SSIC) along the lines of the Sunni community. The SSIC's president is to be the equal of the Sunni Mufti.
1995	Law 449 of 17 August 1995, 'Arrangement of the affairs of the 'Alawi Islamic community in Lebanon'	Officially established the 'Alawi community and its internal regulation.
1995	Law 450 of 17 August 1995, 'Establishment and administration of the 'Alawi Ja'fari courts'	Officially established the 'Alawi courts and their regulation.
Procedural laws		
1962	Law of the Sharia Courts (LSC) of 16 July 1962	A comprehensive procedural law regulating the Sunni and Ja'fari courts (superseding an existing law of 1942). Section 242 defines the law to be used in each: the OLFR and Hanafi law for the former (until 2011, see below); Ja'fari law for the latter.
1983	Law of Civil Courts (LCC), Legislative decree 90 of 16 September 1983, 'The (new) law of the principles of civil judicial process'	The procedural law regulating the civil courts. Important for the sharia courts as they follow its provisions where they have none of their own and because it sets out the processes through which religious court rulings are to be executed by the state. It also speaks as to the powers of the civil courts to rule on personal status law in some instances.
2011	Law 177 of 29 August 2011, 'Modification of section 242 of the Law of Organisation of the Sunni and Ja'fari Courts'	Effects a fundamental change in the authority on which the Sunni courts' rulings are to depend. Changes section 242 of the 1962 LSC to direct the Sunni judge in the first instance to the resolutions of the Sunni community's Supreme Islamic Sharia Council, opening the way to codification of Sunni family law.

also reckoned as part of the state, but are distinct; Christian tribunals have recognition but are not part of the state in the same way. This somewhat variable institutional landscape reflects the gradual and piecemeal development of the legal underpinnings of Lebanon's confessional political accommodation.

That confessional legal system is, however, well-established, and grants wider institutional autonomy within a civil republic to a number of officially recognised religious communities. Those include the Sunni and Twelver Shi'i communities, which are both numerically and politically of the first significance. These religious communities have official establishments: governing bodies, bureaucratic institutions and hierarchies of leaders and functionaries. While the laws governing them have developed over time, they have done so in reference to each other, 'mirroring' one another in Henley's phrase. Despite long-standing debates over the appropriateness of the notion of a 'clergy' in Muslim contexts then, such a clerical class of 'men of religion' (*rijal*, sing. *rajul*, *al-din*), Muslim and Christian, is clearly apparent in Lebanon. Or as Greek Orthodox Bishop George Khudr put it, 'the French Mandate in its Catholic culture . . . made the clergy master over every sect . . . and set up in return muftis in Christianity.'[72]

Official religious authority thus emerges in reference to the state. Despite the notorious 'weakness' of the Lebanese state, its presence is in this sense inevitable and ubiquitous: all other claims to authority are defined through and against it.[73] And despite the secularists' sentiment that it is the religious class that, among other things, retards the emergence of a properly secular, unified Lebanese nation state, Lebanese unity and common citizenship are constant themes of the official religious class.[74] Of course, communitarian, not to say sectarian solidarity is the potentially darker side of the same coin. And the creation of an official religious establishment also further creates its obverse: independent claims to authority as representing the authentic tradition rather than an ersatz, state-co-opted, version. There is a considerable range of Sunni and Shi'i religious actors and organisations beyond the fold and control of the official establishments – indeed Hizballah, for instance, rather overshadows the official Shi'i community. For them, as Henley says, the establishment is 'traditionalist', while for the establishment, its rivals

72 This was as part of comments in response to the 1998 debates over civil marriage in Lebanon, reproduced in Traboulsi 2000: 308 and cited at greater length in Clarke 2009: 62. See also Henley 2013: 32–33.

73 See Ghamroun 2014.

74 As Henley well describes for the Mufti of the Republic and the Patriarch (2013: 168–208).

are easily labelled opportunist and 'political' rather than authentically 'religious'.[75] This perception that standing apart from the established, official line perforce means being considered 'political' is one that we will see borne out below.

The civil state defines itself in opposition to religious community; official religious community defines itself in reference to but in contradistinction from the state, with an eye also to the claims of 'authentic' tradition; unofficial religious authority defines itself as authentic in contradistinction to the state-mandated official religious establishment. The sharia courts are situated at the intersection of official religious community and the state, of which they are legally defined as a part. A duality in the state legal system (civil vs. religious) is mirrored by a duality in the array of religious authorities (official vs. unofficial). The boundaries between these positions are of course more porous than this bald schematic summary suggests, and individual actors can shift between them, as we will see. But these tensions and oppositions will carry through into the ethnographic descriptions that follow. My account is one of religious actors and dynamics. But we should always also keep in mind – as those religious actors cannot help but do – the broad swathes of people disinterested in, dissatisfied with or downright opposed to the privileged position that religious institutions enjoy in Lebanon's political structure. That is the theme of the next chapter.

[75] Henley 2013: 234–236.

2 The Consequences for Civility

The multiplicity of personal status law entailed by Lebanon's confessional political and legal structure has become one of its distinctive features, affirmed in the constitution, as we quoted Lebanese legal expert Ibrahim Traboulsi as saying in the previous chapter. But, as Traboulsi also notes, this is a closed regime: there is a corresponding compulsion to belong to one of the communities specified in 60LR.[1] This has obvious and fundamental implications for what I am calling 'civility', the ways in which people with different identities, commitments and interests are understood to be able to live together in a shared polity.

Religious courts have the exclusive right to hear cases concerning marriages contracted in Lebanon by Lebanese citizens, whether they are religiously committed or not. A case can be brought even if the parties are not resident in Lebanon: given the huge Lebanese diaspora, and the popularity for emigres of marrying 'back home', the religious courts also see many cases involving Lebanese residents abroad, where one party has sought to make the other subject, willingly or not, to religious law.[2] Civil (i.e. non-religious) marriages in Lebanon are not legally recognised.[3] Despite the earlier promises of the law 60LR of 1936, one cannot opt out of the system and the currently officially recognised communities are seen as exhaustive of the field of communitarian identity. That entails the impossibility for members of unrecognized faiths to marry at all, as is the case for Baha'is, for instance.[4]

1 Traboulsi 2000: 32–34.

2 Following section 75 of the 1983 Law of Civil Courts. It is sufficient here that one party is Lebanese; they can then raise a case in Lebanon regardless of the nationality of the spouse or where they live (Qazzi 2007: 28).

3 The 1951 law stipulates in section 16 that, 'Marriage of a Lebanese Christian or Jew in Lebanon before a civil court is null', as does the analogous section in the Druze law, although the sharia courts do not have an explicit such clause. Further, the personal status records offices forbid the registration of marriage contracts arranged in Lebanon which do not bear the acknowledgement of the religious authority which contracted the marriage (Qazzi 2007: 14).

4 Zalzal 1997: 38 and Farha 2015: 36.

On the individual level, this can be painful. One may not be religiously committed and resent having to be under the authority of religious leaders in such an intimate and fundamental domain of one's life. One may indeed be an avowed secular nationalist, opposed to the confessional regime with which the religious courts are bound up. Or one may find the content, especially the generally patriarchal nature of religious family law unacceptable. Or perhaps you just fall in love with someone who, according to religious law, you shouldn't have fallen in love with.

Mixed Marriages

'Mixed' marriages between people of different communities are stereotypically seen as socially 'problematic'. A Sunni lawyer told me that in his father's generation it was even said that 'someone from Basta Fawqa can't marry someone from Basta Tahta', referring to two neighbouring areas of Sunni West Beirut.[5] But beyond social pressures and prejudices, mixed marriages raise religious-legal issues bearing directly on inter-community civility. Marriage to 'idolaters' (sing. *mushrik*) is forbidden for Muslims. But a Muslim man can marry a woman from 'the people of the Book' (*ahl al-kitab*), that is, a Christian or Jew. A Muslim woman, however, may not. A Christian man and a Muslim woman would thus have to marry in Church, where admissible: not all Christian communities allow marriage with the non-baptised. The marriage would not be recognised by the Muslim courts; and in the Christian courts, should the marriage break up, the Muslim wife's rights would be less than those of a Christian woman.[6]

Under Druze law, Druze may only marry other Druze. So a marriage between a Druze and a non-Druze would not be possible in their courts. And should the non-Druze be a Sunni or Shi'i Muslim and the couple try to marry in the sharia courts, other problems might arise, according to one lawyer I spoke with. Although in the terms of the communitarian system the Druze are one of Lebanon's five Muslim communities, the Druze faith is commonly considered within the wider Sunni and Shi'i traditions as beyond the pale of Islam. In sharia-legal terms, Druze could thus be argued to be neither Muslims nor 'people of the book'. A Sunni or Shi'i judge might therefore, the lawyer suggested, require a Druze

[5] In his no doubt unscientific estimation, '95 per cent' of such marriages fail. Anne Weber (2008: 15) cites statistics from the 1970s showing the extreme rarity of such marriages, especially between the broad religious groupings of Muslim, Christian and Druze, where they number 1–2 per cent of marriages. See also Farha (2015: 45–52), who notes the fluctuating nature of such patterns given the changing dynamics of sectarian concerns.

[6] See Weber 2008; Mikdashi 2014 and Farha 2015: 34.

woman coming before their court to marry a Sunni or Shi'i man to say the *shahada*, the Islamic profession of faith, before notarizing the union, although I should say immediately that I never saw such a thing.[7]

Another example: the Shi'i scholarly tradition finds the permissibility of a Muslim man marrying a Christian or Jewish woman doubtful, some authorities going so far as to rule it out altogether, others enjoining caution, making not doing so best religious practice.[8] The Lebanese Ja'fari courts, on the other hand, register such marriages, and seem to have done so for decades.[9] The actuality of the practice of civility in the courts would thus appear to run ahead of much of the religio-legal discourse. Such excesses of incivility – while feasible in terms of legal theory – would be highly discomfiting in the Lebanese context.

Another, perhaps even more sensitive, concern is over marriages between Sunnis and Shi'a. There may be social pressures in play here, but this is not formally an issue in legal terms.[10] In so far as it could be, it would be under the heading of *kafa'a*, the equality of status of the couple. According to the Ottoman Law of Family Rights, a bride's guardian (*wali*) – usually her father – could demand the breaking off or annulling

[7] See the discussion by one ecumenically-minded Shi'i scholar ('Atwi 2004b: 19), who finds it sufficient that a Druze not affirm or perform anything which denies the fundamental principles of Islam.

[8] This is in the case of a permanent rather than a temporary marriage (the latter being seen as less problematic; a further consideration is as to whether this is a second marriage, 'on' a first, Muslim wife). Enjoining not contracting such a (permanent) marriage out of caution as to its permissibility is the position of the currently influential Ayatollah Sistani (2002 vol. 3: 68), as well as his celebrated mentor Khu'i (1975 vol. 2: 370) and also Khomeini (1989 vol. 2: 259). Current Iranian Supreme Leader Khamenei reportedly rules it out altogether, which would appear to be the majority view (Mir'i 2003: 176). Lebanon's Fadlallah, liberal in such matters, suggests that caution be recommended but not obligatory (Fadlallah 2002–3 vol. 3: 416; 2005a vol. 1: 256; see also 2005a vol. 2: 422–3). It is worth noting here that for the (Sunni) Hanafis and Shafi'is marriage to a Christian woman is *makruh* (detestable) even if permissible (Zuhayli 2006: 6653–6656).

[9] Muhammad Jawad Mughniyya, head of the Ja'fari courts in the 1950s, wrote that the Lebanese Ja'fari courts register such marriages as fully legal (Mughniyya 1979: 314–315; see also Mughniyya 2003: part 5, 230–233); but a subsequent court president, 'Abdallah Ni'ma (1996: 21), thought that the majority view (*al-mashhur*, generally held to be that applied in the courts) is that it is forbidden, also reportedly the view of Muhammad Mahdi Shams al-Din, long president of the Supreme Shi'i Islamic Council (Farha 2015: 33n5). The Shi'i judges I worked with dismissed the latter position as rare and practice as otherwise. A venerable Shi'i lawyer pointed to the eight Christian wives in his family alone, married some thirty-five to forty years.

[10] For statements of the formal legal position see Ni'ma 1996: 23 and Mughniyya 2003: part 5, 238–239. As testament to the currency of the issue beyond the courts see the 'Q&A' in Fadlallah 2005a vol. 1: 256, 258. Fadlallah finds that, although marriage within the *madhhab* is 'first and best and preferable' as most harmonious, there are some considerations which point the other way, regarding rapprochement (*taqarub*) and mutual understanding (*tafahum*) between Muslims (Fadlallah 2003 vol. 3: 416–417; see also 'Atwi 2004b: 18–19).

of a marriage if this condition was found not to be met. This is, apparently, vanishingly rare in practice. It was, however, one of the grounds of a significant recent case – 'the case of the century', as one of the lawyers involved put it to me.

The story, as related by the husband in a newspaper article his lawyer produced to put pressure on the courts, is this: a Shiʿi man and a Sunni woman wanted to marry, but her father refused.[11] 'I did not arrange to meet her secretly and I spoke to her family openly', he says. 'And because I am Shiʿi and do not possess great wealth [later, 'my two great sins'], her family rejected my request.' In the teeth of such opposition, the couple enacted a marriage contract with a Shiʿi shaykh, with two witnesses, outside of the courts. The wife became pregnant, later delivering twins. They then went to a Shiʿi court to register the marriage officially, as normal; in the case of a mixed marriage, the courts of the husband's community have jurisdiction.[12] The wife's reluctant family sought to and succeeded in having the couple's application to have the marriage registered refused, at both the initial and appeal court levels. According to the article, the bride's father claimed to the judge that these interventions were made 'in the spirit of courtesy and good relations between the Sunni and Shiʿi communities'. The initial court ruling, according to the article at least, asserted that 'a lack of equivalence [in status]' (*'adam al-takafu'*) had been established. The husband appealed; the appeals court confirmed the initial ruling.

The husband now tried a different approach. On advice, he converted to Sunnism. This is in fact a common means for people to get round the strictures of religious law, whether to marry someone they could not otherwise, or indeed – for Catholics, for example – to obtain a divorce. Such conversions are a well-attested means of forum shopping, famously employed by some high-profile political personalities. Legislation has been enacted to limit these possibilities, but they endure.[13] The couple then registered the marriage, and the by now delivered twin babies, in the Sunni courts, and thus with the state, without problem. But her father

[11] The article was posted in the Islamic affairs section of *Al-Liwa'* (Beirut, 1 May 2006). I rely on a photocopy given to me by the lawyer in question. The name of the husband is given as author, but seems better withheld here.

[12] As per section 15 of the law of 2 April 1951.

[13] On the legislation see Bilani et al. 1985: 272. Pertinent is the stipulation that the court where the marriage was first contracted has jurisdiction (as per section 14 of the law of 2 April 1951). On such conversions see Weber 2008 and Mikdashi 2014. Celebrity converts include Druze leader Walid Jumblatt (to Sunnism to marry his Sunni wife) and several former Sunni Prime Ministers, including Riyad al-Sulh, Husayn 'Uwayni and Salim al-Hoss (to Shiʿi Islam in order that their daughters not be disinherited) (Courbage and Todd 2011: 31; Mikdashi 2014: 283 and Farha 2015: 38n21).

pursued them nevertheless, bringing an opposing suit. According to the article, this was on largely procedural grounds, which were that the Sunni court did not have jurisdiction and could not overrule a pre-existing Ja'fari court ruling, especially concerning an on-going case.

The newspaper article directs its thrust at exactly the civility – empty or otherwise – of relations between the two communities. Entitled 'Is there one Islam or two?' (*A-Islam wahid am islaman?*), its author, 'a Muslim, of the people who hold to the unity of God upon the religion of Muhammad, God's peace and prayers be upon him', addresses himself to the then Prime Minister, Fu'ad Siniora (as ultimately responsible for the sharia courts), and the two Muftis and heads of the Sunni and Shi'i communities, then Shaykhs Muhammad Rashid Qabbani and 'Abd al-Amir Qabalan: 'two sects which practice one religion and recite one [holy] book'. The author asks them rhetorically whether they can accept that 'the principles of etiquette [*mujamala*, also 'civility', 'courtesy', 'flattery'] between the Ja'fari sharia courts and the Sunni sharia courts prevail over the word of truth?'

They told me that the Sunni and Ja'fari sharia courts are regulated by one law, so I obtained a copy of it and there read section 242, 'The Sunni judge issues his ruling according to the weightiest statements of the school of Abu Hanifa [i.e. the Hanafi school], except in those cases where the Ottoman Family Law of . . . 1917 speaks, whereupon the Sunni judge applies the rulings of that law; and the Ja'fari judge issues his ruling according to the Ja'fari *madhhab* and, where it is in harmony with these schools, from among the rulings of the Family Law.'

And when I was one of the followers of the Ja'fari school, before the beginning of my tribulations, I went to the book *Dalil al-qada' al-Ja'fari* [Guide to Ja'fari judgment], written by the late Shaykh 'Abdallah Ni'ma, previous president of the Supreme Ja'fari Sharia Court, and in it, on page 70, section 189, I read: 'There is no guardianship [*wilaya*] of the father and paternal grandfather over the sane, adult virgin; rather, her instructions regarding her marriage are entrusted to her, and their soundness does not rest on his permission.' Just as I read in section 190: 'If the father and paternal grandfather stood in the way of their sane virgin daughter and prevented her marrying someone of equal status, despite her wish to marry them, then their guardianship lapses; and she may marry, even if her guardian detested that.'

So if these were the rulings of the Ja'fari school, then why was my case to establish my marriage rejected before the Ja'fari judge? And when I became a Sunni, then I went to the rulings of the Hanafi school, and I read in the book *Fiqh al-Sunna* by Sayyid Sabiq,[14] on page 88 of volume two: 'And Abu Hanifa and Abu Yusuf

14 One of the best known and most approachable twentieth century digests of Islamic law, its author, Sayyid Sabiq (d. 2000), a distinguished Egyptian scholar associated with the Muslim Brotherhood.

think that the rational, adult woman has the right of carrying out the contract by herself, whether she is a virgin or non-virgin.' Then I studied the [Ottoman] Law of Family Rights, and I read there section 50, which stipulates: 'Further, it is permitted for the courts to annul the marriage for lack of equivalency [*kafa'a*] before the manifestation of pregnancy.' Does this not mean that it was no longer possible to annul my marriage, given that my wife had delivered her two children?

As for saying that I am not her equal [*kafw*], that is a matter that needs pausing on: for I am an Arab Muslim in gainful employment; I possess enough to maintain my wife for more than [the requisite period of] two months by far, and not by doing anything illicit, even if I do not possess the wealth that my wife's family does. This is as regards wealth; as for reputation, many have borne witness to my good character.

His wife's father's suit was successful nonetheless. This was tragic, not only for the couple's sake, but also for that of their twin children, who were now officially considered illegitimate, a very material problem in Lebanon:[15] 'making my legal marriage into adultery [*zina*] – God forbid! – and of the *nasab* [legitimate filiation] of my two children a complete ruin', as the husband puts it in the article. The husband's lawyer told me that he had felt impelled to tell the president of the Sunni courts that this ruling, 'against the sharia and the law' (*dadd al-shar' wa-l-qanun*), was one of the three times he had truly grieved in his life (the other two being the deaths of his father and Jamal 'Abd al-Nasir).

The piece ends:

Representatives of the State, Excellencies ... [*Ashab al-dawla wa-l-fadila*] do you defend this excess of etiquette between the Ja'fari and Sunni courts, as though these courts are peaceable, contractual, conjoined, neither overstepping the bounds of what the other sets down? Do you think there is one Islam and another Islam? Or do you think that you refuse any path which divides Islam into two Islams and God's sharia into two sharias? Integrity [*amana*] refuses to be divided into two. Is not judgment a matter of integrity? ... 'Blessed are the believers ... who are true to their trusts and promises'. [Quran 23: 1]

This is strong stuff. But it speaks loud and clear to the different dynamics of civility in play and their tensions – between men and women, between generations, between citizens and the state, between Muslims of different communities and between different religious establishments.

Resistance: Marriage Abroad

Conversion, then, is one way to attempt to achieve what would otherwise be impossible under the religious family legal system. But, as we have

15 See Clarke 2009: 76–80.

already noted, the other is to escape the system altogether by leaving Lebanon and contracting a civil marriage abroad, very commonly in neighbouring Cyprus, but also further afield.[16] Again, one might contract such a marriage simply because of the transnational nature of many Lebanese lives. Many living and marrying abroad then register the marriage in Lebanon as well; or perhaps only one party does, commonly the man – for religious law generally favours his interests.[17] In the light of influential contemporary notions of healthy gender relations, however, the rulings of religious law can be seen as outmoded. Civil marriages could correspondingly also be a statement of principle, modernism and secular civility: 'In the unwavering confessional atmosphere still prevalent in Lebanon, civil marriage constitutes a most meaningful political act.'[18] They can further be a necessity when a couple could not otherwise marry.

For instance, one lawyer I worked with, nominally a Sunni Muslim but an avowed atheist, showed me photos of his family. 'Here is my son [also a lawyer] with his fiancée. He wants to get married in France, a civil marriage. Of course he could marry in the sharia way, and have more rights [as a man], but it would be shameful [*'ayb*]: we don't believe in it.' The civil marriage is then registered in Lebanon through the Lebanese embassy. They will then go through the motions of a sharia marriage 'for society'. But, as lawyers, they can say they will register the resulting paperwork themselves, and then just not get around to it, leaving the French civil marriage to stand alone. He pointed to a picture of his rascally grandchildren: 'That's my son, so how will these ones be?! In fifty years' time this [i.e., sharia courts] will all be over.'

These rights are not enjoyed equally by all. Leaving aside the relative expense and bureaucratic complications of marrying abroad – which restrict the option to certain social classes – the sharia courts can claim jurisdiction over marriages contracted by Muslims abroad in some cases: where the country where the marriage is contracted follows Islamic marriage law; where two Lebanese Muslims or a Lebanese Muslim and a foreign Muslim marry in a country applying civil marriage law; and, more debatably, the marriage between a Lebanese Muslim and a

[16] See Qazzi (2007: 8, 17–18), who provides a detailed examination of the complex legal issues involved. According to Lebanon's Ministry of Foreign and Expatriate Affairs, 560 Lebanese civil marriages took place in 2014 in Cyprus alone (Chamas 2015).

[17] On such issues (including whether the civil courts can try religious marriages contracted abroad), see Qazzi 2007: 51ff. Here the prevailing view has been that, despite the specific injunction of the law of 2 April 1951 that the first contract has priority, a religious contract trumps it, based on the notion that it demonstrates intent.

[18] El-Cheikh 2000: 161.

non-Muslim foreigner in a country applying civil marriage law.[19] Section 79 of the 1983 Law of Civil Courts begins, 'The Lebanese civil courts have the right to examine disputes arising from a marriage contract which was completed in a foreign country between two Lebanese people or between a Lebanese person and a foreigner in a civil fashion as stipulated in the law of that country.' But it ends, 'And the rulings of the laws pertaining to the jurisdiction of the sharia and Druze courts are observed if both of the spouses belong to Muslim communities [*al-tawa'if al-muhammadiyya*] and at least one were Lebanese.'[20]

In the absence of a Lebanese civil marriage law, then, marriages abroad are the only way of entering into civil marriage. But then the question arises as to how they are to be tried. In practice, although there is no specific law to this effect, they are tried according to the law of the country where the marriage was contracted. In the words of one well-known activist civil court judge who specializes in personal status, John al-Qazzi, 'Because the legislator, who does not recognise civil marriage in Lebanon, goes back on himself, and recognises the effects of this marriage when a Lebanese contracts it abroad', that leaves the Lebanese judge faced with 'the laws of all the world': 'So the Lebanese judge has come to the point of ruling in the name of the Lebanese people in following the stipulations of foreign law!!' And his useful manual on civil marriage in Lebanon provides as an appendix the relevant clauses of some of the daunting list of laws he has thereby found himself applying: those of Cyprus, Britain, Ivory Coast, Argentina, Switzerland, the Russian Federation, Belarus, Romania, Brazil, Turkey, Ukraine, the State of New York and Venezuela.[21]

Personal Status Law Reform

These are the concerns of a nationalist judge: the lack of a Lebanese civil marriage law abdicates sovereignty to the laws of other countries. To this we can add the unease at the extra-territoriality of many of the ultimate

[19] Section 18 of the Law of Sharia Courts excludes from their purview cases involving foreigners of their *madhhab* (i.e. Sunni or Shi'i) but from countries where personal status is subject to civil law, 'unless one of the spouses is Lebanese'.

[20] See Qazzi (2007: 25ff.) for examples of cases where he (a practising civil court judge) applies this. For the text of the law see Musawi 2007: 14. The latter clause is ambiguous in ways which give the Muslim courts considerable potential claims to jurisdiction, according to Qazzi's (2007: 29ff.) detailed analysis. See also Bilani et al. 1985: 269–271. Professor Talal Khodari suggested to me that the crucial issue is whether recourse to the sharia courts here is compulsory or voluntary.

[21] Qazzi 2007: 7–8, 140ff., 174ff. As Qazzi says (ibid.: 173), this still leaves some awkward questions, not least as to how, as a Lebanese judge, one should interpret these laws.

sources of authority for the official religious communities: the Vatican for Maronite Catholics or the foremost *marja'* in the world for the Twelver Shi'a, for instance.[22] More broadly, given the importance of the religious tribunals for the confessional political system, contestations over their power remain at the heart of nationalist activism. To these impetuses for reform can be added the struggle for increased gender equality.[23] Rather than taking the form of piecemeal reform of individual pieces of religious legislation, however, until recently this has largely taken the form of joining the call for a unified, civil, Lebanese law of personal status.[24] Even from a religious perspective, the forced nature of recourse to the religious courts could be seen to lead to a trivialisation of religious commitment, as in the conversions of convenience alluded to earlier in this chapter.

We have already noted the attempts under the French Mandate to institute some form of civil personal status regime.[25] These were not just a colonial imposition. Such projects continued after independence, part of a long-standing anti-confessional movement, formally adopted in the 1989 Ta'if accord that brought the horrors of civil war to an end: the amended Lebanese constitution states, in a 1990 addition, that 'The abolition of political confessionalism shall be a basic national goal'.[26] For instance, the demand for a civil marriage law was material to the strike called by the lawyers' association in response to the 1951 marriage law, mentioned earlier in this chapter; a text was drafted but never adopted.[27] There were further such debates in the 1960s and 1970s, a serious proposal coming from the Democratic Party in 1971; in 1997, another was made by the Syrian National Socialist Party. But the most important recent initiative was that put to parliament in 1998, backed by

[22] Farha (2015: 42) points also to the intervention by the Saudi Higher Sharia Council in the debates in Lebanon in 1998 over a voluntary civil marriage law. On this point see also Maktabi 2013: 299.

[23] Maktabi (2013: 287) notes the importance of the joining of women's rights with human rights discourse in the 1990s, and thus also the impetus to reform given by the UN Convention for the Elimination of all forms of Discrimination against Women (CEDAW) of 1979, an impetus which, unlike in many other contexts in the region, led to little in Lebanon, for reasons Maktabi describes. Maktabi usefully draws attention to other domains where pressure for change has been brought, including Lebanon's law of nationality and penal code (ibid.: 298; see also Ghamroun 2014: 65–67).

[24] On the calls for reform by women's rights activists see Zalzal 1997, Shehadeh 1998, Zuhur 2002.

[25] See also Kanafani-Zahar 2006.

[26] www.presidency.gov.lb/English/LebaneseSystem/Documents/Lebanese%20Constitution.pdf, accessed 6 January 2016.

[27] See the detailed account based on research into the association's records given by Traboulsi (2000: 25ff).

the then president, Elias Hrawi. This was for a voluntary civil marriage law (it did not cover inheritance and it did not seek to replace or abolish the religious courts), and attempts were made to minimise its conflict with religious precepts, although one of its aims was to improve the legal status of women. It is worth noting – as several Muslim religious professionals did – that marriage in Islam is more akin to a civil contract than it is to a sacrament, in the manner of Christian marriage (a point I take up later). However, with regard to the legal ramifications of marriage, there were a number of areas of conflict with sharia precepts: its implicit permission of a marriage between a Christian man and a Muslim woman, its clear prohibition of polygamy, its granting of equal rights to divorce between women and men, and its recognition of adoption, for instance. And the proposed law did become the subject of intense opposition from religious quarters, which led to its being shelved.[28]

Opposition was led by the Sunni religious establishment and its then leader Mufti Rashid Qabbani, who described secularism as a 'germ' (*jurthuma*).[29] Besides the objections to the law's specific legal provisions, it was argued that this was a battle over the march of secularism and thus the defence of religion more generally. With civil marriage would come the demise of family values, cohabitation, illegitimate children and the legalisation of homosexual marriage. This 'apocalyptic' vision, which resonated with the prejudice, not to say misunderstanding, towards what 'civil marriage' might actually entail, succeeded in whipping up popular opposition and angry demonstrations.[30] Despite the initially less vehement reaction from some other quarters of the religious communities, the political pressure brought to bear was such that they largely followed suit. The law's failure became inevitable – an echo of the similar fervour over such projects under the French Mandate. Many commentators observed that the outcry was at root due to the intimate relation between the religious personal status regime and Lebanon's wider confessional political settlement. Passing the law would lead to further calls for the abolition of confessionalism. 'Is the country ready for such a probability at the moment?', asked former and

[28] El-Cheikh 2000; Zuhur 2002; Farha 2015: 38–43. There were also of course objections from Christian quarters, as in the possibility for divorce the draft law envisaged. For the text of the law see Traboulsi 2000: 277–296 (Traboulsi was one of those involved in its drafting). For a compilation of religious reactions to civil marriage in Lebanon, including those of some of the figures cited above, see Traboulsi 2000: 297–324 and 'Amili 2007.

[29] Farha 2015: 41.

[30] On popular perceptions of civil marriage see Weber 2008: 23 and Farha 2015: 43–51. 'Apocalyptic' is Nadia El-Cheikh's (2000) term.

future Prime Minister Salim al-Hoss. As far as the political class is concerned, the answer would seem to have been no.[31]

Similar efforts continue, however. In 2011 civil society organisations submitted another such draft law to parliament, but it was not debated. More significantly perhaps, in 2009, it became possible for Lebanese citizens to remove ('strike out', *shatb*) their confessional identity from their identity papers and records. Many did so. But legal complications ensued, and the campaign faltered to persuade a mass movement to bring about the end of confessionalism from the bottom up.[32] But, the point was, people with no official confessional identity could arguably be seen as falling under the relevant provision of 60LR, 1936, which makes those not belonging to one of the historical communities subject to civil law in matters of personal status. (Others have called for a nineteenth official community to be created, a secular one.) In 2012, supported by a civil society organisation, Khulud Sukkariyya and Nidal Darwish became the first couple to be wed in a civil marriage in Lebanon itself. After the marriage was eventually ruled legal by the Supreme Judicial Council, the then Interior Minister signed off on it: a subsequent Minister, however, ruled out any continued registration of such marriages, trapping a number of couples in bureaucratic limbo. The scene does not seem set for mass imitation at this point, then. But, as ever, the precedent aroused fury in some religious quarters. Extraordinarily, Mufti Qabbani issued a fatwa in response to the phenomenon stating that any Muslim official who supported calls for a civil marriage law would be considered an apostate, not to be ritually washed and not to be buried in a Muslim cemetery.[33]

Working within the System

Reform of family law in a plural, confessional political environment thus seems inevitably to become tied to both the fate of the political settlement itself and to the status of the religious elite who form part of its armature, with near paralysis as the result.[34] However, even in the

[31] El-Cheikh 2000: 149–157 and Maktabi 2013: 298–299. Farha (2015: 39–40) points to the vested economic interests of the religious establishment in the communitarian settlement. On the entrenchment of sectarianism in post-war Lebanon see Salloukh et al. 2015.

[32] Mikdashi 2014: 288–290. One might also note the resonances of this campaign with notorious incidents during the 1975–1990 civil war, when people were killed because of their confessional identity as listed on their identity card.

[33] Mallat and Howayek 2013: 283–284; Muhanna 2013a, b; Saadawi 2013; Chamas 2015 and Farha 2015: 52–53.

[34] See the helpful discussions in Maktabi 2013 and Ghamroun 2014.

absence of a civil marriage law, that does not mean that all matters of personal status have left the civil courts' purview. As we have noted, the religious courts are exceptional to the wider civil legal regime: all issues which the law does not explicitly assign to the religious courts remain with the civil judiciary. And some civil judges, like John al-Qazzi, are willing to eat into territory that may conventionally be considered as that of the religious tribunals. One example that drew wider attention was his ratification of an adoption.[35] While full adoption is ruled out for Muslims (although fostering, *takafful*, is not), it is possible for Christians and was previously considered a matter for the Church courts, following clause 4 of the law of 2 April 1951. In the case at hand, however, which involved a Lebanese Catholic couple married in a civil marriage in Cyprus, Judge Qazzi claimed jurisdiction on the grounds that section 79 of the Law of Civil Courts gives the civil courts jurisdiction over cases 'arising from a marriage contract which was completed in a foreign country between two Lebanese people ... in a civil fashion as stipulated in the law of that country'. The decision was controversial and indeed came after the same request had been previously denied by a different judge. But it was executed by the relevant offices of the state.

Closer to home for the sharia courts was the emergence in 2007 of a civil court judge responsible for cases involving children who was prepared to overrule sharia court rulings, not least in the controversial area of custody: the sharia presumes a father's right to custody of his children at strikingly early ages to contemporary eyes. As Samer Ghamroun describes, this judge had seen his powers enlarged after a law was passed in 2002 giving protection to endangered children and making reference to the 1989 UNICEF Convention on the Rights of the Child, which Lebanon had adopted in 1991. The new law could be interpreted as allowing the restriction of the competences of the religious courts. And the judge proceeded to do so in a number of cases in order to protect a child threatened with 'danger' or to safeguard 'the better interests of the child'. The religious courts were incensed. I myself saw a lawyer preparing such a submission before the civil judge ('a judge with a neck tie', as he put it), but who was going to get a colleague to put it through the system rather than do it himself, because 'the shaykhs hate this judge'. The Court of Cassation found in favour of the judge's rulings in two

[35] The ruling was published in a number of Lebanese newspapers, not least *al-Nahar*, under the title 'A special and courageous decision for personal status law'. For the ruling and commentary see Qazzi 2007: 36–50. See also the discussion in Traboulsi n.d.

appeals; but communitarian pressures within the civil court system led to a change in direction. The moment was over.[36]

It is not, however, that there is no impetus towards reform of religious legislation itself. Religious reform from within, as led by Islamic scholars, even if often in response to external pressures, is of course a pronounced feature of the modern (and pre-modern) era.[37] But such movements have until recently left little trace in the law applied in Lebanon's courts, at least since the reforms of the Ottoman Law of Family Rights. One glaring exception that threw the previous immobility into sharp focus was the recent reform of the law applied in the Sunni courts in response to protest by women's groups. In Ghamroun's account, this was again in response to the perceived injustice of the sharia precepts applied regarding custody, which, in the Sunni courts at the time, presumptively awarded custody to the children's father once they reached a certain age: seven for boys and nine for girls.[38] (In the Ja'fari courts – also the target of protest, in this case unsuccessful – the standard applied is even more favourable to the father.[39]) Debatable in itself, this also provided men with powerful levers in legal disputes with their wives and ex-wives. After a long campaign targeting the central Sunni religious institutions, including demonstrations outside Dar al-Fatwa itself, the women won change.

Ghamroun notes that this is a relatively unusual mode for women's activism, targeting the authorities of the community rather than the Lebanese state system itself. More 'traditionalist' feminists thus criticised the movement for in a sense legitimising the place of religious communities in Lebanon's personal status system, as well as abandoning the opposition between secular and religious norms. But the activists instead targeted the plurality of opinion within the Islamic legal tradition itself. As we have seen, at that time clause 242 of the 1962 Law of Sharia Courts directed the Sunni judge, where the 1917 Ottoman Law of Family Rights does not speak – as it does not on the question of custody, to the preponderant opinions of the Hanafi School, a diverse and contested field of discourse. Ghamroun quotes one of the movement's members:

[36] Ghamroun 2014: 69–77. See also Maktabi 2013: 299.

[37] On such movements in the Ottoman Syrian provinces see Commins 1990; on Lebanon's Twelver Shi'a see Mervin 2000.

[38] Ghamroun 2013. The debates and court practice seem to assume solar years rather than the lunar years of the Islamic calendar (10–11 days shorter), which I presume was the reference point of the classical literature.

[39] Two years for boys and seven for girls being the usual position. I discuss this further in Chapter 14. The protests are ongoing. Some Shi'i mothers have gone to prison rather than give up custody of their children, as in the high-profile case of Fatima Hamza in 2016. See Hamdan 2017.

> Abu Hanifa [the eponymous founder of the Hanafi school] says seven years for the boy and nine years for the girl. At that time, the child needed its mother so long as it could not look after itself. At the time, at seven years old the child would go with its father to work. Now the mother stays with her child until the *brevet* [school exams taken at the age of sixteen] to teach it – if she doesn't it will fail. Then Abu Hanifa changed opinion, [saying that] the girl stays with her mother until her marriage and the boy until puberty. But the Sunni courts adopt the opinion of the first Abu Hanifa: seven years and nine years.[40]

The movement achieved progress: in 2009, Dar al-Fatwa had sent a proposed law to the Council of Ministers adopting many of the movement's proposals, with many influential political supporters, not least the Hariri-led Future Movement. However, once the law came to be debated in Parliament, the characteristic communitarian sensitivities of Lebanese politics came to the fore. In angry reaction to the notion that Sunni Islamic precepts could effectively be decided upon by the Lebanese Parliament, a new legal project was advanced instead to transfer control over the law applied in the Sunni courts to the community's Sharia Council. This law was passed in 2011. After further lobbying of the council, the women finally achieved their objective. The age of custody for mothers was raised to twelve years for both sexes, in a decision by the council that was ratified in 2012.

The law in question, Law 177 of 29 August 2011, 'Modification of Section 242 of the Law of Organisation of the Sunni and Ja'fari Courts...', in theory represents a fundamental change to the way in which the Sunni courts operate. Section 242 has now been changed so as to direct the Sunni judge in the first instance to 'the resolutions issued by the Supreme Islamic Sharia Council regarding the personal status of Sunni Muslims', and only after that, 'in the event of there not being any [such] text', to the OLFR and then the Hanafi school as before.[41]

[40] Ghamroun 2013: 210–211.

[41] Many thanks to Samer Ghamroun for sending me a copy of the text, which reads in full:

> Section 1: Section 242 of the Law of Organisation of the Sunni and Ja'fari Courts, issued on the 16 July 1962, and its modifications is changed to the following form:
>
> The new section 242:
>
> Firstly: the Sunni judge issues his ruling following the rulings laid down in the resolutions issued by the Supreme Islamic Sharia Council regarding the personal status of Sunni Muslims and pertaining to the regulation of the affairs of religious communities according to the first section of the rulings of legislative decree no. 18/55, as altered by the resolution issued on 21 Dhu al-Qa'da 1386, corresponding to 2 March 1967, and the law issued on 28 May 1956 and published in the official gazette on 30 May 1956, number 22. In the event of there not being any text, the Sunni judge refers to the Ottoman Law of Family Rights of 25 October 1917, and otherwise rules according to the preponderant statements of the *madhhab* of Imam Abu Hanifa.

(There is no change to the situation of the Ja'fari judge.) This is a radical shift in the formal chain of authority, opening the way to more extensive reform. As the law post-dates my fieldwork, its practical effects and consequences in the courts are beyond the scope of my knowledge and thus of this book. But the Sharia Council has already issued a thirty-eight-clause resolution outlining reforms to the principles of not only custody, but also *mahr* (the husband's marriage payment to his wife, discussed further below) and maintenance. Although the resolution is entitled, 'System of family law' (*Nizam ahkam al-usra*), it is not yet a comprehensive such code. But it clearly could become one.[42]

Conclusion

We have seen in this chapter some of the consequences of the way Lebanon's confessional family legal system seems to saturate the field of possibilities for Lebanese citizens. For some, that marriage, divorce and all their consequences are subject to religiously inspired law and authority is in principle unproblematic; for others it is an unwelcome, even outrageous presumption. Some of the consequences can be worked around, through manipulation of the religious court system or – for those with the means to do so – by marrying abroad. But there are many who see this as something more than just a personal obstacle, as rather a systemic, political problem that goes to the heart of what they perceive as the flaws of Lebanon's confessional accommodation. The obviously political nature of any discussion of reform of those confessional legal and political structures has frustrated most such debates – not just those

Secondly: the Ja'fari judge issues his ruling according to the Ja'fari *madhhab*, and where it is in harmony with this *madhhab*, from the ruling of the [Ottoman] Law of Family [Rights].

Section Two: the rulings of this modification apply to cases which are still under review at the initial and appeals level, and the rulings of this modification do not apply to cases in which a definitive ruling has been issued.

Section Three: this law is to be acted upon at the moment of its publication in the Official Gazette.

42 I must thank Moussa Abou Ramadan for supplying me with a copy of this resolution, dated 1 October 2011 (with subsequent modifications in 2012) and published in the Official Gazette on 12 January 2012. I detail the reforms it enacts at the appropriate junctures below. See also Mallat and Howayek 2013. It is worth noting that, according to one previous president of the Sunni courts, Shaykh Salim Jalal al-Din, later Mufti of the South, there were several earlier but unsuccessful attempts from within the Sunni courts to introduce a codification of the sharia principles to be applied, including one in 1979 backed by the then Mufti Hasan Khaled (Jalal al-Din 2003: 137–138).

over proposals for the possibility of civil legal personal status legislation, but also over reform of the actual laws currently applied in the religious courts. This backdrop of contestation and politicisation should be borne in mind as, in the coming chapters, we turn more towards the point of view of the Muslim religious professionals who work both within and outside the sharia courts.

3 Becoming a Shaykh

In order to understand the ways in which the sharia is invoked in Lebanon, we also need to understand the motivations and capabilities of the Muslim religious professionals who invoke it, both inside and outside of the sharia court system. If we can grasp something of the general expectations people have of a shaykh, then we will better comprehend the tensions and temptations of the more rarefied roles of sharia court judge and independent legal scholar. So, having laid out in schematic form the legal framework within which Lebanon's Muslim communities and their institutions are embedded, in this chapter and the next I present an account of one shaykh's ambitions and activities and the social context in which they are played out. Of course, any single instance is necessarily in some ways a particular one. My example here is of a young man, with a predominantly young, male audience. He has a vigorous style, his rhetoric as passionate and committed as his personality. Others – and we will meet others in the course of the book – might be gentler and more compromising, or more otherworldly perhaps, or less passionate and engaging. Here, as throughout, we have to bear in mind the range of possibilities that the Islamic tradition can sustain. But shared concerns nevertheless emerge.[1]

In particular, by examining our shaykh's efforts to shape both himself and his youthful congregation into virtuous Muslims, we will gain a sense of what I am calling the ethical aspects of the sharia-centred life and the pedagogical nature of the shaykh's vocation, in what emerges as something akin to a pastoral role. These compulsions are not always easy to reconcile with the bureaucratic work of official institutions. Through examining those pedagogical efforts, we will further see how Islamic discourse can be made to resonate with the contemporary realities of life, but also the potential risks of such 'relevance' at a time of considerable social and political tension. Our shaykh is part of the mainstream.

[1] See Antoun 1989 and Gaffney 1994 for comparable cases and points.

But the committed pursuit of a shaykhly vocation – being a 'real' or 'true shaykh' (*shaykh haqiqi*) as some put it – may lead to friction with the establishment. And while such commitment should nominally be total, to live up to an Islamic calling in an environment like contemporary Beirut, saturated with competing and often incompatible values, is no easy task.

Portrait of the Shaykh as a Young Man

I first met Shaykh Muhammad in 2004. He was working in Dar al-Fatwa, the official administrative centre of the Lebanese Sunni community situated in the heart of West Beirut, responsible, among other things, for looking after converts to Islam. Many are foreigners, some converting in order to marry a Lebanese Muslim (a Muslim woman cannot marry a non-Muslim man, as we have seen), others simply drawn to the religion. And Shaykh Muhammad was a good choice for the job: young, then only twenty-five, very personable and with a fair knowledge of English, gained initially from his education at Seventh Day Adventist and Baptist schools – missionary education has a long and distinguished history in Lebanon and retains a certain prestige.[2] Open and sincere, he is also highly determined, not to say insistent, and, he told me, known to some of his friends as 'the hammer' for just that quality. As an expert in foreigner liaison, Shaykh Muhammad immediately approached me when I visited Dar al-Fatwa in search of information for my then project on Islamic medical ethics, and we became friends. His career was to blossom, and through his generosity I was able to involve myself in many of his activities, in particular his work as imam of a nearby mosque, where he busied himself with the religious education of his congregation through regular lessons, and as an assistant to a judge in the Sunni sharia courts where I did much of my court-based fieldwork.

Shaykh Muhammad is the second son of four children: three boys, then all still single, and one married daughter, the eldest child. Framed photographs of them all stand on the ornate side tables of the living room of the family apartment, where the three sons and their parents live together on the first floor of a building in a 'mixed' (Sunni, Shi'i and, in earlier times, Christian) neighbourhood within walking distance of Dar al-Fatwa itself. On the wall hangs a photograph of his grandfather, a shaykh himself, wearing the turban-wound tarbush that marks the qualified scholar, although he gave up the life of the religious specialist

[2] See e.g. Thompson 2000: 78–79, 282–283.

for employment in the state security services. Middle class then, albeit respectable rather than wealthy, both parents are proud of having been born in Beirut, mark of Sunni urbanity, and observe the norms of Islamic decorum, as they see them at least. 'Thank God, we are conservative [*muhafizin*]', says Muhammad. Male guests sit apart from the women of the house; his mother wears a headscarf when out and about. This is a marked choice, for certainly not every family in the apartment block or the area does likewise.

His father, gentle and affable, owns a mini-market, none too profitable in the economic climate of the time. Commerce, heavily valorised in Sunni Beiruti middle-class circles, runs in the family: Muhammad's uncle is a respected and successful real estate developer, and Muhammad himself started out in trade when he was just eleven, working in his father's shop. He then built up his own independent venture importing and selling on soap, shampoo and other personal hygiene products. When I first met him I would accompany him, often on the back of his moped, on his rounds chasing up late payments from his customers in West Beirut. This was in addition to his day job at Dar al-Fatwa and helping out as imam in the mosque. As his shaykhly career blossomed his available hours diminished, as did his range of action: nipping about on the moped, for instance, became potentially embarrassing – he had to borrow his cousin's SUV instead. He handed on his business to his brothers. While of course aspiring to knowledge of their religion, both are pursuing academic means of advancement, higher degrees in mathematics and engineering, in combination with hopes of commercial success ('Bringing things from China and selling them in Dubai', as the youngest would have it). More recently, under the influence of a shaykhly mentor – 'He's so generous!' – Muhammad has tried to unlearn his commercial instincts, to spend and tip without thinking: 'Of course, I could talk for a day about a price, haggle them down. I studied commerce.' But now, in imitation of his new model, he 'doesn't think about money'. His new vocation required new virtues and reflexes.

Muhammad's religious calling had not come straight away. He had studied mathematics at university for a year before being drawn to his present vocation. Living by a well-known mosque, he would hear the call to prayer every day, and begged the mosque's custodian to let him have a go. It was then that he decided to make the switch to religious studies.[3] He completed a four-year undergraduate degree – a *licence*, following the French model – in sharia studies at the Sharia College of the Islamic

[3] Cf. e.g. Antoun 1989: 75–89 and esp. 88.

University of Beirut, affiliated to Dar al-Fatwa, with a final year dissertation on the place of Christ in Islam. He then devoted another year to a higher degree, the *diplome* in Islamic studies, finally graduating in 2003. After that he started work at Dar al-Fatwa, clearly having won the good favour of his teachers.

He began helping out as a mosque imam, officiating at the least convenient and well attended – if most rewarding – sessions, the dawn prayers. There is a magic to being at one's religious work so early, and to walking the uncharacteristically empty streets in earnest discussion with one's comrades. But he was then appointed as the imam proper of a distinguished mosque, not far from his home in Beirut's Sunni heartlands, just past Dar al-Fatwa itself. First and foremost he is responsible for leading the prayers: chanting the requisite formulae and Quranic extracts from memory, and setting the rhythm of the prostrations. Too fast and you've hardly time to finish saying '. . .' (part of the prayers during the prostration) before you have to get up, and then before you have said '. . .' (the next formula) they are off down again, as some of the men of the neighbourhood complained of one shaykh, over their evening sweets in the local sweetshop. Ideally one has a pleasing voice. Shaykh so-and-so's is so beautiful, the conversation continued, that one of them had seen tears rolling down the face of another shaykh once when he was listening to him.[4] Shaykh Muhammad has worked hard on his own abilities. Sitting in his flat, he would play me calls to prayer and other snatches of Islamic musicality stored on his polyphonic mobile telephone. 'Listen, listen – all with one breath!', he marvelled, as he played me a good ninety seconds of enchanting recitation, pure of tone but with heavy vibrato. 'I couldn't possibly do that', he said regretfully. While some go to music college expressly to achieve such skills, Muhammad laboured at home, listening to tapes of famous reciters and copying them. Through intensive practice at high volume he 'widened his throat'. I imagined a world of young men swapping downloads on their mobiles and practising in their bedrooms, as my friends and I had guitar riffs. Even at this level, the job requires craft and talent.

He was later also entrusted with giving the Friday sermon, no small matter in this relatively prestigious mosque, and worthy of an extra stipend. His role as shaykh and imam brings other responsibilities to the community, such as saying prayers over the dead, mediating disputes, visiting the sick and answering the myriad questions of his congregation, in person and on his mobile telephone. Such commitment and

[4] For discussions of weeping during prayer elsewhere see Mahmood 2005: 129–131, 146–148.

energy, over and above the formal requirements of his paid role, is well appreciated. A shaykyh is 'not like the priest, paid to do community work', but a deeper duty to perform such a pastoral role is shared, according to Shaykh Muhammad at least.[5] 'My official work is just here in the mosque. But it's God's work.' Another young shaykh, also very energetic, commented that, 'sorry to say', most shaykhs view their role as a job, to earn a living. They lead the prayers, then leave the mosque and shut up shop. But the shaykh's work should be 'twenty-four hours a day, seven days a week'.[6] Muhammad's cousin, a committed Sufi recently returned from California where he had had his own Islamic centre, scoffed at 'the Islam of the books', 'without spirit' (*ruh*), just what they teach them in college. For him, these 'shaykhs' (and he might include his cousin Muhammad in this category) aren't shaykhs at all. So too the efforts of the official sharia court, which he calls the 'pub' (in English): they sit around doing nothing. But the shaykh who chairs the devotional sessions he himself attends, does he sleep? Hardly, he works so hard. Sitting with a man who has committed adultery and wants to know how he can escape damnation, for hours, maybe a whole day – this is hard work! 'My shaykh, sometimes he goes two days without sleep.' To follow a vocation, and to be recognised as so doing, is not the same as 'just doing a job'. To be a shaykh is to hear a spiritual calling, not just to perform a paid intellectual task. It should take you over totally.

To walk down the street with Muhammad, or to be with him in the mosque, is to see him continually hailed, people rushing up to shake his hand, even pulling up their cars or motor scooters to do so: 'I know everyone from here to Tariq al-Jadida' (another Sunni neighbourhood some way down the road), he boasts. '*Salam 'alaykum*', he calls out, '*Ya khayy*!' – 'Hey brother!' – 'Are you coming to the mosque today? Why weren't you at the lesson last Saturday?!' '*'Alaykum al-salam*', they reply, '*Ahlan wa-sahlan*' – 'Welcome!' – inviting him for some of the wares of the shops that line the street: falafel, ice cream, pizza. 'What, I say I love the shaykh and don't invite him?!', as one sweet shop owner put it. But Muhammad is wary of accepting such hospitality. He usually says right away, 'no'; and if they persist then he leaves. He could eat everywhere for free, but 'no way'. That would destroy his reputation. No doubt not every shaykh inspires such trust and affection. 'It's about personality:

[5] The term 'pastoral' might be seen as having a specifically and distinctively Christian connotation. No doubt there are significant differences between the Christian and Islamic traditions on this point. Nevertheless, in the context of plural Lebanon, the link that Shaykh Muhammad makes might be suggestive of some conversation between the two. Whatever the case, I think my use of the term can stand here.

[6] Cf. Gaffney 1994: 197.

people like me', he ventured. Whether or not that is so, the notion that shaykhs are seen as loveable is worth remembering, given their often rather forbidding image in the wider world.

Having made such a good account of himself, he is entrusted by individuals with charitable donations, some clearly of quite considerable sums, which allow him to help the needy: 'It's a lot of work believe me.' He already had a project of his own for Palestinian street children in the refugee camps, where he planned to rent a room for a school. In 2007, he took on two further responsibilities. First, he won the authorisation to tend to the spiritual needs of his co-religionists in prison. He finds the work rewarding, if sometimes intimidating: 'There are drug addicts there, gays, murderers.' One, a huge Palestinian man covered in tattoos was in for a four-year stretch for beating up a gang of a dozen soldiers who had attacked him. 'We were sitting there – I thought it would be like one of those American films: he would pick up the desk and smash it on my head.' But 'The guy says, "I want to grow my beard, I want to become a Muslim."' He was surprised to find so many there with 'beard, perfume [*'atr*], everything – perfect Sunna', that is, the example given by the Prophet. On the way back from the mosque some evenings I would find him shopping for provisions for the inmates; and he arranged for the mosque to host a charitable sale of goods the prisoners had made. Such work is inevitably political. Many of the prisoners were Sunnis sent to prison as 'troublemakers', at a time when unrest on the streets seemed to Shaykh Muhammad and his flock to be organised by Shi'i youth groups and paramilitaries, and retaliation only natural. Others had been arrested as potential 'terrorists', a still more sensitive and problematic topic.

Second, he was made assistant to an important judge within the central Sunni courts: 'Now I will marry and divorce people', as he put it. His duties entail recording the sessions, maintaining the case notes and other bureaucratic functions, and he is also regularly employed as a court-appointed marriage officiant, supervising wedding ceremonies and contracts, which by and large take place outside of the court itself. These latter are an important additional source of income for a shaykh, and Muhammad is doing well by local standards. By 2008, he was earning about $1400 (US) a month, mostly paid by Dar al-Fatwa, but including $300 or so for writing marriage contracts. He was lucky, he remarks: from the very start working as an imam he was bringing in around $800. Not all shaykhs get that by any means. It depends. He is *Imam al-khatib*, an imam who also gives the Friday sermon. Others might just do the prayers. Some are just part time. Relatively speaking, this is a good salary, more than you would get as, say, a starting engineer. With the downturn in the rest of the economy, Muhammad is the family's main source of income, and he subsidises his brother's Master's degree. He is not ashamed to say that it is he who looks after the family, he told me, with the implication perhaps that this was not quite the natural order of things. He is certainly assertive within the household – everyone calls him 'shaykh' – but when I attended one of his Friday sermons with his father, Shaykh Muhammad greeted him with proper and traditional reverence, kissing his hand.

He has done well for himself in his new vocation. He even has a much-coveted official shaykhly identity card, which Dar al-Fatwa has stopped issuing: everyone wants one; they're like gold dust. But he has bigger ambitions. For one thing, being in the courts has made him wonder if he could not become a judge himself in the fullness of time. In order to get on, you need to stand out from the crowd, and one plan is to attain a higher degree, a doctorate in Islamic studies, preferably from abroad. Where Egypt's Al-Azhar might once have been the summit of such ambition, now the West seems more prestigious. 'Britain [in this respect] is the best', he told me. (I am British, admittedly. But France was the ideal of the older generation and the United States by now perceived as just too hostile.) In terms of employability, Islamic banking and finance seems a tempting specialisation. The Lebanese Islamic banking sector is expanding, with a number of banks scrambling to get a piece of the market. The banks need a shaykh on board to ensure the legitimacy of their Islamic products, and he would be well rewarded: $2,000 or $2,500 a month for an afternoon's work, Muhammad reckoned. And if he wants a loan, he will get one interest free. Of course, such studies could be very expensive, and the family would miss his material support. The volatile political situation was pulling him between whether it was better to stay or go. And, he felt, his congregation would not understand: 'Oh he's off to Britain to enjoy himself, they'll think.' All the rapport he had built up and all the progress he had made in inculcating good Muslim values in them might be lost. And he still needed to finish the 200-page Master's thesis on which he had lately embarked, but which was dragging on. He was none too enthusiastic about the topic, on 'Calling to Islam [*da'wa*] through organisations in Lebanon', and wished he had been able to choose a subject himself rather than being told what to do.

Learning

Irrespective of formal qualifications, Muhammad's vocation calls for scholarship and he is a voracious reader of Islamic literature. Often I would go round to the flat to find him sat cross-legged on the carpet of the living room, surrounded by books, reading up for a lesson or sermon he was about to give, or just for his own interest. Study has to be fitted in around his day job, now at court, from 8:30 AM to 1:30 PM, prayers at the mosque and all the rest that comes with his calling. But he manages six or seven hours a day, and night – for he often works well into the early hours. Not highly computer literate, he is not a big consumer of the Internet or the profusion of searchable CD-ROM-based scriptural materials now available, which, it has been suggested, presage major shifts in patterns of religious learning and authority.[7] He prefers books, and to memorise and embody his learning in the way still expected of someone with pretensions to knowledge (*ʿilm*).[8] 'You have to be ready at any moment' for people's questions, he told me.

A scholar needs a library, and in 2008 he proudly showed me a smart new bookcase, right by the front door and thus in a sense indicative of his pre-eminence in the family home. This joined another large one round the corner: 'These shelves are for hadith', the transmitted reports of the words and deeds of the Prophet: 'Bukhari, Sahih al-Muslim [famous collections] . . . These are for *tafsir* [Quranic exegesis].' He pointed out a compendious classic, al-Qurtubi's (d.1272) exegetical work, which he deemed very useful: it's a *tafsir*, but it gives you information on law (*fiqh*) too. Then there are the legal works of all four Sunni schools: the Hanafi School is applied in the courts, but at college, at the Mufti's insistence, they had also studied Shafiʿi law. Of course he wanted to keep going, and he also knows some Hanbali and Maliki law. One visit discovered a new set of volumes he had acquired at a cost of over $100, the renowned treatise on Hanbali law *al-Mughni* of Ibn Qudama (d.1223). He was also gradually accumulating, at some expense, the many volumes of the fatwas of Ibn Taymiyya (d.1328), the prodigious Hanbali scholar so important to modern Salafism. He loves the richness of legal discourse, the diversity of opinions, the way one school or scholar argues one way and then another comes with a different argument. The sheer breadth of the sharia is beguiling.[9]

Such a collection represents a considerable financial investment, certainly hundreds, if not thousands of dollars, even if religious publishing is heavily subsidised. But a visit to many an ambitious shaykh's apartment would no doubt find the same. One Sunni judge showed me his seemingly very extensive collection with some diffidence – he had just sold off a portion, he told me apologetically. His friend, on the other hand, has a library 'worth half a million dollars. *Al-hamdu li-llah*, he has means.'

[7] See e.g. Anderson 2003.

[8] On this older, but enduring motif of embodied scholarly mastery, see e.g. Messick 1993.

[9] Cf. Antoun's (1989: 95–101) fuller account of another preacher's library.

A Shi'i judge's books were all in boxes, packed for his move away from his old flat in the southern suburbs, damaged in the 2006 Israeli bombardments ('We had a rocket through the window!'). He drove me, in the course of a tour of the war's ruination of the area, to his new one, still in construction, in a quieter part of town. Here he will have his own study on a separate floor: a deliberately modest desk, a wardrobe for his shaykhly robes, a little kitchen to prepare tea and coffee for his guests, and plenty of book cases – I could, he promised, come and use his library when all was ready. A room of one's own remains an important ambition.

The shelves housing Muhammad's collection nearest the front door are clearly arranged for display. Most of these huge, multi-volume religious tomes are printed in attractive hardback sets, with gold-embossed writing stretching across the spines of the individual volumes, so that when they are arranged in order they spell out the title and the author of the work. Like everybody who has a passion for collecting such literature (including myself), he had gone to some trouble to make them look right. In the other bookcase down the corridor, they were not quite so beautifully arranged – 'I must do these too', he muttered.

He was also taking private lessons in *fiqh* with a shaykh outside Beirut, 'not a famous one, a young guy. But he knows so much.' They spent more than an hour on just one page. 'Analysing this point, that point – taking from here and here and here.' But knowledge is not just a matter of book learning, and Muhammad is not the unworldly type. Although he is in principle available to anyone in need, as a relatively young man he especially understands the problems of the youth (*al-shabab*). They in turn trust and turn to him in particular. He is inundated with their problems, even in the middle of the night: '2.30 AM, even!', his mobile phone will ring – '*Shaykh-na, su'al*' ('Our shaykh, a question . . .'). Our conversations were continuously punctuated by such calls: 'Sorry, let me take this one.' It was a girl who was engaged to someone, but now apparently he is leaving her. Muhammad told her that he knew that the guy has issues, but 'she was really upset.' His congregation, young men and women, besiege him with affairs of the heart. While he is, as he acknowledges, not always the best qualified to answer, as a committed virgin before marriage, he has learnt much from such conversations with them, and latterly also from his work in court. 'Before then I would never have believed that a man could ask his wife for such things.' Drawing on this experience, he has evolved his own 'philosophy'. As he told a friend, who was anxious that his girlfriend might not be able to wait for her parents to become reconciled to them marrying, 'Love doesn't last.' All human relations, he told me, are based on self-interest (*maslaha*). That doesn't mean that's bad, but that's the way it is. Only the love of faith is not like that, the love of one's brother in Islam. Take one of our mutual acquaintances: he only knows him from the mosque, but would do anything for him. 'This is real love.' Isn't that also based on self-interest? 'Yes, but *true* self-interest [*al-maslaha al-haqiqiyya*]: it's eternal.'

Of course he should himself marry at some point. Especially as a 'man of religion' (*rajul al-din*), you cannot be going around with your eyes popping out of your head every time you pass a girl. But it would be no easy matter to find the right one. Far from every woman wants to be married to a shaykh, and of those that do, not all would be attracted by a shaykh like him, one of such restless energy, uncompromising seriousness and openness to life. For most Lebanese girls, life with him would be unbearable, he reckons. He secretly admires fearless, 'crazy' women, like the young Western journalists for whom Beirut is a relaxing base between trips to Palestine or Iraq, totally committed to their own calling but so full of zest for life. If only one of them could embrace the light of Islam and join him in his life's work. He is not short of offers, for sure. Religious networks offer many such opportunities: a shaykh he met by chance on a visit from Saudi Arabia offering to gift him the money to furnish a flat and find him a potential bride; Lebanese émigrés keen to marry off their daughters – 'I'm not going to America! She can come here!'; and, more realistically no doubt, colleagues who knew suitable young women in Beirut and would whisk him off to someone's house, where he would unexpectedly find himself swapping words with a girl. He met one such, attractive and respectable, studying for a doctorate in education and with ambitions to set up a nursery. She was perfect: but there was no spark between them, for him at least. He asked God for guidance (*istikhara*), performing two prostrations, pondering the matter and seeing what answer came to his heart.[10] It was not to be. He is just not sure if now is the moment. He has so much he wants to achieve, so much study that needs to be done if he wants to become a real scholar (*'alim*). Just courting, let alone starting a family, would take so much time, of which he already has so little: sometimes he would feel compelled to leave me alone in the living room just to snatch a few moments alone with his mother in the curtained snug, or else he would never see her.

[10] Such forms of divination, which have a deep history, will come up again and need some explanation. Muhammad's technique is orthodox by Sunni standards. We will later see other practices in Shi'i circles, including consulting the Quran. Another common technique is to sleep on the matter, hoping the response will come in a dream or in some other form. See the entries on *istikhara* by Goldziher and Fahd in *EI*^{1} and *EI*^{2} respectively, and also Aydar 2009.

Even if studying abroad remains only a theoretical possibility for the moment, Shaykh Muhammad already has wider horizons than Beirut. He has been a regular visitor to Saudi Arabia for the Hajj and ‘Umra, of course;[11] he needs to get closer to God for a while sometimes. He fondly reminisces about times spent turning up in Mecca with nothing and sleeping in the streets and mosques, fed by the faithful. And business had frequently taken him to the Gulf, where he could broaden his knowledge of the world in ways impossible at home. In Dubai, in the hotel, he heard music and was told there was an all night party. ‘“What, here?!” [i.e. in Arabic/Muslim Dubai] So I went and had a look, and saw the people dancing. You need this kind of experience.’ But in Lebanon, ‘No one would believe it was just for research purposes.’

He has family scattered across Europe, and in late 2007 was invited to travel to Spain and Italy in order to give lectures to the Arabic communities, also taking the opportunity to visit relatives in Germany. This trip to Europe was a formative one. He realised that his thinking about the way of life there, especially regarding relations between the sexes, was off the mark. One time he was entering a mall with his aunt and they met a friend of hers, a woman, who kissed his aunt in greeting. And then, before he could react, she embraced and kissed him as well. He was shocked. But he understood that this was an uncomplicated, friendly gesture, with no deeper meaning.

> This opened my eyes a lot – like the [European] woman who was sitting next to me on the plane who talked to me all the way through the flight, about my work and Islam and everything, and then, when we parted at the airport, wanted to hug me goodbye! I had to explain, ‘No look, I can’t, this is my religion, it’s nothing personal’. Before, some years ago, I would have been shocked: what, you only know me for half an hour and now you want to hug me?! But now I understand. It is not like people here think!

I remarked that similar insights had surely been available to him in Lebanon, where after all Christians hug and kiss each other in greeting in just the same way. He had to confess that until recently he had had no Lebanese Christian acquaintances at all. But lately he had made the effort to get back in touch with some he had known at school. They were somewhat taken aback: ‘Wow, you’re a shaykh now!’

11 The latter being the ‘lesser pilgrimage’ (*al-hajj al-saghir*) to Mecca, a personal act of supererogatory piety that can be performed at any time, where the Hajj proper is a religious obligation that takes place at a set time in the Islamic calendar.

Sunna

He certainly looks the part. He wears his hair and beard in religiously recommended modes, the Sunna, or exemplary mode of the Prophet: short, close-cropped hair, normal enough, and a definite beard, not very bushy, but in the chin-curtain fashion with closely clipped upper lip characteristic of contemporary Sunni style. The Prophet is in fact thought to have had an impressive beard and worn his hair long, covered by a cloth, but to imitate the latter is, unfortunately, 'unacceptable' in contemporary Lebanon ('Maybe in Afghanistan.'). It is the cropped upper lip that has become totemic of today's 'serious' Sunni Muslim, obviously distinct from mainstream facial hairstyles (clean-shaven, moustache or close full beard), and for which the barber – the time I sat in at least – uses a dedicated electric clipper. As a graduate of the sharia college, working as a religious functionary, Muhammad is entitled to wear official shaykhly garb, the 'turban' (*laffa*, a cloth-wound tarbush), and robe (*jubba*), although he rarely does. He should when at work in court, although, like most of his peers, he finds the turban heavy, uncomfortable and perhaps somewhat pretentious, and he leaves the robe at the court in his locker. Out and about he normally dresses like any other Lebanese man in shirt and trousers, with a jacket if the weather is chilly. But when he goes to the mosque or another religious function, to serve as shaykh and imam, he adopts 'Islamic' apparel. This means at least donning a long, dress-like robe (*dishdasha*) and cap, both usually in immaculate white (his mother's work, no doubt). Sometimes he affects still more exotic, 'authentic' (if seemingly improvised) touches such as, weather permitting, sandals (not generally worn by Lebanese men), or a North African-style, hooded *dishdasha* and a cane.[12] In the winter this might be supplemented by a sleeveless body warmer and a woolly hat. A touch of perfume completes the ensemble: for the mosque the very expensive, non-alcohol based 'Arabic' scents, which he occasionally receives as gifts; otherwise a squirt of a standard man's aftershave.

But such superficial religiosity is just the start. As he put it to me:

> I'm at the beginning of the road. I'm in the car, I've got my clothes on, I'm ready to go. But it's not just about the appearance, the clothes, the beard. Yes, those are good. But it's also about morals . . . It's got to be about both appearance [*al-zahir*] and what's beneath it [*al-batin*, the deeper reality]:[13] what you can see must match what you can't. Someone might have a beard like this [miming a big,

[12] See Gaffney 1994: 212–213 for a comparable example of such sartorial improvisation.

[13] These terms have much deeper metaphysical resonance. See e.g. De Smet, 'Esotericism and exotericism', in *EI*^{3}.

bushy one], but then might have hairy armpits. The Prophet shaved his armpits. Look, I shave mine [he showed me]. Or he might have loads of hair here [miming a great mass of pubic hair]! We don't know, we can't see. It's no good having the right clothes and then stealing or lying ... God chose Jesus, Moses and Muhammad because they were the best men of their age. I want to be like that. I'm not saying I am, but that's who I want to imitate, not just a normal man.

Faith is evinced in both word and works (*al-iman qawl wa-'aml*), according to Muhammad at least. For this is the subject of some of the most pressing theological debates of this and other times: 'This has split Islam.'[14] While it may at root be a matter of doctrine (*'aqida*), to be able to question someone's faith as a Muslim by dint of their actions has huge political implications. Some contemporary Salafis argue that those in political office who claim to be Muslim but damage Muslim interests, by allying themselves with the United States for example, have rendered themselves unbelievers (*kuffar*, sing. *kafir*). It becomes not just a matter of hypocrisy (*nifaq*), but rather of apostasy (*ridda*), in Islamic thought a crime punishable, under certain conditions, by death. This then provides a theological justification for violent insurrection: apostasising (*takfiri*) *jihad*.[15]

This is an intellectually fascinating, but politically dangerous topic, and Muhammad is careful to distance himself from such extremism, or 'severity' (*tashaddud*), even if he enjoys reading around the subject: 'I am not a fanatic!' He sees himself within the mainstream, the Lebanese Sunni establishment. In that context, Salafism is beyond the pale: open adherents to Salafi currents are apparently barred from access to official employment and patronage. The Sufi practices that Salafis anathematise are, on the other hand, and perhaps in reaction, much more acceptable in establishment circles. Indeed I thought official Sunnism in Lebanon of a somewhat Sufi inflection, although that might be a misreading: certainly, Sufism remains a matter of private devotion rather than public policy, even if everyday forms of enchantment are commonplace enough in the mainstream – dreams of the Prophet, or the miraculous preservation of a copy of the Quran in a car torched during the events of May 2008.[16]

[14] Muhammad's formulation is historically a 'Hanbali' one, and orthodox. From the earliest times, there were Islamic movements that maintained the sufficiency of the profession of right belief for the constitution of recognisable faith (the Murji'a), and others with a radical insistence on right religious and moral action for claims to Muslim identity (the Kharajites). See the entries by Della Vida ('Kharidjites'), Gardet ('Iman') and Madelung ('Murdji'a') in *EI*[2]. Contemporary Salafi discourse often depicts those Muslims not of their way as the Murji'a of today (Haykel 2009: 40).

[15] See e.g. Wagemakers 2009: 95ff.

[16] See Clarke 2014 on this theme in Lebanon and e.g. Mittermaier 2011 (on Egypt) for elsewhere.

Muhammad, however, is dismissive of what he sees as Sufism's unworldly and thus apolitical implications. He bitterly resents the injustices of Israeli and Western occupation and murderous aggression in Palestine, Iraq and Afghanistan. But that is of course a position shared by all his peers and a commonplace of political discourse of all stripes in the region. Sometimes, he told me, when he is at home performing the dawn prayers, he reads some verses from the Quran and thinks of all the Muslims in the world being oppressed and suffering. He prays to God to help them and he weeps. But he is convinced, because he has 'read it' in the texts, that Islam will defeat its enemies, despite their present seeming strength. God works in mysterious ways.

His encyclopaedic knowledge of the minutiae of subjects like classical Islamic rulings on the criminal punishment of apostasy is largely redundant. 'Nobody else studies this stuff. People say to me, "Why do you study such things?" Because I might need them in the future.' Talking in the sort of vague utopian terms shared by many, even if with very different aspirations no doubt, he says that, even if there is no Islamic state (*dawla islamiyya*) now, 'Maybe it will come. I hope and pray it will come.' So all this reading is just in case – even if it might be unlikely. Nevertheless, 'I am free, personally. I can grow my beard and pray. I can make an Islamic state in my house.' Sometimes on satellite television there are things that there shouldn't be: naked women. If there was a proper state they wouldn't be allowed to transmit them. But you can decide for yourself, 'Turn the TV off, change the channel.' If only it were so simple. Leaving aside the blandishments of Satan – walking back from the mosque, Muhammad told us how he himself had struggled to get up for the dawn prayers: 'There was this voice saying "Go back to sleep!"' – it is not always easy living up to Islamic ideals in a society which, for these committed Muslims, seems in many ways an unsympathetic, not to say hostile, environment. Muhammad had forgone trying to walk on the Corniche, the seafront boulevard popular for family outings or promenades, after he had been (accidentally) showered with beer. Reaching the flat one time, we found two young women waiting outside the neighbour's door. These were not 'veiled' (*muhajjaba*) girls by a long way. Muhammad took pity on them and invited them in to wait. One, already showing a good deal of her midriff, without thinking rearranged her clothes, taking off her wide belt to do so. Her companion chided her: 'Ooh, watch it, the shaykh!', and they both giggled. After they had gone, we had a good laugh over this. 'What she's taking her clothes off in front of us!', joked Muhammad. 'Well never mind', I said, 'they're good sorts.' 'Yes', he said, '"natural"'.

There are more sinister forces at work. He had himself been harassed by members of al-Ahbash ('the Ethiopians'), the cultish Sunni group suspected of involvement with foreign intelligence services, once by a policeman who made him open his bag.[17] 'I know your type', he said. Muhammad went to the police station and made a complaint: he is a shaykh at Dar al-Fatwa after all; you can't mess with him like that. Another time, he saw a fellow committed Muslim (that is, in Muhammad's telegraphic description, a man with a big beard) being jostled on the street. Muhammad was about to go to help, but a group of men suddenly appeared and started beating up the bearded man badly. Muhammad did not want to get beaten too, and ran off. He felt terrible afterwards, 'crying inside'. He went to prayers and could not stop weeping with shame, the people asking him all the while if his tears were from love of God.

And inter-community relations in this religiously mixed neighbourhood had become more and more tense. On the main road, near the turning for the flat, stands a huge billboard poster of Hizballah's Secretary General, Sayyid Hasan Nasrallah, with fist raised; as one leans over the balcony, one sees a picture of the toils of Husayn, grandson of the Prophet, whose martyrdom lies at the centre of the Shi'i rituals of 'Ashura; the flat is hard by the local Husayniyya, where these distinctively Shi'i practices are hosted and from where the voice of the resident shaykh grates over the PA, pumping people up, as Muhammad would have it. Day-to-day relations seemed cordial enough, Muhammad swapping pleasantries with a burly lad who he later told me was a member of the other dominant Shi'i political movement, Amal: 'They call him the ghost [*shabh*], because he makes so many problems.' 'God bless', he called down from the balcony. 'Cheers mate!' ('*Habibi*!', lit. 'Darling!'), the lad shouted in return. I remarked on his bulging physique. 'Yes. These people [i.e. body-builders] are empty inside', said Muhammad, moving to a favourite theme, the spiritual emptiness of Lebanese youth, Sunni or Shi'i, Muslim or Christian, in this irreligious age.

But the family feared that were there fighting, they would be right on the front line, defenceless, and at the highpoint of the crisis in 2008, as the politicians' rhetoric escalated, they seriously considered moving house. Several times I would arrive at the flat to see Amal-affiliated youth running from police; a tank was posted on the corner; I would occasionally be stuck there waiting for the roads to be cleared of burning tyres. Come the events of May, with Hizballah's take-over of Beirut, these

[17] See Hamzeh and Dekmejian 1996; Kabha and Erlich 2006 and Rougier 2007: 113–127.

youths went on the rampage, smashing up cars, although Shaykh Muhammad and his family seem to have emerged unscathed. Looking as obviously 'Islamic', and more especially 'Sunni', as Muhammad does could attract unwanted attention. Religious professionals, with their distinctive garb, are emblematic of Lebanon's various religiously defined political communities. Another young Sunni shaykh driving me through Beirut would take off his turban when passing through certain areas to avoid trouble; and a Shi'i judge who sometimes gave me a lift home would avoid passing through the heart of the city altogether, slowing our progress considerably. And for Muhammad, walking to the mosque and on other business, some routes are better taken than others.

4 Lessons in the Mosque

Muhammad described the mosque where he served as imam as 'old', although it dates to only thirty or so years ago: few Beirut mosques survived the civil war intact, and most are of recent provenance. While the latest affect an antique style, this one is in the modernist mode of angular, whitewashed concrete with a green-lit tower, the recipient of an international Islamic architectural award in its time. Downstairs is a well-appointed basement Islamic centre, the venue for lectures and other events, as well as providing overspill for the thronging Friday prayers. The mosque sits on a crossroads on a large arterial road in a densely populated part of Beirut and attracts a sizeable congregation. We are in the heart of the Sunni community, just down the road from Dar al-Fatwa and the sharia college; Egypt's prestigious Al-Azhar University has a school nearby and shaykhs from al-Azhar's visiting delegation frequently pray here; the Mufti himself lives a few blocks away.

Come time for the best attended, sunset (*maghrib*) prayers after work, Shaykh Muhammad's arrival is eagerly anticipated by his protégés, young men mostly, who he is setting or keeping on the straight and narrow. Teaching, as well as learning, is vital to the shaykhly vocation.[1] The lessons are part of Muhammad's wider pedagogical efforts, especially focused on his closest adepts, with whom he would sometimes go to the graveyard after dawn prayers to meditate on the inevitability of death and (in my terms) help shape God-fearing selves.[2] I would be waiting too, usually sitting chatting with the mosque's caretaker, most concerned with my lack of spiritual progress, and some of the other regulars, older men from the quarter who seemingly spend their leisure time in the mosque – praying, reciting the Quran, studying and chatting. Muhammad cuts things fairly fine, usually getting there just before the prayers

[1] Another young shaykh had a higher degree in education to complement his degrees in sharia studies and ran a primary school within the mosque where he served as imam.

[2] On other such 'technologies of the self' see e.g. Mahmood 2005; Hirschkind 2006 and Clarke 2015.

themselves: there is quite an interval (perhaps twenty minutes) between the first call to prayer (the *adhan*), a recording from Saudi Arabia broadcast by loudspeaker from the mosque's tower to summon the faithful, and the *iqama*, the second call to arrange the rows for the prayers themselves, usually sounded by one of the regulars with a particularly strong voice. In the interval, people carry out the two sets of prayers (*ruk'as*) that are enjoined by the example of the Prophet as a 'greeting' to the mosque, and sit and talk. If Shaykh Muhammad arrives early, there is an opportunity to pay one's respects, or ask him a question. 'Shaykh', one young man asked him, 'isn't it forbidden for a woman to go to a swimming pool, even a women's only one?' It could well be, Muhammad told him – it depends what the women are wearing. Are they all in covering swimsuits or bikinis? 'Shorts!', cried the man's young son, who had been turning cartwheels on the mosque carpet, miming their length. But what about the others – are they in bikinis leaving the belly exposed? Are they looking at each other, commenting on what nice bodies they have? Maybe they will say as much to their husbands.

When the *iqama* is called, everyone gets into their ordered rows behind the leader, and there is much fiddling and pulling people into place. Latecomers dash up so as not to miss anything – if they do then it must be made up afterwards. I would usually sit quietly at the back, just behind the old men, who sit on a row of plastic chairs well behind everyone else for the prayers, as their knees or backs are not up to the energetic prostrations. An old fellow might roll in late in his pyjamas and dressing gown. Men bring their little sons, and sometimes their little daughters too, who run around, look lost, or imitate everyone else, slightly unsure of themselves. Then Shaykh Muhammad will lead the prayers, melodiously chanting the Fatiha and other Quranic verses, often lengthy passages. Should another shaykh be present, there will be a pantomime struggle as to who should take charge – the senior man should of course be pushed unwillingly to the fore. Prayers completed, hands are shaken and supererogatory prayers performed.

For most of the year, between these and the subsequent, evening (*'isha'*) prayers, there is an interval of about an hour or so, which offers a convenient slot for some form of religious edification or instruction. The two prayers and the intervening session thus form a seamless whole of religious endeavour. Such events take place in the evenings on most days of the week in this mosque, and in other mosques. They might include lessons in Islamic law, training in Quranic recitation or celebrations of the Prophet (*mawlids*), like the weekly session chanting praise poetry amid Sufi *dhikr* led in this mosque by a prominent judge in the sharia courts, or one-off special events with a 'band' (*firqa*) and a PA.

The latter included official-seeming events, moments of establishment mobilisation, but also privately funded parties, to mark the move to a new home, for example. There is no officially set curriculum or text: such lessons are personal initiatives by those with the appropriate expertise, the mosque forming the stable ground for a shifting set of devotional and pedagogical practice. No fear here, so close to Dar al-Fatwa, of the mosque being 'taken over' by undesirable forces, even if one nearby was known to have been commandeered, in this case by the Ahbash. But nevertheless, in paranoid times, one never knows who is listening.

I had already seen Shaykh Muhammad earlier in his career give an impromptu talk at another mosque elsewhere in Beirut. We had nipped over there together on the moped, because he had agreed to lead the prayers, filling in for a friend – 'substitution!', he joked. He then gave a little talk at the end – 'If you don't mind listening brothers' – perhaps five minutes about the evils of putting things off for another day, which most stayed on to listen to. Another talk in Ramadan in 2004 had especially pleased him: 'They were shaking afterwards.' Now, with his own mosque and congregation, he could institute a much more ambitious programme. In 2007 and 2008 I regularly attended what had become a weekly hour-long lecture, or lesson (*dars*), on Saturday evenings.[3] Again, it is not a prerequisite of his job, but he feels it his duty. A less committed, energetic and studious shaykh would perhaps shirk such a responsibility. 'It's a little extra', he put it to me modestly one time. It is a lot of work though, he acknowledged, preparing such things, researching a topic, finding a suitable hadith (saying of the Prophet) to make the point.

This is in addition to his role as preacher of the Friday sermon, which is, by contrast, a formal, official function. For the Friday prayers, the mosque is much busier than usual, full upstairs and down, with shoes spilling out onto the steps outside, and people noticeably better dressed. On the one occasion I attended, Muhammad seemed transformed, standing at the top of the high pulpit between two cream flags adorned with green calligraphy, beautifully dressed in a pale grey suit and white shirt with matching robe and his turban. He spoke without notes, for perhaps twenty minutes, distanced from the audience, as it seemed to me, by his stern tone, stereotyped material and elevated linguistic register. The official nature of the event resonated in other ways too: before

[3] I attended six in 2007, of a possible nine, and received accounts of the contents of the other two. In 2008, I attended five of the weekly lessons and had knowledge of a sixth, before the change to a shorter, daily lesson, in reaction to the Hizballah-led opposition movement's takeover of Beirut. My accounts are drawn from notes taken from memory immediately after the lessons, and checked with Shaykh Muhammad, usually on the following day.

initiating the prayers, he announced a lecture to be held in the cultural centre downstairs in the coming week on citizenship (*muwatina*); afterwards, a very old but distinguished gentleman in a suit was pointed out to me – former Prime Minister Rashid al-Sulh;[4] as I left with Muhammad and the lads, we met the judge to whom Muhammad is an assistant, who gave his verdict on the sermon (a couple of grammatical mistakes but good overall); at the door a political pamphlet was thrust into my hand by affiliates of Sa'd al-Hariri, the Sunni political leader at the time.

Muhammad's lessons, then, are a different, if allied genre: less formal, freer, more personal.[5] In 2007 he could tell me proudly that he had been giving the lessons for two years and had hardly ever missed one. This continuity is very important to him, building a relationship with his congregation and a core group of followers. Attendance was variable: the older regulars would usually stay for the lesson; and Shaykh Muhammad has, as noted, a group of *shabab*, young disciples, many of whom would be present; and there were always a few other interested men in their prime. A typical audience in 2007 might have been between twenty and thirty men, with perhaps the occasional woman upstairs in the gallery, although on more than one occasion he remarked upon an unusually large crowd (once of sixty). In a particularly purple patch, his parents came proudly to see their son performing. In 2008, the head of the delegation from Egypt's al-Azhar university and one of his colleagues were regular attendees, which surely betokened success, but also implied some measure of scrutiny, even if gently phrased. One time they left the lesson half-way through, troubling Muhammad: 'You didn't like it?', he asked later. 'No, no. It was very good', said the Egyptian shaykh, praising Muhammad's approach to politics, which he deemed sensitive. 'God opened the way for you for this lesson, no doubt about it.'

After the prayers, when I had been sitting at the back, I would move to near the front. Shaykh Muhammad would sit on a chair with a lectern, miked up, in the *mihrab* (the niche indicating the direction of prayer), and would start almost as soon as prayers were over; the audience would lean against the mosque walls and relax. As he talked, a little boy of eleven or so dressed in a sparkling white *dishdasha*, who I thought of as

4 Born 1926, Prime Minister 1974–1975, 1992.

5 While, therefore, there is a good comparable literature on contemporary Islamic sermons (Antoun 1989; Gaffney 1994 and Hirschkind 2006, for example), such differences in genre need to be borne in mind. Mahmood 2005 deals with mosque lessons like those I describe here. The divisions between these different instances of pedagogical discourse – lessons, sermons, stories – should not be seen as sharp, however. For discussions of premodern cases see Berkey 2001 and Jones 2012.

the mosque mascot, would plead to be allowed to carry out his weekly duty: to go into the cupboard at the front of the mosque where the PA equipment resides, and where is kept a big box of sweets – in this case lumps of rock sugar – which he would then take around the audience, offering them each a lump in turn. Occasionally, some of the lads might have clubbed together and got biscuits and soft drinks that they could hand out at the end. In such politically tense times, my presence did not always feel comfortable. I sometimes felt exposed, challenged even, by a passing reference to the meddling of the Western powers, say, or the need to be wary of strangers in our midst. But this is one of the classic tactics of the preacher, to test the consciences of his congregation, and I stuck it out.

For the basis of the lesson, Shaykh Muhammad advanced progressively through a text, turning on the life of the Prophet or 'the Muslim personality', for instance. When I first started attending the lessons seriously in 2007, he was using the *Zad al-ma'ad* of the famed Syrian Hanbali scholar Ibn Qayyim al-Jawziyya (d.1350).[6] This is, then, a text of hundreds of years ago, although Ibn Qayyim seems fresh, and is a favourite of revivalist ('Salafi' in a broad sense) discourse. It is, as usual, a massive work, of many volumes and hundreds of pages: 'It will keep me going for years!', Shaykh Muhammad told me. But come 2008 he was using a new text, the *Lawaqih al-anwar* of the Egyptian scholar and Sufi 'Abd al-Wahhab al-Sha'rani (d.1565).[7] These core texts are supplemented by his copious and eclectic extra reading, 'bits from here and here and here', he would say, miming plucking things from all around.[8] 'I study all week for this lesson.' But he does not just produce the stuff by rote: the Quranic verses and the hadith reports of what the Prophet said and did of course; 'maybe I won't get every word right, but . . .' But as for the rest of the material, he reads it and then comes up with his own ideas. 'Take this story about the Prophet Muhammad before the battle of Badr', he enthused. They are eating before the battle, and someone offers him a date – he dismisses it impatiently – he wants to get on with stuff. Here we

[6] In full, *Zad al-ma'ad fi hady khayr al-'ibad*, 'The provision of the hereafter in the guidance of the best of worshippers', that is, the Prophet Muhammad.

[7] *Lawaqih al-anwar al-qudsiyya fi bayan al-'uhud al-Muhammadiyya*, 'The gleams of the sacred lights in describing the ages of Muhammad'.

[8] So, for instance, for a lesson on the battle of Badr, I found him preparing with the popular modern biography of the Prophet *Al-rahiq al-makhtum* ('The sealed nectar: a study of the life of the Prophet'), by Indian Shaykh Safi al-Rahman al-Mubarakpuri al-Fawri, which featured a map of the battle, and Ibn Kathir's (classical) *tafsir*. He does not just use these by any means: he cited Qurtubi's *tafsir* as very important to the lessons, and Tabari's history as well; and he uses other books on the life of the Prophet, that by Syrian scholar Shaykh Muhammad Sa'id Ramadan al-Buti, for instance.

see his love of God and the next world, not this one – he wants to get there as soon as possible; he doesn't even have time to eat a date. What about us?! We eat like cows!' Sometimes sections of instruction in Islamic law are included, drawn from a relatively 'contemporary' (*mu'asir*) text.[9]

These are an eclectic range of sources, and speak to the need not to imagine a world of too neatly classifiable 'Sufis' and 'Salafis', or 'traditionalists' and 'modernists'. Shaykh Muhammad's interests and imagination, like those of most Muslims no doubt, ranges more widely across the field of discourse than that.[10] And there is a correspondingly interleaved, almost haphazard feel to the lessons. They almost invariably begin with a reference to the core text, summarizing last week's theme and stating this week's: 'Last week's lesson was about what the Prophet wore, this week's is about what he ate'; 'Last week was about the call to prayer and how the muezzin has a special place in heaven. This week we are continuing with our book and we're looking at washing for prayer.' The book would be with him, the page marked (and sometimes he might have brought another text as well), and he might read a section, although very often he would paraphrase his prepared material from memory. But the theme might be postponed, or be interspersed with digressions and asides (see Table 4.1). There was relatively little sense of an unfolding narrative to the lessons, although there was clearly a point to them.

The material mined from these texts, presented in the elevated and self-consciously 'grammatical' (*nahwi*), sometimes archaic register of *fusha* ('pure', i.e. literary or 'classical' Arabic) which is a mark of his learning, is then related to the contemporary everyday lives of his audience through references to Lebanon's consumerist, materialist society, popular culture and international politics, all in the local dialect. 'You have to do *da'wa* ["calling" to Islam] in a language people understand.'[11] Again, knowledge is not just a matter of book learning. He draws on his experience, including his work in court and as a prison visitor. He seeks to be engaging: he cracks jokes; he asks the audience questions; and they talk back – but all in good humour

[9] The example he gave being *al-Fiqh al-manhaji*, a modern Shafi'i text.

[10] See also Antoun 1989: 97.

[11] Another young shaykh told me of the lessons he gave in downtown Beirut in the house of a 'very rich' man, the manager of a major company, for this grandee and his wealthy peers from the managerial class. He rapidly came to realise that despite these men's high social station, 'If you give a lesson in *fusha*, they don't understand a thing!' On the politics of this linguistic and cultural diglossia and its rhetorical uses see e.g. Armbrust 1996: 37–62.

Table 4.1 *The Subjects of Shaykh Muhammad's Lesson Series*

Weekly, from May 2007	Subject
Lesson 1 (of a series underway)	The marriages of the Prophet; their large number; types of marriage allowed in the pre-Islamic era but rejected under Islam; the adoption of Zayd and his divorce of his wife; the strategies behind the Prophet's marriages.
Lesson 2	The Prophet's wives, Khadija, 'A'isha; a diatribe against 'hypocrites' (*munafiqin*); contemporary conspiracies against Islam; prison visits.
Lesson 3	Rejecting aspersions against Islam's rulings on women, e.g. inheritance, the bridal gift (*mahr*), polygyny, physical chastisement and divorce; the situation of women in the West.
Lesson 4	The migration of the Prophet's followers to Ethiopia; the conspiracies against the Prophet in Mecca.
Lesson 5	The ulama and their confrontation of unjust rulers (historical examples); the fickleness of paid retainers; the nature of Hellfire; under what conditions the killing of unbelievers is legitimate.
Lesson 6	[Content unknown to me]
Lesson 7	The Prophet, his appearance and special powers of knowledge.
Lesson 8	The battle of Mu'ta and its martyrs; what the Prophet ate and drank and how he slept; the amazing nature of the Creation; God is always attentive; the three things the Prophet loved; the ingratitude of women.
Lesson 9	The activities of the Prophet, commercial and otherwise; Islamic legal rulings on ritual ablution.
From Feb. 2008	[Again, I resumed attending a series underway]
Lesson 1	The call to prayer [?].
Lesson 2	Prayer; ritual ablution, the opinions of the different legal schools; the application of *hadd* punishments (the divinely prescribed, capital and corporal punishments) to Muslims outside of Dar al-Islam; conditions for the execution of non-Muslims.
Lesson 3	The companions of the Prophet; alms (*sadaqa*); commanding right (*al-amr bi-l-ma'ruf*); the difference between a messenger (*rasul*) and a prophet (*nabi*); fornication (*zina*); the relative worth of the grateful rich man and the ungrateful poor man; envy; the relative worth of the strong, libertine ruler and the weak pious one.
Lesson 4	The scholar (*'alim*) in Islam [?].
	[A two-week break]
Lesson 5	Muhammad was the most beautiful of men; the need to call others to Islam; the need to learn; knowledge is tested on Judgement Day; the need to be politically aware; choose your marriage partner wisely.
Lessons 6 and 7 (?)	[Two weeks I have no knowledge of]

Table 4.1 (*cont.*)

Lesson 8	The Muslim is twice born; the Muslim is a stranger (*gharib*) to others; against materialism; the dangers of the marketplace; the stand (*mawqif*) for judgement before God; Muhammad's mode of greeting; the plight of contemporary Muslims.
	[Lesson cancelled]
Lesson 9	Explication of a Quranic verse enjoining strict adherence to the word of Muhammad; the question of Muhammad's infallibility, e.g. re the release of prisoners after the battle of Badr and the method for fertilising date palms.
Lesson 10	[The political situation prevented my attending]
Lesson 11	The problems of the argument from analogy (*qiyas*); the temptations of Satan; explication of a Quranic verse concerning Adam; today's Satan, television.
	A switch to shorter lessons in response to the political situation (explained at the end of this chapter)

('That was Hajj so-and-so. Don't worry, he really loves me!'). After a lesson, he was always keen to know my opinion: 'Did I come across as full of knowledge? Self-confident? Was there too much information maybe?'[12]

By way of contrast, every now and then the leader of the al-Azhar delegation would be present in the mosque and feel inspired to give a lesson himself, a desire to which Muhammad would of course accede. There is great popular affection and respect evinced towards 'Egyptian shaykhs' in Lebanon, a measure of the historical standing of al-Azhar, long the paradigm of learning in the Sunni world although tarnished by years of government control and no longer the aspiration of an ambitious student like Muhammad. This Egyptian shaykh had a traditional, enchanted, 'Sufi' persona, which resonated with popular expectations (although not necessarily the norm for al-Azhar or Egypt more widely): he would be asked for *awrad*[13] and blessings; he would constantly call for recitations of the *Fatiha* in supplication; during the tours of Lebanon's sacred geography I occasionally enjoyed with him, he fed me titbits from his plate for the blessing (*baraka*) they contained. He is of the old school. So in his lessons he employed the traditional rhetorical mode of rhyming

12 See Gaffney 1994: 172, 208–237 for a comparable (Egyptian) example, among a diversity of possible styles.

13 Sequences of prayers and formulae for repetition that unlock stations of spiritual progress.

prose (*saj'*)[14] as used in the Quran, in a monotone and highly elevated linguistic register; and he confined himself to safe, establishment themes with none of Muhammad's immediacy or familiarity with his audience. I found the lessons hard to understand, if mercifully short, although others seemed attentive and respectful enough. Muhammad would congratulate him heartily afterwards, the two, very different to my eye (and ear) but colleagues, in a sense validating each other.[15]

A Typical Lesson

To give a feel for a typical lesson by Muhammad, I present selections from one in 2007, summarised from my field notes and with commentary:[16]

> This lesson was supposed to be about the food that the Prophet ['Peace be upon him!', here and throughout] ate, following on from last week's lesson, which was devoted to what he wore. But before that we began with an account of the crucial battle of Mu'ta, a village east of the Jordan river, where three thousand Muslims dispatched by Muhammad – 'How many?' He held up three fingers: '3000!' – faced 200,000 [!] Byzantine troops.[17] How did they do it? Through faith. How do you defeat the Americans? Is it with RPGs? [Miming firing a shoulder-held rocket launcher] No, through faith. People are afraid of the Muslims because of this. He then discoursed for a while on the evils of the enemies of Islam [in his account, 'the Jews' and America], and the blood of the Muslims that has been shed in combating them. 'God have mercy on their souls!', cried an old man sat beside me. Faced with Muslim deaths, Muhammad continued, 'Who cares?', they say. 'There are plenty of them: they have lots of children.'

Present and past fuse into one sacred narrative.[18] The travails of the Prophet and his early community resonate with those of today's Muslims in Iraq, Chechnya, Afghanistan and Palestine. The first Muslims had 'sanctions' imposed on them when Mecca was cut off and there was nothing to eat, 'just like in Iraq'.

> This brought us to martyrs [*shuhada'*]. They want to die. Nobody wants to live again after they have gone to Paradise except martyrs, who want to come back, to

[14] This style has been much criticised for its obscurity by modernists. See e.g. Commins 1990: 99 and Hirschkind 2006: 150, 238n6–7.

[15] Gaffney (1994: 194–207) also presents an example of a 'formalized' preaching style to set against his more 'creative' one. Interestingly, contrary to my case, his formalized example comes from a younger shaykh and the more creative one from an older man.

[16] Lesson of 23 June 2007. Here and below, I should say, I could not claim to be rendering his words verbatim, as they were noted from memory, albeit immediately afterwards and in conjunction with later consultation.

[17] See the entry on 'Mu'ta' by Buhl in *EI*[2].

[18] What Gaffney (1994: 53) calls 'metonymy', I think. See also Fischer 1980 for a classic (Shi'i) example.

fight and to die again and again, because they know God will give them reward. There were many such martyrs at Mu'ta. We took the example of Ja'far al-Tayyar, ibn Abi Talib, brother of the Prophet's cousin and son-in-law 'Ali ibn Abi Talib and standard-bearer of the Muslim army. They call him 'two wings' [*janahay*], because in Paradise he is like a bird. Why? Because in the battle he was fighting and using his right arm and it got chopped off. So then he used his left and that also got chopped off. So then he held his sword with the two stumps. Then his head got chopped in two, split apart. [All acted out]. And so Muhammad, peace be upon him, said that in Paradise he is like a bird, with two wings, in the place of his arms.

This sort of martial subject matter and gory detail[19] was common in the lessons, not as some form of 'radicalisation' – the political tropes are unremarkable, in local terms – but more the particular enthusiasms of a relatively young male crowd. Going through his library with me, Shaykh Muhammad would pull out a volume like 'Issues in the jurisprudence of holy war' (*Masa'il fiqh al-jihad*) to show me especially: 'Look at the sections: assassination in Islam; when you can make an alliance with the infidel [*kuffar*] in order to fight the infidel; the fate of spies.' Or he would explain a topic like retribution (*qisas*): 'The majority of scholars say it should be like for like: so if someone is killed with electricity – arrgghhh! [He mimed sticking some cables into someone and then shuddering under electrocution] – then you kill them the same way.' Shaykh Muhammad deemed this action-packed style, with much shouting and violent episodes, important to keep people on their toes and stop them falling asleep. Other speakers would no doubt take different approaches.

Discussion of the battle, its ethics (under what circumstances you can and cannot kill non-Muslims) and its miracles complete, we moved on to the promised topic of what the Prophet ate. He ate everything. That's the key thing. He ate everything, including humble food such as bread and oil. But he also ate meat and chicken and honey and dates and the like. How did he eat? Not just shovelling it all in [mimed with much comic effect]. He ate with his hands of course, but not all five fingers; no, he used three fingers (the thumb and the first two fingers). And amazingly modern science has proved that if you eat a mouthful then stroke your beard, as he did, it improves the digestion. How amazing is it that the Prophet knew that?![20] Even if he ate with his hand, that doesn't mean that if you see someone eating with a fork you should say 'don't do that!' [The audience chuckled.] No – but eating with fingers is Sunna [i.e., recommended practice, as the practice of the Prophet]. Also, when he drank, they tell us he drank sitting down. That doesn't mean that if you see someone drinking standing

19 'Cinematographic' perhaps, in Gaffney's (1994: 225) terms.

20 For this sort of 'functionalisation' of religious discourse in dialogue with the prestige of modern scientific knowledge see e.g. Starrett 1998.

up you tell them off. No, but drinking sitting down is Sunna. He slept on his right side on a mat. It was hard; it made a mark on his shoulder. 'Umar [the second caliph] saw that mark and cried! Not like now. Now people say 'I can't sleep on this, bring me a mattress from Sleep Comfort [a much advertised local purveyor of luxurious bedding]!'

The perils of such 'worldly' (*dunyawi*) materialism were an important theme throughout Muhammad's teaching: 'If [the famously ascetic second caliph] 'Umar saw what we have today, he would be shocked: not just one phone, two! Not just one car, two!' Explicating the theme of 'the grateful rich man': 'Who is that? The man who sticks his money in his pocket [which he mimed], and says "Thanks be to God, I've got millions in the bank!" [everyone laughed]? No – it is the one who gives to charity.' Illustrating envy: 'You say "Why has he got a Mercedes and I haven't?" "Why have I got an old Nokia and he's got a new one? I need the new one!"' These touches of resonant detail were always very popular with the audience.

[After much further discussion of the Prophet's attributes, including his treatment of his nine wives] he finished by affirming that all you really need do is say 'There is no God but God' and giving a stern warning about heaven and hell. There's just those two: it's either heaven or hell. Everything you've done is written down. On your right shoulder is an angel recording it. And if you've looked on the wondrous nature of the cosmos and said, 'There is no God', then you're going to Hell.

The torments of the wicked were frequently invoked in fearsome fashion: hell fire is fanned to red for a thousand years, then a thousand years more to white heat and then finally to burn so hot that it burns black; pornographers would be crushed under foot on the day of judgement like insects, this mimed with a heavy stamp. And gender relations were also a common theme of the lessons, close to his young male audience's hearts and an important site of contemporary Muslim apologetics. More than one lesson was devoted to refuting 'Western aspersions' in this regard: the number of the Prophet's wives was a repeated trope; but Shaykh Muhammad also dealt with the unequal inheritance provisions for women, polygyny and the permissibility of beating one's wife. Other preachers perhaps make more of the possibilities within the Islamic tradition for a progressive discourse on gender – the tone of some of the lessons, such as one on the 'ingratitude' of women, seemed coloured by the preoccupations of his mostly male crowd. Discussions of marriage and divorce allowed Shaykh Muhammad to bring in accounts of his experiences in the courts, especially the sad fragility of matrimony in these fallen times: 'Think carefully before marriage, choose wisely. Don't just rush into it [driven by lust], and then we see you in the courts a couple of weeks later: "*Talaq* please, *mukhala'a* please"' (referring to two common types of Islamic legal divorce).

Throughout, he would mark an important distinction between Muslims in name only and proper Muslims, 'the faithful' (*al-mu'min*), who he was hoping to mould. The *mu'min* does the ritual ablutions (*wudu'*); the *mu'min* prays; the *mu'min* feels it when he has done something wrong, 'It is like a paving slab [*blat*] on his heart.' The real Muslim is a rarity in a hostile and uncomprehending, even if nominally Muslim society:[21]

> The Prophet (peace be upon him) said that the Muslim should be as a stranger [*gharib*]. What does it mean, that he should be a weirdo?! No, of course not: you will see that the true Muslim, if he comports himself correctly, will be a stranger amongst his family even. We see this: if he becomes a serious Muslim, people in the family may not accept it. 'What are you doing?!', they say. 'What is this backwardness [*takhalluf*]?!' That is especially for girls, if they take the veil. If they say to their mother or father, 'I want to wear *hijab*', they'll say, 'Oh, why not wait till you've grown up? Why not wait until after university, wait till you've got a job, wait till you've got married.' People try to pull you away from the path. You want to do the dawn prayers – they try to keep you up all night. 'Let's go and eat some burgers. Let's go to the cinema – there's delicious popcorn! There's this new computer game ... [he knew the name, which the lads appreciated].' At work: people look at your clothes, your beard, and they think you're weird. One of those communists, he's got hair out here [miming a huge mass of bushy hair], a beard like this [miming a big, messy, tangled beard], he hasn't washed for five days – you can smell him from the other side of the room – he is wearing 'hippy' clothes ... And they think Muslims are weird! [The audience rolling with laughter.]

Just as sacred and mundane time were fused, so were the high register of religious discourse with the resonant actualities of the everyday lives that he and his congregation shared. Islam appears 'total' in that it can be woven into the whole fabric of life. And yet Muhammad and his peers felt marked apart also, as authentic Muslims struggling to lead authentically Muslim lives in inauthentic times. The total experience of Islam must remain an aspiration, in pessimistic mood, perhaps even inevitably out of reach.

Legal Discourse

In the course of his lessons, Shaykh Muhammad also sought to impart knowledge of Islamic legal discourse (*fiqh*). Sharia talk thus did not stand alone, but was folded into the rest of his presentation of what it means to

[21] This section taken from another lesson, 12 April 2008.

be a Muslim today. This instruction was not solely for the immediate audience's benefit. The point of learning such material, he told them, was also so that they could teach others. Those who know, teach. Those who don't know, learn. Pedagogy is an imperative. A common theme was the intricacies of the rules around ritual purity (*tahara*) and the ritual cleansing that is required before prayer (*wudu'*) for worship to be accepted by God.

You go to the toilet and there's some [ritually polluting] urine or faeces [using technical terms] on you, what do you do? Say 'never mind' and go into the mosque to pray? No! You must wash. How do you wash? He quoted from the relevant Quranic verse [5:6]. First, 'Wash your faces' [*fa'ghsilu wujuhakum*]. What's that? From here [the top of the forehead], to here [the chin]; and from here to here [ear to ear]. Not just this [indicating washing round the eyes and nose alone]. 'Ooh, the water's cold!' [Everyone laughed] Nor, if it's hot, do you do it like this [miming throwing loads of water over oneself, again to much laughter]. Then one's head: not the whole head – look how easy Islam is! – just four fingers worth [from the top of the forehead up into the hair]. Your hands, past the elbow. Look: lots of people stop before the elbow. Maybe they've got on a $100 jacket. 'Let's not roll it up all the way', they think. Or, 'I've just bought a new shirt from [a famous designer label].' No. Then the feet.[22]

Of course, behind this relatively simple presentation there lies a whole world of scholarship. How exactly do you define the extent of the hand (*yad*, shading into the arm) or foot (*rijl*, extending into the leg) in Arabic, for instance, or even 'the face'? He explained the latter in another lesson:[23]

What does *wajh* [face, sing. of *wujuh* in the Quranic verse above] mean in the Arabic language? It means 'facing', 'opposite', so that's why your face is *al-wajh*. So it's from the brow to the chin to the ears – according to al-Shafi'i [the great jurisprudent and founder of the Shafi'i school], this white bit [the exposed skin between beard/side-burn and ear] is where you go up to; according to [another famous jurisprudent] it's this bit here. Does it include the beard, if you've got a proper long beard? According to such-and-such school it does: you have to give it a wash. According to these others [he listed them], you don't. But it is Sunna [the Prophetic example] to give it a wash. The beard: it's the whole beard; you wipe it with three fingers. Can you do it with one finger three times? Yes, but that is just trying to be clever!

And then there is a whole set of other legal concerns, as to the quality of water one is using, for instance. It should ideally be pure water. Stuck on a boat, say, you could use sea water. Water that has been left out in the sun and developed a scum on top is permissible, but discouraged.

[22] Lesson of 30 June 2007. [23] 16 February 2008.

What about water contaminated with other substances, like urine (polluting), as when a baby has done a pee in your bath? That is no good, unless it was a sufficiently large quantity of water to dilute the impurity to negligible levels.

Here both his own authority as an expert, but also the majesty of the sharia, in terms of its depth and breadth, were communicated. Muhammad sought to impart something of the richness and diversity of Islamic legal discourse that so fascinated him: 'There are rulings, proofs and traditions [i.e. of the Prophet and companions] for everything. Look at these writers: so-and-so's book is twenty-something volumes on just one subject. Many, like Ibn Taymiyya, were in prison when they wrote them. Amazing!' The topic of ritual purity is a good one for such purposes, complex – notoriously, even ridiculously so for some – but also of direct and continual concern for his audience.[24] *Fiqh* 'can be useful' too. But he ended this lesson by bringing it all back to fundamentals.

> Look how much Islam focuses on cleanliness. Why? For the nobility [*karama*] of the Muslim. If you don't wash for a month and then go to work, people will stay as far away from you as they can! Some extra things: you should shave the moustache. You see some guys, regrettably, who have bushy moustaches. No – the point is that it gets in the mouth. You shouldn't have anything going below the lip. You should shave the armpits [giggles from the younger men]. Not, Amazon! [Holding his arms up in air, indicating huge bushy growths underneath]. Like in Africa, a big jungle. And the pubic hair. Because if you're married, it's nice for the wife [giggles again]. You boys aren't married yet, so you can't talk about this yet. When you're married... You must cut the nails, not have huge fingernails with three kilos of dirt underneath, or so long that you poke someone's eye out with them! OK, if you're going to Afghanistan or Iraq ... [a joke – met with laughter]. Are there any questions? No? Because I will test you, I'll give you an exam!

Indeed, during Ramadan the year after I left, he told me (over the telephone) that he was holding a competition based on his lessons, with some impressive prizes donated by well-wishers: first prize was an all-expenses paid Hajj pilgrimage, worth about $4,000; and there were to be second and third prizes, the second possibly $500 worth of books to start your own library. People would have to know thirty hadiths, with their accompanying chain (*sanad*) of authenticated transmitters; and they would have to explain them. The competition had, he reported, proved very popular.

[24] On the compelling nature of the sharia's 'legalism' see Clarke 2015. For the complexity of the Islamic discourse on purity see Katz 2002 and for Western fascination with it see Reinhart 1990.

After the lesson ended, the lads swarmed round him with masses of questions, as usual: 'Can you use Kleenex?'; 'How do you wash your feet exactly?'; 'Do you clean in between the fingers and toes?'; 'What about the mouth?' This interest in the specifics of ritual was typical, along with other preoccupations, not least the proper behaviour for the young women that these young men had nominal responsibility for: their sisters and other female dependents. Can girls wear trousers exposing the calves? What about perfume? What is the legal position on feelings of love? ('Well, it's OK, love is good, a positive emotion ...' 'But what about telephone calls shaykh?') But this day, one of the older regulars had a particularly tough question:

> Look, what's this about peeing in the bath making the water polluting? A barrel [*barmil*] of water weighs a load: a litre of water is a kilo; a barrel is 200 litres, 10 tanks [i.e. car fuel tanks, a standard measure] – so it weighs 200 kilos. And a bath is a barrel's-worth. I know, I've studied this: Shaykh so-and-so told me that a bit of pee in the bath wouldn't affect it.

Shaykh Muhammad was nonplussed – 'There's 200 kg of water in a bath?!' (an over-estimate, but not radically so) – and had to have recourse to his book of law. 'Mmm, "a great quantity of water" is so many so-and-so's [an archaic unit], which makes 165 kg.' So it looked like the old boy was right. As a budding scholar, you have indeed to be on top of your game.

Real Shaykhs

The events of May 2008, when Hizballah and the opposition movements took over the streets of Beirut, were traumatic for the whole community. Fearful for their lives and property, many from Muhammad's congregation also felt they had been humiliated, powerless in a conflict that had often explicitly sectarian overtones: the fragile patterns of Lebanese civility were breaking down. Some, Muhammad reported, came to him saying, 'I want to fight.' 'With what?', he would reply. 'How? You don't even have a gun, let alone know how to use it.' Returning to the mosque after the worst was over, I found localised trouble lingering on the streets around. The army had to intervene after some Amal lads blocked the road and there was something of a scuffle. The continued provocation was just too much: 'This is our area!' 'It's Dar al-Fatwa!' Muhammad felt too drained to give his usual lesson, and convened instead a circle of the *shabab*, asking each of us in turn for our thoughts on the situation. Many voices were of the opinion that the Sunni community needed a strong leader (*qa'id*), like the Shi'a had in Hizballah's secretary general Hasan

Nasrallah for example, and shaykhs who were not just functionaries (*muwazzafin*) with the requisite qualifications on paper, but 'real' (*haqiqi*) shaykhs.

Having gone round the circle, Shaykh Muhammad was now inspired to some exhortation. This was like what the early Muslims did. The Prophet Muhammad took advice from his companions; they were his advisors. Everything had to start, he urged, with good religion: it would take self-sacrifice (*tadhiya*); worldly (*dunyawi*) considerations, cars and mobiles, must be left behind. Shaykh Muhammad quoted a parable of sacrifice, that of one of the Prophet's companions who returned to Mecca from a mission to the Ethiopians to find the Muslims very ill-treated; offered the protection of a local man, he declined, putting his trust in God, and an unbeliever put him to the test, punching him in the eye. 'That's nothing, punch me in the other eye', he said. Now that's self-sacrifice! They could make a start themselves, Muhammad continued. There were ten good guys here. The leader could emerge from among them. 'It could be you, or you; it could be me.' Or it could be someone from another group. 'But what's important is that we are virtuous.' That they come together, their little circle, and build on it. Such activity was, however, not something to be advertised, with its possible overtones of radicalism: they didn't want one of their wives to be gossiping about it on the phone to their friends. 'Real Muslims' can be seen as suspect. (One joker noted wryly that it could be good too: people would think them pious.) The circle broke up with the call to prayer, but immediately after the devotions, Muhammad sat at the front and gave a very quick talk, which many people stayed for: 'Some lads and I were sitting here talking, saying how we need a good leader to emerge, a Muslim leader. We don't know where they'll come from: it could be one of you. What is needed though is a real sacrifice', and he told the same parable.

This was to become a pattern. One response to the crisis for the community was a striking return of people – and especially men – to the mosque en masse. Prayers were packed. As a consequence, Shaykh Muhammad changed the rhythm and focus of his teaching. He moved to a much briefer (five minutes or so), daily lesson directly after the evening prayers, often standing in front of the congregation rather than sitting, maximising the numbers he could engage with and the impact of that engagement. Instead of a relatively small circle, now he was regularly speaking to a crowd that more than half filled the mosque. This was at the cost of Saturday's full-length lessons, which he regretted; but getting the material together for a lesson every day was exhausting enough. Now he had all these people coming, he could not let them down: even one day off might break the flow. These new lessons had a different focus, more plotted. He told the story of the early political history of the Muslim community and its travails in the face of the hostility of its opponents, obviously (to me) standing in counterpoint to the current travails of their own community: the battle of Badr, when the Muslims were seventy-five men amongst three hundred unbelievers; the sceptics who wanted to give up on the cause; the threats to the Prophet of assassination by the intelligence services of the day.

I could not attend them all, and came to see less of Muhammad as his commitments grew denser. My fieldwork came to an end. But when I visited again the subsequent year (2009), it was to find that from this highpoint had come a fall from grace. He had been expelled from the mosque by the committee (*lajna*) of local grandees that ran it. Apparently, they had said that he had been getting above himself, displaying too much pride in showing off his knowledge. He felt that it was actually because he was becoming too strong and independent, with his coterie of lads and his financial backers. The committee wrote to Dar al-Fatwa asking that he be removed and he was. As one of his young regulars put it to me, 'There are Muslims who aren't faithful [*mu'min*]. Shaykh Muhammad was expelled because of corruption [*rashwa*]. They [the ubiquitous, anonymous 'them'] don't want the real Islam, the real shaykhs.' Muhammad succeeded in being assigned by the Board of Endowments to give a weekly lesson at another well-known mosque in an important commercial district. But the committee there did not want him either, and tried to block his appointment. He made some ill-judged comments in response as to what he and his coterie of lads – some with 'big muscles' – would do if he was not allowed to preach, and the mosque authorities complained to the Mufti. Summoned to explain himself, Muhammad was asked if he had really said what they alleged. Yes, he replied, but not for his own sake, 'for the sake of religion'. 'Like Moses', he told me, 'when he saw them worshipping the cow, he threw down the Torah.' I do not know the other side of the story. But, whatever actually transpired, it speaks to the tensions that the path of being a 'real shaykh' might be thought to entail.

Conclusion

In this chapter and the previous one, I have given an account of what it means for one young aspirant to follow a shaykhly vocation, and the context within which such endeavours unfold. Having heard the call, he undertook formal, university-style education in sharia studies. Such qualifications are necessary to employment as a religious professional within the ambit of the official institutions of, in this case, the Sunni community. They are not, however, in themselves sufficient to satisfy people's expectations. First and foremost, to put oneself forward as a shaykh is to make claims to religious learning, including knowledge of the sharia, and one must be ready to be tested. Book learning, and the ability to call upon it away from one's texts, is thus indispensable. But one must also obey the injunction to share one's knowledge. The faithful must be formed, and pedagogy is an essential element to the shaykhly vocation. Sharia discourse represents a part, rather than the whole, of this pedagogical and pastoral project. Success in this field takes engagement, and especially with the youth. Muhammad can deal with them in their own terms, drawing on his worldly experience and his intense social work; he is available at any hour to help people solve their problems. All these efforts take great commitment and energy. But they bring rewards: gainful employment, the prospects of advancement, and also a loyal following. A successful shaykh can accrue the financial and human resources to institute individual projects of their own. Such potential power can, however, prove threatening to others. Being a 'real shaykh' may bring one into conflict with the establishment. It also brings tensions with wider society. How can one hope to meet with integrity such total demands, in what is a complex context of competing values? There is a duality here between the committed, 'faithful' Muslim and the rest of the world, to which she or he appears as a stranger.

This is one particular example, and one sort of model, of what it means to be a shaykh. It is a colourful, and perhaps at points an idealised one. I did not see every side of Muhammad's life, and no doubt it did not always measure up to the image and ideals he sought to communicate to me. One need not be so noisy and confrontational. There are less uncompromising exemplars than those that fascinate Shaykh Muhammad; and I knew quieter young men (as well as older ones) who had chosen Islam as their vocation. But the essential principles of commitment, learning, pedagogy and engagement seemed to me shared. So too do I find of more general importance the tensions that trying to live an exemplary life entails. I have focused here on the Sunni community. The Lebanese Shiʿi community has its own dynamics. But I would argue that my broader points as to the shaykhly vocation would still hold. They should be borne in mind as we now turn to the state-sponsored sharia courts, which constitute a major bulwark of employment and influence for the scholarly class.

Part II

Sharia within the State

5 Introducing the Sharia Courts

In the first part of the book, we learned not only of Islam's place within the legal structure of the Lebanese state, but also something of what it means to be a shaykh, an Islamic religious professional, ideally engaged with the people around them and committed to their education and assistance. There it was a question of the work of such a professional in the wider community, but more especially in the mosque, privileged site of Islamic religious practice. In this chapter, we turn to the chief subject of this book, Lebanon's sharia courts, setting the stage for the discussions of legal practice that will follow. Here shaykhs serve as judges (*qudat*, sing. *qadi*), adjudicating family legal disputes and applying the sharia as state-sanctioned law. This is the post to which our young Shaykh Muhammad aspires: he already works as an assistant to one of the judges, an important point of entry into a career in the courts and the official religious community. From judge, the fortunate few might become consultant judge – consultant, that is, to the courts' president, the final rung in the court hierarchy, which in its turn might open the way to something still grander.[1] We will need to consider the particular demands of the judgeship, while bearing in mind the more general expectations of the Islamic religious professionals who assume it.

There is a certain ambivalence within the deeper Islamic tradition about the position of judge. Witness such well-worn sayings as, 'He who undertakes the judgeship slits his own throat without a knife' and 'Of three judges, two are in hell' (one shaykh, a judge himself, joked during a mosque lesson I attended that 'Nowadays some say it's all three!'). The judge's proximity to potentially corrupting temporal power and income from the state were perceived as dangerous, as was his necessarily imperfect instantiation of the ideal sharia in mundane form.

[1] Thus Shaykh 'Abd al-Latif Daryan went from Sunni court president to Mufti of the Republic in 2014. See too Shaykh Salim Jalal al-Din's (2002) presentation in his memoirs of his journey from initial court judge, to consultant, to head of the Sunni courts and then Mufti of the South.

This was still more the case within the Shi'i tradition, long excluded (they would argue) from power and pessimistic as to the possibilities for justice in the absence of the Hidden Imam.[2] Such concerns resonate for today's judges, indeed could be seen as still sharper for them, working as they do in Lebanon within a civil republican legal system and paid from the taxes of what could be perceived as a morally dubious state, one that licenses nightclubs and allows the sale of alcohol, as one mischievous lawyer pointed out. The politics of obtaining such a desirable position could also be suspect; and once in place, the judge may be subject to pressures and temptations when people of influence come before him. Allegations of corruption are, in a banal way, rife, although the criminal courts have a much worse reputation (many of the lawyers I knew eschewed practice in them for that very reason).[3] But, as one lawyer had it, the civil judge writes, 'In the name of the people' (*bi'sm al-sha'b*) where the sharia court judge writes, 'In the name of God' (*bi'sm allah*) – 'So it's got to be right!'

Greater religious prestige is nominally given to scholars working independently of such compromising institutions, rather than as a state 'functionary' (*muwazzaf*, 'civil servant', 'employee'), as it is put in contemporary terms.[4] But regardless of their standing in a grander religious hierarchy, for today's Lebanese sharia court judge the post accrues all the benefits of high civil office, and the judgeship is thus a major milestone in a shaykhly career, even if in some ways a distraction from the scholarly efforts that would be required to scale its very heights.[5] As Shaykh Muhammad put it, being a judge is maybe the best thing in society, the highest status – except a government minister or president of course.

2 See Coulson 1956, Calder 1979; Madelung 1980; Messick 1993: 142–145; Reinhart 1994; Moussavi 1996: 64–73; Vogel 2000: 19–20; Masud et al. 2006: 10–11 and Gleave 2008.

3 Lawyers had many colourful tales of dubious dealings. But serious allegations require careful handling. One lawyer praised the way the courts had dealt with one such, where the judge he was finding unreasonable had a very weighty reputation and position. The lawyer asked that the case be transferred to a different judge, but the court authorities rejected that as implying that the judge was in the wrong, and instead changed the assignment of responsibilities for different types of case. I also saw one uncompromising judge have his duties rearranged after a case involving a relative of a very high profile politician landed on his desk.

4 The Law of Sharia Courts (section 455) specifically refers to the sharia court judges as such. Former president of the courts Shaykh Muhammad Kana'an was atypical in baldly stating to me that the judge 'works for the state, he gets paid by the state, so yes, he is a *muwazzaf*. His job is judging that's all.' But he did add a nostalgic note: 'In the Islamic era, judges were more independent, more valued. They could judge the ruler if need be.' Not so now, he concluded.

5 The Law of Sharia Courts (section 455) stipulates that the sharia court judge receive all of the salary and benefits given to judges working elsewhere within the wider legal system.

A judge gets a good salary, about $3,500 (US, per month),[6] and a special passport: wherever you want to go you can get a visa at the airport. You get security, a bodyguard. If you want a loan, $100,000 even, you can get it. But then again, he mused, alluding to the tradition cited above, were he to become a judge it would also be a 'disaster', 'because if you don't do it right then you will be in Hell'.

The role is a materially rewarding but potentially uncomfortable one then. And a shaykh might not feel wholly at home in the courts for other reasons too. In the mosque, one is mostly dealing with the faithful, or at least the willing, and centred on devotion and right living. But in the court one is faced too with the non-committed and often decidedly unwilling, and much of one's time – beyond the continuous focus on conflict – is spent on paperwork and bureaucracy. That the sharia courts are embedded within the larger structures of the Lebanese civil state, at some sites literally under the Lebanese flag, is keenly felt. Emblematic of Lebanon's dual legal system, these are in many respects hybrid institutions or assemblages, bringing together religious professionals and sharia legal precepts with civil legal personnel and laws, as well as other state paraphernalia: the policemen who serve as guards; the stock forms and stamps. And while this assemblage functions well enough in practice, it is imagined by the religious professionals who serve within it more as split than as blended, its duality highlighted rather than glossed over, if cast in somewhat different terms from those introduced so far.[7] For these shaykhs, the master trope of this rhetorical dichotomy is one of sharia (divine law) versus *qanun* ('law', i.e. civil state law), a distinction which ramifies in various ways throughout the life of the courts, as we will see.[8]

In some respects, we might see this as a means of managing the tribulations of instantiating God's sharia as mundane law in fallen times. For many of the clients of the courts, the religiously non-committed, this may be a rare and unaccustomed encounter with the sharia, and it may not meet their expectations, or their liking. And for the pious, it can equally be a disappointment. As one committed young Muslim woman

[6] I heard a variety of estimates. Another knowledgeable commentator told me a judge earned about $2,000 a month at that time, which seems more in keeping with the modest amounts state employees might earn more generally. A reviewer of this book, on the other hand, reported that they heard much higher figures.

[7] That is to say, the duality, or plurality, of Lebanon's legal system is carried into the sharia courts themselves. On sharia courts (in Malaysia) as 'assemblages' see Peletz 2013; for the tropes of hybridisation and blending (in Iran's family courts), Orsanloo 2006.

[8] This rhetorical framing has Ottoman antecedents: see e.g. Ergene 2014. Of course, analytically one might well be suspicious of such dichotomies, as in the Ottoman cases (ibid.). But ethnographically in my own field context these rhetorical distinctions were very real.

sitting in her lawyer's waiting room, deeply frustrated by her own experiences in the courts, put it to me: 'It's really a civil [*madani*] court. It's political. Maybe it's 20 percent religious.' A Sunni shaykh working in official marriage arbitration was still more downbeat: he thought the work of the sharia court judge was '90 percent law and 10 percent sharia'. Another Sunni shaykh, a judge's assistant, told me, 'You won't see the sharia in the courts – maybe only five percent', and advised me to look in books instead. After all, 'Here you see the problems of those who don't apply Islam.' A Shiʿi judge maintained that I would not learn anything at all about the right handling of divorce by sitting in the court. While not being wholly captured analytically by this binary rhetoric, I do see this tension between 'sharia' and 'law' as a key element of the characteristic flavour of Lebanese sharia court practice. And so I foreground it here and invoke it at many points subsequently.

Into the Courts

Let us start by following our young friend Shaykh Muhammad to his place of work in the Sunni court complex at the Imam ʿAli Mosque in Tariq al-Jadida, a quintessentially 'Sunni' part of West Beirut, for Sunnis at least. This is a core institution within the Lebanese religious courts system, housing not only the Supreme Sunni appeals court, but also the office of the president of the Sunni courts; it is home too to the president's consultant sharia judges (*mustasharin*), who sit with him on the appeals court panel, the inspector general of the sharia courts, who is a civil judge, and a number of initial Sunni courts, where I was a regular attendee. The court complex is situated in an annex to the large, modern mosque, which throngs with worshippers on a Friday, when the courts are closed. The courts are accessed from an entrance at the rear, just up from a little arcade of shops, one selling religious materials such as copies of the Quran, cassettes of leading Sufi 'singers' (*munshidin*),[9] perfumes, honey (a Prophetically advised foodstuff and medicine) and prayer beads; another, more prosaically, sells bathroom fittings.

The narrow street is usually closed, as a security precaution no doubt, but also allowing the untroubled arrival and departure of the judges, who may have an attendant driver. ('Have you noticed', a lawyer complained to me, 'there is not one religious court in Lebanon with a car park? Not one!') The standard judge's transport is a black Mercedes of varying vintage, although other luxury saloons are also favoured, along with the

[9] Technically 'singing' (*ghinaʾ*) is illicit; Sufi *nashid* is, although melodic, formally different – 'chanting' perhaps.

occasional SUV. From a shaykh's car, it was suggested to me, and his home should I be invited to see it, one might gauge his honesty: to be too flashy would attract the suspicion of corruption. Nevertheless, a judge occupies a distinguished position in society and also has to live up to it. As one Shi'i judge told me: 'A judge has to keep up appearances. This is in Lebanon, just in Lebanon. In [a no doubt idealised] Iran a shaykh could be a farmer, a peasant, tilling the land. In Lebanon, no way. You see a judge riding a motor scooter – oh! Word would be around the whole country in minutes. Shaykh so-and-so was riding a moped!'

Once through a security check at the door, one mounts the stairs inside, past offices on the first floor and the wardrobe full of headscarves and black cloaks for women otherwise 'improperly' dressed to don, as a sign advertises, and up to the courtrooms on the second floor. First, the supreme appeals court, grand and capacious. In common with the rest of the courts, following the dictates of the 1962 Law of Sharia Courts, these sessions are open to the public.[10] Unlike the initial courts, however, this appeals courtroom has been designed with public attendance in mind. Lavishly panelled in wood, subsequent to a recent refurbishment, with calligraphy reproducing apposite Quranic verses, the setting is marked as 'Islamic', although the atmosphere is hardly devotional, even if the proceedings open with the *basmala*, 'In the name of God the Merciful and Compassionate', after the usher has bade all rise as the judges enter with the call of 'Court! (*Mahkama!*). Here the appeal court judges, the president and four senior consultants, sit in their shaykhly robes on imposing chairs at a raised platform. There is a seat for the recorder, who takes dictation by hand, from the president; and to the right sits the prosecutor general (*al-na'ib al-'amm*),[11] the representative of the civil legal apparatus, dressed in his own distinctive crimson robes of the French style (and, in my time, without a beard). He attends to ensure that the overarching civil legal constraints upon this court are honoured, and is available for consultation, a possibility frequently taken up during the proceedings. Legal representation is mandatory at this level, and here the lawyers must wear their professional robes, black gowns with ersatz ermine trim. The high theatre rather belies the lack of drama: at this level, one has the feeling that the action takes place elsewhere.

Away from the appeals courtroom, one enters the bustling heart of the court complex, ringed with the various judges' offices. The corridors

[10] Section 171. Cf. Agrama 2012: 99–100, 131–132, 137 on Egypt.

[11] The *parquet général* of the French tradition, either by direct transmission, given the colonial legacy, or indirectly through Ottoman precedents or the influential Egyptian model (Hill 1979; Messick 1983 and Rubin 2011: 133–152).

around throng with plaintiffs and respondents and their families and other sources of moral support; a few benches allow respite during what can be hours of waiting. In the Sunni courts, junior shaykhs, many fresh out of sharia college, others older men seeing out an unspectacular career, serve in a variety of administrative positions, and the courts bristle with energetic bearded young men, as well as the more usually clean-shaven or moustached 'lay' (my term) functionaries (*muwazzafin*), that is, those without specialist training in the religious sciences or pretensions to such learning. Here too is the lawyers' 'mess', as one lawyer with a military background described it to me: a small room where lawyers can sit between cases, chatting over tea or coffee, and brokering deals between themselves.

Other courts were of an almost identical pattern. The Ja'fari (Shi'i) courts mirror these in form and organisation, with a supreme court complex in a tall apartment building in al-Ramla al-Bayda', an upmarket part of Beirut on the sea, some way from the Dahiya, the southern suburbs of Beirut which are now the heartland of Beirut's Shi'i communities and home to the Supreme Shi'i Council. I attended an initial court here, as well as ones in the southern suburbs (at Musharrafiyya and Harat Hrayk). The Sunni and Ja'fari courts lead a largely separate existence: people working in both systems were curious about, and thus more or less ignorant of, the other; I was often requested to offer a comparative judgement as to their relative merits, all part of the discourse of confessional relations crucial to a certain vision of Lebanese civility. In the Ja'fari courts, shaykhs only serve as judges: all the other functionaries, including the judges' assistants, are laymen, not wearing clerical robes.

In both systems, I largely devoted my ethnographic efforts to the initial courts: at the appeals level one tends to see little in court but allusive and elusive lawyerly wrangling. In Jami' Imam 'Ali, the initial court offices are separated from the corridor by an outer office, with a desk or two manned by a lay functionary and, when not on recording duties, one of the judge's shaykhly assistants. On those days, two or three times a week generally, when the judge has sessions (*jalsat*, sing. *jalsa*), an usher (*mubashir*) guards the entrance, calling out the names of parties to cases. These were the days when I would attend: it would have been rather odd for me regularly to sit watching the judge do paperwork, as on the other days. The judge's office within takes a conventional format: there is a desk, behind which sits the judge, guarding his various stamps (which he should not leave unattended), and to the side of which, on his right, sits his assistant and recorder (*musa'id al-qadi / katib*). In the Sunni courts, a junior shaykh serves as assistant and recorder; in the Ja'fari courts, it is a lay functionary who does so. Here there is no civil legal representative present to advise the judge. There are easy chairs and sofas in a black leather finish round the sides, where lawyers and parties to cases can sit and wait for their case to come up (and where I sat): a judge may be more or less amenable to this, although lawyers cannot, in point of principle, be excluded. These offices are not, generally speaking, very large, and easily become crowded and noisy, arousing the ire of a hard-pressed judge: one, asked if he would not like more chairs, growled, 'No, preferably none at all'.

People, especially women, will often come with the moral support of relatives: their mother, father, other relatives, a female friend maybe. If there are children they may have to come too: a babe in arms along with all the associated paraphernalia to be wrestled up the court stairs; a little boy with a balloon standing forlornly by his mother's side. They might be material to the proceedings: the judge might want to see them, and even speak to them if he needs to gauge their ability to make informed choices. People are of all sorts, although the wealthier classes will more usually be represented by their lawyers: soldiers in uniform (perhaps saluting the judge); even sometimes prisoners with marital problems, brought in handcuffs and accompanied by guards, which adds a hint of excitement to the proceedings. The far-flung nature of the Lebanese diaspora often gives a cosmopolitan atmosphere. As one judge said, faced with yet another defendant living in the United States, 'Let's open a court in America!' But there might also be Filipina ladies, come to work in domestic service, sometimes only knowing English, or Russian wives, speaking Arabic but not able to read it. Translation raises its own problems: the judges' language skills are largely not those of more cosmopolitan classes.

The sessions are generally scheduled to begin at 9 AM, but a judge would more usually arrive at about 9:30. Until then, everyone must sit and wait. Given the need to settle down, chat to the recorder, peruse the schedule and the files, and drink one's cup of morning coffee, the sessions proper might not start until ten, although many judges are keen to get stuck straight in, especially when faced with a packed schedule. An average day for a judge handling one of the main caseloads, maintenance for instance, might have twenty or more sessions scheduled, although I rarely saw a day where as many actually took place.[12] (One judge's

[12] Actual sessions heard would average more like ten, although much paperwork would also be transacted. One old hand flicking through the register said that 'in the old days', they had only had one case a day. In total, a judge might have a hundred or more files in process. One judge commented that he had two hundred files on the go. 'Not even a judge in the Courts of Justice [*'adliyya*] gets that.' What was often perceived as an overly high caseload was blamed on a shortage of personnel, especially in the Ja'fari courts: not

usher complaining to another, 'We've got thirty-seven cases now! It's not on.' 'Well, we've got thirty.') Nevertheless, no one might turn up at first, certainly not till later in the morning. People well know the sluggish rhythms of bureaucracy. Large sections of my field notes read, 'A long period where nothing really happened.'

The general impression, however, is one of lively business, and a judge may complain of being hassled and overloaded. He might even take a break from the sessions, or at least call for refreshments. People are continually popping in, needing something signed or explained: the judge signs off or stamps forms requesting cases. Visitors unconnected to the immediate work of the court might drop in, shaykhly colleagues, for instance, bringing news or greetings after a trip abroad or to discuss business of the clerical class. Telephones ring continuously: the office will have at least one, sometimes more; the judge will have one or more mobiles, often with religiously themed polyphonic ringtones; the judge's assistant will have one too, as will most of the people present, many of whom will have neglected to turn them off – although respect for the court enjoins diligence in this regard, busy lawyers are often prepared to test the judge's patience. I recall vividly the image of one judge regularly dealing with court business while simultaneously holding two telephone conversations, a phone to each ear. One judge had to chastise his assistant for pulling the office telephone's cable out of its socket, tired of its repeated ringing and the judge's picking up and slamming down of the receiver. Occasionally a judge just does not feel up to the daily grind. 'Sometimes the routine is killing' (*al-rutin qatil*), one judge confessed. 'Please stop sending people in!', another shouted in desperation, and we had to sit in silence for a while for him to recover, as he contemplated his briefcase bursting with files requiring processing.

The court is not an environment obviously saturated with Islamic symbols. In the case of the initial courts at least, this is a generic office space. There is little or no personalising of the offices, beyond the shaykh's nameplate, usually in black calligraphy on a brass background mounted on a wooden plaque on the desk, as normal elsewhere. Even the bookshelves remain largely empty: the judge will but rarely check a dog-eared copy of the laws on court procedure; consultations of volumes of *fiqh* (Islamic jurisprudence) take place in the judge's own library at home,

enough judges and functionaries for too many cases. One judge working in the suburbs thought they needed four or five judges in their initial court rather than the two they had. A Sunni judge estimated that overall they were fourteen posts down. New posts need parliamentary approval (see Zayn 2003a: 106–111 for previous such changes): but the political paralysis in the country left little prospect of remedying the problem.

where he writes his rulings (*ahkam*, sing. *hukm*), carrying the files to and fro in his briefcase. Halfway through my major fieldwork at Jami' Imam 'Ali, the offices were redecorated in a prolonged process that upset settled ways and coincided with a routine reshuffle of the judges' duties: 'There are other things I'd like to see renewal [*tajdid*] in first,' joked one judge. A knowledgeable observer commented that these moves were of a piece, designed to consolidate the new President of the Court's grip by reminding his judges of the ephemeral nature of their positions: 'Not even your desk is your own. Because if a judge stays in the same place, he does everything for people: marrying them, registering their children.' Too well established, a judge could become too powerful. The offices emerged immaculate but even more impersonal.

Religious decoration is correspondingly rare: several offices have a calligraphic wall hanging citing a Quranic verse, say, or there might be a sticker on the door, 'I love God's prophet' inside a heart; there will be a copy of the Quran on the desk; but not much more than that. This is not a deliberately over-determined 'religious' or 'Islamic' environment. That is less true of the more emblematic appeals courts, which are, however, conversely more 'formal' (*shakli*) or procedure-bound in terms of their practice. The daily routine is, it is true, punctuated by the call to afternoon prayers that comes towards the end of the working day. At Jami' Imam 'Ali, the courts are attached to a mosque and when the call came many of the younger shaykhly functionaries would dash down there; the majority of judges do not, preferring to perform their prayers later at home. In one of the Ja'fari courts I worked in, the judge's assistant would perform his prayers right there and then in the office. But the call would not interrupt sessions, if they were still ongoing. In the Ja'fari courts, it is true, some judges – 'ones known for faith [*iman*] and spirituality [*ruhaniyya*]' – are known to practice Quranic and other forms of divination (*istikhara*), performed by telephone in between sessions, and sometimes even there and then for court employees.[13]

Shaykhs as Judges

But the main marker of religiosity lies in the person of the judge himself. He is a shaykh, a 'man of religion' (*rajul al-din*) trained in the religious sciences, and thus represents the sharia in his person as well as his

[13] As discussed in the relevant note to the previous chapter, *istikhara* covers a range of different practices, not all regarded as legitimate by all. Quranic divination was common in the Shi'i circles I frequented; Sunnis favour other forms.

rulings: he is dressed – and bearded – accordingly.[14] Like the appeals court judges, the initial court judge wears, in principle, his formal shaykhly garb, in its most official form. In the Sunni courts, that is a robe (*jubba*) over either a shirt, trousers and waistcoat or a white *dishdasha*, depending on the judge's style, and the 'turban' (*laffa*, *'imma*), the paradigmatic symbol of the religious classes, formed of the red Ottoman tarbush hat, or fez, wound round with a generous length of white cloth.[15] In what is the most striking superficial difference from the Sunni courts, the Shi'i judges wear their own distinct Shi'i clerical regalia, that includes a robe over shirt and trousers or, more commonly, a *dishdasha*, but is distinguished by a full turban of wound cloth alone, rather than a winding on top of the red tarbush, reminiscent of their unofficial status within the Ottoman system perhaps. The standard such turban is white. Those shaykhs who are also sayyids ('sirs', recognised descendants of the Prophet) wear a black turban, and are referred to as 'sayyid' rather than 'shaykh'. This elevated status grants no formal precedence in the judicial hierarchy, however. It is worth noting that, unlike that of the Sunni judges, this garb is, more or less, common to all Shi'i clerics and not confined to 'official' ones, as the Sunni equivalent is. Hizballah's clerical cadres dress in much the same way, for example. The distinction between officially engaged clerics and those working outside of the state-sanctioned institutions is thus not at all apparent, where it seems marked in Sunni contexts.[16]

To wear this full dress throughout a busy morning of sessions is onerous, particularly in summer; the turban especially weighs heavy. Consonant with the high prestige of the clerical class among the Shi'i community, I never saw a Shi'i judge remove their turban or robe, except

[14] The Law of Sharia Courts (section 474) states that, 'Sharia court judges must wear their religious dress [*thawb-hum al-dini*].'

[15] Shaykh Muhammad told me that in principle every shaykh who has graduated from a suitable religious college can wear the turban, but you wouldn't unless you had a post, in the courts, Dar al-Fatwa or the Religious Endowments (*Awqaf*) offices. Officially you are a shaykh 'once you have responsibilities'. I was sitting with one young shaykh when his new turban was delivered by the man who winds on the cloth. The shaykh had provided the cloth and the tarbush, and this man had wound on the cloth for the princely sum of $20. This garb, he told me, has its roots in Ottoman times, when all men were required to wear the tarbush, and so shaykhs wrapped white cloth round it as their mark of distinction. This mode of (Sunni) shaykhly dress thus extends across the former empire, although the Lebanese version has a considerably fuller winding than the more modest version of Syria and Egypt, say. 'In Lebanon it is very big, *mashallah*!', the shaykh joked. See also Gaffney 1994: 86.

[16] See Mervin 2000: 98–100 on the Shi'i turban from a deeper historical perspective (characteristically bigger than its Sunni equivalent, noted French High Commissioner Puaux).

briefly, in public. Several Sunni judges, however, would put aside their headgear and robe when at the business of judging or, more often, in the more relaxed and private part of the day when the sessions have finished. Nevertheless, the president of the Sunni courts felt the gravitas of the office requires that the turban be worn at all times, by judges and by their shaykhly junior assistants alike, 'for respect for the profession', as Shaykh Muhammad put it.

In practice, it is very rare for the assistants and other junior shaykhs in the Sunni courts to do so. Most just wear the *jubba* over a shirt and slacks or *dishdasha*, sometimes not even that. The very most proper would first ask the permission of the judge to disrobe, and then re-robe if they were to leave the privacy of the office, 'Or it will be a shame on us [*'ayb 'alay-na*].' The turban is said to be too heavy – it is 'too hard' – but perhaps also seems presumptuous. Their beards (some extravagant) and dress do mark them out as religious specialists, albeit not of the same standing as the judges, and they may in any case be known as such by locals frequenting the courts. They are addressed and address each other as 'shaykh'. More contestable is the relationship between these junior shaykhs and the lawyers, who may know the ropes better and may in any case have gained better grades in school. They might not be very deferential at all. In the Ja'fari courts, as we have noted, shaykhs only serve as judges, and the judges' assistants are laymen, not wearing clerical robes, but, by dint of experience, are often very knowledgeable.

Judges are owed respect, and are, to greater and lesser extents, jealous of their station. I found it all too easy to slight one by favouring another. Official letters of introduction required a panoply of titles,[17] and had to be evenly distributed (one judge congratulated me on my knowledge of 'protocol'). When people are called on the PA to the judge's office, they are called to the room of 'His Excellency Shaykh/Judge so-and-so' (*fadilat al-shaykh/al-qadi*), and they might address the judge as such;[18] someone with an ear for politeness would address them in the plural form;[19] lawyers commonly call out '*ra'is*!' ('president' of the court). However, they are not always addressed so formally, and the Lebanese idiom often favours a rather familiar style: 'Shaykh Muhammad', or

[17] E.g. *Janab ra'is al-mahkama al-Ja'fariyya al-'ulya fadilat al-qadi al-shaykh* so-and-so; *Janab musta'shar al-mahkama al-Ja'fariyya al-'ulya fadilat al-qadi al-'allama al-sayyid* so-and-so.

[18] Or *hadarat al-(q)adi* (or *fadilat al-qadi, samahat al-shaykh*).

[19] One middle-aged lady did so and then, clearly somewhat overwhelmed, also addressed the lawyer opposing her in the same way. The judge commented drily, 'He's a lawyer not a judge.'

shaykh-na, 'our shaykh'.[20] Most commonly, and as I did, one refers to *mawla-na*, roughly, 'Milord'.[21] For some, the university educated and secular-minded say, this gesture of deference may grate. Eating in court is disrespectful, as is smoking as a general rule, although two of the Shi'i judges I sat with (but none of the Sunni ones) were smokers themselves and would often share a smoke with a lawyer or acquaintance. A man slouching with his hands in his pockets may be told, by the judge or his usher, to stand up straight, or to take off a baseball cap: 'This is a court!'

Such respect is no doubt due the civil judge or court too. But the other key marker of these environments as 'Islamic' – itself commonly spoken of as a matter of 'respect' (*ihtiram*) for the judge and thus in its own way a form of civility – is more distinctive: the modest dress (*hijab*) that women are required to don, with varying degrees of effect. Rather rarely, even in the Shi'i courts in Hizballah's heartlands, does one see stereotypically modest apparel: a black *'abaya* and veil, for instance. Once or twice I saw women in full face-covering *niqab* and gloves. Much more common was the modern pious look of a tight-fitting headscarf, combined with a more or less modest or extravagant array of skirts, trousers and tops. It is not unusual to see combinations of, for instance, high-heeled sandals encrusted with rhinestones or calf-length leather boots, with skin tight jeans, a studded denim jacket and a pink head-scarf, perhaps topped off with sunglasses. But most common of all was to see women wearing jeans and a T-shirt, say, with a scarf draped over their head as a concession to the court, perhaps thrust upon them by the court officers. Very far from all Muslim women in Lebanon wear a headscarf. Various makeshift improvisations may serve: the hood of their sweatshirt; a child's T-shirt borrowed for the moment; a New York City beanie hat. The most egregiously unacceptable outfits – a strappy crop top or the like – will require the use of an encompassing black robe from the cupboard, much to the amusement of accompanying friends and relatives.

The judges are generally fairly tolerant, at the most perhaps asking, 'Cover your hair please', if a loosely draped scarf slipped off –'Whoops, sorry our shaykh!' It would no doubt be rather beneath their dignity to make more notice, although some might comment: 'She's got to come dressed like Muslims do!'; 'They are laughing at the judge'; of a woman

[20] See also e.g. Antoun 1980: 461 on Jordan.

[21] Literally, 'our lord'. These conventions may be local: a visiting Iraqi civil official heard me refer to one of the Shi'i judges I worked closely with as *mawlana* and found it most peculiar. Another source, however, tells me that it is common as mark of respect at Egypt's al-Azhar.

with a head scarf, but wearing a T-shirt and pedal-pushers, 'What, cover the head and reveal the body?! They've no respect. They're coming to court not a soirée.' More likely it will fall to a court official or junior shaykh to make a stern comment: 'Pull down that skirt!' While many female lawyers adopt a pious look, many also maintain a very different secular Lebanese model of the female professional, with stiletto heels and make-up, a token gauzy cloth slipping off their heavily styled hair. A few make no concession at all and appear without any hair covering, and I heard no comment made.

For many women, especially those not previously acquainted with the courts, this imposition is clearly resented: one can see them tearing off the cloths in annoyance as they leave. People do sometimes become infuriated by this forced encounter with the sharia, for some perhaps their first such acquaintance. (Two such, seeing a shaykh, whispering: 'Is that a judge?') Our young Shaykh Muhammad heard someone cursing God and told him to shut up. '*Kufr* [disbelief] is bad enough but this is the sharia court!' It became a bit of a scene and he almost got in a fight; he had to excuse himself before the court president.

Lawyers and Civility

The 'shaykhly judge', in my terms – the sharia court judge who is a shaykh, marked as such in dress and aspect – in some sense clearly stands for the sharia aspect of the sharia courts. Lawyers on the other hand, who are a ubiquitous presence in the courts and have their own official robes (which they by contrast rarely wear, despite also being formally required to do so), can be seen to represent the law, and more especially the civil law and the republican tradition. Relations between the lawyers and the shaykhly judges are thus in many ways emblematic, or at least symptomatic, of the deeper relationship between the sharia and civil legal traditions that constitutes the courts themselves.

The law is a respected and prestigious profession and the lawyers' association (*Niqabat al-muhamiyyin*) a force to be reckoned with. Among other things, the law can be a gateway to parliament: at least one of the venerable lawyers regularly to be found in the sharia courts had served as a deputy; another was mayor of the municipality (*baladiyya*) of one of the courts I frequented. The most distinguished figures write books and publish cases, which provide a literature and a commentary on the courts (which I refer to), and in some senses constitute interventions in the legal system. Lawyers need to be treated with some respect too, and are referred to by the honorific *ustadh* (approximately, 'Master') also used of university lecturers and other intellectuals.

First and foremost, however, they are jobbing professionals plying their trade in the courts. Many people, even those without great means, do hire a lawyer. Their services can be obtained relatively cheaply. 'Do you imagine that lawyers in the sharia courts charge a lot of money?', Shaykh Muhammad scoffed. '$100.'[22] Some cases may offer richer pickings. Even the richest find it hard to avoid the courts in family matters, including inheritance, and I knew of lawyers working on the estates of men of fortune who expected a very decent portion. A divorce too may result in large sums of money changing hands: 'The lawyer will take a cut', one judge (and thus not necessarily a wholly reliable witness here) told me. Judges would often quietly advise people not to get a lawyer, or mock their decision to do so when they were arguing over whether or not to pay out in the case at hand: 'What, you were arguing over $100 and now you want to get a lawyer?!'; 'Why don't you just pay her half what you owe instead of engaging a lawyer. Do you think a lawyer can get you out of having to give her her due?' But faced with the intimidating and confusing courts, some, especially vulnerable women, feel they do need someone to stand up for them: 'I haven't got anyone. I want to ask someone, a lawyer, so as not to make a mistake.'

The shaykhs are on principle suspicious of the lawyers, whose task it is, they would point out, to argue either side of a case with equal conviction. 'Lawyers are liars', was an English jingle often quoted to me with great amusement. One shaykh cited the saying, 'Of three judges two are in hell', and added, 'But *all* lawyers are in hell!'[23] In practice too, they feel, lawyers often seem to drag out cases to inflate their fees. They are 'materialistic' (*maddi*), as one judge put it. So they try to prolong the case, where 'we' judges try to get it done quickly. Most of these cases could be solved rapidly, he claimed. But lawyers slow things down. Their alleged (by the shaykhly class) rapacity contrasts with the shaykhs's supposed material disinterest: a judge dispensing advice as to how to write up a will or a case might remark, 'This is for free. Not like a lawyer. How much does a lawyer charge for a consultation?!'

22 A monthly maintenance of $2,000 was being aired in court one time. 'Do you earn that much as a lawyer?', joked the judge. 'I wish!' One lawyer told me that he had represented poor people for years. He estimated that he earned $4–5,000 a year, but was 'not interested in money'. Other sums bandied around were considerably larger: one woman told the court she had paid $1,700 to a lawyer; another party mentioned the sum of 4–5 million LL (about $3,000).

23 Another saying I heard often, attributed to the Prophet, was '*al-wukala' fi-l-nar*', which could be interpreted as meaning, 'The lawyers will be in hell.' See also Messick 1993: 224.

But as such banter also indicates, despite the structural tension, everyday relations are generally cordial, especially with those lawyers who are sharia court regulars. They might shake the judge's hand, kiss his assistant, even sprinkle some jasmine flowers on their desk in season. Some have connections with shaykhly milieux, whether intellectual interests in the sharia itself or, more commonly, through kinship. One regular was the daughter of a famous shaykh, one of three out of his four daughters who had become lawyers: the law is known as a good profession for women because of the favourable hours, the courts closing at lunchtime. Many are from well-known and well-connected families. Lawyers and shaykhs might have been schoolmates. Familiarity does breed a certain ease, some feeling free to leaf through the files or grab a tissue off the desk. And, it should be said, the initial court judges I worked with do maintain a relatively relaxed atmosphere, for instance by generally not insisting that lawyers mark their profession and privileged position in the courts by wearing their robes as required. As one judge put it to me, 'I could not allow them to speak unless they are wearing their robes. But we make it a bit easier.' But, when tensions come to the surface, such formality can be insisted upon: 'It's not clear that you are lawyers', one judge complains. 'I'm sorry milord, it's the first time I've appeared before you.' 'We're easy on you', chips in the judge's assistant.

Given the power of the civil law that the lawyers stand for, such good relations are desirable: 'Respect for the lawyer is good, so there's no conflict between them and us', a judge told me. The lawyer does have legal privileges, and may well be more at home in exercising them than the shaykhly judge, who is not a civil legal specialist. Lawyers may refuse to be cowed by the aura of respect due the judge and a dangerous trial of strength can result: one of the judges I worked with was the subject of an official complaint brought by a lawyer that had him thrown off the case. It should be said that not all lawyers are so fearsome a prospect. A judge might even help out a confused beginner or occasional practitioner in the sharia courts, or note an egregious failure in the 'tactics' employed. And lawyers do of course have their uses. One judge was sanguine: 'There are good ones, especially the religious ones, who take it very seriously, and there are bad ones.' A good lawyer, on this reading, is one who tries to engage in healing his or her client's problems. And lawyers are also useful for soaking up people's limitless appetite for questions and advice: Shaykh Muhammad, being badgered by someone in the corridor, saw a couple of the regulars – 'Thank God, there are some lawyers. Ask them.'

Lawyers are not all of a type of course. One helpful contact was a committed atheist – 'Don't get him started on the *hijab*', his female assistant joked. Another was straightforwardly 'religious' in style, but a modernist rather than a traditionalist, director of a centre for comparative legal-Islamic studies with publications to his name: his assistant wears a headscarf; his office prominently displays a copy of the Quran in a gilded case. Another, my most generous colleague, as well as running his own legal office was also a legal academic (with at least two posts) and an activist for reform of the courts. But the most imposing figure of all, in the Sunni courts at least, having practiced there for forty-two years by his account in 2008, was staunch in his commitment to the established form. 'The shaykh of the lawyers' (*shaykh al-muhamiin*), one judge called him – 'This is not praise', observed his recorder wryly. When I finally persuaded him to let me interview him, I asked his opinion as to the need for reform (*islah*). No need, he told me. 'The courts are sound [*saliha*]: they follow the rulings of Abu Hanifa.'

The Vulnerability of Authority

These two professional classes can lay claim to their own particular forms of knowledge and authority. The sharia court judge is a shaykh, and is trained as such, in the religious sciences. He has no (civil) legal training, a common source of criticism from the lawyers. The lawyers have, by contrast, been through law school – for many, a more prestigious and demanding a choice than sharia college – and are trained in the civil law and not in the religious sciences. They mostly practice across the various courts of the Lebanese legal system, although those most often seen in the sharia courts have developed a specialist practice in the area. From a lawyers' perspective, then, the shaykhly judge's legal authority is contestable. As one put it to me:

> Look, how long does it take to become a lawyer? Four years' law study plus three years' work-experience – the latter is effectively four because it takes a year to get a place with a lawyer. If you want to be an appeals court lawyer, that needs another one. So that's nine years and another five years' experience, let's say. So if you start at eighteen you will be thirty-two. What about the sharia judge or the court functionary [*muwazzaf*]? First, they don't study law. Second, there is no work-experience. He does four years of sharia studies. Does he study 'The principles of the sharia courts' [*usul al-mahakim al-shar'iyya*, i.e., I assume, the LSC]? No. Does he study 'The principles of the civil courts', because when there is no text in the sharia court law then you go to the civil law code?[24] No. Does he study international private law, for when there's a conflict between different laws?

[24] Section 444 of the Law of Sharia Courts states that where there is no text stipulating the required procedure then recourse must be had to the Civil Procedures Act of 1983. This covers items such as postponements, notification and summons. 'But they totally ignore it', as another lawyer told me.

No. So how can they have judicial culture [*thaqafa qada'iyya*]? He learns on the job, like a doctor who practices on his patients.

And he had suitably horrific tales to tell of instances when judges had thereby erred egregiously. In another lawyer's pithy verdict, 'They are more shaykhs than judges.'

Even on the shaykhs' own ground, their claims to knowledge may be vulnerable. For one thing they have less of a monopoly over religious learning than their class once did, in an era of mass literacy and higher education, religious television programming and searchable Internet and CD-ROM-based scriptural sources.[25] And in any case most initial court judges would hardly pretend to have reached the most exalted heights of scholarship. Few, save the most senior, especially the highest, consultant judges, seem to find the time to research and author the scholarly works a more elevated status would require.

Some observers are indeed critical as to their level. One venerable lawyer working in the Ja'fari courts likened the current generation – 'shaykhs of the end of days' (*mashayikh akhar al-zaman*) – to 'battery chickens', processed through a new array of local, modernised sharia colleges and seminaries in a few years: 'They don't know anything.' This is, let it be said, in many respects hyperbole and nostalgia. One can point to a generational difference for Shi'i clerics here: the older generation, now in its last gasp, having studied in the prestigious seminaries of Najaf before Saddam's Iraq became too dangerous; the younger having studied in the reformed institutions of the Islamic Republic of Iran in Qom, swollen with students after Najaf's wane, or in new modern seminaries in Lebanon itself.[26] This generational difference has its analogue among the Sunni religious professionals, an older generation having aspired to study in Egypt's al-Azhar, a more recent one more commonly educated in Lebanon's new Islamic colleges.[27]

[25] There is a very considerable literature on such transformations and their consequences for the authority of the clerical class. See e.g. Eickelman 1992 for one classic discussion.

[26] See e.g. Abi-Saab 2006. The Law of Sharia Courts (section 450) specifies that the Ja'fari judge has to have graduated from Najaf 'or any Islamic university' (*jami'a islamiyya*) with a higher certificate of religious studies (or indeed from a law college where the rulings of the Islamic sharia are taught). Prior to modifications made to the law in 1986 and 2000, this section further stipulated that precedence in appointing judges be given to those who bore the title of 'absolute *mujtahid*' (*mujtahid mutlaq*) (Zayn 2003a: 99).

[27] So too here the Law of Sharia Courts (section 448) specifies that the Sunni judge has to have graduated from al-Azhar or a law college where the sharia is taught; section 449 then added that someone possessing a certificate from the sharia college in Beirut can also apply if they have worked as a judge's assistant for at least six years, although Zayn (2003a: 98–99) notes – somewhat confusingly – that this section was annulled in 1994.

But in any case, as we will see, the vast majority of cases heard before the courts are not the 'difficult', and thus 'interesting', cases that might require pronounced intellectual exertion. The 'selection effect' that makes law seem excitingly contested from an academic perspective privileges the small minority of such cases, in itself a selection of those most often heard before the highest courts, rather than the great mass of cases routinely resolved at the lower levels.[28] Court life is in fact rather 'boring' (*mumill*) from this perspective, as one shaykh wearily affirmed. The range of sharia precepts drawn upon is correspondingly restricted. As one judge put it to me, after a hearing with an embarrassed lawyer representing a particularly obstinate husband, there isn't actually much room in the sharia court for the lawyers to manoeuvre. They are 'limited' (*munhasir*). Is he going to say a father doesn't have to pay maintenance for his children? No. As another judge had it, most lawyers don't specialise in the sharia. They do civil and criminal law. So they don't go into the substance of the cases; they just make arguments about form. (And still stronger: 'Positive law is the creation of lawyers. Most of the legislation they pass is for the benefit of their profession.') While we will have more to say about this characterisation in due course, it is no doubt true that relatively few lawyers are in fact prepared to enter into detailed debate over the sharia with the shaykhly judge. There are exceptions of course, dangerously learned advocates, some activists. But the 'formal defence' (*daf' shakli*) is indeed a ubiquitous move, especially at the appeals court level. As one judge told a frustrated party before them, 'We have to get the procedures right, I am afraid, because we have the appeals court over our heads.'

Besides these technical difficulties, which most judges, it has to be said, seem to rise to without that much problem, there is the deeper problem of trying to act as a shaykh, following the expectations of the vocation described in the previous chapter, while also attending to the minutiae of bureaucratic detail. That is, as it is more commonly phrased in the court, the imperative of maintaining the 'humanity' (*insaniyya*) of the proceedings, the pedagogical engagement with couples' problems that chimes with expectations of the shaykh's role more broadly: a judge might be praised for being especially 'human' (*insani*, *adami*). 'Look master lawyer [*ya ustadh*]', the judge will remind them, 'these are human affairs [*umur insaniyya*]. We don't want to talk about laws [*qawanin*] here.' These courts, they would argue, deal with something very different from other areas of law: 'The family, the heart of society.'[29] For a

[28] See e.g. Schauer 2009: 22–23, 157. The seminal article on the selection effect is Priest and Klein 1984.

[29] A distinctively modern notion, let it be said. See Asad 2003: 231–232.

shaykhly judge in the family courts to devote himself to getting the paperwork right and neglect the 'humanitarian' demands of his vocation is to run the risk of being perceived as being nothing more than a civil servant (again, *muwazzaf*), 'just stamping papers', as one committed Islamic activist working outside of the official establishment put it to me, or, in a judge's words (evoking similar thoughts we encountered in the previous chapter), 'just doing his job as a job'.

In the coming chapters, I explore in some detail the workings out of this opposition between the 'humane' (*insani*) on the one hand and the 'dry' (*jaff*), 'wooden' (*khashabi*) nature of the law on the other. This contrast between the humane and the 'formal' or 'procedural' (*shakli*) often elides into that between the divine sharia and mundane, positive law (*qanun wad'i*) that I introduced earlier. This tension runs through the aesthetics, rhetoric and practice of sharia court judging in Lebanon and is in some senses arguably crucial to it. It is bound up too with the duality of law in Lebanon (civil versus religious), the duality of religious authority that flows from this state recognition (official versus unofficial), and the related, but not identical boundary between what is of the state and what is not. Producing these courts as recognisably religious 'sharia courts' as well as functioning elements of the Lebanese state and its legal system is hard work.

6 Marriage before God and the State

In the previous chapter I introduced a distinction often invoked in the sharia courts between 'sharia' (*al-shar'*) and man-made, civil law (*qanun*). This was largely as a feature of professional discourse. Most ordinary people who come to the courts would not necessarily feel confident as to where one begins and the other ends. Indeed, for those who worry about the sharia's standing in today's world, that is in part precisely the problem: flawed human law might be confused with God's ideal vision. But in other ways the (related, although not identical) distinction between what is required by God and what is demanded by the state is a more familiar one. That is so in the case of marriage, for instance. God demands a religiously correct marriage for sexual relations to be licit: sex without marriage is a mighty sin (*zina*), one of the mightiest of all. The state, on the other hand, demands a legally correct marriage for its own purposes: so it knows what is what and who is who. (And, beyond that, society has its own demands.) The notion that one could be married in one sense, but not the other, is not such an obscure one.

Marriage is thus a good place to start our exploration of the courts' business for more reasons than one. Given that the bulk of that business is made up of disputes that arise subsequent to marriage, it in any case makes sense to start where those disputes ultimately have their roots. Marriage is of course a manifold social phenomenon – a process – involving a large number of different occasions, relationships and material exchanges. I do not discuss here engagement (*khutba*), for instance, which does occasionally come to the courts' attention if a dispute arises over gifts made, or the wedding celebration (*'urs*), or the whole complex skein of property transfers that marriage entails.[1] I concentrate instead on

[1] On engagement, the OLFR (section 2) stipulates the return of goods that constitute an advance potion of the *mahr* agreed; others should be considered as gifts. I only heard of one such case (noteworthy due to the large sum of money and high social status of the parties involved) and never saw one in the courts. On the complexities of marital property transfers, see e.g. Moors 1995, Mundy 1995 and Singerman 1995 for examples in Palestine, Yemen and Egypt, respectively.

the marriage contract (*'aqd al-zawaj*), which, in both Islamic and Lebanese law, is what institutes the marriage, rendering sexual intercourse permissible, assigning legitimate kinship relations (*nasab*) to any children issuing, and instituting rights of inheritance as well as other rights and duties between the spouses. From a legal perspective – sharia and civil legal – the contract is fundamental. And from a social perspective the performance of the written contract (*katab al-kitab*) is certainly a key moment in the larger marriage process. But we should remember throughout that it is only one moment within the multiplicity of events that constitute marriage in the Lebanese context, necessary but not sufficient, perhaps not even the most important: the subsequent public celebration and consummation are definitive.

As far as the larger argument of the book is concerned, marriage exemplifies the tension between what is required by God and what is required by the state, as well as the complex work of assembling the religious and the bureaucratic that the sharia courts and their staff perform. The supervision of people's marriage contracts is a paradigmatic enactment of the authority and indispensability of the shaykhly class. But it is also a paradigmatic way in which the uneasy union between religious community and nation state in Lebanon is produced.

Marriage before the Shaykh

Imagine a couple, accompanied by their families, come before a shaykh in the Ja'fari sharia courts in order to be married. I have dwelled slightly more on Sunni contexts so far, and it is thus in order to redress the balance and pay closer attention to Shi'i ones for a while. Nevertheless, as we will see, the focus here on the Ja'fari courts is not otherwise arbitrary: the tension between the religious and state-legal aspects of marriage is cast there in somewhat sharper light. The first thing to note about our imagined couple is that in coming to the sharia court to marry they have made a choice. The choice is not so much to have a 'religious marriage' rather than a secular one. Admittedly, as we saw earlier, there are many who resent and reject Lebanon's system of religious family law, and some who have the means and sufficient resolution to travel abroad – usually to nearby Cyprus – in order to contract a civil marriage instead. But within Lebanon, there is no such possibility. A religious marriage is all you can have.

Nor is the choice in question that to be married by a shaykh, an Islamic religious professional, although here too there is a theoretical possibility to do otherwise. As also noted, it was remarked in the context of the debates over civil marriage – by shaykhs as well as activists – that marriage in Islam is merely a contract between two consenting parties and is thus in this sense 'civil' rather than a religious sacrament, as in Christianity.[2] For the marriage to be recognised by God all that is required is the mutual consent of the parties involved, contracted in the proper way. This then raises the further question as to whether a religious professional has to officiate, as in the case of the Catholic priest. There would seem no basis for such a requirement in the sharia, even if it might be advisable, in order to ensure that the contract is correctly performed. As we will see, there are various essential formulations and components that a layman might be ignorant of. But irrespective of what learned debate has to say on the matter, most Muslim popular sentiment in Lebanon sees marriage as something sacred and the *katab al-kitab* as one important locus of that religiosity. The writing of the contract is thus, not least by popular demand, almost invariably presided over by a religious specialist, a shaykh. In social practice, this is a distinctively 'religious' moment as well as an officialising one. When I suggested to our young Shaykh Muhammad, for instance, that because marriage in Islam could be viewed as a civil contract a shaykh would not in fact be required, he was unimpressed: 'Marriage is something sacred [*muqaddas*], they think. They want a shaykh.'

Given that the supervision of a religious authority is not required for an Islamic marriage to be sound, the opposite question arises as to whether that of a civil authority counts in religious terms. With the country's huge expatriate population, a more pressing issue for many than the debates over a Lebanese civil marriage law is whether civil marriages contracted abroad, recognised by the Lebanese state, are valid and binding in terms of the sharia, with regard to 'the permitted and the forbidden' (*al-halal wa-l-haram*). Will the couple's sexual relations be licit? Will resulting children be bastards in God's eyes, if not the state's? Many Lebanese couples living abroad thus choose to enact an Islamic marriage contract alongside a civil marriage. Some indeed visit Lebanon to contract the marriage there. Subsequent disputes may then come to follow different tracks, civil and sharia, foreign and Lebanese, simultaneously.

But even if the oversight of a religious professional might not be compulsory under the sharia, it is for Lebanese law, which demands that marriages be registered with the appropriate state authorities. Following

[2] See Donahue 2008 for a discussion of the complexities lying behind this common contrast. As Ali (2008: 11) says, despite the fact that in the Islamic legal literature the contractual dimensions of marriage take precedence over its broader religious significance, some Muslim scholars have considered marriage to be in part an act of worship (*'ibada*) rather than purely a worldly transaction (*mu'amala*). See also Zuhayli 2006: 6519–6521.

the Ottoman Law of Family Rights and the 1962 Law of the Sharia Courts, the sharia courts formally require the writing of marriage contracts to be supervised and registered by a religious specialist appointed by the court, either the judge or a deputy authorised by him. By dint of Lebanese law, the state-sponsored sharia courts thus nominally monopolise both the civil and the religious aspects of marriage, despite being theoretically dispensable for both purposes. People are, however, well aware that this state requirement is not a 'religious' one. Or as a Sunni judge put it to me, they view performing the contract as though it was for God, but know that registering it with the state is not. 'They separate religion and state.' Non-compliance in this regard, however, is a criminal matter.[3] Nevertheless, it is not legally stipulated that non-compliant marriages are thereby null and void as marriages. A couple could thus in theory bring a case asking for a marriage that has been conducted unofficially to be established formally (*ithbat al-zawaj*). They might have got married independently of any religious authority; or their marriage might have been supervised by a religious specialist not officially licensed by the courts. They might even never formally have got married at all, although this had better be glossed over. If anything, the courts tend to prefer to err on the side of generosity and assume the best – that a couple is married – rather than the worst, that they are not and thus living in sin, their children bastards (*awlad al-zina*).[4]

By far the majority of marriages are legally above board of course: that is the norm. But some are not. Not registering a marriage with the state will cause problems later on down the line, however. A distinction opens up between being married in God's eyes – 'in the sharia' (*shar'an*), right and proper as to 'the permitted and the forbidden' – and being married 'in law' (*qanunan*).[5] I saw, for instance, one lady, not well off, in a Ja'fari

[3] According to: section 37 of the OLFR, on which see also Anderson (1951a), who notes the corresponding amendments to the Penal Code; sections 348–356 of the 1962 Law of the Sharia Courts; and sections 2 and 22–29 of the 1951 law on the registration of personal status documents (Zayn 2003a: 30, 33), which speaks of the judge as the spiritual authority (*ra'is ruhi*) or religious power (*sulta diniyya*) under whose hand the contract was completed. Mandatory registration of marriage has a deep history in the region, enjoined by a sixteenth century Ottoman Sultanic decree. See Welchman 2007: 53–59; Sonbol 2008: 97; Tucker 2008b: 59–60.

[4] On the former point, see one published case before the Sunni courts where a marriage not presided over by a religious specialist was ruled as established because completed 'according to the sharia principles', rejecting the argument of one side that 'the witness conducting the contract was not authorised or delegated to perform the contract, because that delegation and authorisation are not among the pillars of the marriage contract or its conditions' (Homsi 2003: 80). On the latter score see ibid: 111–114 and Barakat 2005: 107 for examples.

[5] See e.g. Homsi 2003: 17.

court with her child, wanting to divorce her husband. They had done the *katab al-kitab*; the husband was supposed to have registered the marriage but had not, it seemed, got round to it. The judge immediately noted a problem: the child was a year and two months old, and registering the child with the state – vital to obtain basic services – requires a civil court case after the age of one. And she had as yet no proof that she was even married. 'I want a fatwa for my daughter', she said, appealing to the most well-known form of Islamic legal authority. 'That's not how it works', the judge told her. Before she could do anything else she needed to bring a legal case to establish the marriage (*ithbat al-zawaj*). She would have to go back to the shaykh who had performed the *katab al-kitab* and get a copy of the contract.[6] For in some cases the supposed husband might deny the marriage ever took place at all.

Given the number of people wanting to get married, one can imagine the organisational challenges to processing them all. At this point a difference between the Sunni and Ja'fari court systems presents itself. Following the letter of the law, the Sunni system requires the writing of marriage contracts to be supervised and registered by a religious specialist appointed by the court. Except in the most exceptional circumstances ('if [the groom] doesn't have a house, for instance'), this now generally takes place outside of the court, in the home – 'otherwise we would be doing nothing else', as one of the functionaries told me.[7] The couple obtain a marriage licence from the court: they will then be assigned a shaykh who will supervise the contract for them and fill in the paperwork. The marriage is then registered. This marriage procedure costs, according to my source, $100 (US), of which some goes to the court and some to the shaykh.

By contrast, the Ja'fari courts do not require marriages to be contracted by an agent specifically authorised by the state, although they do expect the supervision of an appropriate religious specialist and require that the marriage be registered with the courts subsequently.[8]

[6] Interestingly, one infers that these out of court shaykhs are presumed to keep records. See Barakat 2005: 11–12 for an example of such a case.

[7] Since about 2003–2004, my source estimated.

[8] This would in theory include 'temporary/limited marriages' (*al-zawaj al-mu'aqqat/munqati'*), less politely known as 'marriages of pleasure' (*zawaj al-mut'a*), one of the highest profile distinctively Shi'i institutions and a heavily politicised topic. While much 'modernist' rhetoric sees great wisdom in the practice, and such marriages certainly take place, they are not a matter for public openness in Lebanon (Mervin 2008b; see also Weiss 2010: 172–174 on the French Mandate period.). I very rarely saw or heard of them in the courts, although one does find the odd pertinent published case: e.g. Barakat 2005: 105, where a judge registers a temporary marriage in order to ensure the registration of a child.

Notwithstanding its practical conveniences, this is presented as a principled stance. There is a difference here between the law and the sharia, as one judge put it to me. In the sharia you don't need such state authorisation of the shaykh presiding, and that is the position they adopt. The supervision of any Shiʿi shaykh known to the court will be sufficient surety for them to register the marriage. 'We might make a little investigation [*tahqiq*]', the judge told me, 'but if we know the shaykh then no problem.'

The more liberal attitude of the Jaʿfari courts to the contracting of the marriage fits with a wider pattern, which lawyers like to point to, that, 'For Sunnis, marriage is hard and divorce easy, for Shiʿa, marriage is easy and divorce hard'. This refers most directly to the question of witnessing. Sunni precepts require that the marriage contract be witnessed by two witnesses to be valid, and this is stipulated in the Ottoman Family Law (section 34).[9] Shiʿi law, on the other hand, does not formally require witnessing of the marriage contract – although it is recommended (*mustahabb*) and general practice, certainly in court.[10] With regard to divorce, however, the opposite applies: Sunni law requires no witness, where Shiʿi law does. The lawyers tend to think the Sunni position better in the first regard and the Shiʿi better in the latter. Such comparisons between the court systems – but styled as between 'Sunnis' and 'Shiʿa' – are all part and parcel of Lebanese civility (and incivility). But they also point to the plurality of the Islamic tradition and its resources. And here they indicate a more general feeling on the part of the legal establishment that that which brings marriage and its consequences more clearly under oversight and control, and more particularly under the jurisdiction of the state, is better.

The choice that our couple has made, then, is to come to court to perform the marriage contract. Most prefer to do so outside of the court's busy and bureaucratic environment. In less pressed circumstances – at home perhaps – there is an opportunity for a more elaborate service: extended prayers, verses from the Quran, perhaps even a little sermon of guidance, fitting the pedagogical nature of the shaykh's role. Or a couple may want the blessing of a particularly distinguished figure. A good portion of my research was devoted to one such, Sayyid Muhammad Husayn Fadlallah, who I discuss in detail later in the book. One day a week in his schedule was reserved for performing marriage contracts:

9 See Homsi 2003: 73–74 for a case where the Sunni courts refuse to recognise a marriage contracted outside of the courts due to the absence of witnesses on the record of the contract.

10 Mughniyya 1979: 297; Niʿma 1996: 11 and Ali 2008: 17.

only one day, as 'otherwise the Sayyid would never do anything else'. A slot opened up and became an opportunity for me to meet with him for other purposes (to present him with my doctoral thesis, which had discussed his opinions at length). Waiting in the hall outside the reception room, I chatted to one of the many understandably nervous-looking grooms also waiting their turn (the brides have a separate entrance). You have to book a month in advance, he told me: to do the contract with the Sayyid brings great blessings (*baraka*). Through the just open doors I could see a marriage taking place: the bride coming in through the other door, the brief ceremony being videoed. It is an opportunity for guidance, one of his staff told me, but the Sayyid only has time for a few brief words: something along the lines of, '[Groom's name], this woman is a trust [*amana*] from God to you; [bride's name], this man is a trust from God to you. A trust – that means, she has rights against you [*'ind-ha huquq 'alayk*].' People want more of course – they would like to have the whole Quran recited, he joked.

Our imagined couple, however, prefers to come to see one of the shaykhs working as judges in the court: perhaps because they like and trust that particular shaykh, and that is where he is to be found; or perhaps because it makes the bureaucratic process simpler – no need subsequently to go through the hoops of registering the marriage. Two of the judges I worked with were especially well trusted and frequented for this purpose. Given my regular presence, I thus came to see many such performances of *katab al-kitab* in the courts. The twenty marriages I observed admittedly constitute a relatively small sample, but nonetheless an informative one. They were of course in some ways a distinctive set of instances: all Shi'i for one thing; but also the performance of the contract in court no doubt highlighted the more administrative sides of the marriage process, while constraining the possibilities for more extensive devotional and pedagogical accompaniment. That should be kept in mind.[11]

Katab al-Kitab

The writing of the contract would be fitted in between court sessions in a quiet moment, indicative of its secondary status with regard to court business at least. The wedding party might well have made an appointment, but also often seemed to have turned up on an opportunistic basis.

[11] As the contract has to be performed outside of the courts for Sunnis, I did not see that process on such a regular basis. The one instance I did observe was somewhat different, but not radically so.

The couple would almost invariably come in person, although that is not strictly necessary: either party could be represented by someone else instead, usually a relative. Most brought some relatives along for support: their fathers, mothers, aunts, uncles, siblings and maybe more; some parties were large, filling up the judges' spartan and cramped offices; others were much smaller, maybe just numbering the couple and their two fathers. They might be dressed up smartly, but not always – and certainly not in 'wedding dress', which would be reserved for the *'urs*, the wedding celebration proper. In all these respects, the groups I saw were varied: there was no rule. The mood would most commonly be festive, if somewhat nervous, the bride usually, if not invariably, shy, consonant with customary expectations; sometimes there might be some tears. The judge, sitting at his desk filling out the requisite forms, might crack a few jokes to lighten the mood. Many times he would know the families, resorted to by them for this very reason.

Before proceeding, the shaykh presiding will want to check that all is present and correct, not least with regard to the paperwork. A series of bureaucratic and Islamic legal conditions have to be satisfied. He has before him a form, the standard marriage contract, which effectively dictates them.[12] He will want to know, for instance, that the appropriate medical certificate from a licensed doctor (*tabib shar'i*), has been produced, in accordance with a law of 1983 (modified in 1994), which requires prospective couples of all communities to provide the results of examinations for various sexually and genetically transmitted diseases and conditions. The sharia courts are, for their part, responsible for enforcing this.[13] 'Ah, thank God, there's nothing wrong with the bride!', the judge might joke to lighten the tone. The couple's identity papers and personal status records (*ikhraj al-qayd*) are required. We dealt above with the question of the spouses' religious identities: none of the marriage contracts that I observed were between (religiously) 'mixed' couples (although a fair number of the cases that I saw pursued in the courts were), so I could not speak to the protocol on this point. But there is also the matter of the consent of the bride's guardian (*wali*), usually but not always the woman's father, and usually present. 'Even an Ayatollah comes with their father', growls the judge. Where the *wali* is not present to sign in person, their consent can be recorded at the office of the local district mayor (*mukhtar*) and the requisite certification produced.

While the need for the consent of the bride's father, or that of another guardian, is in the general course of everyday practice unremarked, in the

[12] As per section 349 of the LSC.
[13] Zayn 2003a: 37–38. This is also common elsewhere. See Welchman 2007: 55–56.

context of wider debates over Islam and women's rights it is controversial. Why should an adult woman need her father's formal permission to marry?[14] One lawyer and advocate of reform told me how he had, some years previous, helped a fifty-five year-old woman to conduct a marriage contract in the Sunni courts, represented by her son – first in line as guardian under Hanafi precepts, which the Sunni courts broadly follow as we have seen.[15] 'I mean, come on. I can understand a virgin who has no experience of marriage needing to be represented, but this is a woman! A grandmother!'[16] In another instance, a woman in her forties wanted to divorce her (younger) husband in return for giving up financial rights owed her. The judge demanded the assent of a guardian. 'This is ridiculous', the lawyer commented. 'What can I say to my female colleagues? They can represent someone before a criminal court who will be hanged but they can't renounce their own bridal portion [*mahr*]?!'

As it happens, there is in fact a range of opinions within the Hanafi school on this point: where the woman is of age the permission of the *wali* is, according to the majority opinion, recommended rather than obligatory.[17] But the Sunni courts, as we know, must in the first place follow the Ottoman Family Law of 1917 where it makes explicit provision, as it does here. Section 8 states that 'If an adult woman of more than nineteen years of age asks to marry someone then the judge shall announce that to her guardian, and if the guardian does not object or it is reported that there is no objection from him, then he should allow her marriage.'[18] The upshot is that the Sunni courts take a stricter line on this issue than does the Hanafi School which they nominally follow. Or as one self-styled modernist shaykh working outside of the courts put it, 'The courts apply Shafi'i law here, and in a strict form [*bi-l-tashaddud*].' If we return to the notion of a distinction between what God requires and what the state does, in purely 'religious' terms a Sunni marriage could thus arguably be contracted without the father's permission. The sharia's plurality counts.

14 See e.g. Welchman 2007: 69–75 and Tucker 2008b: 144–149, 166–167.

15 Zuhayli 2006: 6703.

16 The distinction between virgin (*bikr*) and non-virgin (*thayyib*) he alludes to is indeed significant in the Islamic legal discussions on this point.

17 Mughniyya 1979: 321; Zuhayli 2006: 6572–6574, 6698–6699 and Ali 2008: 14–15. For historical examples see e.g. Tucker 2008a on Ottoman Syria and Palestine. As we have seen, the *wali* may further ask that a marriage conducted without his permission be annulled if it does not satisfy the need for 'equivalence' (*kafa'a*) between the status of the groom and that of the bride, as stipulated in the OLFR, section 47.

18 Zayn 2003a: 131. But see section 47: 'Were an adult woman to conceal matters from her guardian and marry herself to another without obtaining his consent, and it is apparent that she has married suitably [*kufu'an*, i.e. with regard to status equivalence (*kafa'a*)], then the contract is binding.'

But that would have to be done outside of the official system. Such unofficial, often secret marriages do indeed sometimes take place, as we will see later in the book, but are, as one might expect, highly stigmatised.

In Ja'fari law, opinions are also varied, and there are those authorities who hold that an adult woman (virgin or otherwise) is free to contract as she pleases, including in the case of marriage, and that the guardian's permission is thus not required. Among them was Sayyid Fadlallah, introduced earlier. This was in keeping with his broadly 'contemporary' and progressive legal style, which we will discuss later. This granting of permission to women, including ones who are virgins, to contract a marriage as they please, even a 'temporary', time-limited marriage (a possibility for Shi'a, but not Sunnis), was, however, especially attention-grabbing, not to say scandalous, and was later moderated.[19] More mainstream Shi'i opinion finds that due religious caution would indicate taking the permission of the guardian into consideration.[20] Certainly that seems to be court practice in Lebanon, although Shi'i judges made clear to me that they were entitled to – and sometimes did – overrule an unreasonable father.[21]

To proceed: the judge will also ask the parties what they have settled on for the *mahr*, the bridal gift or 'dower', commonly referred to colloquially as a woman's 'right' (*haqq*).[22] The *mahr* is conventionally paid in two instalments: prompt (*mu'ajjal*), paid on marriage and often, if certainly not always, a token sum or gift, such as a copy of the Quran; and postponed (*mu'ajjal*, *mu'akkhar*), to be paid upon the end of the marriage

[19] See Fadlallah 2002–2003 vol. 3: 451; 2005a vol. 1: 255, vol. 2: 425–426. See also Ali 2008: 15 and Mughniyya 1979: 322; 2003: part 5, 259–263. On the scandal see Deeb and Harb 2013: 22, 81–82

[20] That is the position of Iraq's Ayatollah 'Ali Sistani, for instance, currently probably the most widely acknowledged authority worldwide. See Sistani 2002 vol. 3: 28, and also Mir'i 2003: 165–166 for the same position on the part of an array of other leading authorities.

[21] A 1998 ruling from the Ja'fari Supreme Court suggests that their position is that a virgin bride does require the guardian's permission (Barakat 2005: 134), even if the legal discourse is more varied. Shaykh 'Abdallah Ni'ma, one-time head of the Lebanese Ja'fari courts, for instance, finds in his authoritative legal handbook that there is no such power of guardianship over a virgin's marriage choices, but follows this with a three page footnote speaking to the complexities and contestations over this point (1996: 70–73).

[22] Sometimes also termed *sadaq*. There is no wholly satisfactory translation, although 'dower' is common and certainly superior to e.g. 'brideprice' or 'bridewealth' (see the useful discussion in Moors 1995: 77n1). Tarabey (2013) presents an interesting account of *mahr* in the Druze courts.

by divorce or the death of the husband.[23] The delayed *mahr* portion thus generally constitutes the wife's greatest hedge against divorce. The size of the *mahr* is also in some sense seen socially as reflecting her 'worth'.

It will be helpful at this point to have an idea of the sums involved. It would perhaps be misleading to speak of average amounts, although I gathered *mahr* figures for seventy-one marriages I saw discussed in the courts and can thus provide a rough notion for the purposes of orientation. Older marriages are hard to compare due to the enormous inflation of the civil war years, which raises problems of its own. There are those who argue that such *mahr* values need to be adjusted accordingly, a controversial position that was at this time not favoured in the Sunni courts (this changed more recently), although it had had some success in the Ja'fari system.[24] Second and re-marriages have much lower sums. Different social classes have different expectations: very high bridal gifts are to be found among the rich (I had one instance of a million US dollars) – but then so are token amounts; very high sums are also occasionally to be found amongst the poor (in one case, 'her weight in gold'). But excluding the older, pre-inflation figures, exceptional sums and cases where I had some doubt as to the details, combined totals of the advanced and delayed *mahr* ranged between about US $3,500 (uncommonly low) and $60,000. The average over the forty-seven cases thus included was $24,000.[25] Again, these figures are highly approximate and only designed to give a broad impression. But we are generally

[23] This division is common to the Levant and Egypt and has wider historical depth and breadth, although we should recognise how its uses can change even in recent times. See e.g. Tucker 1988: 168–173, 1998: 52; Moors 1995: 92–150; Mundy 1995: 229n32; Hoodfar 1997: 67–68, 266 and Sonbol 2008: 90, 95. When it becomes due after the husband's death, the wife may be forced to bring a case to obtain her *mahr* from the husband's estate as a debt owed: see Homsi 2003: 100, 104–106; Barakat 2005: 179–185, 197–199.

[24] On the latter score see Barakat 2005: 201–208. The Sunni courts' position shifted subsequent to the change in 2011 to the law they are to apply, which is now to follow in the first instance the decisions of the Sunni community's Supreme Islamic Sharia Council (see Chapter 2). In 2012 the latter ratified a partial family law code including provisions on *mahr* values, which are now to be re-calculated in proportion to the price of gold at the time of the contract (section 2, resolution 46/2011, 'System of family law', as modified by resolution 15, 5 May 2012).

[25] This is rounded to the nearest $1,000, and includes no doubt crude conversion of the value of gold coins, commonly employed. This average figure seems quite high in the light of my own recollections: many (18 instances) cluster around $10,000; there is another group around $20,000 (11); and then higher ones around $30–40,000 (5) and $50–60,000 (8). The average for Sunni cases ($24,000) was only just higher than Shi'i ($23,000), with both in any case rounded to the nearest $1,000, the former up and the latter down, and thus to all intents and purposes the same.

talking in terms of very considerable sums for most Lebanese men, especially given the dire economic situation at the time.

There may thus be a certain diffidence about stating the amount, consonant with its actual material and social importance, being in a sense a marker of the standing of the bride and her family. And the judge may, again, attempt to keep the tone light. 'What have you agreed on?', he will ask. 'How much is the *mahr*, the rights I mean?' The advance is, say, a copy of the Quran and one 'English gold pound', a commonly employed measure of gold. In this case, the groom has British citizenship. 'It's an English pound, but that's not because of the British passport', jokes the judge. 'What about the delayed portion [*al-mu'ajjal*]?' 'Whatever', shrugs her mother, who seems to be in charge. 'Come on!' 'Twenty-five.' 'Twenty-five what? Thousand dollars?' No, it was 25 million Lebanese Lira, which equates to about $17,000. (This is a common sort of elision: '50 million.' 'I thought it was 50 thousand', the other party teases. The judge, later: 'So what was the *mu'ajjal* again, 50 million dollars?!') The judge might ask the bride, especially a young one, if they know what it is for. 'You get it on death or divorce. A long time away hopefully.' Or he might ask if they have received their advance portion yet. And the groom's sponsor might joke, 'Do you want me to hand it over now?!' (And I did sometimes see it handed over there and then.)

The shaykh can then complete the marriage form in order to proceed with the ceremony. The only other qualification might be if there is an additional condition (*shart*) to be placed in the contract. Such conditions are seen by many, Islamic legal reformers as well as academic and activist commentators, as an important means for a woman to render the contract more equitable.[26] For example, the contract could be made subject to the condition that the marriage be dissolved if the husband takes another wife (not common, but possible), or that the husband deputes to the wife his power to pronounce divorce (*tafwid*), placing that power 'in her hand', as it is said.[27] However, such conditions seem not to be common: one Sunni judge commented that before that year he had never seen one (but this year he had seen three), an impression shared by another Sunni judge's assistant; I myself saw but a handful of instances in the Ja'fari courts. 'Reformist' shaykhs mourn this rarity and attribute it to a lack of education as to the possibilities the sharia offers. Other judges

[26] See Welchman 2007: 99–102; Ali 2008: 21–23 and Tucker 2008b: 61–63. For comparative contemporary and historical examples see e.g. Sonbol 2008 and Zulficar 2008 on Egypt, Wynn 2008 on Saudi Arabia and Mir-Hosseini 2008 on Iran.

[27] Tucker 2008b: 91–92, 118–119. For published Lebanese cases see Homsi 2003: 81–82 and Barakat 2005: 173–176.

are less keen, feeling that such conditions point to a lack of trust between the parties. Take an instance of a *katab al-kitab* before one Shi'i judge: a young couple, the girl sixteen and, to my eyes, clearly pregnant, accompanied by her father; the lad represented by his older brother. The atmosphere was tense and terms had been agreed (the advance a copy of the Quran, the delayed portion half of a shop and $20,000 – 'Anything else', the judge asked the father wryly, as there had clearly been a lot of wrangling). It was announced that there was to be a condition in the marriage contract: that 'divorce is in her hand'. 'Are you in disagreement?', asked the judge. 'Because this points to a lack of mutual understanding here.'

Performing the Contract

Once the form has been filled, the couple, the guardian and two witnesses, who could be the judge and his clerk if necessary, sign the paper. Now the actual performance of the contract can finally take place. The shaykh will begin with some prayers, in the rhyming chant of a distinctively religious register: *Bismillah al-rahman al-rahim, al-hamdu li-llah rabb al-'alamin, sali allah 'ala Muhammad wa-alih al-tahirin al-tayyibin*, 'In the name of God the Merciful and Compassionate, thanks be to God Lord of Humanity, God's prayers be upon Muhammad and his family, pure and good', and on it goes. This is not, in legal terms, an essential part of sealing the marriage contract. Rather, it is 'for a blessing' (*li-l-baraka*), as one judge put it. Again, if the marriage were done outside the court, he told me, the shaykh would recite an appropriate passage from the Quran and give a little talk about marriage, perhaps taking quarter or half an hour, but here the pressures of court business do not permit.

In classical Islamic legal theory, the only unanimously agreed essential element to the contract of marriage, besides the couple themselves, is the offer and its acceptance (*ijab* and *qubul*). The offer is conventionally made by the bride's party and accepted by the groom's. There is some legal debate over the possible wordings of these statements. They should be in the requisite linguistic form, the past tense, as this (in Arabic) signifies that the act is completed rather than a future commitment. The OLFR (section 36) specifies that the offer and acceptance should be made 'with clear expressions' (*bi-l-alfaz al-sariha*), 'such as *ankahtu* and *tazawwajtu*' (both, 'I married').[28] We should note the comparatively

[28] Zayn 2003a: 133. Anderson (1951a: 119) comments that article 36 'represents the Shafi'i view, as against the rather broader rule of the Hanafis, Malik and Ahmad ibn Hanbal, who allow certain other expressions also'. See also Ali 2008: 13–14. For the

elevated linguistic register in play here, with its formal grammatical endings and somewhat rarified, religio-legal vocabulary.

In the practice I observed in the Ja'fari courts, the judge will commonly act as the bride's agent (*wakil*) and perform the offer for her. This is supposedly because the bride is generally incapable of reliably enunciating the offer sufficiently and distinctly due to her proper shyness and modesty. Even if brides very often did appear diffident (although sometimes they cannot quite stop themselves from beaming with excitement), they hardly seemed incapacitated to my eyes. But this acting on the part of the bride is not a necessary part of the ceremony. It is just 'To make things easier, nothing more', as one judge put it to me, although it sometimes seemed to me to make it rather more complicated than it might otherwise have been. It requires the judge first asking the bride formally if she consents that he acts as her representative in the matter of the marriage at hand, its details carefully specified, including the *mahr*. Given the highly elevated diction and unfamiliar procedure, the bride might well not understand what is being asked of her, and it will have to be explained. She will then reply, as instructed, 'You are my representative' (*anta wakili*).

The shaykh then proposes marriage to the groom with the specified *mahr*, as in the bride's case preceded by sonorous and pious formulae (*A'udhu billah min al-shaytan al-rajim, bismillah al-rahman al-rahim*, 'I take refuge in God from the accursed Satan, in the name of God the Merciful and Compassionate') and in the highest linguistic register. The man must then consent, using a formulaic and grammatically formal phrase such as 'I accept and consent' (*qabiltu wa-radayt*). ('Do you know what to say?' 'Yes, *qabiltu al-zawaj*.' 'Oh, you've done this before!' Laughter.) The judge will brief him on what is required: 'You heard how I am the *wakil*. I'm going to ask you if you accept the marriage. You say: *qabiltu wa-radayt*. And you must start with the *qaf*!' – that is, the Arabic letter '*q*', the point being that it is not usually enunciated in Lebanese colloquial Arabic. There is usually some pantomime – especially with one of the judges, who was very exacting – around this expression of acceptance, as one must eliminate any doubt as to its validity. The *qaf* of *qabiltu* is generally the sticking point. The shaykh will often chide the groom on this point and ask him to repeat it several times, to occasional amusement. The acceptance must then further be repeated in a different formulation (e.g., *qabiltu al-tazwij*, 'I accept the marriage'), just to ensure that it was definitively pronounced. 'No, *qaf*! *Qabilt*!'

Ja'fari courts (which do not have to follow the OLFR) see Ni'ma 1996: 9–11 and Mughniyya 1979: 293–296.

'We want it in Arabic not Lebanese [*bi-l-'arabi mish bi-l-lubnani*]!' 'Mm, that wasn't very clear, do it again.' If the groom is just too nervous or incompetent to get out this unfamiliar mouthful under pressure, then he in his turn might even have to depute someone, such as the judge's clerk, to do it for him ('as a precaution', the judge might suggest).

Having got through all this, the shaykh will then say congratulations (*Mubarak inshallah*) and the groom will kiss the father of the bride (not the bride!). There may be embraces all round (except between the bride and groom), even of the shaykh (and he might also get slipped a tip). And a happy parent might pass some sweets around.

Conclusion

In this chapter I have started my account of the sharia courts' activities with an analysis of marriage, the act that underpins most of the cases that come before the courts, which are largely marital disputes. I ended with the moment at which a marriage is agreed, under the supervision of the shaykh presiding. In this rather elaborate enactment of the ceremony, I perceive a corresponding enactment of the authority of the Islamic professional religious class. The involvement of a religious professional is in theory not required in sharia legal terms. But it is generally seen socially as indispensable. The performance of religious blessings (also not a prerequisite), the knowledge of the proper form of the ceremony and the contract, and the mastery of the tongue-tying highest register of Arabic that are foregrounded in the *katab al-kitab* all go towards establishing the necessary authority of the professional religious specialist. Indeed the shaykhs seem to make the case for their indispensability through their practice in insisting not only on the need for, but also the difficulty of getting the requisite phrases exactly right.[29]

Furthermore, the involvement of a licensed religious authority is required by state law – with criminal sanctions for non-compliance; and, when the marriage takes place in court, the bureaucratic trappings and requirements of the process in themselves further mandate the authority of the state-sponsored shaykhly judge and his functionaries. Religious and state authority are here fused, although neither is in fact necessary for marriage in God's eyes. Other relations of authority are also very apparent at this moment, in particular that of the bride's father, or *wali*, whose consent is effectively required. This enactment of patriarchy – whether in token or real form – foreshadows the heavily gendered

[29] Again, these are a specific set of instances and this particular practice may not be universal, but it is surely symptomatic.

structure of the family legal conflicts that come before the courts, but is itself contested and controversial. Analytically, we will want to keep an eye on the various threads of this knot of religious, state and patriarchal authority, which sometimes seems in danger of unravelling. Most often, however, it is unremarked, the normal course of things.

Given the possibility of being legitimately married in religious terms but not those of the state (and vice versa), a distinction opens up between what is sanctioned by the divine sharia (*shar'an*) – a plural field of possibilities – and what is established in human law (*qanunan*), or otherwise put, between a God's eye view of the law and that of the state. This is rhetorically akin to the contrast between sharia and *qanun* that I described in the previous chapter, although that was more bound up with the aesthetics of legal and bureaucratic process. Here we are faced with a more substantive difference between different legal domains, perhaps even ontologies.[30] This does not only apply to marriage of course. Divorces too – easily performed by a Muslim husband without recourse to the court – can have been properly enacted in Islamic legal terms but not established to the Lebanese state's satisfaction. Or, conversely, a woman who has succeeded in obtaining a divorce from a state court abroad, somewhere in Europe, for example, will not be divorced in religious terms and thus unable to marry again without thereby sinning grievously. As we will see, in Islamic law, women usually require a judge's intervention in order to obtain a divorce against their husband's wishes. And so, in order to be divorced in God's eyes, a wife may be forced also to bring a case in the Lebanese state-sponsored sharia courts.

In one such instance I saw, involving a woman of Lebanese parentage who lived in Germany and who married and then divorced a Turkish migrant there, the *katab al-kitab* had been informally conducted in a mosque and never registered with the Lebanese consulate. Her father had come to consult a judge in Beirut, along with her proposed new husband, his nephew. As the judge told him, in terms of God's sharia (*shar'an*), a civil divorce is not the same as a sharia-compliant divorce. A new marriage would be null and void and, from the perspective of 'the permitted and the forbidden' (*al-halal wa-l-haram*), she would be committing adultery. If the marriage had not been registered in Lebanon as the father said, then she would not be able to get a divorce in the Lebanese courts – as far as they are concerned, she is not even married.

[30] So, what from one sort of actor's perspective (someone wanting to get married) might look like a plurality of legal options, from another could look more like a radical disjuncture between normative and ontological orders.

First they would need to bring a case establishing the first marriage. Then they could raise a case of judicial divorce (and the judge thought that the existing divorce in Germany would be enough to prove it, although that would be contestable, I think). One gets a sense of just how complicated – perverse even – these intertwinings of religious and state law can be.

7 Bringing a Case

I now turn to the bulk of the sharia courts' business: the family legal disputes that arise subsequent to the marriages we have just considered.[1] It is sad to move so swiftly from marriage to its breakdown, although that is indeed the impression that the courts give. Many of those working in them reported thinking that their experiences must be symptomatic of some wider social malaise, or finding their impression of married life jaundiced as a result. One highly experienced lawyer told me that he had never married for that very reason.

Relations between spouses break down for a wide variety of causes. In the most tragic instances, which made for painful hearing, wives and children were fleeing violent and abusive husbands and fathers. Domestic violence is properly a criminal matter, and many cases featured official documentation of such complaints, although it should be said that women's organisations have campaigned against what they argue is the laxity of the law and its enforcement in this area.[2] At the other end of the spectrum, some couples simply found themselves incompatible, emotionally, socially or sexually. But the most common underlying reason for stress within a marriage, I would say, was the harsh economic climate. One direct consequence of people's straightened means, a very common complaint, is that the husband may not be able, or willing to provide adequate housing: in the courts' terms, a legitimate home or residence (*maskan/bayt shar'ī*), one of whose most important characteristics is that it be independent. Very commonly instead the couple would be living with the husband's parents (or the parents living with them). The housing and economic situation in the southern suburbs was especially bad,

[1] Again, this is not the entirety of their concerns, as they also handle inheritance, guardianship and religious endowments (*waqf*), amongst other things.

[2] Concerns continue despite the passing of a new law on domestic violence in 2014. The Lebanese NGO KAFA ('Enough [violence and exploitation]') has documented and campaigned on this issue extensively. See www.kafa.org.lb. Tarabey (2013) provides a powerful account of the causes of the failure of marriages, including abuse, among the Druze community. See also Human Rights Watch 2015 on the religious courts more generally.

subsequent to the 2006 Israeli bombardment that levelled much of the area. Living with others creates friction: women often complained of being abused by their husband's family, and especially their mothers-in-law. Sometimes couples stated that they were happy with each other, but found the pressures from wider family unbearable, especially where the contracting and sustaining of the marriage had depended on their financial aid.

While gender expectations and modalities of course vary from one area, community, class or individual to another, being unable to provide for a family was clearly felt by men to constitute a failure of masculinity, for which the husband might overcompensate in other ways. Judges frequently complained that men in this 'masculinist society' (*mujtama' dhukuri*) were wrongly interpreting Islam's granting to men certain modes of authority over women in the context of marriage, privileging customary ('Eastern', *sharqi*) understandings of gender roles over the true import of the sharia (which is of course the subject of much debate). The *qiwama*, the famous Quranic verse (4:34) on marital relations that begins, 'men are the guardians of women' (*al-rijal qawwamun 'ala al-nisa'*; the translation is open to discussion), was often cited.[3] 'But', as one judge asked, 'in what sense? Military?' 'He wants to define what I eat, when I can go to the bathroom', one wife complained. Some men would work two or more jobs, 'From morning to midnight', in order that their wives did not work outside of the home, even when they wanted to. 'Every woman, everywhere in the world, if they are locked up gets frustrated', a judge in the Ja'fari courts reminded one husband, whose wife had fled back to her father's house. 'We are European!', her father had exclaimed to the husband: that is, rhetorically at least, forward-thinking and egalitarian in gender matters in comparison with the husband's retrograde 'Eastern' notions. This points too to the cultural intimacy of such matters.[4] Western criticisms of Muslim and Arab patriarchy are well known locally; expectations of modernity are formed in their light; judges often wished to ensure that I understood where the lines of 'custom', 'Islam' and individual failing lay. Failures in the man's expected (socially, religiously and legally) role as provider were paralleled by the frequent failure of men's expectations of their wives' proper duties: a man wants to come home from work to find his dinner ready for him; a working wife might, it was suggested, be too tired for sexual

[3] The verse goes on to discuss financial responsibilities, a wife's duty of obedience and the proper response from the husband if his wife behaves otherwise, including the legitimacy of his striking her. Unsurprisingly, its interpretation has been the subject of long debate and contestation, in scholarly circles and more widely. For a discussion from a more liberal Muslim perspective see Wadud-Muhsin 1998: 136–138.

[4] An allusion to Herzfeld 1997.

relations. With regard to the latter, men's frustrations were often expressed in the form of sexual jealousy and suspicion.

The dire financial situation further leads many men to seek work abroad. Lebanon is a country of emigrants, the global diaspora far outnumbering the population of the homeland. (Their country is their suitcase, as one lawyer put it to me, quoting Palestinian poet Samih al-Qasim.) Very often a man will marry and then leave to find work, his wife commonly having to stay behind. Communication often then ceases, the husband having built a new life in his new land, and many cases are thus brought by deserted wives, frequently left with children to bring up. Even if the husband does take his wife with him, that can also be problematic: the life of an immigrant worker can be a hard one, whether in Europe or North America, or still more the Congo or Ivory Coast.[5] Wives might return home, disenchanted.

If, for whatever reason, a marriage breaks down, the wife will commonly move out, most often back with her parents. Attempts at mediation and reconciliation often ensue, involving relatives, family councils or other mediators, very commonly including members of the shaykhly class. Such mediation could be seen as a religious duty: the Quran (4:35) famously urges that, 'If you fear a breach between a man and his wife, appoint an arbiter from his people and another from hers. If they wish to be reconciled, God will bring them together again. Surely God is all-knowing and wise.'[6] These shaykhly mediators might be acting as respected individuals within the community, or as members of larger organisations such as Hizballah or the Jama'a Islamiyya, the Lebanese Muslim Brotherhood. We should thus remember that the institutions and personalities we are concerned with at this point are embedded in, and to a certain extent compete with, a larger sharia-oriented context. Court proceedings may be initiated subsequent to, in parallel with or independent of other, related processes.

For those who do have recourse to the courts, bringing a case, and still more so, getting a verdict, especially the one you had hoped for, is generally a laborious and fraught undertaking. As one judge said to me, 'People think when they enter the court that their problems are over. No, the problems start when they enter the court.' For one thing, the bureaucratic procedures required are often onerous. Given the volume of the courts' business and the number of discrete stages involved, cases take months if not years to process. For those without the money or

5 West Africa was a common destination for Shi'i migrants in the twentieth century, where many made fortunes. See e.g. Leichtman 2013.

6 In Dawood's 1951 translation.

inclination to hire a lawyer, these processes require a very considerable investment of time, in often desperate circumstances. They also impose a distinct rhythm and tone to proceedings that colours the experience of both those before the courts and those involved in running them, not least the judges. The very process of going through legal proceedings can thus lead to further deterioration and complication of the personal relationships that are their object: 'Your hearts will harden,' as the judge warns. Although the work of the courts requires some form of engagement between the parties at odds and, as we will see, their bias is towards reconciliation, this work of mediation is far from facilitated by the apparatus of an adversarial bureaucratic court system. Very often, going to court is the end of a marriage, even if a nominal legal resolution is found.

In the terms of the broad contrast I have been elaborating between the 'sharia' aspects of court practice and the merely 'legal' ones, the pressingly bureaucratic nature of this process, not least in its materiality of files, stamps and papers, is rhetorically assigned by those working in the courts to the mundane domain of human law.[7] In this chapter I explore its frustrations in some detail, from the perspective of the courts' clients as much as their staff. Consonant with the vision of the shaykh's vocation that I have described, the divine sharia is associated rather with the work of personal engagement with the couple and their problems on the part of the judge and others, an engagement often frustrated by the mechanics of the legal process. Perhaps counterintuitively, satisfaction of the shaykhly judge's role – his job well done – can be seen to lie more in this Quranically sanctioned work of mediation than in his powers of legal decision. That is the subject of the next chapter.

Marital Disputes as Legal Processes

Entering the court system is a challenge in and of itself then. One has to know how to do so, that one has to bring a case (*daʿwa*) for sure, but also what sort of case, and then what procedures have to be followed. One might engage a lawyer, although that is not everyone's first move – a relative or friend might be able to help, or the local district mayor (*mukhtar*), or else perhaps a familiar shaykh with the requisite knowledge and connections. Or one might simply turn up at court. Here one's first port of call will be to one of the functionaries in the confusing and busy

[7] Matthew Hull (2012) has directed attention to the ways in which the material aspects of bureaucracy, paradigmatically in the form of the file, take on something of a life of their own. Such a careful exploration of the social life of paper lies beyond the scope of my study here, although it would no doubt be illuminating.

offices. Court functionaries thus play a crucial role in the definition of the cases that come before the courts. Especially for those functionaries in the Sunni courts who are also shaykhs (remembering that this is not the case in the Ja'fari courts), this may be an opportunity not just for bureaucratic advice, but also for pedagogical intervention.

In Jami' Imam 'Ali, such enquiries were often (although far from always) directed to one of the most senior of the judges' assistants, clerk to one of the most respected judges. While Shaykh Tayyib, as I shall call him, was certainly well placed to give appropriate advice as to process, he was also wont to dispense moral and religious encouragement. One lad was brought to him to ask about divorce – his nine months' pregnant wife wanted to leave him. 'Don't worry', Shaykh Tayyib told him, 'just get before the shaykh and say, "I will divorce her if she excuses me of the *mahr* and maintenance during the *'idda*,"' the prescribed waiting period after divorce before remarriage is allowed. 'She takes the child, you pay maintenance for it and have to pay for the delivery. But', the shaykh continued, 'does she pray?' No, it seemed. 'Do you pray?' 'Well, I do the morning prayer ... But I make her wear the headscarf – and not the *model* style!'

As we should remember throughout, and as in the case of young Shaykh Muhammad for example, shaykhs working in the courts also have professional lives outside of them. It was not until I attended a substantial, privately commissioned *mawlid*, or celebration of the Prophet, that I realised that Shaykh Tayyib was also a virtuoso Islamic 'singer' (*munshid*): indeed, while now in his forties or so, in younger years he had represented Lebanon in international competition. Cassettes were available in the market place; and his band was reportedly a regular fixture at such events. Flanked by backing singers and percussionists, wiry and intense, he gave voice in powerful fashion with heavy vibrato. Shaykh Tayyib, who also arranges trips to Beirut's seaside and football matches for the faithful, has his own 'Islamic centre' on one floor of an apartment building in the heart of West Beirut, very near Jami' Imam 'Ali, where he holds weekly sessions of *dhikr*, 'remembrance' of God, and an accompanying lesson (*dars*). These are extremely popular, attracting a mixed, if mostly young crowd, male and (in a separate room) female, with an attractive blend of musicality, undemanding Sufism and his highly entertaining speaking style.[8] When I attended, I saw many of the

[8] I attended six of these sessions in 2008. This is a suitable moment to mention the concern of one reviewer that my account of the Sunni courts and wider community makes them seem full of Sufis, which might mislead. It is quite possible that my sample is not a representative one. But my own impression is that Lebanese Sunnism has – in common

lads I knew from elsewhere in the community, like me, tasting from a variety of the different possibilities available. If I missed a session, I would be told I had lost out: 'Where were you?! We were laughing so much!' 'No one comes only once', said one enthusiast. 'If you come once, then you will come every week.'

After chanting poems together in praise of the Prophet ('O God we pray for Muhammad [prayers] in the number of / the leaves of the trees / the grains of the sand / the drops of the rain / all the women and men'), some old classics, some written by Shaykh Tayyib's father and himself, punctuated by lengthy, keening solos from the master and cries of appreciation from the crowd ('Allah! Allah!'), and then some *dhikr*, repeating the name of God and other formulae with the lights turned down, Shaykh Tayyib would give a lesson on what it takes to be a good Muslim in today's Lebanon, 'something that will be really useful. For the women too, so they can teach their kids to grow up like this, so they can ensure their husbands are like this; to people who are thinking of getting married, to people who are married; to divorced people.' He would return again and again to gender roles, referencing heavily his work in the courts and his own family life (he is married with children), tackling themes such as the husband as 'Lord of the home' (*rabb al-bayt*) and the right understanding of the *qiwama*, the Quranic verse entrusting women to men's tutelage. His style is folksy and comic, adopting funny voices and pulling faces to make his point. The audience roars with laughter as he acts out themes of lust or miserliness (*bukhl*).

Just as those who enter the court may have come there as the latest step on a road through the wider life of the sharia in Lebanon, so too others might find themselves sent out to that wider world from the court, as an entry point for the non-committed into the pious community. Another account from my field notes of Shaykh Tayyib's efforts:

A tough looking man in his work clothes, with huge arm muscles, tells Shaykh Tayyib that his wife has just moved out, 'for no reason'. 'Of course there are reasons', says Shaykh Tayyib. 'Maybe for illicit reasons [*asbab ghayr shar'iyya*]', says the man, hinting at some sexual wrongdoing no doubt. Shaykh Tayyib is unimpressed. The man's immediate concern is that his wife wants to take their child with her, as is, much to his bemusement, her right, it still being of a sufficiently young age. Shaykh Tayyib explains the wisdom of the sharia in

with many other Sunni contexts – an important Sufi heritage that continues to be relevant to mainstream religious practice and that a number of leading figures do have interests that might be readily associated with Sufism. See also for example the memoirs of previous head of the Sunni courts Shaykh Salim Jalal al-Din, born (in 1912) to a distinguished family of religious personages, shaykhs of a Sufi order, and whose father was, he tells us, known for his healing grace (Jalal al-Din 2002: 7–17).

accommodating a young child's natural need for its mother and suggests that he ring the man's wife there and then. The man now gets cold feet: there is to be a reconciliation session with lots of family present; maybe they should wait until after that ... Yes, suggests Shaykh Tayyib, why doesn't he surprise her in the meantime, offer to give her some money to look after their child; then she will swell with pride. The suggestion does not seem a wholly welcome one. Shaykh Tayyib then bids him come to his lesson that evening – he will hear things he wouldn't get on any tape in the souk. The man promises he will be there, unless a matter of life or death comes up.

I attended the lesson that night and did not see the man among the crowd, although I might have missed him.

Legal Form and Dynamics

One way or another, then, those seeking recourse to the courts will hopefully find their way to an appropriate legal entry point. Generally speaking, a wife's first legal means to put pressure on her husband, in the hope of forcing a solution of one sort or another, is a case suing for maintenance (*nafaqa*): for herself (*nafaqa zawjiyya*) and, where applicable, for her children (*nafaqat al-awlad*).[9] As a rule of thumb, maintenance thus accounts for the highest proportion of the courts' caseload. Another key, concomitant demand may be that the husband provides an adequate marital home to live in: again, a 'legal residence' (*maskan shar'i*). He in his turn will then normally sue for 'obedience' (*ta'a*, or *ita'a*): that is, that she return to living with him. This does not mean that a husband can use the law either to force his wife to obey his wishes or to force her to live with him. Rather, if his case is successful, and she refuses to return to living with him, then he is not compelled to pay her maintenance as she is considered, in a technical sense, 'recalcitrant' (*nashiza*;

[9] Awards are not substantial. The standard award for monthly maintenance of a wife in my experience was 2–250,000 LL (around $150 US), and for a child 100,000 LL (around $70 US). The 'meanness' of such settlements was a point of discussion and some embarrassment in comparison with the more generous awards of the Christian courts (cf. Shahar 2015: 101 on Jerusalem's sharia courts). Some judges made higher awards, but cases would be brought to lower them, even up to appeals court level. One initial court judge, for instance, awarded a wife a monthly award for her and her two children of 600,000 LL. She wanted more, asking first for a million and then 800,000. The judge told her that even with 600,000 he was afraid the ruling would be overturned; 800,000 definitely would. But judges are also conscious of many husbands' straightened circumstances: what is the point, they would ask, of imposing a sum which he cannot pay – to send him to prison (which could be his fate)? The partial new code for the Sunni courts (resolution 46/2011) covers *nafaqa* in some detail and clarifies that the husband is responsible for his wife's medical expenses, a point of contention previously.

the substantive, 'recalcitrance' or 'disobedience' is *nushuz*).[10] This is thus the most common legal response to a case of maintenance, inaugurating a rhythm of suit and counter-suit that proceeds in predictable fashion. He must, however, have a 'legal home' for them to live in for his case for obedience to be answered positively. Given that these cases, which can rapidly proliferate, are all bound up in one fundamental dispute, the judge may bring them together into one file (*talazum*).

The next step in the rhythm of case and counter-case, where the dispute is not resolved, will very often be to proceed to the question of divorce: '*Tafriq* [judicial divorce] kills *ta'a*', as a lawyer working in the Sunni courts put it. That is, the husband's claim to 'obedience' is formally trumped by a wife's to judicial separation. Divorce may in any case have been the original intention: one lawyer working in the Ja'fari courts estimated that '95 per cent' of suits for maintenance were the first step in an attempt by wives to initiate divorce. As the judges like to remind those before them, the Prophet thought divorce 'the most hateful of permitted things to God'.[11] It is a sign of moral failure, and the shaykhs' default stance towards it is one of regret and disapproval. That there are, or so it appears to all concerned, so many divorces nowadays only serves, in this discourse, to show the distance of this society from the ideal of Islam.[12] People are perceived to rush into divorce, where they should strive to reconcile their differences first, although one sees too that the formal structure of legal proceedings brings its own momentum towards this end. Even if women find their domestic situation unbearable, the judges counsel caution, as divorce is damaging to women, their reputations and their finances. Of particular concern is the plight of the children of these marriages, who may become the subject of bitter dispute. But nevertheless, the judges themselves know that in many cases, even if hateful, divorce can still be the solution, although it may be difficult to persuade a husband of that. Men would commonly appear to see releasing their wife – let alone being forced to do so – as a profound challenge to their self-respect and indeed masculinity.

10 Interestingly, the partial new code for the Sunni courts does not use the term *nushuz*, although it does detail the circumstances in which a wife is not entitled to maintenance, including her refusal to live in the marital home (section 8, resolution 46/2011). The categories of *nafaqa*, *ta'a*, *maskan shar'i* and *nushuz* are shared with other Islamic contexts, if variously constituted. See e.g. Tucker 2008b: 50–56, 63–64, 73–75 and Welchman 2007: 93–99.

11 *Abghad al-halal ila-llah al-talaq*. See e.g. Zuhayli 2006 vol. 9: 6879.

12 I do not have any reliable statistics as to the divorce rate unfortunately. Tarabey (2013) has figures for the Druze courts, which may be suggestive, although not strictly comparable.

Divorce is thus of course a fraught issue. But it is also a legally complex one. Notoriously, under Islamic precepts, the right to effect a divorce varies between the sexes: one must distinguish between divorce initiated by the husband and divorce initiated by the wife. Broadly speaking, the power to divorce is 'in the hand of' the husband (*bi-yad al-zawj*).[13] He can terminate the marriage at will, without his wife's consent and even in her absence, subject to various conditions. (That is, unless she made transferring this right to her a condition of the marriage contract – definitely a possibility within the tradition, but one relatively rarely taken up in contemporary Lebanon, as we have seen.) This is termed *talaq*, often translated in this technical sense as 'repudiation', but also used in lay discourse in Lebanon as a blanket term for divorce more generally.[14] The husband must, however, then honour his wife's financial rights. Most importantly, these include the as yet unpaid portion of her *mahr*, her bridal gift, again, commonly referred to colloquially as her 'right' (*haqq*). She is also owed maintenance during the period she must wait before she can legitimately remarry another man (the *'idda*, usually three months, or rather, menstrual periods).

Remembering that we are generally talking here in terms of thousands of dollars, very considerable sums for most Lebanese men in the current economic climate, this is, then, a powerful disincentive for a man to divorce his wife. Indeed the man may not be willing or capable of paying the *mahr* at all. In such cases after a divorce, the wife may have to pursue her claim to her financial rights through the courts, not necessarily an easy business, especially if the husband is living abroad.[15] Arrangements may be made for the *mahr* to be paid in instalments.[16] Or, when realisation dawns as to the financial consequences of his divorce, a man may reconsider and take his wife back before the *mahr* becomes due, as is his right during the *'idda* waiting period.

A wife seeking divorce may therefore propose that her husband divorce her in exchange for her giving up these financial rights (*tanazul 'an haqq-ha*), most commonly in a form of divorce termed *khul'* (or *mukhala'a*), divorce in return for a consideration.[17] This requires his agreement and

[13] Zuhayli 2006 vol. 9: 6877.

[14] Hallaq 2009: 280 thinks the translation of *talaq* as divorce 'useless'; but it is hard to avoid.

[15] European courts, for instance, have a hard time knowing how to deal with *mahr*, whether it should be treated as alimony, a debt, a gift or otherwise. See e.g. Jones-Pauly 2008 on Germany and Freeland and Lau 2008: 334–336 on the UK.

[16] *Taqsit*, in legal terms. See e.g. Barakat 2005: 209–210.

[17] See Tucker 2008b: 95–100, 113–114, 127–128. In Lebanon, *khul'* takes the mutually agreed form known to the classical Islamic legal tradition rather than that of recent attempts elsewhere to institute judicially imposed *khul'* as a way of reforming the

involvement. For unlike the husband, the wife cannot end the marriage unilaterally, unless she has been specifically granted that power as a condition of their marriage contract. This puts her at a dangerous disadvantage, for under Islamic precepts a man can have more than one spouse, and can thus marry another woman without having first to be divorced, leaving his first, spurned wife in limbo, or 'in prison' as both husbands and wives were wont to put it.

Where the husband is unwilling, then, a wife seeking divorce will need to obtain either an annulment (*faskh*, on various grounds such as medical conditions, including impotence, or the husband's apostasy), or, more commonly, a judicially imposed divorce for desertion or maltreatment, against the husband's wishes. Judicially imposed divorce is perhaps the most contentious issue before the courts and very differently construed between the Sunni and Ja'fari systems. Judicial divorce on the grounds of marital strife (*tafriq li-l-shiqaq wa-l-niza'*) in the Sunni courts is a relatively straightforward, if costly, time-consuming and bureaucratically demanding procedure, and one of the most commonly encountered cases. We will come back to it in more detail, but for now we can note that marital strife must be established, usually by witness testimony, and arbitration sought. Two court-appointed mediators will meet at least twice with the couple, attempt to reconcile them, and, if no reconciliation is effected, produce a report as to relative responsibility for the marriage's failure. Divorce will ensue and financial liability will be imposed following the arbitrators' recommendation. While the legal categories and processes of *nafaqa*, *talaq* and *khul'*, for instance, evince a deep historical continuity, *tafriq li-l-shiqaq wa-l-niza'* is in many respects a more recent innovation, set out in the Ottoman Law of Family Rights.[18]

In the Ja'fari courts, not bound to follow the OLFR, the equivalent is divorce by the judge (*talaq al-hakim*). But here establishing maltreatment or desertion lacks a similarly routinised procedural form and is consequently much more problematic. Further, the *hakim*, or judge, required is stipulated to be a religious scholar of the very highest rank, a

inequitable state of divorce law, as in Egypt and Jordan, for instance. See Welchman 2007: 112–122 and Tucker 2008b: 128–130.

[18] The provisions of the OLFR (section 130) represented a reform in the face of the notoriously restrictive position on this matter of the Hanafi school, drawing on the provisions of the other Sunni schools (Anderson 1951b: 272–274, 285; Tucker 2008b: 107–109, 119 and Welchman 2007: 109). As we will see below, the 1962 Law of Sharia Courts (sections 337–343) also legislates here, in a substantive reform amplifying the provisions of the OLFR. For the deeper history in the immediate region of the other legal categories mentioned see e.g. Tucker 1998.

mujtahid, the highest position in the Shi'i religious hierarchy. This infusion of charismatic authority is consonant with the gravity assigned to a judicial divorce without the husband's consent. But it raises the bar problematically high, not to mention that it poses the problem of who can legitimately claim such a status. These considerations make this an extremely difficult case to make and win and one very rarely awarded. I return to this in a later chapter, but for now we should note that this gives men much the upper hand, as they will most often have to be cajoled into agreeing to a divorce, most commonly through the wife giving up her *mahr*, or even by paying him a consideration over and above that; and so for the wife of a Shi'i husband to obtain a divorce prolonged negotiations will very often be required. This gives a rather different dynamic to the flow of proceedings in the two courts, which are otherwise largely identical.[19]

The structural imbalance between men and women's rights to divorce makes this issue a key one for women's rights campaigners. As one middle-class Sunni woman put it to me in discussing divorce in Lebanon (and in fact referring to the plight of a Shi'i friend in particular), 'It's worse than Saudi Arabia'. Civility between the genders is directly at stake, as is national pride, and indeed comparison between the Sunni and Shi'i schools. Such issues also arise around further cases that may then arise after divorce where children are involved, those of custody (*hadana*) and visitation (*ru'ya/mushahada*). As we have already had cause to note, under Islamic precepts fathers are awarded custody of children at strikingly young ages, to Western and indeed contemporary Lebanese eyes: at the time of my research, seven years for a boy and nine for a girl in the Sunni courts (now twelve for both), and two and seven years respectively in the Ja'fari courts. This gives a husband still further leverage against his wife in any divorce negotiations, and has been a major focus of recent reform activism, as we have seen.

But such debates notwithstanding, disputes are inevitably presented to the court through these particular legal forms. The categories of cases that are available impose a standard structure on proceedings, an adversarial exchange framed in terms of certain stereotypical issues. They also impose a potential teleology with its own momentum that extends through to divorce and beyond.

[19] One Sunni judge told me that if a Sunni woman wants to marry a Shi'i man they advise her to make it a condition in the marriage contract that it will be the Sunni court that will have jurisdiction in case of divorce. He also told me of a case he had where a Sunni husband converted to Shi'i Islam in order to have greater control over his wife.

Paperwork and Procedure

This dynamic and rhythm is further structured by the demands of procedure and the constraints of the courts' timetable. A summons (*istihdar*) needs to be filed, the relevant documents – the marriage contract, personal status records – provided. Papers need to be stamped, and a court session (*jalsa*) arranged. These need to be booked weeks if not months in advance due to the volume of cases. A judge will need to sign off on such a request. A spare moment has to be begged, or the forms given to one of the judge's functionaries, his usher perhaps. A stack of such papers is taken in and thrust under the judge's nose to be signed, in the course of his other business. If the judge gets the chance to read it, he might spot a problem: the case is being brought in an inappropriate jurisdiction, say; or, very commonly, he is not the right judge for this type of case.

In a court the size of Jami' Imam 'Ali, each judge handles only cases of a specific sort, the responsibilities divided up between the judges, in ways that can be opaque to the uninitiated. 'I do marriage, not annulment of marriage'; 'I do divorce initiated by the man: Judge so-and-so does it initiated by the woman'; in a case of custody, 'How old are the children?' 'How old are the kids?' the dogsbody shouts outside. 'Four', comes back the answer. 'Below the age milord.' That is, below the age of legal majority, because another judge handles custody of children who are of age. Different types of cases are more or less common, and thus these judicial assignments, which are an administrative matter rather than one of professional specialisation, carry very different case loads. Come a reorganisation, I would suddenly find that one of my favourite judges had hardly any cases, and another who I had thought of as of a different status was now very busy. Such a reshuffle of duties causes considerable bureaucratic upheaval, not to mention delay for plaintiffs and respondents: cases have to be started afresh with the new judge; papers can go missing in transit.

The appropriate fees must be paid and the requisite stamps obtained. Just about every document submitted to the court seems to need a stamp. You can see lawyers licking and sticking great piles of them. The fees are not very considerable, although for the poor they are no doubt a material factor.[20] They depend on the case and the court: appeals cases are more expensive. But, one judge estimated, even the highest charge for the most expensive case will not reach $50 US. That may not be the end of the

[20] The Law of Sharia Courts makes provision for legal aid (section 266). But I also saw one judge resort to (surely illegally) paying one old lady's fees himself via a trusted lawyer.

expenses, however. The court may commission someone, usually the judge's assistant, to conduct an investigation: as to whether or not the marital home a husband is claiming to provide meets the minimum legal requirements, for instance; or the whereabouts of someone not replying to a summons. And he will need to be paid, the charge generally stipulated in the written record in order to stop him charging what he likes. The court appointed mediators in a case of *tafriq* need to be compensated. Expert testimony, from a doctor for instance, may be needed and will incur a fee.[21]

Notification (Tabligh) Of crucial administrative importance is that the respondent party, or their representative, must be given notification (*tabligh*) of the case being brought against them.[22] If they have not been so informed, as recorded in a paper in the file, then the case cannot progress. An account of the legal stipulations surrounding this practice will very quickly give an idea of its complexities and serve as an illustration of the pains of legal bureaucracy more generally.

In the first instance, within Lebanon, notification must take place in person, through a court official (or the police when necessary), at the addressee's given address, abode or place of work.

> Section 138 of the Law of Sharia Courts: All judicial papers and resolutions are to be sent to the relevant party in person wherever he is or to his representative or at his address or his abode or his place of work through the usher.[23]

Lawyers know to tip the court functionary, to make sure they have enough to cover their travel expenses and a little bit more besides, as they otherwise have little incentive to make the extra effort that may be required. I saw one judge having to go back through all the files for several months because of a functionary just signing off on a tranche of summonses without actually having done the work necessary to serve them.

If the addressee is not present at those locations then, if someone suitable is to be found, the papers can still be served:

[21] The standard such fee for a court official in the course of my research was 100,000LL (about $65); a case of judicial divorce (*tafriq*) in the Sunni courts requires multiple sessions of arbitration, which may total 3–400,000 LL, although the judge may take a plaintiff's financial circumstances into account and discount that. It should be said that although payment of such fees is required from the plaintiff in advance, they may be recovered in part or whole from the respondent subsequent to the court's ruling.

[22] For examples of appeals based on the claim that it was performed incorrectly see Homsi 2003: 63–64, 107, 139–140.

[23] For the relevant sections of the LSC see Zayn 2003a: 64–66.

LSC section 140: Where notification pertains to someone not to be found in his place of residence or his place of work ... then it proceeds according to the principles of the civil courts ...

Section 400 of the Law of Civil Courts:[24] If the usher did not find the person whose notification is sought at his address or his abode, it is permitted for him to give the paper to he who declares that he is his representative or works in his service or is one of his cohabitants, from among spouses and kinsmen and affines, from those whose appearance indicates that they have reached eighteen years of age, on the condition that the interest of the one whose notification is sought is not contrary to their interest. In the event that any of those persons stated above refuse to accept the papers the usher is to leave the papers for him and considers notification as at that moment legally obtaining, even if they refuse to sign the record.

If no one is to be found, or the functionary is refused entry, or if normal notification is impossible for some other reason, then 'exceptional' (*istith-na'i*) means are to be employed (LSC section 142).

LSC section 145: Exceptional notification is performed by sending a registered letter to the person whose notification is sought for their attendance at the office [*qalam*] of the court, so that they may receive the document addressed to them. This letter is to be sent in an envelope stamped with the seal of the court to the last known address or abode or to their designated address. And if the addressee refuses to accept the letter, then the postman returns it without delay to the office of the court appended with an indication of their refusal; and this is included in the file of the case so that it may stand as indication of notification having been obtained. And if the postman did not find the person to whom the notification is addressed at the address indicated, then he explains that event and returns the letter without delay to the office of the court. And in this event, just as in the event of the address being unknown, a copy of the paper is to be attached to the noticeboard on the door of the court for a period of twenty days and a notice announcing to the person whose notification is wanted that there is a notification concerning him in the court is to be published in two daily newspapers of wide local circulation. And testimony from the clerk establishing the completion of twenty days from the attaching of the copy and the publication of the announcement is taken as a substitute for the record of notification.

In many instances the respondent (and sometimes also the plaintiff) will be living abroad. Their notification is potentially still more problematic.

[24] I.e. *Qanun usul al-muhakamat al-madaniyya*. See Musawi 2007: 50. The identification of section 400 as the relevant one is my own. Zayn (2003a: 64) refers in a note to section 140 of the LSC to section 403 of the LCC, but this concerns the procedures for informing members of the army, merchant navy, etc.

LSC section 147: Notification in foreign countries proceeds via a registered letter or in accordance with the documented principles in the law of those countries, except if there were an agreement which stipulates a special procedure. And notification is considered as obtaining from the day of the signature of the one to be notified attesting to knowledge of its arrival or from the day of his refusal to sign or accept [the letter]. And if the letter were returned without notification having taken place or the legally required period expired without the letter being returned or knowledge of its arrival, then it is allowed for the court to consider the person addressed as of unknown address.

At this point one further needs to know the definition of the legally required period to wait. Section 104 of the LSC defines the standard period for court processes as one month. However, as detailed in section 107, if the party concerned is abroad then a further period must be added to that: 30 days in the case of Syria, Egypt, Iraq and Jordan; 90 days for the countries of America, Oceania, Japan and the Philippines; 60 days for all other countries. Establishing someone as of unknown address requires a resolution from the judge in the light of an investigation conducted by the clerk through questioning of the addressee's relatives and neighbours and the *mukhtar* of the area where they were last known to reside (section 148). And then exceptional means will have to be mobilised.

One readily perceives the obscure (from a litigant's perspective), complex and potentially problematic nature of these procedures. An uncooperative respondent, especially one that can convince their friends, colleagues and relatives to cover for them, can evade a summons and force the plaintiff down the time-consuming path of 'exceptional notification'. A wife, say, with an estranged husband abroad, may have to wait months before the case can proceed. Should the plaintiff not follow the requisite procedures faithfully to their end, then the whole process will have to be begun anew. If the case gets handed to a different judge then that process will have to be repeated. Each step requires further visits to court and further financial outlay. The whole business can seem costly, endless, not to say pointless: 'But I know he's been informed, because he told me he couldn't come'; 'I don't understand – I see him every day when he comes to see the children'; 'Can't you just phone him?' Some give up.

Of course, if you have the money to hire a lawyer, then much of this annoying work can be taken care of for you. But representation carries its own administrative burden. Lawyers (or anyone else acting as a representative – a father or brother, say) need to produce their official document of representation (*wikala*), with the requisite stamps and seals. I saw many a case postponed because it had been left in the lawyer's office or was missing a stamp. And let us remember that the standard court postponement is for a month. A man come representing his wife suddenly found the missing document amongst his papers – 'Here you go!' No, it wasn't acceptable; it has to be submitted according to the regulations. What was wrong with it? It hadn't got the requisite stamps. He could go and get them there and then. 'At the next session.' 'But if you happened to be free today.' No, the judge was not free that day. And that was that, another month lost. The document of representation has to be specific to the case or action in question, which, as things develop, it not always is, leading to further frustration.[25] And it is specific to the lawyer, and not to their assistant or colleagues in their office without further documentation, raising more potential pitfalls for lawyers spread thinly across several cases and courts. Too narrow an insistence on this sort of bureaucracy is thus a concern even for the lawyers. One respected practitioner, exasperated when his assistant was sent back, went down to the court to complain in person. Why make things so difficult? 'There is laziness and there is stupidity.' He quoted a saying of the Prophet: '[You have been sent to] make things easy, not hard.'[26]

Sessions

Let us assume that the painful business of getting the paperwork right has been achieved. The plaintiff (or their lawyer) will then finally get their day (or rather, minutes) in court. Formal and procedural considerations come into play here too.[27] The parties to the case, along with, or substituted by, their lawyers are to stand facing the judge: the plaintiff on the judge's right; the defendant on the left. The largest offices might have lecterns for them, but, given the constraints of space, most do without. If both parties and their lawyers, if any, are present, then the session (*jalsa*) can proceed. If only one party is present then a decent interval must be allowed for them to turn up, at least one hour after the scheduled time, according to the law of procedure. ('In the sharia' by contrast, one judge noted drily, 'the court is waited upon; it does not wait.') The judges understand the vagaries of life and Lebanese transport as well as anyone else. Once the appointed hour has passed, however, the judge can rule *in absentia* (*hukm ghiyabi*). Even if they are to be represented by lawyers, the judge may insist on seeing the parties at least once in person (*bi-l-dhat*, or

[25] See e.g. the case cited at Homsi 2003: 82–83. For a case where non-production of the document of representation resulted in losing the case and being fined see Barakat 2005: 223–226.

[26] *Bu'ith-tum muyassirin wa-lam tub'ath-u mu'assirin* (Sahih al-Bukhari vol. 1 book 4 hadith 219).

[27] On the following legal points see LSC sections 193–199.

muwajahan, 'face to face'), to get to the bottom of things and in order that they demonstrate their seriousness (*jiddiyya*) in the matter. This is potentially a powerful source of leverage. An opposing lawyer may request such a personal appearance to bring tactical advantage, as when, for example, a party lives abroad. For one thing, it may be inconvenient, or impossible, for them to come. For another, once in Lebanon it may be possible to trap them there with a travel ban (*man' al-safr*), a common, and potentially very powerful, way of exerting pressure: they may be in Lebanon for the summer holidays and need to get back to work elsewhere, or be in the middle of proceedings to gain a coveted foreign nationality or work permit.[28] An often given reason for such a ban is the fear that one parent might take the children abroad and then they would be lost to the other; or a woman might be afraid of violence from a husband, for instance.[29]

As we have already noted, the Law of the Sharia Courts follows civil procedure in stipulating that court proceedings are public (*'alaniyya*), despite the intimate nature of the matters discussed.[30] This relative transparency, it was commonly brought to my attention, contrasts with the procedure of the Christian courts, which are not only closed to the public, but also, reportedly, frequently to lawyers as well. The publicity of the sharia court hearings was thus an important marker of their relative civility, in the narrow sense of their impartiality and the broader sense of their incorporation into the institutions and modalities of the Lebanese state. (Intimate discussions – whispered exchanges – violate this supposed impartiality and are disapproved of.)

However, this publicity can become too apparent. The audience may become obviously involved, especially in the larger courtrooms: a protracted instance of mud-slinging on the part of the wife might attract amusement or condemnation from the crowd, as might a particularly sullen husband's intransigence in response ('Shame [*'ayb*]!'). People are understandably reluctant to discuss intimate matters in public. But before the judge, they are required to talk. A private, or secret, session (*jalsa khassa / sirriyya*) can thus be requested or imposed, where matters of greatly felt sensitivity are involved. Such requests are readily and frequently granted, for generally stereotypical reasons, such as an

[28] I even saw one case where the husband worked for the Lebanese port authority. A travel ban meant he could not enter the port to go to work, as it counted as outside the country's borders.

[29] More legalistically, an appropriate reason is to obtain their response to a case (*istijwab*) or secure payment of maintenance owed. See LSC section 21 and e.g. Homsi 2003: 95.

[30] Section 171.

intimation or accusation of sexual infidelity or other dramatically immoral and irreligious acts such as drinking alcohol, on either party's account, or else an embarrassing (i.e. sexual) disability.[31] The court, usually just a small office after all, will be cleared of all but essential staff (I was often, but not always, allowed to stay). Lawyers cannot, in principle, be excluded, even if not actually involved in the case, another marker of the privileges claimed by the civil law that they most closely represent.

Just as the publicity of the hearings is based on a civil precedent, and lawyers, who in many senses represent the civil legal aspect of these nominally sharia courts, cannot be excluded, so conversely it can be argued, as by one judge, that the private session is 'something *shar'i*', that is, here, pertaining to the sharia. The sharia seeks to preserve the secrets of the family; religion enjoins modesty (*satr*, 'veiling', 'shielding'). He quoted a famous hadith: 'He who shields a Muslim, God shields him' (*man satara musliman satara-hu Allah*).[32] Beyond the courts, mediation between couples occurs in any number of private sessions. Such efforts at private, personal engagement and the shielding of intimate matters through relationships of confidentiality and trust can thus be readily styled, in opposition to the publicity of the courts, as a characteristically, if not uniquely, religious concern, one more mode of expressing the distinction between ideal sharia and the flawed reality of the law.

In any case, the parties are sometimes intimidated by the judge and his court, and he may adopt a light-hearted approach to put them at their ease, cracking a few jokes or engaging in some banter. But sometimes the requisite respect may be lacking. People can be difficult; the judge may become exasperated. Obviously it is stressful for the parties involved. Sometimes they shake with anger, tears or anxiety. Some women have very good cause to fear their spouses; and the judge may advise them to linger in the court for a while until the husband is well gone. While most sessions pass without incident, occasionally arguments break out, even – rarely – brawls. The court's policeman may have to be called, a potent reminder that the courts are an arm of the state.

Having finally got before the judge, the parties will at last get the opportunity to air their grievances. A litany of bitter complaints will most likely tumble out; the other side will want to butt in – 'That's not true!' The extent varies to which the judge will hear them out: some might

[31] The LSC (section 171) cites concerns for public order (*al-nizam al-'amm*), decency (*al-adab*) or the sanctity of the family (*hurmat al-usra*).

[32] See e.g. al-Nawawi, *Riyad al-salihin*, book 1 hadith 244: ... *man satara musliman satara-hu Allah yawm al-qiyama*.

demand a written submission in lieu of hearing an exhaustive such account. The wife starts: 'It was one day in Ramadan ...' 'We don't need all this detail now in the court. He's got to talk as well. We'll be here for hours! Write it all down on a piece of paper and submit it next time.' The husband's turn: 'That day in Ramadan ...' 'Look, how long have you been married?' Two years eight months. 'Right, if I have to listen to all these details, it will take two years eight months! Write it down!'

The court's time is limited, and the case and its sessions have their formal dynamic. Each party should take their turn to speak: the plaintiff presents their case first; then the respondent should produce their reply (*jawab*).[33] They have the right to postpone to do so; they can also postpone proceedings for the purposes of engaging a lawyer; the first time a lawyer attends they have the right to postpone in order to examine the files of the case; every time a document is submitted the opposing side has the right to postpone to consider it; if another related case is pending proceedings may be postponed in order to see the result. The court must adjourn and meet at the next available session, which could be in several months' time. The long-awaited *jalsa* may thus prove something of a disappointment.

Such postponements can of course be used tactically, to frustrate the other party. Take a case of 'obedience' brought to trump a wife's suit for maintenance: the wife's lawyer in her separate suit for judicial separation announces loudly to the judge, 'I am not a lawyer [*wakil*] in this case'; and the wife then asks for a postponement in order to engage a lawyer in this new one. As the lawyer then explained to me rather loudly (part of the plan I think), they were playing tactics (*tactic*), trying to upset the husband. 'She has the right to a lawyer [in this new case]. So now she will ask for me to become her lawyer: it takes time, delays the case.'

Building a File

As the proceedings progress, the case will become sedimented as a file (*mahdar*). A great pile of brown envelopes, each containing the notes to the case and scrawled over with the dates of the various hearings already held, will tower on the judge's desk. During the sessions, they are taken up one by one, the papers extracted, the notes scanned by the judge and then passed to his assistant, who will record the judge's dictation by hand into the file. A computer stands on the desk in many judges' offices, but is rarely troubled. In a long-standing case, notes might have been taken

[33] See too Dupret 2006: 165.

in a different court during previous sessions, or by a different recorder – the judge might squint at the unfamiliar handwriting, or bemoan some grammatical errors as the recorder reads from the file, perhaps correct his own assistant's mistakes in this regard.[34]

Notes are dictated and taken during the proceedings in *fusha*, nominally 'classical' Arabic, although in this case of a distinctly legalistic rather than literary variety. Mastery over the Arabic language is the traditional mark of learning, and something that a shaykh in particular, immersed in scripture, should command.[35] A learned debate over the correct Arabic for an SMS text message, for instance, offers the chance for a judge to show his cultivation (*risala hatifiyya*, or 'telephone letter', it was agreed). Many, perhaps most, lawyers (and certainly most clients) are incapable of such a register in sustained speech, or at least do not trouble themselves with attempting to reproduce it in court, although legal documents certainly affect it and a few distinguished figures all but dictate to the recorder themselves, in the highest-flown language. The judge may enjoy the opportunity to correct a slip in a submission. Outside of the dictated notes, however, the proceedings take place in the commonplace register of everyday speech. One young woman, overawed but good-humoured, wondered, 'What, do I speak normally [*bahki 'adi*]?!'

The record taken is thus a version, or summary translation of what is spoken. A long list of renewed grievances might be dictated as: 'And it emerged that the plaintiff' – for the individual person becomes subsumed by their role – 'repeated her demands.' On the first meeting the judge will want to see the marriage contract and ask if there are any children: 'And it emerged that the two spouses were married in such-and-such court on such-and-such date with a prompt dower of such-and-such and a postponed dower of such-and-such, and that they had three children.' Again, each side is to speak in turn; while in fact they may be talking over each other, the judge will distil from the wrangling what he deems the salient

[34] I saw a judge become suspicious that a ruling he was presented with had been forged because the handwriting was too good. 'It's nice [*hilw*], very clear, not like mine.' And so, he later commented to his clerk, it could have been the judge's assistant who had written the ruling rather than the judge himself. (Previous Sunni court president Salim Jalal al-Din [2003: 163–166] provides an account of just such a case in his memoirs.) Like the proverbially inscrutable script of the doctor, the higher the status of the professional the more illegible the handwriting, it seems. Notwithstanding the possibilities of print (and digital) modernity then, manuscript culture remains current (cf. Messick 1993; Clarke 2010 and Hull 2012).

[35] It is not necessarily, however, that command of the highest linguistic register is automatically associated with the highest social status. See e.g. Haeri 1997 on Egypt. Let us remember too that Islamic religious professionals are not themselves necessarily associated with the highest status or social origins.

points. 'And the plaintiff stated that the respondent does not maintain her and has neglected her for so-many years.' 'And the respondent stated that all of this was untrue and that he had provided a legal home for the plaintiff in the region of such-and-such.'

Claims will need to be substantiated. As the Islamic principle runs, the burden of proof is on the plaintiff and the one denying (the accusation, i.e. the respondent) should take the oath (*al-bayyina 'ala-l-mudda'i wa-l-yamin 'ala man ankara*).[36] But, as judges would point out to me, family cases are such that it is often hard or impossible to establish the facts of the matter: 'proof is hard' (*al-dalil sa'b*). As one judge said, 'In matters of marriage, there is no right and wrong [*haqq wa-batil*], no case – or they are very rare – where it is clear like the sun. Usually they are confused [*mukhtalat*]. It's hard to judge someone: how do I know what sort of man this guy is, when he is standing before me for ten minutes in a hearing?' And as he put it another time, 'In such matters, family matters, there is a sort of mystery and faith and religious belief [*naw' min al-ghayb wa-l-iman wa-l-'aqa'id*]'. For the judges, as we will see again later, family law is marked out as different in kind: its intimacy and privacy in some sense puts it beyond the domain of law, which, in Islamic terms at least, is concerned with the apparent (*al-zahir*) as opposed to the internal (*al-batin*), whether that be the truth of a person's intentions or indeed that of the intimate domain of the home. There is, according to this judge at least, some form of enchantment to married life as a legal object.

Nevertheless, evidence can be submitted to the court in a variety of forms, from personal statements, through to bank records and (in the Sunni courts) sworn testimony.[37] The judge may require that some investigation be done, usually by his assistant or one of the other court functionaries – to see if the *maskan shar'i* a husband is claiming he has provided really matches up, for instance. Expert testimony could include medical evidence; other sources include paperwork from another case, such as a criminal case as in instances of domestic abuse, or bank statements, pay slips or photocopies of passport pages in evidence of a party's movements. Written submissions (sometimes handwritten, depending on the claimant's means) have of course to be adorned with the relevant stamps and copies provided for the other side.

Given the nature of the cases before the court – largely marital disputes – the parties are often keen to establish the immorality of the other.

[36] See Brunschvig, 'Bayyina', in *EI*².

[37] The Shi'i tradition, I was told, takes a different position on the value of such evidence, and the LSC, section 184, gives the Ja'fari judge a choice in the matter. In practice the Ja'fari courts do not, so far as I am aware, admit sworn testimony.

This is especially so in cases of custody, where one seeks to prove the unsuitability of the other party to serve as guardians. Photographic evidence (often on a mobile phone thrust towards the judge), audio recordings or telephone records are sometimes produced: photographs of one or other at a party, drinking; the husband alleges the wife is having an affair and produces telephone receipts showing a high number of calls 'to a man' and a picture of that man with her and the man's wife at a Lebanese holiday resort. There are, however, strict conditions associated with such evidence. Permission is required from the public prosecutor (*al-na'ib al-'amm*) for its collection, as the judge will inform them. And the judges are well aware of the possibilities for manipulation that modern technologies bring. Judges were invariably uninterested in such submissions, often averting their gaze to avoid seeing them, and I myself never saw them play any significant role in the proceedings.[38] What is relevant, from a legal point of view, is not necessarily what people assume. The law has its own expectations, and judges have to honour them.

[38] But see Tarabey (2013: 159–162) on the Druze courts.

8 Rulings and Reconciliation

Moving directly on from the previous chapter, I now propose to focus on one type of case in more detail: judicial separation for reason of discord (*tafriq li-l-shiqaq wa-l-niza'*) before the Sunni courts, a common and high profile, if also relatively complex category. Again, this type of judicial divorce is particular to the Sunni courts. The Ja'fari courts' version, 'divorce by the judge' (*talaq al-hakim*), is much more rarely encountered and gives rise to a distinct set of issues, which I discuss below. But the more general themes that *tafriq* raises, those of the bureaucratic nature of sharia court practice and a corresponding counterbalancing emphasis on the work of mediation and attempted reconciliation, are shared between the two court systems.

Tafriq li-l-Shiqaq wa-l-Niza'

As we briefly noted in the previous chapter, this form of judicial divorce was introduced in the 1917 Ottoman Law of Family Rights, drawing on precedents from the Maliki school to expand on what was possible under Hanafi law, and then modified in the 1962 Law of Sharia Courts (sections 337–347). It could thus be considered for a traditionalist in some sense a hybrid form, a legal assemblage, certainly an instance of modernist reformism – although its reformist credentials may now seem somewhat threadbare. For wives, although it does provide a ready avenue to divorce when wanted, it is a relatively lengthy and costly process;[1] for some husbands, on the other hand, it represents – or so they claim – an outrageous attack on their patriarchal rights.

[1] Say 2–250,000 LL for the cost of bringing the case and notifying the respondent, including taking out adverts in the newspapers, and then say 300,000 LL for the professional arbitrators. One judge estimated such a case takes at least a year. Another thought it had become easier of late ('We're the easiest sect', i.e. to get divorced under, he said), more a matter now of three to six months rather than the previous six months to a year. His clerk scoffed: he had just seen a case ongoing on for three years. 'The folder is that thick!'

Here too it is worth paying attention to the letter of the law. First the OLFR:

If strife and discord [*niza' wa-shiqaq*] arises between the two spouses and one of them applies to the judge, the judge shall appoint an arbitrator from the family of the two parties [again, following the Quranic injunction]; and if there is no person to be appointed as an arbitrator from the family of the two parties or one of them, or there is, but they do not possess the proper qualities of an arbitrator, then someone who suits them from outside [their families] shall be designated. The family council [*majlis al-'a'ila*] formed in this manner shall scrutinise the testimony and defence of the two parties and shall strive to reconcile their differences [*islah dhat al-bayn*]. If reconciliation is not possible, then if the fault is on the part of the husband the judge shall divorce [*yufarriq*] them; and if it is on the part of the wife then a mutually agreed divorce [*mukhala'a*] will take place for the whole of the *mahr* or a part of it. (OLFR section 130)[2]

And in a significant addition, the LSC (section 337) stipulates that

Both spouses may ask for separation [*tafriq*] because of harm [*darar*] arising from discord [*shiqaq*] or ill-treatment [*su' al-'ishra*, 'bad relations'] such as beating [*ka-darb*] and verbal abuse [*sabb*] and coercion to perform a prohibited act [*ikrah 'ala muharram*] or practice what is prohibited [*ta'ati al-muharram*].

The judge will thus first seek to ascertain if harm has been caused, and whether there is discord between the spouses, evidence of which might include (but need not, given the qualification 'such as', indicated by the prefix '*ka-*') beating, verbal abuse and prohibited practices.[3] Wives seeking a divorce may well allege that there is discord, that their husband beat or abused them, or drank or gambled (religiously prohibited), or forced them to have anal intercourse, for instance.[4] ('That's not on!', 'She can't say that!', the husband might cry; the judge will shut him up: 'You'll get your turn.') But again, given the intimate nature of married life these may not be so easy to prove. In the worst cases there may be medical evidence of beatings or criminal charges against the husband, which will obviously suffice.[5] But usually the wife will have to provide witnesses. 'Were there

[2] I have benefited here from El-Alami and Hinchcliffe's (1996: 166) translation, with some modification. The text in Zayn 2003a: 140 has *mukhalasa*, which cannot be right: Anderson notes the use of the term *khul'* in the course of his own translation (1951b: 285). On this section, Anderson (ibid.) comments, 'This provision is pure Maliki doctrine'. See also Tucker 2008b: 121.

[3] Here and below compare Dupret's (2006, 2007) 'praxiological' account of establishing *darar* in an Egyptian divorce case.

[4] See also Mir-Hosseini (1993) for much the same tactics in the Iranian courts. While the law allows both spouses to sue for divorce on these grounds, I only saw one such case brought by a man, which one functionary thought due to the husband's reluctance to pay the *mahr* that he would otherwise owe.

[5] See e.g. Homsi 2003: 36.

any witnesses to this?', the judge will want to know. 'Bring them. I want two.' Two Muslim male witnesses are required; the testimony of two women can stand for that of one man. In the latter case, the two women give their testimony together, confirming their account and jogging each other's memory. (This gendered hierarchy of powers to bear witness is enjoined by the Quran [2:282], but another bone of contention for critics of the courts.)

That raises immediate problems: where to find the witnesses? Certain categories of relatives are excluded, but others are not; one might turn also to friends and neighbours. Then they must be brought to court and persuaded to endure the hours of waiting. People cannot necessarily take the whole morning off work. And also, because of all the frustrating bureaucratic hurdles and delays, this effort can often be brought in vain. Parties and witnesses may arrive at court, only to find a case postponed or rearranged. The witnesses will have to be marshalled again on another occasion: some drop out.

But let us say that the witnesses do finally appear before the judge, then their details will be taken, their religious community established (non-Muslims cannot testify against Muslims)[6] and they will be sworn in. Everyone in the office stands – an unparalleled indication of the gravity of the undertaking – and they have to repeat, 'I swear by Almighty God that I bear witness with sincerity without addition or omission' (*wa-allah al-'azim aqul al-haqq wa-ashhad bi-l-sidq min dun al-ziyada wa-l-naqsan*). And then the judge will question them, asking how relations were between the spouses. 'Was there discord between them?' 'Does he beat her?' (*Byadrabb-ha shi?*) 'Does he abuse her?' (*Byasubb wa-yshtum 'alay-ha?*) An affirmative response would build the file: 'And the first witness stated that the respondent abused the defendant.' 'How is her condition? Fine or damaged [*mutadarrara*]?' 'Damaged, of course.' The judge dictates: 'The witness stated that she is damaged by this situation ... And [the plaintiff] asks for the establishment of strife and discord, and because there is harm to her and because of the principle "No harm in Islam" [*la darar wa-la dirar fi-l-islam*] the presence of strife and discord is established.'

As Baudouin Dupret has said, 'unlike ordinary conversations, the order of a speaker's turn in judicial settings is fixed, as is the type of each speaker's turn. Within this system of turn allocation, both the judge and

[6] Another point of criticism from various perspectives, but also a potential frustration for someone bringing a case who had been living in a religiously mixed area: if all the neighbours were Christian, say, then admissible testimony could be hard to obtain (as I saw in one case).

the witnesses are oriented to the production of information that may be legally relevant and credible.' A more extended example:

WITNESS 1: The defendant is bad.

JUDGE: Like what, he curses her?

WITNESS I (PARAPHRASED): He doesn't fast in Ramadan. And he stops his kids doing so. He doesn't let anyone visit his family in 'Id – there is no 'Id. He insults the family. He beats his children. And he blasphemes. He stopped her going on the Hajj and 'Umra. He says he would divorce her if she went on the Hajj. He forbids her to read the Quran, or to have the television on a religious programme. One time she rang me – 'He's beaten me. I went to the police station but they wouldn't do anything without evidence.'

. . .

WITNESS 2 (IN TURN, PARAPHRASED): The husband was originally Christian. He converted in the court when they got married. And he says he's a Muslim now too, but . . . He is useless. Their son is afraid to pray in front of him. They are forbidden to go on the 'Umra. He forbids them from fasting. We hear blasphemy. We avoid visiting them so as not to hear his blasphemy [*kufr*]. Memorising the Quran, that's forbidden. He forbids the children from registering for religious studies, and from listening to religious programmes on the television: no way, immediately.

THE JUDGE DICTATES: He forbids his family from their religious duties [*al-wajibat al-diniyya*].[7]

Given the difficulties of finding suitable witnesses and getting them to court, judges may be more or less disposed to less onerous means of establishing marital discord. If a dispute is an enduring one, then that might constitute evidence enough. One judge, for instance, told me that six months separation between the spouses would suffice as proof of discord. It could even be argued that bringing such a case is evidence enough in itself. Such positions are, however, the minority, or perhaps more a matter for academic conversation than practice, as some lawyers scoffed.[8]

[7] This judge seemed generally receptive to the notion that a husband's irreligious behaviour and its impact on the religious commitment of the family, especially the children, constituted evidence of discord. My impression was also that he was more stringent in this respect with regard to converts to Islam, although, when I put that to him, he thought not.

[8] I have no such rulings in my own collection, although it is far from exhaustive, let it be said.

During this process, the husband, or his lawyer, if present, must be careful. Too intemperate or argumentative a response to what may be infuriating allegations could itself be taken as evidence of discord; and an experienced lawyer acting for the wife might encourage her to provoke him for just this purpose. As one seasoned practitioner (whose ‘tactics’ we saw above) told me, ‘The woman has ruses: sometimes we ask the woman to cry abundantly of course!’ Or she can try to provoke her husband, ‘Either in the home, so the neighbours hear, or in public. Even in court. About his sexual inadequacy. A woman said to a man in front of the judge, “You do not have the power to take me”, and he slapped her. That immediately establishes that he beats her.’ I saw one session where the wife slapped her husband herself, after he claimed that her statement was ‘lies’. The judge made a note in the record, but the husband was careful not to react. ‘I want to finish with him [*biddi akhlas minnu*]!’, she shouted. ‘Don’t you want to finish with her?!’, the judge asked him. ‘This is your married life?!’ ‘I love her’, the man replied, not very convincingly. The judge dictated for the record that he was issuing a resolution establishing discord there and then, on the basis of the behaviour in the session. Afterwards, the wife was not impressed at all by how things had gone and was complaining bitterly about the process. But the judge had of course helped out with his resolution, even if his efforts had gone unappreciated.

Another case involved a prisoner, a young man of twenty or so, serving seven years for theft but brought from prison to court in handcuffs. His wife’s mother put forward their case: they were prepared to excuse him from paying her ‘her rights’, the *mahr* owed, if he would divorce her. ‘What about my rights?!’, he asked. ‘So you refuse the divorce?’ ‘Yes. And I demand . . .’ ‘You can’t demand anything – you are the defendant, not the plaintiff. That is the law. Do you have anything else to say?’ ‘Her mother abused my father in court!’ He was led away, but, as the judge commented afterwards, ‘Regrettably, establishing strife and discord is more significant than the abuse of his father.’ The man had thought he was being clever – putting the other side in the wrong – but actually this just went to add to the evidence of the bad relations between the families. Another husband also thought he was being clever, in this judge’s assessment, when he had claimed that his wife did not do the housework, as she worked outside the home. His expectation was that the Islamic judge would have been ill-disposed to his wife’s liberties. But he had instead simply demonstrated the strife between them. Another man reacted to his wife’s lawyer’s production of a list of proposed witnesses by saying, foolishly, ‘I have witnesses too. I have witnesses that they beat me!’ Her lawyer swiftly countered that this just went to demonstrate conflict and requested a resolution to that effect, which the judge granted.

Arbitration (Tahkim)

Once the judge is satisfied that harm due to ill-treatment or discord has been established he will issue a resolution to the effect and, following the LSC (section 338), enjoin a period of one month for attempted reconciliation (*sulh*) between the couple. After this more or less welcome (depending on the party) further delay, the case now moves to its next stage, an evaluation of the relative responsibility of the spouses for this discord on the part of arbitrators (*hukkam*, sing. *hakam*). Remembering the Quranic injunction that, 'If you fear a breach between a man and his wife, appoint an arbiter from his people and another from hers. If they wish to be reconciled, God will bring them together again' (4:35), this formal stage of arbitration is thus built upon a notion of a process of potential reconciliation, as are indeed the whole court proceedings, as we will see later.

If one recalls the passages from the OLFR and LSC setting out the principles of *tafriq* cited earlier, one will recall that while both laws formally envisage such arbitrators being sought in the first place from the families of the parties concerned, as in the Quranic verse, they also, following the Islamic legal tradition, allow them to be drawn from outside the family.[9] And the Sunni court system prefers indeed to work with professional arbitrators, drawn from its networks of religious specialists, as the judge will make clear. So, for instance, the judge asked one lawyer if there was anyone in the family who could act as an arbitrator. The lawyer, slightly nonplussed (and thus no doubt not familiar with this sort of case): 'Well there's the uncle.' 'Is there someone who knows the *shar'*? Who can act as a proper arbitrator [*hakam*]?' 'Yes, he's known [*ma'ruf*, i.e., of good reputation].' 'No, it's not enough to be known, he has to know the *shar'*. Is he experienced in conducting sessions of arbitration?' 'No.' And then the judge could dictate, 'He answered negatively. And in law if there is no-one in the family of one of the parties who can do it then the court decides on arbitrators. And so are appointed Shaykh X and Shaykh Y. And the side is charged with paying the sum of 300,000 LL.'[10] I heard one woman asked, 'Is there anyone in your family who can adjudicate, who knows law and sharia [*qanun wa-shar'*]?' After a moment's thought, she replied that her sister works in the Interior Ministry and is a lawyer. The judge swiftly dealt with this suggestion: 'Well, it's known that someone who works in the Interior Ministry can't

[9] On the legal discussions over the requisite qualifications of arbiters and the process of arbitration more generally see Zahraa and Hak 2006.

[10] The fee to be paid to the arbitrators varied according to the means of the plaintiff, but was generally of the order of 2–400,000 LL for the two of them.

take on other work.' She then had another suggestion, her (female) cousin, who was also a lawyer; but that was also discouraged. The judge decreed the case was to go to two specified shaykhs instead. In another case, the wife's lawyer suggested a shaykh of their own, but was overruled. He did not like the outcome, questioning the expense and that she has to pay it. 'They are experts [*khubara'*]', the judge replied. 'But our shaykh has expertise [*khibra*] in reconciling families', said the lawyer, indeed (note), 'by the sharia and not by means of civil law [*tariq al-qanun al-madani*].' He did not get his way.

The plaintiff will have to make contact with the arbitrators in the first instance, and inform the respondent of the session (raising yet again all the attendant problems of such official notification). I attended five such. One took place in Dar al-Fatwa, the central institution of the Sunni community and thus an 'official' setting, even if the shaykhs concerned were not wearing their full shaykhly attire and the session took place outside of office hours. But the other four were held in the apartment of one of the court's most frequently utilised and respected arbitrators, who I shall refer to as Dr F: sometime dean of the sharia college, professor at a number of Lebanese universities and author of a whole shelf of books on varied topics.

The more homely setting of Dr F's office-cum-sitting room, sitting before his desk in front of the bookshelves lined with books, suits the wider aesthetic of the session: this is, it is said, all about sharia, not law, by which is meant an emphasis on the personal over the procedural. In my first session, Dr F's colleague (two arbitrators should attend), a shaykh but not robed, was of the opinion that, while in the sharia court the work of the judge is 90 per cent law and 10 per cent *shar‘*, theirs was the inverse, '90 per cent *shar‘* and 10 per cent law'. He drew my attention to the closed nature of their sessions (recall our discussion of closed and public sessions in court). Not even the lawyers have a right to attend. Here they dealt with 'the secrets [*asrar*] of the people', the details of what goes on in the privacy of the home. When people did come with supporting family or lawyers, Dr F would feel free to tell them to remain in the adjoining room, so that the arbitrators could talk to the couple alone: 'They don't need a lawyer, him and her, because here it is all *shar‘*.' In a homely counterpoint to this intimacy, however, Dr F's wife would not only bring refreshments, but would also feel free to intervene with homily and encouragement; even Dr F's (grown-up) son popped in to comment occasionally.

In contrast to the sessions in court, Dr F would start with the *basmala* ('In the name of God the Merciful and Compassionate') and a little homily on love and marriage, quoting a Quranic verse perhaps. He would explain the proceedings, that he and his colleague were charged first and foremost with reconciliation (*islah dhat al-bayn*), and then, if it came to it, managing a divorce. And then both parties were to speak in turn, as fully as possible, 'including secrets [*asrar*], because we need to know everything. Nothing must be left unsaid.' Certainly the resulting discussions were more intimate and free-ranging than the court standard, with extended discussions of the husband's sexual inadequacies in one case (when he was not present). In the less cosy surroundings of Dar al-Fatwa too, the shaykh presiding also opened the session with a *basmala* and then gave a brief explanation of what would happen, quoting the famous Quranic verse on arbitration. When the husband asked if he could bring his witnesses, he was told, 'We don't talk about law [here], we talk as shaykhs' (*ma bnihki qanun, bnihki mashayikh*). When the husband stated that he (unusually) was seeking *tafriq* on his wife's responsibility (*'ala mas'uliyyat-ha*), he was asked, 'Where did you get this phrase? This isn't a humane [*insani*] expression. You got this from a lawyer.'

Consonant with our impression of the shaykh's vocation, Dr F's ethic is 'to help the people'. At his home, one might find someone waiting who has come to ask a question or beg a favour. He dispenses advice, or assists with the paperwork: he writes the summons for them, puts on the stamps, tells them where to go in the court, all 'for free', he noted. Overheard on the telephone: 'Go to the *mukhtar*, get the marriage certificate drawn up, go to the court and raise a case of maintenance. And tell the *mukhtar* that Dr F says hello, then he won't charge you too much.' His learning was widely admired: he had studied at Egypt's distinguished al-Azhar university at the same time as the then Mufti of the Republic, who he no doubt knew well, although he had chosen to study for a doctorate in Arabic language rather than sharia studies (much harder, it was said to me). By rights he could be addressed as 'shaykh' – and those in the court (and his wife) did refer to him as such – but he prefers 'doctor', as on his name plaque in his office, and eschews a shaykh's robes. One colleague even told me that, 'He thinks doctor is above shaykh, better. He doesn't like it if you call him shaykh!' Dr F's less procedural, nominally more sharia-friendly role is accompanied by a down-playing of the formal trappings of the Islamic religious professional.

Two sessions are the minimum – otherwise, I was told, the appeals court could criticise the soundness of the case – but Dr F has, he told me, done as many as four. Each session represents a further attempt at reconciliation, punctuated by time for the couple to reflect and to try to work things out. 'Now', he would say, bringing a session to a close, 'I am talking *shar'i*, we as arbitrators are supposed to work to resolve the conflict. So, what if I said to you, why don't you try living together for a month?' The wife – who was there without her husband – was adamant: 'No way!', she said. Her sister, who had accompanied her and had herself been through a divorce, sought to put the request into context. She had also, she said, been taken aback by the way that those involved in her case had continually pressed for reconciliation. Even now the thought of her husband, an 'animal', caused an involuntary shudder. 'But now I understand that's just procedure.' And there is the rub: attempts at reconciliation may sit better with the aura of the sharia than the legalistic proceedings of the court, but, given that most such cases are a long way down the line, they themselves become just another bureaucratic hurdle, to be participated in more or less constructively.

For all the open and engaged style of the proceedings, their final product is a report (*taqrir*), which then goes to the judge, with a copy sent to the lawyers, and joins the case file, which the arbitrators have before them for reference. Notes are taken, in the usual bald, legalistic form: 'They attended and we opened the session with the *basmala* and recommended reconciliation and listened to the wife.' 'I asked the wife what her opinion is and she refused to excuse him from the *mahr*.' The arbitrators' central finding is that of relative responsibility for the breakdown of the marriage, expressed as a percentage (which will translate into a percentage of costs and compensation). The judge has some power to alter the arbitrators' recommendation, but it is nevertheless significant. As ever, as one lawyer confidant told me, these formal processes can be manipulated. 'They will ask the man if he is angry with her, does he want to separate. He will say, "No, no!" Because he doesn't want to divorce, as then he'll have to pay. Then they will ask her. She does want to separate. But if she says so, she will be held responsible and will have to pay.' Certainly I noticed the exaggerated care that one man took continuously to stress his desire for reconciliation and to express his affection for a wife who was complaining about his behaviour bitterly. So too a lawyer acting on a husband's behalf, when allowed in, was sure to radiate enthusiasm for reconciliation: 'Have we reconciled now then?!' But in the arbitrations I saw – and this pattern was borne out in the rulings of *tafriq* I knew of – there was always deemed to be some fault on both sides, with the majority residing with the husband. Even in the case of a husband who had never turned up to any of the court or arbitration sessions, the wife had to take some of the blame. 'What will the responsibility be, 100 per cent his?', she asked. 'No, there is no such ruling', she was told. 'We rule between 50 and 70 per cent. We can never give 100 per cent to the woman because it is her choice' (i.e. to get divorced).

Judgements and Agreed Settlements

Once the process has taken its course, and if the dispute has not by now been resolved through an agreed settlement (dealt with later in this chapter) or fallen into abeyance, then the judge will have to rule. The very word, *hukm*, has a certain gravity. So gasps a lady of a certain age: 'Who will give the *hukm*? You, shaykh? Oh! Have mercy on us, shaykh [*rahham-na*]! God bless you [*Allah yubarik fik*]!' The judge will take the case file home to determine his verdict and write it up in the appropriate fashion. They are mostly, or so I was told, originally handwritten by the judges, and then typed up by a court functionary. (One progressive judge in the Sunni courts was indeed praised to me by a lawyer as 'the only one who types his own cases.') These are not huge documents, generally running to three or four pages say; the briefest might be a couple; exceptionally long ones might run to nine or ten. A session is then arranged for the summary verdict to be (brusquely) read out to the parties, or they will be otherwise notified. A copy of the ruling can then be taken to the (civil) chamber of execution (*da'irat al-tanfidh*) for implementation. It can also be appealed: a ruling is thus not necessarily the definitive moment that it may seem to some rhetorically.

Rulings take stereotypical (but not uniform) form. Headed 'Lebanese Republic, Prime Minister's Office, Sunni/Ja'fari Sharia Courts', they open (unlike the judges' sessions themselves) with the *basmala* – 'In the name of God the Merciful and Compassionate' – following the specific injunction of the Law of Sharia Courts (section 238). They are thus marked as different in kind from civil rulings, which are issued 'In the name of the Lebanese people'. They note the court, the judge presiding and the assistant attending before moving onto the ruling proper, typically made up of three sections: the first describing the details of the cases, ascertained from the parties and other sources of evidence ('Under examination', *lada al-tadqiq*);[11] the second marshalling those circumstances into points of legal significance (*bina'an 'alay-hi*, 'based on that'); and the third stating the derived ruling (*li-dhalik*, 'therefore', or, rarer, *li-hadhihi al-asbab*, 'for these reasons'). The Law of Sharia Courts states that the ruling must make clear both the sharia and legal basis on which the ruling is made – and they are thus by necessity a hybrid form.[12]

[11] In appeals court rulings, *lada al-tadqiq wa-l-mudhakira*: 'under examination and deliberation'. Appeals court rulings also more formally mark out sections devoted to form (*fi al-shakl*) and substance (*fi al-asas*).

[12] Section 240 of the LSC, which makes a series of detailed stipulations as to what a ruling must contain and thus no doubt helps shape the stereotyped nature of the genre.

Let us take an example ruling of *tafriq li-l-shiqaq wa-l-niza'* before the Sunni courts.[13] At four pages it is neither especially long nor short, although it will have to be somewhat abbreviated for our purposes here.

In the name of God the Merciful, the Compassionate.

In the council convened in the Sunni Sharia Court of [...] under the presidency of the Judge Shaykh [...] and the presence of the judicial assistant Shaykh [...].

Under examination:

It is apparent that A on [a date in April 1999] alleged against B, both of them from [...], that on [a date in 1991] there took place her marriage to him for an immediate bridal gift [*mahr*] of three million Lebanese Lira [then just over US $1000 at a time of savage inflation] in lieu of the furnishing of a bedroom and a postponed one of two million Lebanese Lira, and that the respondent treated her badly with insults and beating [i.e., the terms required by the LSC for establishing 'harm', *darar*] and was mean in maintaining her. And she asked for judicial divorce between her and him on his complete responsibility, and accompanied her petition with a copy of her marriage contract to the respondent.

(Again, one imagines the exchanges in court that were distilled into this formal and compressed account, introduced by the eminently legalistic, 'It is apparent that ...' [*yatabayyin an*].)

And in public session in person the respondent replied, acknowledging that the plaintiff is his wife and that he had consummated the marriage with her and had not been blessed with a child by her. And the court resolved on [a date in April 2001, so two years later] to listen to the testimony of two witnesses, X and Y. And very damaging [*mushayyina*] testimony came from both of them as to the harm [*darar*] arising from ill-treatment [*su' al-'ishra*, again the terms of the LSC]. And it appears that the representative of the respondent, the lawyer P presented a document in response, dated [July 2001, two months later], in which he stated that the plaintiff had reconciled with the respondent after she had brought her case and agreed to live with him and give him a chance, and then after that the situation between them became aggravated, which necessitates the rejection of the case formally [*shaklan*]. That is, the plaintiff had dropped her case when she accepted reconciliation with her husband and return with him to his home. And what the plaintiff slanders him with, that her husband beat her and abused her, and that he is mean, is not true, and there is no evidence of it. So too did he object to the stated record of the testimony of the stated witnesses because they drew their information from the statements of the plaintiff's side, pointing to the fact that the stated witnesses were relatives of the plaintiff, and so their giving sworn testimony was not legally admissible. That is, one of them is the paternal cousin of the plaintiff and the other is the husband of her maternal aunt. That necessitates disregarding their testimony and ignoring it. And he demanded the

[13] An unpublished ruling, copied for me by one of the lawyers involved.

rejection of the case on formal grounds, and if not, on substantial grounds, for the lack of its seriousness and legality; and he also demanded that the plaintiff pay the charges and expenses and fees and costs in full.

It is also apparent that [in July 2001, one week later] the court made a resolution establishing the harm arising from the bad relations between the two parties and to adjourn for a period not less than a month for reconciliation. And this [latter] resolution proved impossible, as it had before. And so the court [in August] designated His Excellency Shaykh M as an arbitrator for the plaintiff and His Excellency Shaykh N as an arbitrator for the respondent, so that they might bring the spouses together in a family council, in which they shall attempt mediation and reconciliation between them, and failing that, shall then put forward a detailed report of what they arrived at. And they submitted their report [in September, two weeks later] proposing the necessity for divorce between the spouses due to the impossibility of married life between them, and that the husband bear 70% of the responsibility for the failure of this marriage, due to ill-treatment.

In a session a month later, which the husband did not attend (nor his lawyer I presume), the wife's lawyer asked that the resolution be revisited and the arbitrators explain why 30 per cent responsibility had been attributed to her client. An appendix was duly added (two weeks later) now stating that the failure of the marriage was to be solely attributed to the husband, because the majority of the fault lay with him, and that the wife should thus receive the entirety of her (financial) rights. Their leniency towards the husband, they explained, had been due to his difficult economic situation, which affected their marriage; he had only beaten her once or twice, rather than habitually [sic]; he was ready to do anything to be reconciled with her, while she persisted in demanding divorce. In a final session later that month (at the end of October now), the two sides stuck to their positions and an end was thus declared to the proceedings.

The ruling continues:

And since the plaintiff brought a case demanding judicial divorce between her and the respondent.

And since the court resolved that harm between the parties had been established after listening to the testimony of the witnesses X and Y and adjourned for a month for reconciliation, and that proved impossible.

And since the court regards what the respondent's representative, the lawyer P, put forward in the written response dated [...] as falling outside of its legal place for the reasons that follow:

1. The return of the plaintiff to living with the respondent does not mean the lapse of the case and its abandonment, but rather the procedures stipulated in sections 216, 217, 218, 219 and 200 from the Law of Sharia Courts must be

followed for a case to have been abandoned and thence its lapse legally, and likewise the section 212 of the stated law.

2. The court resolved on [a date in 1999] to strike the case off the roster of proceedings, looking to the lack of attendance of the parties. And this striking off does not entail loss following the effects of the procedures of section 193 from the Law of Sharia Courts. Then, on [a date in 2000], the plaintiff requested renewal of the case ... and that is what section 212 from the same law stipulated ...
3. The request of the representative of the respondent for the ignoring of the testimony of the witnesses on the grounds that they are the plaintiff's relatives is rejected because not all kinship is a bar to testifying. Rather the bar applies to the testimony of ascendants and descendants and spouses. And as for the testimony of a paternal cousin or maternal aunt's husband, that is acceptable in law [*shar'an*] as the books of *fiqh* stipulate ...

The relevant books of *fiqh* are not detailed, however: the position of the sharia – here mentioned for the first time – can in some sense be taken for granted. The other objections to the witnesses' testimony are then discussed and rejected. The ruling continues, noting that the resolution of the arbitrators placed the responsibility for the divorce on the shoulders of the respondent, which entails that the judge should rule with judicial separation, and that the *mahr* and maintenance during the *'idda* are owed to a divorced wife.

And since the documents produced established that the plaintiff's prompt dower was 3 million Lebanese Lira in lieu of furnishing a bedroom and the postponed was 2 million LL, and according to sections 80, 81, 82, 103, 117, 130, 131, 139, 144 and 145 of the Law of Family Rights, and according to sections 16, 17, 19, 20, 91, 112, 117, 238, 239, 240, 242, 260, 264, 297, 337, 338, 343 and 344 of the Law of Sharia Courts,

Therefore:

We rule as follows:

1. With judicial separation between [the spouses A and B] with a first, single, final divorce – of the lesser finality,[14] so that the divorcee is not licit to her divorcer [for sexual relations] except with a new marriage contract and bridal gift. And that is on the responsibility of the respondent. And it is on the divorcee to honour the legal waiting period of three menstrual periods or the delivery of a pregnancy if she were pregnant, considered as from the date of this ruling. And that is to be noted on their marriage contract document.
2. Obligating the respondent to hand over bedroom furnishings to the value of her prompt dower and pay to her the sum of two million Lebanese Lira, the value of her delayed dower.

[14] *Baynuna sughra*, as opposed to the 'greater finality' (*baynuna kubra*) of a third divorce, after which the couple could only remarry after the wife had first been married to and divorced from another man.

3. Obligating the respondent to pay the plaintiff the sum of 1 million Lebanese Lira as maintenance during her waiting period for however many days it totals.
4. The rejection of all demands at variance with this ruling.

And all charges and costs are charged to him, as a contradictory judgement [*hukm wijahi*, i.e., I think, not an agreed one or one by default] according to the right of the parties, issued at the initial level, open to appeal, read out and made known publicly according to the principles on [the date, in both the Hijri and Gregorian calendars, in a final touch of explicit hybridity].

Hard Cases and Boring Cases

Baudouin Dupret has well analysed similar rulings in Egypt, where one also expects personal status law to be 'Islamic', albeit constituted as such in different ways.[15] He notes the predominance of procedural concerns, as I do here. As Dupret says, such a 'procedurally impeccable ruling' constitutes an achievement in itself. The judge demonstrates his command of the demands of his job. In so doing, he has in mind an audience looking over his shoulder, attentive to these points of procedure as potential avenues for argument, perhaps even in order to over-turn the ruling.[16] Let us recall one judge's comment that procedure must be got right because 'we have the appeals court over our heads'. Appeals court rulings certainly give a sense of scrutiny of the rulings made by the initial courts. But one imagines the judges thinking of the lawyers here too. Lawyers' submissions give a powerful sense of this mutual conversation, similarly organised as they are into cumulative arguments, here starting with 'the facts' (*fi al-waqa'i'*) and then moving to the law (*fi al-qanun*) before stating their claim ('therefore', *li-dhalik*).[17] A formal dialogue unfolds along conventional lines. Those judges that are unable properly to participate, through not having yet learnt the proper legal style, are the subject of carping gossip and successful appeals.

Our ruling is tightly justified in terms of legal procedure. But there is almost no reference at all to sharia discourse per se, aside from 'the books of *fiqh*', which can, it seems, be taken for granted. This is, I would say, a

[15] Dupret 2006, 2007. Egypt no longer has 'sharia courts' restricted to family law. Rather the sharia is formally taken as the fundamental source of all Egyptian law. See e.g. Dupret 2000 and Lombardi 2006.

[16] Dupret 2006: 154–155, 2007: 88.

[17] I had access to a good number of lawyers' submissions, from summonses to arguments in response to appeals, in both civil and sharia court settings.

more common pattern. Sharia discourse is relatively infrequently referred to, except in the vaguest terms: 'the books of *fiqh*', 'the books of the *madhhab*', 'the rulings of the noble sharia'.[18] Of the supreme rhetorical power of the Quran or hadith, say, only very occasional use is made.[19] So too Dupret comments of his Egyptian rulings – admittedly, again, a somewhat different case – that, 'At the very place where it is supposed to be massive and overwhelming, that is, in personal status law, references to Islamic law are conspicuous for their paucity.'[20]

Here we might first remember that the vast majority of cases before the court are not 'hard cases' in the terms of legal discourse, those 'when no settled rule dictates a decision either way', in Dworkin's words. On the contrary, in legal and sharia legal terms they are generally straightforward, 'easy cases':[21] a husband owes his wife maintenance; he must provide a satisfactory marital home; he has the right to divorce her. Most (but not all) such provisions can be found in the Ottoman Law of Family Rights, by which the Sunni courts are still to a large extent bound, and which is correspondingly frequently cited.[22] The Ja'fari courts, however, are not so bound: but their rulings are, if anything, still more exiguous in terms of sharia discourse. It is vanishingly rare to find any citations of Islamic legal reasoning at all, even in the most knotty cases.

On the other hand, that these are 'easy' cases does not mean that they are not cause for legal citation, of the Law of Sharia Courts and the OLFR in the main. Unless one were to argue that these, or at least the latter, could be seen as in some sense of the sharia in genealogical terms, which would be a reading against the grain, then we must reckon with a different treatment being given to sharia discourse in comparison. For one thing, as has been often remarked, classical sharia texts do not suit the civil legal style: 'According to sections ...' This no doubt explains the occasional references I have found in published rulings to the well-known nineteenth century codification of Hanafi status law by the Egyptian Muhammad Qadri Pasha (d. 1888), *The Rulings of the Sharia on*

18 Homsi 2003: 18, 132, 133; Barakat 2005: 40, 'And since the *shar'* obligates the father to maintain his child'; (77) 'And since the mother's request ... is in its sharia and legal place' (*fi mahall-hi al-shar'i wa-l-qanuni*).

19 See e.g. Homsi 2003: 123, 131. More common perhaps are legal maxims: 'Do not harm a mother through her child' (*la tudarr walida bi-walad-ha*); 'Punishment hobbles rights' (*al-jaza' ya'qil al-huquq*); 'No inflicting of harm nor repaying one harm with another' (*la darar wa-la dirar*, admittedly originally a hadith but quoted as a 'rule' or 'principle' [*qa'ida*]).

20 Dupret 2007: 97.

21 Dworkin 1975: 1060 and Schauer 1985, 2009: 157.

22 Custody (*hadana*) would be an exception, for instance, but detailed references to *fiqh* are not significantly more common in rulings on it than on other categories of cases, I would say.

Personal Status (*al-Ahkam al-shar'iyya fi al-ahwal al-shakhsiyya*).[23] These citations can sometimes come together with those of the LSC and OLFR, bound together as 'law'-like one feels, in the final summary of a ruling: 'based on [*sanadan li*] sections 70, 92 and 94 of the Law of Family Rights and sections 160, 161, 173 and 184 of the Rulings of the Sharia on Personal Status'; 'based on sections 189 and 466 from the Rulings of the Sharia on Personal Status and sections 92 and 99 of the Law of Family Rights.'[24] But works of *fiqh*, Islamic legal discourse proper, never do. This vagueness as to 'the books of *fiqh*' must say something at least of that imagined audience reading the ruling over the judge's shoulder. For them an explicit stipulation of *fiqh* sources is unnecessary it seems. Can it be taken as read for the Islamic religious professional audience perhaps? Or as over the lawyers' heads?

With regard to the latter, however, it is not necessarily that the lawyers, in the Sunni or Ja'fari courts, eschew sharia discourse as 'non-legal' and the judges, constrained by their legal setting and audience, follow suit. Several of the legal submissions I have copies of make broad appeals to 'the Quran and hadith' or cite some secondary source on Islamic personal status law, and it is clear from the rulings, which *inter alia* summarise the proceedings, that some lawyers attempt still more technical arguments.[25] One lawyer working in the Ja'fari courts who I spent many afternoons with prided himself on being 'the only lawyer who also writes *shar'*', his long (thirty pages even) submissions rich in arguments (*ijtihadat*) 'that have been lost', 'forgotten', by the mainstream, from venerable sources like Shaykhs Yusuf al-Bahrani (d. 1772) and Muhammad Hasan al-Najafi (d. 1850).[26] 'I show the judges I've got knowledge by using the old sources. And they're good, powerful.'

[23] Homsi 2003: 18, 21, 66, 82, 124, 125, 127, 131, 158. Qadri Pasha's codification is notably also referred to as 'The law of the rulings of the sharia for personal status' (*qanun al-ahkam al-shar'iyya li-l-ahwal al-shakhsiyya*), and, despite its unofficial status, Zayn notes the Sunni courts' 'reliance upon it' in his comprehensive sourcebook (2003a: 5). The same applies in Egypt (Dupret 2006: 150) and Jerusalem's sharia courts (Shahar 2015: 36). The Ottoman *Majalla* is also occasionally cited. See Homsi 2003: 35–40 for a contested example.

[24] Homsi 2003: 124, 125. I have never seen the approximate equivalent for the Ja'fari courts, former court president Shaykh 'Abdallah Ni'ma's (1996) *Guide to Ja'fari Judgement* (*Dalil al-qada' al-Ja'fari*), reportedly much used by lawyers, cited in this way. I imagine that the new partial family law code (resolution 46/2011) will, however, now be referenced in this manner in the Sunni courts.

[25] Or see e.g. Barakat 2005: 130, where a lawyer appeals an initial court ruling of annulment (*faskh*) on the grounds that, although it supplied a legal justification (which was merely to the clause of the LSC that defines the sorts of cases the sharia courts have jurisdiction over), it did not provide a sharia legal one.

[26] On the latter see Mottahedeh 2016: 342.

But these attempts at arguing through *fiqh* are effaced in the rulings. In a case in the initial Ja'fari courts involving the controversial issue of recalculating a woman's *mahr* to offset the savage inflation since her marriage for example, her ex-husband cited the authority of perhaps currently the highest profile scholar in the Shi'i world, Ayatollah Sistani of Iraq. The ruling found in his favour, but mentioning only the vaguer 'opinions of jurists' (*ara' al-fuqaha'*) in the discussion and with no sign of any Islamic legal considerations at all in the final summary. However, the supreme Ja'fari court is in favour of such 'changing of *mahr* values' (*ta'dil al-muhur*), as they state in a ruling on another such case, albeit in the baldest of terms, noting merely that this is 'the reasoning of this court' (*ijtihad hadhihi al-mahkama*).[27] That reasoning takes place off stage.

It is not that there are not 'hard cases' then. I refer to a number of published volumes dedicated to them (the work of lawyers), along with copies of some of the rulings and arguments of which judges and lawyers I worked with were most proud. The courts – and, consonant with the contestable nature of the issues, these are generally the appeals courts – are faced with having to decide matters such as the attribution of religious community to the children of an apostate and thus the right to their custody, whether it is legitimate to gain custody of child by changing their religious affiliation to a legally more favourable one, whether the use of magic counts as sufficient reason for divorce, or the question of the obligation and calculation of the waiting period after being widowed or divorced for a convert to Islam from Orthodox Christianity and thus the legitimacy of her subsequent marriage.[28] Such less routine cases do allow judges to display their learning, and while some involve complex points of civil law, others turn on discussions concerning the sharia. Then a ruling might, in my Sunni cases at least, cite in passing such venerable Hanafi sources as the Damascene Ibn 'Abidin's (d. 1836) nineteenth century *Radd al-muhtar 'ala al-durr al-mukhtar* or the seventeenth century *al-Fatawa al-hindiyya*.[29] One appeals court judge, Shaykh Faisal al-Mawlawi (d. 2011), who enjoyed a high profile as the head of the Lebanese Jama'a Islamiyya, or Muslim Brotherhood, even published a

[27] Barakat 2005: 189–191, 205–207. I return to these issues below.

[28] Homsi 2003: 27–28, 60–62, 69–73; Barakat 2005: 227–234. This is just a limited selection.

[29] See Homsi 2003 passim. Other classic Hanafi sources cited therein include: Sarakhsi's 11th c. *Mabsut*; Kasani's 12th c. *Bada'i' al-sana'i'*; Zay'ali's 14th c. *Tabyin al-haqa'iq*; Kardari's 15th c. *Fatawa bazzaziyya*; Ibn al-Humam's 15th c. *Fath al-qadir*; and Ibn 'Abidin's *al-'Uqud al-durriyya fi tanqih al-fatawa al-hamidiyya*. But this is an eclectic mix, hardly to be characterised as sustained Islamic legal argument of the order encountered in the dedicated *fiqh* works we will consider later.

book devoted to one of his cases, as to whether or not someone who denies the prophethood of Adam is an apostate and should thus have their marriage dissolved. The court had sought the opinions of the Muftis of Egypt, Syria, Jordan and Lebanon, and the book – a fascinating document in itself – includes their detailed deliberations.[30]

But such windows onto the vast realm of sharia discourse must be counted as exceptional rather than the norm. Most cases are, again, in legal and sharia-legal terms, 'easy'. The courts are not, generally speaking, the venue for intellectual fireworks. Their activities are, as one shaykh wearily assured me, 'boring' (*mumill*). However, I doubt that their protagonists would accept them as 'easy' in any but the most limited of intellectual senses. We have already gained a sense of how hard they are for the parties involved. And we have also touched on the laborious nature of the processes for the judges. Beyond the bureaucratic, however, there is another domain in which the judge is bound to exert himself. He should engage with the parties to the dispute, ideally bringing them towards some form of reconciliation, or at least an agreed settlement (*sulh*), a theme to which we now turn.

*Reconciliation and Agreed Settlements (*Sulh*)*

There are, formally speaking, two chief paths to resolving a dispute: a ruling (*hukm*) by the judge in favour of one party; and an agreed settlement (*sulh*). The notion of *sulh*, meaning both the process of reconciliation and the amicable settlement that might result from it, has a privileged status and noble genealogy within Islamic legal discourse, lauded in both Quran and hadith.[31] 'Reconciliation is lord over rulings' (*al-sulh sayyid al-ahkam*), as the saying goes.[32] It also fits with key aspects of the ideal type of the shaykh – a committed, engaged and expert mediator – as well as the nature of the cases before the courts, which

[30] Mawlawi 1996. The case involved the Ahbash, who we encountered earlier. They had, in Mawlawi's opinion, defamed him by attributing the appeals court ruling that denying the prophethood of Adam does not constitute apostasy to him as a personal fatwa – and thus, in their eyes, apostatising him too. Hence his wish to set the record straight in published form and recourse to such high-level, official authorities for support. It is tempting to liken this to the qadi's more usual recourse to a mufti in 'hard cases' across pre-modern Islamic legal history (see e.g. Powers 2002), although that feels anachronistic – this is the only such example I have.

[31] 'Settlement is best' (*al-sulh khayrun*, Quran 4:128). See Othman 2007: 68–69.

[32] See Hallaq 2009: 162. One judge would commonly dictate, 'Reconciliation is lord over rulings and among the foremost duties of this court' (*al-sulh sayyid al-ahkam wa-huwa min ula wajibat hadhihi al-mahkama*). Other oft-quoted sayings include: 'A losing settlement is better than a winning case' (*sulhun khasir khayrun min da'wa rabih*), and 'mutual agreement beats the judge' (*al-taradi ghalab al-qadi*).

concern intimate and complex knots of family relations. Legal scholarship, including academic scholarship on Islamic law, tends to focus on judgements. But we should not allow that to induce us to see negotiation and attempts at reconciliation as something apart from the court's business, even if they do very often proceed outside of the court sessions themselves.[33] The Lebanese sharia court judge is required by the LSC (section 164) to enjoin an attempt at reconciliation upon the parties at their first meeting, and may well involve himself in that attempt. We have already seen that this period for reconciliation may not be the only one during the legal process, and we should further remember that such processes in the courts take place in parallel with other interventions, within the extended family but also within the wider Islamic professional community.[34] *Sulh* is stressed morally and legally then, as the judge's first obligation. While I have inverted that order by taking it up last in this chapter, that is not so as to diminish its importance.

Section 164 of the LSC further stipulates that if an agreement is reached between the parties through this initial attempt at reconciliation then this is to be documented; the judge is then to issue a resolution (*qarar*) ratifying it, which has the status of a ruling (*hukm*) but is not open to appeal. An amicable settlement thus holds distinct legal advantages – it constitutes a definitive resolution of a dispute, both in the sense of not being open to appeal as a judge's ruling is, but also because, if properly arranged, it would cover the totality of points at issue and potential sources of further dispute. A well-drawn up agreement very often brings an end to a whole set of different cases – another powerful motive for pressing for it. It also extricates the judge from the morally and spiritually hazardous business of imposing his potentially fallible decision on the parties before him.[35] Beyond this initial invocation of *sulh*, the LSC (section 172) thus also allows the parties to a dispute to reach an agreed resolution at any point during the proceedings and record their agreement (*ittifaq*) in the file; the court can then ratify their settlement if there is no legal obstacle to so doing.[36] And although no agreement should

[33] Aida Othman (2007: 65, 68–72) has pointed this out most forcefully. Antoun (1980) talks of an 'ideology' of reconciliation in Jordan's sharia courts. See also Rosen 1989 on Morocco, discussed in more detail below.

[34] For eighteenth century Ottoman cases, Tamdogan (2008: 56) talks of 'a single continuum that links the court with external sociolegal arenas'. Such a joined-up picture of practice would seem overstated for my contemporary Lebanese cases, although not the notion of a wider world of religious professional practice within which the court is embedded.

[35] Othman 2007: 79.

[36] See Hana 1995: 175–179; Homsi 2003: 55 and Barakat 2005: 175–176 for examples. For the status of such agreements in the Christian courts see Traboulsi 2000: 215–216.

entail a conflict with what the sharia (or law) deems lawful and prohibited, it does allow greater flexibility in setting terms than a judge's legal finding.[37]

However, the parties may well already have sat through many hours of such attempts at reconciliation and family councils, having come to the court as a last resort; or the opposing party may be absent, the very source of the problem. As we saw earlier with the process of arbitration, the imposition of a further period for such an attempt – one month being the standard, I would say – often seems like yet another unwanted delay in the legal process; a judge's more or less energetic efforts to pursue such an outcome may not be especially welcome. One man scoffed when told that before proceedings in his case of custody got under way there would have to be a reconciliation meeting with the mother. 'From the beginning of the case? The sharia says reconcile the husband and wife before divorce. But here in the court it's totally the opposite!' The judge chided him: questions of custody have to be resolved through agreement; this is about the children; it is a matter of religion (*din*) and morality (*akhlaq*). Again, there is a strong sense in which discussion and attempts at reconciliation are presented as religiously constituted, as against the impersonal machinery of the law, seen as an obstacle to them.

But as ever, this legal stipulation can be manipulated. A husband being sued for maintenance pleaded his desire for his wife to return to him, which the judge much appreciated. 'Buy her some flowers', he suggested. Her lawyer was not impressed: rather than buying her flowers, why did he not give her her rights? Another lawyer had brought a new separate case in the course of a difficult dispute and argued that because there was now a legally enjoined period of reconciliation in that case, the proceedings at hand had better be postponed to await the outcome. The opposing lawyer was derisive: of course there was no new possibility of an amicable resolution. Fine, said the first, but it should be recorded that her lawyer refused to attempt reconciliation – a sharp enough performance to raise some amusement in the court afterwards. The judge's enjoining of a period of reconciliation can also be more or less serious. It might be accompanied with sermonising and homily. Or such efforts can be merely perfunctory. Either way, it will be dictated into the file: 'We enjoined reconciliation on the two parties' (*'arad-na al-sulh 'ala al-tarafayn*).

[37] Othman (2007: 70, 72–73 and passim) thus speculates that observations of judicial mediation might have contributed to the Orientalist notion of arbitrary *qadi*-justice, a point I return to later.

An agreed settlement could be 'positive' (*ijabi*), where a couple settle their differences and get back together as man and wife – not something I saw very often – or, more commonly, 'negative' (*salbi*), where they agree to divorce according to mutually agreed terms. Even where the parties do not make up, then, that does not exhaust the possibilities for settlement. As we have already noted, very often divorce comes as an agreed process, and there is a strong sense in which a judge's efforts towards enabling that are perceived by the shaykhly class as part of their mediatory role and of the institution of *sulh* broadly conceived.

In such cases, a judge will most often push for 'a complete solution', covering such matters as the financial obligations of the husband, living arrangements, the redistribution of household goods and custody and visitation of children, before having the divorce performed in court. As already discussed, that may be a *talaq*, performed by the husband, or it may take the form of a *khul'*, where the wife formally proposes terms to the husband and he then accepts. Very often, again, such an agreement will entail the wife giving up some of the financial rights owed her, for these are most often the greatest disincentive for the husband to divorce. The careful drafting of terms is vital to avoid problems later: one finds cases where no record of the wife's giving up her right to her *mahr* was recorded and she then successfully lays claim to it;[38] but equally once a wife has formally undertaken to 'give up' her financial rights, they are lost regardless of whether or not the husband keeps his side of the bargain. The wording of the agreement and the sequence of events are vital, still more so if the fate of children becomes part of the negotiation. 'Do not harm a mother through her child' (*la tudarr walida bi-walad-ha*), the saying goes. But people talk about 'giving up' custody or children (*tanazul 'an al-awlad/al-hadana*) as part of these negotiations in the same way as they talk about giving up the *mahr*, even if they are not of the same legal order. Custody is arguably the right of the child, and not that of the parent, and care is needed: if a mother gives up her *mahr* in return for retaining custody of a child who is of the age when a father has rights to them, she could find the father subsequently bringing an unanswerable case for custody and have lost her *mahr* for nothing.[39]

It is in the managing of people towards such a solution that the craft of judging is arguably displayed. As one judge put it to me after a seemingly good-natured session with a couple, the relative harmony had only come after much work on his part over many sittings: 'Now it's "Londonised"

[38] See e.g. Barakat 2005: 187–188.

[39] For a case citing the principle that custody, or perhaps better here, parental care (*hadana*) is the right of the child see Homsi 2003: 58.

[*talandana*], become like you [i.e., a British person], cool [*barid*].' Time and again I saw him nudging people towards some kind of resolution. One time I arrived at his court to find a young couple before him squabbling over their two children. I had seen them before him previously – it was an enduring dispute. From my fieldnotes:

The wife was there with her intense lawyer; the husband hunched and resentful. He wants to divorce; she has raised a case of custody. Their daughter lives with her, their son with him, but she wants them both. So, the judge says to her, you don't want to reconcile? I do, she says. But both their positions seem firmly entrenched. The judge suggests to the man that he gives her their son but arranges to see the children from Friday to Sunday. He says no. 'The boy is my right. She is in the wrong [*ghaltana*], not me.' 'So, what, are you going to punish me for a hundred years? Are you God?', she counters. Her lawyer complains that the husband hasn't changed his position at all. 'But *haram* we separate the children.'

The judge worked on the husband again, asking him what the difference would be: under his suggestion he would have the children three days a week anyway. This is just spite [*kayd*]. At her house at least they will eat. But the man was not budging. The judge lost patience and told them to go and wait outside. 'I've got other cases.' Some people, he remarked to us bystanders once they had left, would take three, four hours happily. After some time the lawyer came back. No, the judge said, let them stand there longer. Four hours and they have no intention of agreeing. 'They are laughing at our time' [*yadhaku 'ala waqt-na*]. And then to us onlookers: 'If a rich man has problems it might come to something. A poor man . . .'

But eventually they got their turn, and now the judge was determined to get the matter resolved. He worked for a complete solution, that is, with divorce. First there was the matter of the *mahr*: the husband did not object to paying it, but would want to pay in instalments. The wife was not keen. Look, the judge told her, don't say you won't take instalments, because then you will have to bring a case to get your *mahr* and it will take you at least two years in the courts. We moved on. Now there was the issue of maintenance of the children. Let's say it's 300,000 Lebanese Lira [$200] a month for the two children, the judge suggested. How much does he earn, her lawyer wanted to know. Good question: the judge put it to him. Not much it seemed. He can't pay that much. So what about 250,000 LL? Now the wife doesn't like it. So now the judge worked on her. Look, he reminded her, he also has to pay for medical expenses and the school, so in fact you're much better off.

Then we returned to the issue of the *mahr*, and they seemed unable to agree how much it was. Her lawyer says $10,000 and he's saying 10 million LL [just under $7000]. The judge is bemused: 'You can't even agree on something written down?!' But now it seemed that he sensed the end was near as he dictated to his clerk for the file that, 'He divorces her with one divorce. . .' Each side, he reminded them, is giving up something. But now the husband dug his heels in: he refuses to give the boy to her, he said, 'He is my right [*haqqi*].' So now the judge sent the wife and her lawyer out and worked on the husband alone. If you leave it to a ruling, he told him, then they can be for high amounts. With an agreement it will be less. Then the wife and her lawyer were brought back in and the judge resumed his dictation, announcing that they had reconciled regarding custody being given to the mother and regarding maintenance ... How old are the children, he wanted to know. Three and four years of age. So how much? 200,000 [LL]? But the man maintained he could not pay that, in the face of some determined attempts to persuade him. 'How much then? 150,000?! What do you want to pay just 1 Lira? It seems you're not serious at all. Just messing with the court!' But he would not budge. So the judge took 100,000LL as read. Look, he said to her, at least you've got that all secure and guaranteed. Yes, she says, but there's such a thing as respect ...

Now they had to agree on what age the children would remain with the mother until. Nine? Seven is what's customary, the man said grumpily. OK, so taking into account the age difference, because we don't want to separate them, until the girl reaches seven and the boy eight. Visitation is his every week from 4 PM on Friday until 4 PM Sunday. He will undertake the transport. Where will he pick them up?

And on it went. Who will the doctor be? Which school will they go to? Who will get which item of furniture? The experienced judge will steer them through it all.

Finally, whether at the end of a single sitting or of a long succession of such efforts, the judge will call upon the man to pronounce the words, 'You are divorced' (*anti taliq*) or 'I divorce you in return for the consideration' (*khala'tu-ki*). A ripple might pass through the courtroom: 'Oh, he's divorced her.' The couple must sign the requisite form. (In the Ja'fari courts, witnesses are required: when the judge sees that the way is clear he presses on, filling out the form – 'Where is the clerk? Bring me witnesses, quickly!') It might, or might not, be an emotional moment. One notably pious (Shi'i) judge would make everyone present beg God's forgiveness ('God forgive me!', *staghfir Allah*), in recognition of its gravity.

Conclusion

This chapter and the previous one have set out to give an account of the workings of cases within the sharia courts. We have seen how messy marital disputes turn into legal categories and files. We have also seen how much hard work goes into making that happen, particularly on the part of the parties to the cases, most often women trying to bring errant husbands to book. A case is a procedural achievement, on the part of the parties to it as much as on the part of the judge and his staff, as the example of the process of notification (*tabligh*) showed. It takes time and money. The procedural mechanisms of the courts constitute their key battleground: lawyers use 'tactics' to frustrate the other side. This interest in procedural legality is reflected in the rulings that judges produce. Much care is taken to satisfy the demands of citation practice, citation, that is, of the laws in effect. Sharia discourse is by contrast muted and non-specific. In some respects that reflects the routine ('easy', in lawyers' terms) nature of the vast majority of the cases before the courts. But even in 'hard' cases and issues, much sharia discursive reasoning takes place off stage. The reasons for this professional intimacy are not immediately apparent, but speak to questions of authority, explicit and implicit: I return to them later in the book.[40]

Baudouin Dupret has argued against what he calls the 'essentialist' attitude of most scholarship on Islamic law. Instead of asking, 'What is Islamic law?', he suggests, we should ask, 'What do people do when referring to Islamic law?'[41] In the settings I describe here, the sharia is more often invoked as elusive ideal than as legal reality. That is despite (because of?) the ubiquitous referencing of the courts' title as 'sharia courts' (*mahakim shar'iyya*). This is not to say that the sharia forms no part of what the courts do in legal terms. Husbands must pay maintenance because that is what the sharia says, uncontroversially. Fathers have custody rights over their children after certain ages because that is what the sharia says, more controversially. A respectable Islamic legal genealogy could be provided for both assertions. But such points of sharia law are not what dominates one's impressions of the courts' daily business and their textual production. The sharia is more often summoned upon in order to take distance from that daily business, associated, by contrast, with human law (*qanun*).

A related series of oppositions are thus made rhetorically (by the shaykhs, if not the lawyers), as we have seen (Table 8.1):[42]

These oppositions do not necessarily map exactly onto each other no doubt. But again, overall one is faced with a broad distinction between divine sharia – highly valorised – and mundane law – more or less despised in contrast. The courts' business is characterised as largely (e.g., '90 per cent') devoted to the latter. In the context of our

[40] Sharia court rulings from other times can also seem sparse. Leslie Pierce, writing on sixteenth century Ottoman Aintab, for instance, refers to the judge as 'textually silent' (2003: 93, cited by Messick 2014: 82). As Baldwin (2017: 68–69) explains, in the context of seventeenth/eighteenth century Ottoman Cairo, such reticence with regard to *fiqh* in particular was because the judge was not supposed to be an expert in jurisprudence so much as procedure. The landscape of Islamic legal authority in contemporary Lebanon works differently; but the comparison would be interesting.

[41] Dupret 2007: 79, 81.

[42] Square brackets mark my own additions.

Table 8.1 *Rhetorical Oppositions Made in the Courts between 'Sharia' and 'Law'*

Shar'	Qanun
Shaykh	Lawyer
[Non-bureaucratic]	Bureaucratic, procedural
'Humane' (*insani, adami*)	'Formal', 'legalistic' (*shakli*)
[Flexible (*marin*)]	'Wooden' (*khashabi*)
Intimate, private, personal	Public, impersonal
Mediation, reconciliation, agreement (*islah, sulh*) [as promoted by shaykhs]	[Conflict, as promoted by lawyers]
Appeal to conscience and morals (*akhlaq*)	Self-interest (*maslaha*), stratagems, deceit, bad faith (*kayd*), 'tactics'
Divine accountability (*al-halal wa-l-haram*)	Legal accountability, the state

exploration of judicial divorce in the Sunni courts, what was marked out as the domain of sharia by contrast was the work of mediation: '90 per cent *shar'*' in the words of one of the shaykhs involved. This personal, non-bureaucratic work of pedagogical engagement is in part what people 'do' then, when they refer to the sharia. That work tallies with key aspects of the image of the shaykhly calling that we explored at the beginning of the book. And at the end of this chapter we saw something of the pride with which the shaykhly judges work towards the allied task of an agreed settlement (*sulh*) inside (and outside) their courts. Counter-intuitively perhaps, in the context of the sharia courts it is thus the 'ethical' aspect of the sharia, in the sense of work on the conscience, that is the more appealed to as opposed to its legal aspect.

This leads us to another key element of our broad opposition, the vocational one between the shaykh – representing the sharia – and the lawyer, representing the law. Where, however, does the judge fit into this scheme? The judge in the sharia courts is a shaykh; but he must also take care of the courts' legal concerns. The shaykhly judge thus straddles both poles of the opposition. In the next chapter, I turn to the question as to how judges try to manage the inevitable tensions of this dual role.

9 The Judge as Tragic Hero

We began our examination of the sharia courts with their uncomfortably dual nature: on the one hand representing the sharia and Islam (either Sunni or Shi'i – marking the difference can be important in the multi-confessional Lebanese context); and on the other representing the civil state. And we then explored how this tension between sharia and civil state law manifests itself in the courts' workings. I now move on to the consequences for the shaykhs who work as judges in the courts. Different shaykhs are impelled in different directions by these forces. Where in the previous chapters I wanted broadly to stress the fundamental similarities of the various tribunals I observed, even if I focused at different points on the Sunni and Ja'fari systems, in this chapter and those that follow the emphasis is on diversity: the diversity of the sharia, and the diversity of the paths one can take as a religious professional devoted to it. Notwithstanding the often monolithic depiction of institutions like 'the judgeship' in the academic literature, different judges have, in my experience, very different approaches, and I start by contrasting the styles of three of those I sat with.

Judicial Styles

1 'Humanity'

Shaykh A is a man of the most kindly demeanour, in his middle age (then in his mid-fifties) with a good, grey beard, the moustache lightly shaven as is considered Sunna (the Prophet's example) in Sunni circles. Shaykh A is not only a judge and a prominent member of the Lebanese Sunni community's religious establishment, but is also shaykh of a local branch of a transnational Sufi order. He leads regular sessions in remembrance of God (*dhikr*) at the order's lodge in Beirut and elsewhere. He teaches at the Sharia College and takes on official functions for Dar al-Fatwa and the Sunni establishment. During the month of Ramadan, like many leading shaykhs, he presents radio and television programs of religious instruction and edification. He is, then, a relatively prominent (and very busy) figure, a leading *da'iya* ('caller to Islam').

Shaykh A does not come from a family of ulama. But his father – notably pious, in a now perhaps old-fashioned, ascetic fashion[1] – wanted his son to be learned. 'And *al-hamdu li-llah.*' Shaykh A studied the sharia in Damascus and Beirut, supplemented by trips in his early twenties to the East to study with the founding shaykh of his order in Iranian Kurdistan: one of the best times of his life, he recalls; 'It was a piece of paradise.' Although Sufism has become a relatively private matter in contemporary Lebanon, in a distinctive and telling addition to the furniture of his desk, Shaykh A keeps beside him a framed photograph of himself as a young man with his late master, taken at that happy time.[2]

Consistent with his Sufi identity, and with what is expected of shaykhs more broadly, Shaykh A is not a man of great material extravagance. Nevertheless it is also expected that one should keep up appearances, and his look is polished and his mobile telephone a new enough model not to look dowdy in what is a competitive field in Lebanon – it rings with an impressive polyphonic rendition of 'There is no God but God' (*la ilaha illa'llah*). He drives a Mercedes of classic vintage, rather than the most luxurious and latest model; he lives in a popular neighbourhood. One can see, as a lawyer pointed out to me with approval, that he is honest, and not on the take.

For Shaykh A, judging is about being shaykhly, about giving humanity (*insaniyya*) and heart to the rules applied in court, engaging with people and trying to lead them back to the right way. He suspects that his Sufism gives him an extra impulse in this direction, although, as we have seen, this is what is expected of the shaykhly class more generally. 'Maybe', he said to me, 'you've seen in your experience in the court that some judges are very harsh, very strict. They totally follow the sharia of course, but . . .' For Shaykh A, that is not in itself enough. As one judge's assistant put it, this is not where the judge's aura (*hayba*) should come from, just talking loudly.[3] Otherwise you could get any old guy from the souk with a megaphone. Even when Shaykh A shouts, he says, it is just for effect, so they will pay attention. 'I don't feel it in my heart.'

He is thus something of a sermonizer in court, ready with pious homilies. 'The Prophet, Praise Be Upon Him, says . . .' To a wife he

[1] He told me that his father would fast almost every day of the year, read the Quran six times through entirely each month, and, all his life, every day, he would get up an hour before dawn to wash with cold water before prayers.

[2] For something more of this Sufi milieu see Clarke 2014.

[3] On the judge's *hayba* see Messick 1993: 165–166.

might note that bearing the trials of marriage with patience will open the path to Paradise. 'Not just that, God will make the door wide open!' To a man, at the end of a session: 'Please, a word of advice, don't wear gold [religiously dubious for men], just silver.' To a notably mean father: 'OK, today beans [*ful*, a stereotypically cheap foodstuff] but tomorrow meat. Not beans today, beans tomorrow and then chickpeas! You give your eye rather than see your children go hungry.' (The man tried to interrupt but his lawyer hushed him: 'The shaykh is giving you good words!')

To sketch a vignette, one day he was faced with a middle-aged couple who had separated, more or less amicably. The wife was suing for maintenance of their two daughters, and while her husband had no objection, the case still needed to be heard. Shaykh A established that one of the daughters, a teenager present, was called Nancy. That is not a very Islamic name, he remarked jovially. 'But God be praised, she wears the veil [*muhajjaba*]!' Well, she was on this occasion as is compulsory in the courts, although it was clear from her dress and that of the family more generally that this was exceptional rather than habitual. Nevertheless, it was a nice touch on Shaykh A's part. He then turned to the couple: 'For the sake of your daughters, reconcile.' The wife was not keen, and with some prompting as to why, it emerged that the husband was a drinker. This then prompted a little sermon. In paraphrase:

> 'God has not prohibited anything useful, nor allowed anything harmful.' Those who say that alcohol has some medicinal value are lying. And one might be drunk and 'the drunkard might have sex with his own mother without knowing.' And as parents we cannot simply act as we please – we are examples to our children. But if it's just the drinking that's the problem then that's simple! Think about your kids. Think about God! You could die at any moment.

Shaykh A came to the judiciary relatively late, and, like most of the shaykhly judges, without any legal (i.e. civil procedural) training. The realm of procedure and bureaucratic nicety seems to him at best a distraction and at worst an impediment to reconciliation or right pastoral care. And yet, as we know, these courts do not function in a vacuum. Their rulings are only binding because they are sanctioned by the civil state. We should remember that a civil judge sits on the sharia appeals court panel, to provide advice and scrutiny on precisely such issues of civil legal procedure, and the appeals court is thus most attentive to these issues. And, as we have noted, it is here that lawyers find their room for manoeuvre, frequently looking to exactly these points of procedure to help their case: the document is missing the requisite stamp; the judge failed to ask the other party's lawyer to produce their power of attorney at the first hearing; no copy was given to the other side of a document submitted to the judge; the ruling is therefore invalid.

However humanitarian and well-intentioned Shaykh A may be, his rulings are, according to my sources, frequently overturned on appeal. As one lawyer put it, he might have a good heart, be humane, but he doesn't know the rules: 'He is more *da'iya* ['caller to Islam'] than judge. Sometimes we say you can't be a judge and a man of religion [*rajul al-din*].'

2 *Efficiency and Legalism*

Another judge working in the Sunni courts, Shaykh B, makes for an instructive contrast, 'more *qadi* than *da'iya*', in the earlier-mentioned lawyer's terms. He comes into the office in the morning, hangs up his robe on the coat peg and puts his turban on its hat-stand. This is not necessarily a matter of secularizing his courtroom, for, uniquely among the judges I worked with, he plays religious CDs (Quranic recitation and Sufi chanting) on his office computer. (It relaxes him – and others, he hopes.) Rather, this is about – metaphorically – rolling up his sleeves and getting down to work. The judge sitting at his desk in a suit, a shirt, tie and waistcoat rather than shaykhly garb, with a close-cropped beard of conventional style rather than the chin curtain Sunna style, seems, to me at any rate, to render his court more explicitly a bureaucratic environment, and Shaykh B is indeed a meticulous and efficient administrator, skills developed during a previous post as secretary to the dean of Beirut's Sharia College. He is also a judge of some experience: twenty years, he estimated.

As something of a fresh air man, Shaykh B often insists on having the window of the courtroom open, and his manner is also bracing, brusque to the point of rudeness on occasion and exacting with regard to bureaucratic minutiae. Where Shaykh A is thought of as a bit of a soft touch by the lawyers, Shaykh B is perceived as 'arrogant': 'Where's the stamp?', he might demand. 'No stamp, no case. Goodbye!' He has a short temper, and the court staff will warn people to tread carefully around him. But he is also known for going by the book. One lawyer thought him tough, 'But fair. Sometimes I say to him, "I know you don't like me, but you've been fair."' He would do no other. He recalled one particularly unpleasant man he had been faced with, whom another judge had been driven to call 'dog' (for which he had been reported to the President of the Courts). But Shaykh B had nevertheless seen the merits of his case and ruled in his favour, because, he said, it pleased God and his conscience.

Although Shaykh B acknowledges his irritable nature, there is method to his brusqueness. By processing cases efficiently and according to due procedure, he reasons, justice will be more swiftly and more surely achieved, and there seemed to me much truth in that. When presented with a case-load of well over one hundred files after the administrative reshuffle, he carefully organised his time, allocating a set number of cases to every day, increasing his days worked and planning ahead so as to process the load as efficiently as possible. He has his own methods and requirements to assist the process. He insists, for example, on written submissions, an exhaustive account (*tafsiliyya mumill*), rather than oral presentations of the parties' grievances. It wastes less of the court's time, he feels. I have already cited his reaction to a couple's bickering about who did what one day in Ramadan: 'Look, how long have you been married?' Two years eight months. 'Right, if I have to listen to all these details, it will take two years eight months! Write it down!'

He seems impatient and unsympathetic: 'Don't tell me all the details about how horrible your husband is,' he might say to a woman seeking divorce through judicial ruling (*tafriq*). 'Just write the key points down and submit it to me as a document. My next available session is in two months time. Goodbye!' But he does not engage with the women's often tragic personal stories because, he feels, he does not need to. Let us remember that in such cases, the major stumbling block for the women bringing them is establishing marital strife. Some judges, like Shaykh B, tend to the opinion that bringing a case of divorce is clear evidence of discord in and of itself, a written statement from the wife more than sufficient, and a husband's written response – usually along the lines that his wife's statement is incorrect if not dishonest – definitive. An emphasis on due process is actually much more helpful in achieving a timely result, and especially in furthering women's causes, structurally disadvantaged in many respects. (More helpful, that is, unless of course dialogue and reconciliation are what are really wanted by the parties to the case.) One colleague commented of his approach that, 'It saves headaches', contrasting it with that of another, 'who opens the door to talk', and was responsible for the pile of over a hundred files handed over to Shaykh B.

Shaykh B's total rigour in such matters can, however, seem inexplicable to bewildered petitioners. A middle-aged man comes with an old lady, who is representing her sister. Did they bring the documents, Shaykh B wants to know? Yes. Translated into Arabic? Yes. 'Right – now you've got to post a summons on the notice-board of the court.' 'What?! We've done it three times already.' It was because of the changing of judges' responsibilities. 'We're going the legal way [*qanuni*]. It's better for you. Believe me, I know. Believe me, I want to finish with this case more than you do! I am working in your interest', this last to the old lady who did not seem convinced. Or in a similar problem in a divorce case: goodness this is turning into a long story, the women plaintiff complains. It won't be less than five months, Shaykh B tells her, and that is with him. Other judges might take two or three years. There is a legal routine that has to be gone through. Another woman now wants to bring a case against her husband for judicial divorce. Inform him, Shaykh B tells her. But she already did, she says. But that was for the case of maintenance. This is a different case. You have to do it again. That is the law. 'This is my way.'

And many find his brusque style upsetting; they complain, even formally to the sharia courts inspectorate. A shaykh should, on common understandings, be understanding and kindly. 'Thanks, God bless' (*yislamu, allah ya'tik al-'afiyya*), one woman says sarcastically after a bracing encounter. 'If the sharia judge is like this', wonders one man. He shouts at you, throws you out. That's not right, complains another. Just following the rules then, however helpful that may be, is not in itself enough.

3 Strategies of Accommodation

Most judges are less obviously close to one or other pole, and all in practice have to try to accommodate both sets of demands. Let us now turn to an example of one such strategy of accommodation, that employed by Shaykh C, a Shi'i judge working in a windowless and airless office in a busy initial court in the mainly Shi'i southern suburbs of Beirut. Shaykh C, somewhat gaunt and harassed looking, is serious in outlook and mien. While dressed in the flowing robes and white turban of the Shi'i shaykh, he bemoans the Lebanese tyranny of appearances. When he arrives at the courts punctually in the morning, he shakes the hands of all the functionaries solemnly in turn before ascending to his office. His reputation for piety brings requests by telephone to the courts for Quranic divination. His reputation for patient and honest advice brings lawyers and petitioners to the court for guidance. As one such lawyer whispered to me, he is good. He does it for religious reasons. You can tell, you can see that he is poor [*faqir*]. He is a teacher. Look, he said, pointing to the case then ongoing, another shaykh would just say 'Goodbye!', but he gives instruction.

Shaykh C reconciles the demands of being shaykh and judge by separating them. So, for example, a couple came before him, in their thirties, the wife with her mother. The wife was the plaintiff, having brought a case suing her husband for maintenance and for the provision of a suitable marital home. 'Right', Shaykh C started, 'did you live together?' 'Yes', she said, 'for one year.' 'No', he countered, 'not even for a day.' Shaykh C let them wrangle on: 'Now we are talking outside of the court', he told them, 'like human beings [*haki insani*].' But as the wife hammered on her point he reminded her, 'Look, we are outside the court session at the moment. But if you want to enter the session then *ahlan wa-sahlan*', the latter an ironic 'you're welcome.' After they had (to some extent) talked themselves out without any progress towards reconciliation, he then said, 'Now we are opening the case', and we now started on the official proceedings, with Shaykh C dictating a summary of what he had heard to his scribe in legalistic language for the file, as is usual. This is Shaykh C's standard tactic: to open the discussion 'outside of the court' (*kharij al-mahkama*), to try to find a solution. He will also try to rope lawyers into the effort: 'The lawyer has to get tired too!', he says. If other involved parties are there, family members for instance, then that is all to the good: 'Outside the session we can talk to you.' Shaykh C will embark on homilies and sermons: 'Is this how the family of the Prophet [*ahl al-bayt*] brought us up? I'm sorry, these are harsh words – but is it?' 'You're a Muslim, but it wants application. What is Islam? Just a system [*nizam*]?' If the couple demure, as well they might, often having already sat through numerous family meetings and other attempts at reconciliation, then Shaykh C threatens to go to the case. 'The language is different: dry [*jaff*].' 'Let's talk first, because judging is harsh [*qasi*].' If the dry language of the session then fails to satisfy, Shaykh C may drop out of it again: 'Okay, before we were speaking in the language of the court session. Now I'll speak normally [*tabi'i*],' 'like a brother' rather than a judge.

This tacking back and forth between the languages of humanity and of the law, and more especially listening to the couples' endless wrangles, is exhausting, and makes for slow progress. An hour or more spent in intense debate might lead just to a request for an adjournment to think things over some more. 'All that talk and we didn't even have a session!' Days spent with Shaykh C in the clouds of smoke from the Marlboro Reds he continuously ignited were exhausting enough for me let alone for him. By the end of the morning he would often be clutching his brow, complaining of suffering from the effects of prolonged, intense concentration. This effort warrants recognition, not always forthcoming, for what it is: a special commitment, as part of a vocation, and not court routine. One petitioner was pressing Shaykh C very hard: 'What do you think I am', he replied tellingly, 'your *muwazzaf* [again, "functionary", "employee", "civil servant"]?!' A man protested a ruling against him. Well, you can appeal it, Shaykh C told him. 'Where?', he asked. 'Look', said Shaykh C, 'I'm not a *muwazzaf* to be asked questions like that! Ask at the court office [*al-qalam*].' For, as he told me, 'The judge can't just be a civil servant. He can't be just doing his job as a job. This is a very hard condition we have', alluding to the Shi'a in particular, for it is a common perception on the part of the Shi'i judiciary (and the lawyers working in their courts) that the Sunni courts are more interested in procedure (*shakl*), accustomed to it as they are from their long centuries of acquaintance with the exercise of power. Whereas, 'Here, it was too bad even to say you were Shi'i, let alone have "Ja'fari court" written outside. There weren't any Shi'i judges. So this is all new.' While my own impression was that attempts at engagement and reconciliation were indeed commonly more exhaustive in the Ja'fari courts, again, I might prefer to argue that this is to a large extent tied to the substantive difference in the law applied in the two court systems rather than their respective judicial philosophies: that is, the relative difficulty for a woman of obtaining a judicially imposed divorce without her husband's consent in the Ja'fari courts.

This adds a certain sharpness to the tensions between sharia and civil procedural precepts shared between the courts. Shaykh C has his own distinctive way here too, as, for instance, in the case of travel bans (*man' al-safr*) preventing their recipient leaving the country, a frequently employed means of leverage in family law cases and within the sharia court judge's power to impose. As Shaykh C explained to a lawyer come to ask about the possibility of imposing one, these raise issues from an Islamic legal perspective, as a deprivation of personal freedom. 'I am talking from a sharia viewpoint of course, not a legal [*qanuni*] one. What do I want with law? I am talking about the law of God [*qanun allah*].' As he told me, when he was about to be appointed as a judge, this was the thing he was more afraid of than anything else, 'before God that is. Taking away people's freedom.' So he has evolved his own compromise solution. One of the key problems as things stand is that the subject of a ban is not informed until they are at the border and their passport is confiscated. Even if the ban was unjust, they will have to bring a case themselves to get the passport returned, which is a very considerable inconvenience. Shaykh C is of the opinion that they should be informed immediately if a ban is imposed, and he keeps his own private notebook recording the instances. 'This isn't part of the law, it's something particular [*khass*, i.e. to him]', he told me.

'If Only There Were an Islamic State'

The shaykhly judge must engage sincerely with the moral difficulties of those appearing before him, in an effort to heal them. This need for 'humanity' is rhetorically opposed to the 'formal' (*shakli*) aspects of legal practice that lawyers are, by contrast, overly preoccupied with, according to the judges' admonishments at least. It is through this sincere engagement that the shaykhly judge becomes recognizable to those he judges as a shaykh, as a true representative of the sharia. And, as the example of Shaykh C makes clear, the judges are themselves wont to merge this distinction between human engagement and bureaucratic legal formality into the further distinction between 'the sharia' on the one hand and 'law' (*qanun*) on the other with which we have become familiar. As Shaykh C told one recalcitrant husband, 'Let's not think about the law. In the war, for fifteen years there wasn't a state in Lebanon. So how were we living?' 'On our morals [*akhlaq-na*]', said the man. 'Right. So let's not worry about the law right now, let's do the right thing. Let's reach an agreement [*sulh*].' But in order to bring these pedagogical efforts to fruition, the shaykhly judge must also of course engage with the legal and bureaucratic requirements of the state-sponsored institution he serves – and do so conscientiously. Otherwise he could be deemed just a *da'iya*, a proselytizer, and not a judge at all.

As we saw in the cases of our first two judges, a neglect of either of these demands imperils the sharia court judge's standing as such. In the third, we saw a distinctive type of practice that attempts to resolve this dilemma by a dramatic separation of the two functions, into a humane, brotherly component 'outside of the court' but tied to the sharia, and the 'harsh' component of judicial practice as 'judge' within the court and tied to the (devalued) law. This drama would seem most readily characterized as a sort of tragedy, in that it constitutes the two demands as fundamentally irreconcilable. Of course, despite my emphasis on the dramatic, it should be remembered that the business of the courts largely proceeds effectively, even if no doubt not ideally. Not all judicial practice offers such a vivid illustration of what is, however, a real tension that is felt, and expressed, to greater and lesser degrees.

These tragic vignettes want a larger narrative. For the sharia-minded, they are readily perceived as acts in a wider tragedy, the nominal eclipse of a sharia-centred polity – of God's law – by the hubristic secular, modern state and its mundane law: 'If only there were an Islamic state [*law kan fi dawla islamiyya*]', as some judges are wont to say mournfully, then such tensions would dissolve. From this perspective, Lebanon's uncomfortable and fragmented hybrid legal system is bound to disappoint. On the latter score at least, much recent academic scholarship would agree, as we noted at the beginning of this book.

My judges' commitment to sharia exceptionalism is understandable, but I would want to qualify it. For one thing, this is hardly a conflict confined to the sharia court. In the context of my fieldwork in Lebanon exactly the same complaints could be heard from civil legal specialists working in the domain of family law. One distinguished lawyer working within the Christian court system apologized for his lateness in receiving me due to a prolonged discussion with a client with the comment that 'Family law demands so much of you! My colleagues in commercial litigation have no idea.' Nor is this solely a 'religious' concern. A judge working within the civil court system but specializing in family law cases made precisely the same observation: family law is unlike other areas of the law in this regard; it demands personal engagement. In the United States, Britain and elsewhere, collaborative (family) law – where couples settle their differences without recourse to litigation – currently enjoys the favour of the legal establishment for precisely this reason. This is, then, I would venture, a broader problem with the application of adversarial litigation to the resolution of family disputes, and, beyond that, of legal standards and bureaucratic procedure to individual lives, not just – if at all – a problem of the eclipse of a sharia-centred polity by the modern nation state, for better or worse. The real tragedy, as the judges I sat with would immediately avow, is the structural violence done, where it is done, to the lives of couples and more especially their children by the bureaucratic court system.

And of course bureaucracy is not the sole preserve of civil law. The historical, pre-modern sharia court was itself a bureaucratic state institution, governed by rules and principles of procedure laid down in the Islamic legal handbooks.[4] Indeed, sharia-based litigation was sometimes seen as overly procedure bound. Alternative judicial institutions evolved in some historical contexts to bypass the sharia courts precisely because of their highly demanding criteria for admissible evidence.[5] Any putative 'truly Islamic' legal system would still need rules of procedure.

I am wary, then, of framing the opposition between bureaucratic procedure and moral engagement as one between positive law and the sharia. There is, however, a prominent strand of academic scholarship on Islamic law that takes this latter opposition seriously, that also sees sharia

[4] See e.g. Hallaq 2009: 342ff. The faithfulness of impersonal legal-bureaucratic writing to complex reality was a source of concern and extensively debated (Messick 1989 and 1993: 212–216). See also Johansen (1999: 36) on how judicial procedure represented a safeguard against the inevitable fallibility of human reasoning.

[5] See e.g. Fahmy 1999a: 236; 1999b: 361–362 on nineteenth century Egypt and, among other things, the emerging use of autopsy reports. This is not just a function of modernization, however. James Baldwin, for instance, has found a similar popular desire to circumvent the demands of sharia court procedure by recourse to local strongmen in late seventeenth and early eighteenth century Cairo; the qadi is here precisely an expert in procedure (2017: 68–71, 105–112). See also Peters 1997: 71, 79 and Powers 2002: 19.

and civil or common law as radically different. On this view, the Islamic judge is to be distinguished by the putative discretion that he exercises, a characteristic emphasis in his work on immediate engagement with the particularities of the cases before him, as against a strict attention to such formal legal and procedural constraints. This 'Orientalist' reading, now perceived as strongly prejudicial, is typified by what is termed the 'Weberian' image of *Kadijustiz* (i.e. '*qadi*-justice'): the Islamic judge ruling according to his whim, or at least general ethical principles as opposed to legal rules.[6] The more academically acceptable – if still decidedly controversial – version of this position is exemplified by anthropologist Lawrence Rosen's recasting of such allegedly excessive judicial discretion as a rational and predictable attention to the repair of the fabric of local social relations, here drawing on fieldwork in provincial Morocco in the latter half of the twentieth century.[7] Another current of revisionist scholarship disagrees strongly with both. On the contrary, the historical Islamic judge did, as part of a wider legal system, have to pay attention to formal, legal constraints, and where he did not, that did not pass without comment, as David Powers has very convincingly described for much the same part of Morocco, but for the fourteenth century.[8]

This is well-trodden ground. But, drawing on my own particular cases, I think it still worth making a number of points in response. First, where, in contemporary Lebanon, the sharia court judge does help the parties reach an authorised agreed settlement (*sulh*), which may not be on the same terms as those that might have been imposed in a ruling in favour of one or other party following the law, while it may indeed show an attention to the restoration of social harmony (which Rosen is right to note), this is not here an exercise in judicial discretion, although it could

[6] It is debatable to what extent Weber intended his employment of the then current trope of *Kadijustiz* (which he took from elsewhere) as an ideal type to be seen as a serious analysis of actual Islamic legal practice. Certainly he does not see *qadi*-justice as limited to Islamic contexts (Crone 1999: 249 and Johansen 1999: 48–49n183). For Weber's position, see Rheinstein 1954: xlviii and Weber 1978[1925]: esp. 976–978 and 1395, but also 795, 813, 823, 980, 1115. For critical discussions of it see Turner 1974: 107–121 and Crone 1999. See also Johansen 1999: 48ff. Rabb (2015) provides a surely exhaustive account of the typically derogatory uses of the *qadi*-justice motif by judges in the US, derived more often from the *Arabian Nights* than Weber it would seem.

[7] Rosen 1980–1981, 1989, 2000: 20–23. For some stern criticisms of Rosen's approach generally see e.g. Mundy 1991 and Abou El Fadl 2002, and on *qadi*-justice in particular Powers 1990: 330n112 and 1994: 366 and 2002 *passim*, Masud et al. 2006: 5–6. For other anthropological work more or less critically following Rosen's line, see e.g. Peletz 2002: 118–123, and, for a historian, Agmon 2006: 171n6.

[8] Powers 1990, 1992, 1994, 2002. See also Gerber 1994: 25–33, on the seventeenth and eighteenth century Ottoman Empire, and, making the same point for the same period but from a rather different direction, Ergene 2003: 115.

easily be mistaken as such. As we noted in the previous chapter, this is an eventuality fully anticipated and indeed enjoined by both the Islamic tradition and the Lebanese law of sharia court procedure.

Second, however, it must be said that the impulse to rule following one's own virtuous perception of where right lies in a particular case, even where it seems to differ from the letter of the law, is certainly one my judges are sympathetic towards. 'I prefer to be appealed by the high court than to be judged by God', as one judge says. A lawyer cited what he thought an egregious example, another judge's granting of child visitation rights (*mushahada*) to a grandparent, which, according to the lawyer, has no basis in Hanafi law. In this case, the ex-husband and father had custody of the child. Generally speaking, the mother nevertheless has clear rights to visitation; but the mother was in France, so the judge gave the right of visitation to her mother instead, in order, he said, to foster the ties of kinship (*silat al-rahm*) as the Quran urges. As the lawyer pointed out, section 242 of the Law of Sharia Court stipulates that where there is no clear provision in the Ottoman Law of Family Rights then you refer to the preponderant rulings of Abu Hanifa. 'But there isn't anything there about the right of the grandmother to visitation!'

But it would surely be wrong to see such impulses as distinctive of sharia-minded contexts. So-called '*qadi*-justice' became a trope of judicial discussion in the West precisely because the impulse to follow the demands of 'equity' is a shared, understandable, and indeed in certain respects admirable one. Discussions of its toils go back at least as far as Aristotle and must be found wherever rules are applied as law, due to what legal philosopher Frederick Schauer calls their 'necessary suboptimality'. No rule can subsume all possible cases within the terms of its original justification: as generalizations, they always imply exceptions. According to Schauer, one can deal with this problematically general nature of rules in two ways: by opening up a conversation when a particular case reveals a given rule not to be fit for purpose (the 'conversational mode'); or by sticking to the rule simply because it is the rule ('entrenchment'). The latter is, for Schauer, the characteristic mode of law. It is by arguing in terms of the rules themselves, rather than their underlying justifications, that one starts 'thinking like a lawyer'.[9] In Schauer's account, entrenchment is a necessary feature of a workable legal system. But it is such 'legalism' that is also the source of much popular discontent with law. What is important to see here is that this has nothing to do with any qualitative difference between sharia and civil law

[9] Schauer 1991: 38–52, 100; 2009: 7–8.

per se. Rather, it is bound up with the way rules work more generally. In other words, the urge to '*qadi*-justice', in Islamic and other legal contexts, is an ethnographic reality and cannot simply be explained away for apologetic purposes. Rather, it can be understood, and we should realise that its attractions are shared.

Third, as the judge's comment above also reminds us, such rulings in Lebanon will almost invariably be overturned by the courts of appeal, which attempt to enforce unified and predictable standards that follow the strictures of the law. Excessive discretion is not permitted in the context in which I worked; where it occurs (which it sometimes does, as we have seen), it is to be rectified. Some have argued that such institutions of judicial review are alien to the authentic Islamic tradition. Others argue that this is yet another Orientalist canard: judicial review certainly did exist in pre-modern sharia-minded contexts, albeit in particular forms.[10] Most likely, such structures of judicial hierarchy and authority have varied through space and time. So-called '*qadi*-justice' is thus surely better seen not as either essential or essentially alien to the sharia-legal tradition, but as a contingent reality in the practice of that legal tradition as it is in others. What appears, then, a theoretical disagreement about the distinctive nature of 'Islamic law' may mask, as so often, an ethnographic or even methodological one. The provincial initial court judge in post-legal modernisation Morocco that Rosen observed in action may indeed have exercised considerable latitude with regard to the letter of the law; David Powers' study of networks of hierarchically ordered judges and muftis in fourteenth century Morocco, as manifested in the texts they produced, has revealed greater constraints. The exercise of judicial discretion within the Islamic tradition – as within others – will no doubt vary from context to context – and from judge to judge.

We must thus make sure that we are comparing like cases with like. We have already noted the 'selection effect' that turns 'hard cases' before the highest level courts into the paradigmatic instances of law in action despite the tiny proportion of reality they represent. Something similar may also be at work in terms of the cases that get selected for posterity and academic attention in historical studies of the sharia. But one has to note as well the process of comparative selection that ends with contrasts between local level dispute resolution forums outside of the West with the British Court of Appeal or the American Supreme Court, for instance. To draw a comparison, as Rosen does, between a metropolitan court of appeals judge in Washington, DC, and a provincial initial court

[10] Powers 1992 provides a good summary of the issues.

judge in Sefrou, Morocco, in the context of a discussion of the differences between the Islamic and common law traditions, surely invites misapprehension.[11]

It is too simple, then, to see the conflict for the shaykhly judge between satisfying the letter of the law and satisfying justice and the pedagogical imperative in individual cases as a matter of a perfect sharia having been contaminated by imperfect 'law'. Such tensions can be intrinsic to the sharia itself; nor are they unique to the sharia-minded. But that is not to say that the tensions between legal obligation and judicial inclination, even if shared between different legal systems, cannot be imagined in very different terms. The sharia's possibilities as a 'total' discipline, encompassing the 'ethical' as much as the 'legal', arguably gives these problems a distinctive shape.[12] In our Lebanese cases at least, a perceived disengagement from the parties before one and pedantic adherence to the rules for their own sake may entail the ruin (rather than the making) of the judge's standing as a shaykh, a virtuous and pedagogically committed representative of the sharia, and his collapse into a mere *muwazzaf* – state functionary, pen pusher and bureaucrat.

To finesse the twin demands of personal engagement and dispassionate and exact rule application requires a certain style, perhaps even a tragic one. 'How many a defeated litigant has salved his wounds with the thought that the law is an ass!', the British judge and jurist Lord Devlin wrote wryly.[13] But the sharia is divine: to think the same of God's law is unconscionable. To think it of the sharia court judge himself, however, is perfectly admissible, as we have seen. There is a sense in which being a shaykhly judge may be an impossible calling, a sentiment amply anticipated, we should remember, in the Islamic tradition. And the history of the Lebanese courts is indeed punctuated with instances of those who found the post unbearable. A previous head of the Sunni courts was, a former colleague told me, so 'disgusted' (*qarfan*) with what he saw there that he retreated to his home, to read and to pray, never again to emerge. 'He does not visit and will not be visited' (*la yazur wa-la-yuzar*), does not even answer the door. That colleague, himself later president of the courts, once sat with this man for two hours trying to persuade him to accept the idea of taking on a still more

11 See e.g. van Velsen 1969 on such 'false comparison' more generally, and Mundy 1991: 189 and Abou El Fadl 2002: 1429, 1431 on the latter point specifically.
12 On which see also Asad 2003: 248–250 and my discussion of his points in Clarke 2012 and 2015.
13 Devlin 1981: 4.

onerous institutional role, that of head of the official community. 'He cried' – and his then junior colleague cried with him.

Another example: Shaykh Muhammad Jawad Mughniyya, renowned Shi'i scholar and sometime head of the Ja'fari courts (1951–1956), was famously pushed out of office, by means of a government decree specially passed for the purpose no less. In his account in his memoirs, that was at the hands of political bosses infuriated by his reluctance to succumb to their blandishments and 'sell his religion' for their benefit (with some further suspicion of the hidden hand of the United States and its 'reactionary' clients). His son writes of how he would put their missives in the bin unopened, in front of their messengers. He also tells of how Mughniyya laughed when an old lady from the country insisted on his accepting a gift of fresh herbs in return for his having performed the quintessential shaykhly task of reconciliation and saved the marriage of her pregnant daughter. The joke was that she could not have known how many inducements of a different order he had turned away. Mughniyya thanked God for having saved him from the job before, as he puts it, the word 'judge' became synonymous with 'sullied' (*mulawwath*), free to turn from the toils of disputes and the 'filth' of politics to writing the succession of books that are his true legacy. He decided that he would thenceforth do nothing expected of a shaykh – not marry people, nor divorce them, not lead prayers or funerals, nor accept the streams of charitable donations that were offered to him – except answer people's questions.[14]

Conclusion

In this part of the book, in examining the mobilisation of sharia discourse within the state, I have tried to present a realistic account of sharia court processes in Lebanon. The cases before the courts are very difficult ones for the people involved in personal terms. But they can also be trying in themselves, in terms of the bureaucratic demands they make. This seemed to me one of the strongest impressions of court life, both for the people coming before the courts and for those working in them. Cases are a hard grind, 'boring' for the religious professionals, and inevitably unsatisfying for at least half of the parties involved. Sharia legal precepts are applied as family law, but it is the laws of procedure that often seem more prominent. As it struck me, the religious professionals manning the courts seek to distance themselves from these negative sides

[14] Mughniyya 2007: 108–118, 502–501. See also Mallat 1988.

to court life by terming them (human) 'law', as opposed to the ideal sharia. Hard work engaging with warring parties and trying to bring them to some form of agreement is valorised in contrast, consonant with widely felt ideals of the ethics and aesthetics of being an Islamic religious professional.

I certainly would not want to imply thereby that the sharia courts are institutionally dysfunctional. The systems work well enough to process hundreds of cases at a time: rulings are made and enforced; agreed settlements are arrived at. Judges apply clearly recognisable sharia legal precepts on a more or less consistent basis; the appeals courts scrutinise those rulings and enforce that consistency. That is not to ignore the fact that local and global observers and activists find much to criticise, chiefly in the relative legal position of wives and children as against husbands and fathers. This critique and the discourse of 'reform' that stems from it is a central theme of the coming chapters. But at this point I wish to highlight more the felt tension between what an idealised sharia should look and feel like and the reality of bureaucratic legal practice.

When people are dissatisfied with the current instantiation of a religious ideal, they are often wont to compare today unfavourably with yesterday. This sort of nostalgia is here frequently accompanied by a vague and utopian harping on a better possible future, framed as a (characteristically modern?) appeal to the idea of the state. 'If only there were an Islamic state', like there used to be, then these problems would go away.[15] No doubt few of my interlocutors would be naïve enough to put it quite so starkly as that. But I certainly picked up something of this vein of discourse in the courts. I have expressed my doubts that either the past or the future could wholly live up to these desires. But I have also noted how both these Islamic religious professionals and many academic commentators frame these tensions in terms of a contrast between the sharia and positive law, if valorised in often wholly opposite fashion.

I find this contrast, as it is usually put at least, misleading. The tension between the application of legal rules and process and the impulse to perceived justice is one shared across sharia, civil and common law and no doubt other legal traditions as well. The sorts of intellectually unexciting cases my judges are faced with, and their attempts to bring the parties concerned to some sort of compromise, would be familiar to similar low-level courts elsewhere. Rather than contrast these sharia courts with idealised, because higher-level, versions of civil and common law courts in other places, I have focused instead on the different

[15] Here one must again acknowledge Hallaq's (2013) strong objections to the coherence of the notion of a post-traditional Islamic state. See also the Conclusion to this book.

approaches one can find among my contemporary sharia court judges themselves, different responses to the same tensions.

Avoiding essentialising the sharia does not preclude the search for patterns in the way that is conceived and invoked. What seems distinctive here is the way that the sharia combines its status as a divine ideal with its legalism and its totalising scope. The former not only makes it easier to criticise the judge than the sharia, it also means that any instantiation of the sharia can be perceived as failing to measure up to its ideal nature. Its legalism pushes one into the logic of rules: the tension between entrenchment and conversation that Schauer describes. Its scope means that it can indeed be applied as law in family law courts, but that it also has a life – under the same name – outside of law courts, in the domain of people's personal ethical lives and their religious experience. But it cannot but function differently in those different domains: sharia applied as law will inevitably look more like law than it will personal ethic and religious ideal. It is this plasticity, under different ecological conditions, that I seek to highlight in this book. That takes my account in the coming chapters to other sorts of contexts where the sharia is invoked, outside of the courts and the state-sponsored establishment.

10 The Wider World of the Sharia

In the previous chapters I have argued that the instantiation of sharia as law gives rise to a particular way in which sharia is experienced, not always consonant with people's expectations of a divine ideal. I now begin to move away from the courts – without leaving them altogether – in order to give a clearer sense of the wider field of religious authority within which they are situated and with which they might be compared. I start by taking up the well-known distinction within the Islamic tradition between the role of the judge and that of the mufti, who gives authoritative guidance as to the sharia but does not have executive power. The latter's pronouncements (fatwas) are thus generally styled in the academic literature as 'non-binding', by contrast with the judge's rulings.[1] The role of mufti does not carry the same ominous associations within the Islamic tradition as the judgeship does, but the title has a similarly grand air.

This is, however, to put things in highly schematic terms, and it is harder to pin down who might count as a mufti in this sense in contemporary Lebanon than it is to enumerate the state-employed sharia court judges. There is, as described earlier (in Chapter 1), an array of 'official' muftis in Lebanon, appointed by the Sunni and Shi'i communities. But these have the role more of community leaders than Islamic legal scholars, even if their offices do also provide legal advice. Here too, to work for the establishment, for a salary, could be seen as having a detrimental effect on one's religious prestige, and one might not expect a truly great scholar to take on what is an essentially administrative function, although these are, like the judgeships, desirable posts for other reasons. But there are then a host of independent religious professionals working outside of the official religious communities who also provide sharia legal guidance: 'answering people's questions', as I quoted the renowned Shi'i scholar Shaykh Muhammad Jawad Mughniyya as saying

[1] See e.g. Masud et al. 1996: 1.

in the previous chapter, contrasting this most essential and least painful of a scholar's roles with the torment of being judge.

Such independent scholars could have greater or lesser reputations. Only the most respected, or presumptuous, might publicly issue a definitive opinion (fatwa) as to matters of the day; but giving advice to those in need is a different matter. Many such scholars, most perhaps, might eschew the title of 'mufti' itself, which could sound rather pompous (and hardly works at all in Shi'i contexts, for reasons I discuss later). As Mughniyya's example suggests, a judge may himself act in such a way on an informal basis away from his court. Shaykhs may thus serve as judges, or as official but essentially administrative muftis by title, or unofficial but publicly recognised muftis in the classical sense, or simply as informal sources of guidance and authority – or even perform several of these functions at once. We have already seen something of this multiplicity of roles in our encounters with young Shaykh Muhammad, or Shaykh Tayyib the judge's assistant, or indeed our judge who is also a Sufi master. All these men who have made Islam the centre of their lives act out that commitment in a variety of ways in a variety of contexts.

For 'the laity' (*al-'amma*), such nuances may be lost, one shaykh much like another representative of a largely undifferentiated 'turbaned' class (*al-mu'ammamin*). But in formal legal terms they are vital. The judge's ruling is binding in this world, to be put into action, even against a party's wishes. The mufti's advice informs autonomous individual ethical action, which will be reckoned in the next world. There is a difference drawn here, roughly speaking, between matters of law and matters of conscience, one that resonates with our earlier dichotomies between 'law' and 'sharia', without being identical to them. Outside of the special demands of an effective court bureaucracy, a more 'conversational' stance towards the ocean of sharia discourse can be taken: its plurality comes back into view. By comparing the sorts of conversations possible inside and outside of the courts, the specificity of the work of the courts will become still more apparent. It should also become clearer why the role and actions of the judge may seem in some ways less attractive than other instances of Islamic authority.[2]

In this chapter, I focus on one particular area of legal discourse as an example, one central to the courts' activities: divorce. Given that it is the diversity of the Islamic legal tradition that is at stake, and appreciating that sharia discourse is a highly evolved legalistic field, we will be faced

[2] This is a question also broached by Hussein Agrama (2010a), although the line of argument I develop here is not quite the same as that he does in response to his Egyptian examples.

with a complex array of nuanced opinions. That complexity is precisely what is at issue, so I make no apologies for the detail of my account. I do limit my discussion somewhat by focusing again on the Sunni tradition in particular. Subsequent chapters turn more to Shi'i contexts. But the detail aside, the crucial points are the plurality of opinion that is available, the expectation that people have of being able to obtain guidance from a shaykh to help them with a dilemma, and the difference – which people may not well appreciate – between what is possible for a shaykh offering general advice and assistance and what is possible for a shaykh acting in an official capacity, and more especially as a judge.

Divorce, Again

As we have noted, under Islamic precepts, a man can divorce his wife at will. This is particularly 'easy' in Sunni law, in as much as there are few conditions attached. A mere pronouncement of divorce, orally or in writing, is sufficient, unlike in the Ja'fari courts where a series of conditions have to be met, not least that there have been two witnesses to the divorce.[3] However, even if the Sunni husband can simply pronounce divorce, a whole set of issues nevertheless arise. What if someone pronounced the divorce formula without intending divorce, as in the case of a legal scholar discussing the issue, for instance? What if it had been a slip of the tongue, like saying, 'You are divorced' (*anti taliq*), when you had meant to say, 'You are a student' (*anti taliba*), for example? What if you had been joking?

The first point to make is that the legal issues here are complex, and the jurisprudential debate thus suitably baroque. The four schools of Sunni law hold different positions, and are differentiated internally as well. An important area of difference is over the significance of the husband's intention.[4] All four schools consider the pronouncement of divorce by one afflicted by madness as invalid. That might be extended to such a pronouncement in a fit of anger or drunkenness so intense that one could be considered to have lost one's mind.[5] Like other

[3] And also, among other things, that the divorce did not take place during the wife's menstrual period. That is because then sex between the couple should be ruled out, which in turns means that this would not constitute a proper test of their resolve to separate. If they have had sex during the current menstrual cycle then a divorce would not stand, as it testifies to the continuity of marital relations.

[4] On intention in Islamic law more generally and in this area see e.g. Messick 2001.

[5] See Zuhayli 2006: v.9: 6882–6884, who comments that this must be considered a rarity, and also Tucker 2008b: 89. But see Hana 1995: 167–198 for several rich cases concerning these points.

modernizing law codes, the Ottoman Law of Family Rights, at the time of my fieldwork still the first legal recourse for the Lebanese Sunni courts, draws on the whole range of the four schools, as well as minority, alternative opinions within the Hanafi School itself, in order clearly to rule out divorce under intoxication and duress, marking a departure from the main Hanafi line. So too in the case of allusive expressions for divorce, such as, 'Go to your father's house!', the OLFR stipulates that, 'the occurrence of *talaq* shall depend on the intention of the husband and if the two parties dispute as to whether or not the husband intended *talaq* the word of the husband shall be taken upon his oath', again a modification of prevailing Hanafi precepts.[6] However, the OLFR could hardly be expected to cover the entire array of possible legal issues and so where it does not, following section 242 of the Law of Sharia Courts, it is the position of the Hanafi School that is to be followed by the Sunni judge (or at least it was at the time of my fieldwork), as we have seen.

Generally speaking, pronouncements of divorce in jest count: 'there is no joking in divorce', to paraphrase a hadith. In the case of a slip of the tongue, however, while for the Shafi'i school such a pronouncement of divorce would not stand because of the lack of intention to perform it, for the Hanafis, as well as for the other two schools, the Malikis and Hanbalis, it would not stand 'in religion' (*diyanatan*), that is, between a Muslim and his or her God, but it does stand 'in judgement' (*qada'an*).[7] Here, in the classical *fiqh* tradition, we have again the distinction between the God's eye view of the law and that of the judge in court, but put not as one between 'sharia' and 'law' (*shar'* versus *qanun*) but as between 'religion' and 'judgement' (*din* versus *qada'*). It turns on the impossibility of the judge knowing the man's true intentions (*al-batin*, 'the interior') but still having to rule on his actions (*al-zahir*, 'the exterior'), whereas God does know and will take account of those intentions come Judgment Day. The judge, if faced with such a case, rules with divorce. But should the couple not take the case to court, whether or not they resume married life as normal is between them and God. Important for us to see here then, this is a constraint seen as intrinsic to the distinct nature of judging itself, and one of the ways in which the Islamic legal tradition distinguishes between ethics and law proper – one preserved in contemporary Lebanese court practice, as we will see.[8]

6 Sections 104–105, 109. See Anderson 1951b: 274–275. On the latter point see also Zuhayli 2006 v.9: 6899–6902.

7 Zuhayli 2006 v.9: 6886–6887.

8 Johansen 1999: 35–37; but cf. Asad 2003: 243–248; and see Othman 2007: 87–89, citing Johansen 1997.

There is more. Generally speaking, divorce (i.e. *talaq*, unilateral 'repudiation' by the husband) is revocable. If, after pronouncing divorce, the husband changes his mind within a set time period (the *'idda*), he can take his wife back without need for a fresh marriage contract. He can do this twice. After the third pronouncement of divorce, however, he can only remarry his wife after she has first been married to someone else. Whether or not a particular instance of divorce 'counts', then, even if it is revocable, is important. But further, it has become common in some circles in Lebanon for a man to use a formula amounting to 'You are three times divorced!' to curse his wife (under the influence, so the judges told me, of Egyptian films). This is a phenomenon of wider currency and historical depth, the so-called 'divorce of innovation' (*talaq al-bid'a*), decried and indeed proscribed under Hanafi and Maliki law.[9] However, should it be pronounced, the legal question arises as to whether it stands as three divorces at once, with the finality that entails, or just as one instance.

All four Sunni schools hold that a triple divorce stands (it has no effect in Shi'i law), although there are subtleties concerning the exact formula used. Where a husband says, 'You are divorced thrice' (*anti taliq thalathan*), for instance, there is agreement that this entails a three-fold divorce. Where he says 'You are divorced, you are divorced, you are divorced' (*anti taliq, anti taliq, anti taliq*), if there is a pronounced break between the three and he claims he intended emphasis by his repetition and not multiplication, then, by agreement between the schools, his intent is considered 'in religion' but not in judgement. There are other differences according to the nature of the expression or if the husband indicated the number through a non-verbal sign (holding up three fingers, for instance). Importantly, beyond the four schools, the celebrated medieval theologian Ibn Taymiyya (among others) thought that in all such cases, only one instance of divorce is entailed.[10] The particular, Hanafi line that the Lebanese Sunni court system follows is thus again more constraining than some. According to the interpretation of the sharia there applied, that more or less casual utterance can carry real and disastrous legal effects, with the couple being thrice divorced and

[9] Zuhayli 2006 v.9: 6926. On debates over this practice more generally see Welchman 2007: 21, 108 and Tucker 2008b: 88, 124–127.

[10] Zuhayli 2006 vol. 9: 6906, 6912 (and more generally, 6905–6919), 6927–6928 and ff. On the latter point, Zuhayli notes that the Egyptian and Syrian law codes rely on this opinion. (See also Tucker 2008b: 88.) Zuhayli goes on to comment that although he finds the opinion of the majority the stronger, there is no problem in giving the more lenient (my term) position as a fatwa 'to make things easier for people' (*taysiran 'ala al-nass*) and to support the bond of marriage (ibid.: 6934–6935).

only able to remarry after the wife has married another man. There are, however, more helpful positions available outside of the court and elsewhere in the Islamic legal tradition.

Where some such problem arises, then, a couple may be best advised to seek the opinion of a mufti (perhaps for them just thought of as 'a shaykh'), someone able to provide general statements of opinion as to the sharia outside of the judicial system, and then to follow their consciences accordingly, without falling foul of the law. In this sort of personal encounter with troubled souls, the mufti can be seen to exemplify that pedagogical engagement that we have seen to be part of the function of a real shaykh, or Islamic religious professional.[11] It is here that the legal consequences can be discussed 'in religion' (*diniyatan*), as a matter of personal conscience, which it is up to the person in question to decide how to effect rather than to have a course forced upon them by someone sitting 'in judgement' (*qada'an*) over them.

Here too, especially in what can now be considered as a 'post-*madhhab* age', where neither scholars nor laypeople generally feel constrained to remain within the bounds of one of the four Sunni schools, one can take the precepts of the sharia in more conversational mode.[12] The vast field of sharia discourse offers many possible responses to such problems, and one answer may fit a troubled person's need better than another. In the sorts of divorce pronouncements we have just discussed, one may want an opinion beyond the Hanafi School. According to a shaykh who worked at Dar al-Fatwa, the central such institution within the official Sunni community, there, unlike in the courts, they can draw on all four schools of Sunni law. This should help in many cases. But Ibn Taymiyya's opinion is not counted as falling within one of the classical schools. Should that be required then, they cannot help at Dar al-Fatwa. So they have to send the couple on to another shaykh, outside of the official institutions. 'Look, they come to you, they're crying, the wife is saying, "Our children! What will we do?!" So you say, "Go to Shaykh so-and-so."'

Responsibility for such matters is not something to take on lightly. I saw a young man come in to court to ask about such 'a sharia question' (*mas'ala shar'iyya*), as the functionary put it in introducing him to Shaykh Tayyib, the judge's assistant and gate-keeper that we met earlier. The young man explained that he had been very angry, had beaten his

[11] As Agrama (2010a) has argued.

[12] On post-*madhhab*ism see e.g. Messick 2005 and Yilmaz 2005. Such conversationality was also of course possible within the *madhhab*s in the 'traditionalist' era of stricter adherence to them.

wife, and then blasphemed and then said to her, '*anti taliq taliq taliq*' ('You are divorced, divorced, divorced'). So what is his situation, he wanted to know? Shaykh Tayyib sent him off to Dar al-Fatwa. Afterwards he commented, 'Why should I put him under my responsibility [*dhimmati*]?', that is, Shaykh Tayyib's responsibility before God for the advice that he gives, by giving this man an opinion to help him out. 'He can go to Dar al-Fatwa, that's their job there. Yes, there is the opinion of Ibn Taymiyya, but I can't give this fatwa. To give a fatwa you need someone really big', or at least with a formal licence (*ijaza*). 'Grant the fatwa, grant yourself Hellfire', he quoted sourly.

But care must be taken by the couple too. Should the matter come to the court's attention, the harder line will prevail. Take a published ruling from the Sunni sharia court of Beirut, for example.[13] Here the wife was seeking to establish that her husband had divorced her, in this case, as he acknowledged, 'with three divorces'. He had obtained a fatwa on the matter, presumably extricating himself from the consequences by arguing that his intention had not been to perform three divorces in one. However, as the ruling notes, the judge is charged with following what is apparent (*zahir al-hal*). As the venerable Ibn 'Abidin says, in the ruling's quotation,

> [The husband's] intention is right [to take into account] in what is between him and his Sublime Lord, because it demonstrates what [significance] his expression bears, so the mufti gives a fatwa that [the divorce] does not come to pass. As for the judge, he does not accept it and he rules that the divorce is effected due to its [i.e., the man's claim of a different intention] being contrary to the apparent [*al-zahir*].

And, the ruling continues, the jurists of the Hanafi School (here citing Zay'ali's *Tabyin al-haqa'iq*) wrote that if the husband were to say, 'You are divorced, you are divorced, you are divorced' (*anti taliq anti taliq anti taliq*) and claimed he intended emphasis, then he is believed 'in religion' and not in judgement: the judge is charged with ruling according to what is apparent, and God is entrusted with the secrets of the soul (*al-sara'ir*).

The judge ruled for the wife here, who presumably wanted to escape the marriage. But worse could be if the couple returned to married life based on the mufti's opinion, but the matter subsequently came to the courts' attention – they could rule that the couple had been living in sin; any children that might have then been born could even be ruled illegitimate, or so I was told. One judge told me of 'a terrible case' where something of this kind had happened: a divorce in 2001 had been

[13] Homsi 2003: 85–86.

deemed not to stand by the local official mufti, a substantial figure; the couple had returned to married life; but then they had differed again and the wife had raised a case of judicial divorce (*tafriq*) against her husband in around 2005. All the details as to their previous differences emerged. Come 2008, a ruling was issued finding that they had been divorced all the time and the husband then demanded back all the maintenance he had paid her in the meantime.

As soon as a judge senses that a couple is about to broach such a story, then, he will stop them in their tracks: 'Wait! Be careful!', he might say, 'If you are about to tell me what I think you are then I can't help you.' In the terms I developed in Chapter 9, the rules of the law, here undeniably those of 'the sharia', present an unavoidable obstacle to ideal moral engagement. I saw a woman and her father come before a (Sunni) judge with a question. The problem was, her husband had divorced her threefold. What is her situation, they wanted to know. In the morning they were drinking coffee and he said '*anti taliq taliq taliq*'. What does it mean? They had asked at Dar al-Fatwa, and the shaykh there had said that it is just one revocable divorce. Well, said the judge, if they felt convinced by the shaykh's fatwa then they should proceed on that basis. 'But we wanted to ask you our shaykh!' The judge's wider shaykhly role in the community outside of the court means that he may be a favoured point of recourse. But, as he tried to explain, 'The court is one thing and the mufti another' (*al-mahkama shi, wa-l-mufti shi*).

The Wider Fabric of Authority

As that example shows, people are well used to relying on the clerical class in times of moral trouble. But they may have relatively little interest in how it is differentiated in terms of formal roles and institutional commitments, and how those differences make a difference. A Sunni sharia court ruling from Tripoli, recorded in a published collection, will serve as a fuller case.[14] I summarise:

A woman came before the court complaining of the impossibility of her married life. Married nearly twenty years, with three children, she had, she claimed, just been divorced by her husband for a third time. On the first two occasions he had returned to married life with her (as is possible with a revocable divorce), but without registering the divorces with the courts, as is legally required. He was now refusing to register this third and thus final divorce, which he had admitted

[14] Hana 1995: 188–198. See also the previous case (ibid.: 180–187), which turns on similar issues and where members of the Badawi Palestinian refugee camp mosques' committee are involved and asked for 'a fatwa'.

to before the (officially recognised) Mufti of Tripoli himself, Shaykh Taha Sabunji. He maintained that he had pronounced the divorce in a state of drunkenness, unaware of what he was doing, such that the divorce does not count. She wanted this third divorce to be legally established (i.e., through a case of *ithbat al-talaq*).

The first divorce had, she said, taken place in Saudi Arabia more than ten years previous. He had said to her, 'May it be forbidden to me in religion, let it be that you are forbidden to me like my sister' (*'alayy al-haram min din bi-anna-ki muharrama 'alayy ka-ukhti*). He then returned her, after 'seeking a fatwa' (*istifta'*, in the technical terms of the ruling) from Shaykh 'Ali al-Tantawi, a renowned Syrian jurist by then living in exile in Saudi Arabia, presumably as to whether the divorce counted and if so whether he could revoke it. The second divorce occurred back in Lebanon a couple of years ago. He said simply, 'You are divorced' (*anti taliq*), and then returned her again, after 'seeking a fatwa' from two named local shaykhs. The third divorce was then recently pronounced in the marital home, with the expression, 'You are divorced, you are divorced, and this is the third time and the final time, and you know that you cannot return to this house again' (*anti taliq, anti taliq, wa-hadha thalith marra wa-akhar marra wa anti ta'rifina anna-hu la yumkin-ki al-ruju' ila hadha al-bayt marratan thaniyya*).

One notes in passing that it seems unlikely that the expression had been quite so grammatically exact. As no doubt the case with his first formula, this is presumably a rendering of a more colloquial register into the legalistic literary phrasing of the courts. No attempt, it would seem, is made to reproduce the colloquial original, despite the importance of the exact wording in such instances.

After he realised what he had done he again sought a fatwa as a 'way out' (*makhraj*). He had recourse to the Mufti and a number of other named shaykhs, but they refrained from pronouncing upon the matter. The wife thus called the shaykhs who had been consulted as witnesses to the divorce.

Altogether five shaykhs gave testimony, along with another man who was present at one of the meetings; the Mufti was not summoned. The first, Shaykh Anwar Bakri,[15] testified that the couple had come to him on the occasion of the second divorce; he had explained to them that they could return to marriage again, but after that there would be only one divorce left. Afterwards he learned that her husband had divorced her again, but he did not intervene further. Next, Shaykh Marwan al-Ayyubi testified as to this third divorce. About a year ago, he said, the husband (who he did not know) came to Dar al-Fatwa (the official fatwa office of the Sunni community in Tripoli) and sought a fatwa concerning divorce. Shaykh Ayyubi told him that fatwas are given only after hearing both spouses, and went with the husband to his house to speak to the wife as well. Here he heard the

[15] This published ruling is, as normal, anonymised as to the parties' names; the shaykhs, however, remain named, speaking to their public status. I follow suit, although I know nothing more about them, save Mufti Sabunji (d. 2015), who was a substantial figure.

husband acknowledge the first two divorces, but claim that he was in a state of rage when he pronounced the third. Shaykh Ayyubi told him that he could not himself give a fatwa allowing the return of his wife and advised him to take the matter to the Mufti.

A third shaykh, Shaykh Ibrahim al-Turk, whose account was corroborated by the other witness, said that some time ago – nine months or a year – he met with the husband in a coffee shop along with some others. The husband said that he had divorced his wife for the third time, and claimed that when he had pronounced the third divorce, he had been angry and drunk. Shaykh al-Turk had explained to him that marital relations with her would only be possible for him if she first married another man. The fourth shaykh, Shaykh Ghalib Sanjaqdar, said that about four months ago the husband came to him seeking a fatwa about earlier divorces in Saudi Arabia, when, he claimed, he had been angry; the wife had then come with one of her family and told him that she had consulted a scholar by telephone and explained how her husband had divorced her, and had been told that the divorce did not stand because of her husband's state of rage. Shaykh Sanjaqdar refrained from giving his own opinion and met with the couple at Mufti Sabunji's office 'in this court' (it is common outside Beirut for the office of the official mufti to be housed within the court complex). The Mufti heard them out and, himself angered, scolded the husband for his conduct, but also did not give his opinion there and then, wanting to have time to study the matter. (We learn nothing of what, if anything, his final opinion was.) In sum, the divorce was the third one and the husband claimed that he had pronounced it in a state of anger and drunk. A fifth shaykh, Shaykh Muhammad Siraj al-Din al-Malik, said he did not remember the couple. (The wife added that it had actually been her paternal uncle rather than her that had visited this shaykh.) There is not a day that goes by, he said, without more than one couple coming and asking about divorce.

To cut a long story shorter, the judge ultimately insisted on the husband swearing an oath that he was not in his right mind when he pronounced the third divorce and did not remember using the extravagant formula his wife reported. (The judge deplored in passing the tendency of the common folk [*al-'amma*], 'who know nothing' of the rulings of the sharia, to use such phrases.) Once the husband had done so, the verdict was that the first two divorces stood (as revocable instances) and the third did not.

One gets a sense of the sheer density of such engagements with religious experts, the reliance on the notion of 'seeking a fatwa' as a 'way out' of difficulties and the delicacy and complexity of such questions. Here the couple sought informal consultations and opinions by telephone as well as having recourse to the Sunni community's official fatwa offices. Some petitioners may understand well the varied geography of the landscape of Islamic legal expertise; some may even try to game the system in a form of forum-shopping. Others may just want the assistance of 'a shaykh' at a time of ethical confusion and crisis.

I saw many such informal encounters between shaykhs and those in ethical need. But in earlier fieldwork in 2003–2004, I also had the opportunity to visit the offices of the official Dar al-Fatwa in Beirut and be given copies of the textual documents ('fatwas'), which they issue for petitioners to take away.[16] It is instructive to compare this genre of official document with the judicial rulings I analysed earlier, with their overwhelmingly bureaucratic framing and content. To take an example, of an average length at two pages, headed with a calligraphic *basmala*, Dar al-Fatwa logo and a Quranic verse ('Then we put you on a path of command [*shari'atin min al-amr*], so follow it and do not follow the whims of the ignorant'; 45:18[17]), it begins with a prayer: 'Thanks be to God Lord of Worlds, and prayers and peace be to our lord and prophet Muhammed, seal of the prophets and messengers, and to his kindred and all his companions and those who follow them with righteousness to the day of judgement', and then continues:

> And if the situation is as the questioner [name removed] states in her question: 'I was married to [...] for six years, during which time my married life was in my father's house, leased [*bi-l-ijara*] from [...], for four years and four months, together with my brother and sister, because my parents died a long time ago, and then, wanting independence, I moved to a marital home in Sanayeh [an area of West Beirut] for a year and eight months. And then I was divorced. And given that I am a woman who does not own a home or property except my father's house where I grew up, I returned to live with my brother and sister in my father's house, which was his by lease and was still in his name. Does the noble sharia permit me to return or does it forbid me to do so? And do I have the right to live in the afore-mentioned house of my father, given that I am a divorcee? I beg you to give me an opinion on this, and may God bless you for it.'
>
> And the answer – and the truth of the matter belongs to God Most High: 'The scholars of the Shafi'i school, may God Most High have mercy upon them, have written in their books relied upon in that school that lease arrangements [*al-ijara*] are not dissolved upon the death of the landlord or the leaseholder. And the benefit rented reverts to the heirs of the deceased. And Imam al-Khatib al-Shirbini, one of the scholars of the Shafi'i school, may God Most High have mercy upon him, said.' (Here follows a quotation to the same effect, if in more detail, with the exact reference to Shirbini's *Mughni al-muhtaj 'ala al-minhaj* given.)

[16] Besides the example I quote in detail here, I was given a number of others, perhaps chosen to give something of an idea of the range of topics that the offices are presented with: a child has a deformed finger – is it permitted to perform surgery on it? Someone very ill wants someone else to perform the Hajj pilgrimage on his behalf: is that allowed? A murderer has become reconciled with his victim's family, but is to be executed: what is the sharia's position?

[17] This is in fact the sole instance of the word-form *shari'a* in the Quran, although cognate forms (verb *sharra'a*, noun *shir'a*, etc.) also occasionally occur.

And based on what the petitioner has stated in her question: Given that the petitioner is the heir of her father, the leaseholder, along with her brother and sister since his death, and that the right to benefit [from the lease] is also inherited, as is the position of Imam al-Shafi'i, may God Most High have mercy upon him, and others among the Imams [i.e., the very greatest scholars of each of the Sunni schools], and given that the petitioner was divorced and has no abode except the afore-stated house of her father, the noble sharia gives the petitioner the right to benefit from the leased property – that is, the house of her father, and the right to live in it as well, just as the remainder of the heirs. And God Most High knows best. May God bless our lord Muhammad, and his kindred and companions, with many blessings, and thanks be to God, Lord of Worlds.

And the fatwa is finally signed and sealed in the name of the Mufti of the Republic himself, Muhammad Rashid Qabbani.

Suitably official looking, and with its own measure of bureaucratic patterning (and a file number), the document nevertheless seems imbued with rather more religiosity than the court equivalent, given its more extravagant religious heading, Quranic quotation and extensive citation of Islamic legal sources. Dar al-Fatwa is a grand building, the signature of the Mufti an overwhelmingly prestigious sign, in official terms at least. The offices are certainly busy, but the process of obtaining such a document can hardly approach the courts in degree of procedural complexity and annoyance. And that process is not an adversarial one. A service is more clearly provided – in this case a solution to a personal problem, a solution that here relies, one notes, on recourse to a school of Islamic law (Shafi'i) other than the Hanafi one by which the courts are bound. One can imagine how the toils of the court and the legal process might seem less attractive in comparison.

11 Reform and Rebellion

If we now turn back briefly to considering the tensions of court practice, we can see that even if the blame for unhappy experiences of the courts largely falls on the judge and the Lebanese sharia court system, there is also a sense in which the sharia itself may be put in jeopardy by being represented by the rulings applied in the courts, in comparison with the greater flexibility on offer elsewhere. The particular line the courts take – which is just one among many possibilities within the wider Islamic tradition – can seem out of step with the moral common sense of the age. Judges know well the pressures the sharia is under with regard to civility between the sexes, for example. In the language of modernity, many (if not all) people with an interest in Islam talk of the need to 'keep up with the times' (*muwakibat al-'asr*) or be 'open-minded' (*munfatih*), rather than appear as blinkered and stuck in the past. But, bound by the entrenched position the law inevitably must adopt, judges are handicapped in this regard. And yet that does not necessarily entail resignation. One can try to 'make things easier' for people by drawing on the possibilities of the tradition. Just like the tensions of judicial practice, however, that impulse can take you in different directions. In this chapter, I contrast the paths taken by two different figures, both frustrated by the status quo. The first is that of another (Sunni) judge, a 'reformist' (my characterisation), driven to challenge those at the summit of the court hierarchy by his felt need to respond to this wider plurality of sharia opinion.[1] I then examine the alternative: forging a career outside of the official system altogether.

The Reformist

Relatively young, more straightforward and less formal than the norm, Shaykh D does not come from a learned, or indeed religious background.

[1] Even if it is my choice to label him a reformist it is not that the category is an alien one in this context. The processes and politics of Islamic reform (*islah*) across the Muslim world have been widely documented and discussed: see Commins 1990 and Mervin 2000 on Ottoman Syria and Lebanon.

But he saw the light, studied at sharia college and went on to become a judge, at the time of my fieldwork posted in Saida (Sidon) in the South. He agrees with those who assert that the sharia court does not match its professed sharia ideal. He told me of an egregious instance of the risks involved, a custody case where the woman concerned cursed the sharia. 'No', he told her, 'curse the *fiqh* of the Hanafi school', that is, the body of legal scholarship and opinion applied in the courts, particularly patriarchal in this matter as we have seen. People see all this as the sharia, he explained to me. It isn't, it's man-made. Only the Prophets are infallible (*ma'sumin*). Normal people make mistakes. When he first started out, as a judge's assistant writing up the cases, he wrote at the top, 'Council of the noble sharia' (*majlis al-shar' al-hanif*). But now he prefers to write, 'Council of the ruling' (*majlis al-hukm*).

For Shaykh D then, the relevant opposition is between Islamic legal scholarship (*fiqh*), which is human and individual, and the sharia, which is divine and universal.[2] People ask for 'the ruling of the sharia' (*hukm al-shari'a*) or 'a sharia ruling' (*hukm shar'i*), but what they get is a jurist's ruling (*hukm fiqhi*). And in this regard, the court's reliance on just one *madhhab* is, for him, outdated. In Lebanon now, he told me, as elsewhere in the Sunni world no doubt, most people are 'non-*madhhab* followers' (*la-madhhabi*). Real traditionalists, the *madhhabi*s, who just follow the Shafi'i or Hanafi school say, are very rare. 'Maybe only one or two people in Lebanon.' For him, the more salient distinction to be made within contemporary Sunni legal thought is between 'strictness' (*tashaddud*), as represented by the traditionalists but more especially the current Salafi trend (also, in his words, 'the fundamentalists', *al-usuliyyin*), and 'making things easy' (*al-tasahul*), represented by the 'activist' trend (*al-tayyar al-haraki*), such as the Muslim Brotherhood and the closely linked, global celebrity scholar Shaykh Yusuf al-Qaradawi.[3] In making things easier for contemporary Muslims, the latter pick and choose positions from the different *madhhab*s, 'patching together' (*talfiq*) bits of the tradition.[4] His sympathies clearly lay with the latter, broadly conceived. He lived in overwhelmingly Salafi Saudi Arabia for

[2] A point which many academic commentators also stress: e.g. Messick 1993: 17; Johansen 1999: 39 and Vikør 2005: 2–3.

[3] On Qaradawi see Gräf and Skovgaard-Petersen 2009.

[4] Such practices could also be found in pre-modern Islamic legal systems, whether as *talfiq* or, more commonly, other forms such as *tatabbu' al-rukhas* ('following dispensations') (Ibrahim 2015). And so the sort of strict adherence to one (in this case Hanafi) *madhhab* that is being critiqued here is arguably relatively modern, as a function of Ottoman state centralisation and Hanafisation (see e.g. Baldwin 2017: 77–98).

six years with his wife, he told me. It proved very difficult. 'I did not find myself in Saudi Arabia. I find myself in Lebanon.'

He shares people's frustration with the courts, and he knows that others do too. 'I can go to the president of the court, the Mufti, they will say the same thing. Everyone does. Everyone says we've got to change the law.' Shaykh D has his own such projects, sharing with me a position paper in which he pointed out that the laws applied to Sunnis had not (then) been changed for a century and the law of sharia courts largely since the sixties.[5] This was prior to the reforms that did come a few years later.[6] But at this point, change was, he felt, urgently needed: to make things easier for the country's citizens on the one hand and to realise the aims (*maqasid* – another characteristically modernist trope) of the sharia on the other. The Lebanese sharia courts system was lagging behind its counterparts elsewhere in the Arab and Islamic world, with their updated codes; its laws needed to be replaced to accommodate the developments in the customs and culture of the Lebanese people, as well as the international treaties which Lebanon has signed regarding the protection of the rights of children and women. And, knowing that this is a long and complicated task, in the meantime people needed to be educated: no marriage contract should be registered without evidence of the couple having first undertaken a course teaching the rights of the spouses and children under religious precepts and Lebanese law. (And he gave me another paper containing suggested such instruction.)

But for the seven years he had then been a judge, he told me, he had heard the same thing. It cannot be done because of the security situation. 'But this isn't the real problem. The real problem is traditionalist thinking [*fikr taqlidi*]', and social and political pressure. Or as a younger colleague had it, such reform would 'never' happen. 'You can take the box, lock it and throw away the key.' You would need a great scholar, with the strength of character to withstand all the attacks that would ensue, and an ability to persuade people like magic. There are none such in Lebanon, he thought. His assessment was unduly pessimistic: as we have seen, change would in fact come in 2011, in the form of the partial new code for the Sunni courts and its reforms to the ways that custody, *mahr* and maintenance were to be judged. But one would not have thought so at the time.

In the meantime, Shaykh D had taken another path, that of ruling according to his conscience within his own court and taking his chances

[5] Entitled, 'Toward improving the personal status system' (*Nahw tatwir anzimat al-ahwal al-shakhsiyya*).

[6] On which see Chapter 2.

with regard to the appeals court. According to the lawyers, Shaykh D was then the most appealed against in the Sunni system (along with another judge but for very different reasons). He has had his cases overturned so many times, he himself told me, had so many arguments with the supreme court, that it has broken his previous awe (*hayba*) of them. Lots of other judges do not trust their own rulings on these issues, a junior colleague ventured, but they are afraid to be as bold. Such activism takes courage. The risks are real enough: I was told of another judge, similarly unlike most of their allegedly 'wooden' (*khashabi*) peers, who had been banished to the far North ('Akkar province, stereotypically rough and 'remote') for not toeing the line.[7]

Shaykh D gave me copies of some of his rulings. All concerned 'interesting' cases, mostly on the hot topic of custody (*hadana*); they are relatively long (the majority, four, of eight to twelve pages in length, another three of five to six pages and only one a more standard three); and they are distinctive in style. His argumentation is explicit, strikingly detailed compared with the others I am familiar with in its legal justifications and sources, both Islamic and civil legal. He cites, uniquely in my experience, the particular editions he is using of the classical texts he refers to. And he thinks of the extensive civil legal argumentation he puts alongside as his own special forte: he sat with a civil court judge to learn the ropes for a year rather than the usual month after appointment, he told me. In one custody dispute where the wife was in France, in possession of a French civil ruling of divorce and custody in her favour, the question arises as to the Lebanese sharia court's right to intervene, a right which he asserts vigorously in a learned discussion of conflict of laws including the principle of *lex fori* and citing also a relevant decision by the Lebanese Court of Cassation. Other judges would have given the same ruling, he thought, but not in the same manner. In another ruling, he does not let one side pull the wool over his eyes through their translation of relevant material from court proceedings in the United States, but checks and cites the exact meaning of 'affidavit' 'in the Oxford Dictionary'. And he 'puts politics' in another case, where a previously Maronite Catholic man converted to Islam in an attempt to win custody of his children, now with their mother in Belgium. They had originally married in the Maronite Church in Lebanon, and, following the

[7] For reasons that I am not able fully to explain, but would guess are in part a function of his sheer ability and energy, as well as a change in the political weather, Shaykh D by contrast prospered, being moved from the provincial South to metropolitan Beirut subsequent to my fieldwork. And much of the content of the new partial family law code for the Sunni courts is in keeping with the positions he maintained.

1951 law that regulates the Christian courts (section 14, which he quotes), in the event of an ensuing conflict it is the court of the original contract that counts. He is, he writes, bound to follow its strictures, even though it 'diminishes the competencies of the sharia judiciary, and makes the efforts which the Muslims in this country gave in repealing decree 60 LR and its supplements lost as dust'.

To take up an example in more detail, one case from 2006 concerned custody of four children. The father now wanted to take custody of the two eldest that had reached the ages of eleven, a boy, and nine, a girl. Let us remember that at this time, controversially, the Sunni courts presumed custody to be awarded to the father at the ages of seven for boys and nine for girls. The other two children were below those ages. The father had taken a second wife; the children's mother was still married to him but had brought a case for judicial divorce. The court had issued a temporary ruling entrusting the two eldest children to the father, but the mother had handed over all four children rather than separate them. A subsequent report from social services on their situation under their father's care indicated problems.

Shaykh D first deals with the question as to whether it is material to a case of custody whether the parents are still married (it is not), citing Qadri Pasha but also the more venerable Hashiyya of Ibn 'Abidin. Next he turns to the crucial point of the age at which the mother's custody ends. He deals first with custody of a male child, sufficing himself with noting 'what is written in *fiqh*', that a mother's right to care ends with a boy's attaining the age of discrimination (*tamyiz*). Since the eldest son has exceeded this age and become able to care for himself, he must be handed over to his father. Now he turns to the question of the daughter. Here he begins by claiming that the position deemed as the actual opinion (*al-qawl al-sahih*) of the eponymous and greatest scholar of the Hanafi school, Abu Hanifa (d. 767), is that the mother's custody of a girl ends when the girl becomes (sexually) mature (*baligha*) – that is to say, contrary to the nominally Hanafi line the court takes (nine years).

In elucidation of this point, he turns to some other classic Hanafi sources, first the *Mabsut* of Sarakhsi (eleventh century), quoting at length, to the effect that once a girl reaches sexual maturity she needs marrying and it is the father that has guardianship over his daughter's marriage, and the sense of honour needed to guard against her temptation and men's lust. Now Shaykh D takes up the later *Fath al-qadir* of Ibn al-Humam (fifteenth century), which refers to a hadith that a girl should be handed over to the father if she reaches the stage of (sexual) desirability (*shahwa*). The question arises as to what age that is. Due to 'the depravity of the time' (*fasad al-zaman*), the later scholars of the school decided that 'the girl of nine was desirable and of five was not desirable, and those of six and seven and eight were desirable if plump, and if not then not.' This gives Shaykh D his point of argument. The later decision of the school's jurists to rely on a less authentic ('weaker', *ad'af*) statement attributed to its imam (Abu Hanifa) was based on temporary considerations of exigency (*asbab maslahiyya aniyya*) tied to that particular time. Or as he put it to me, 'This is the thinking of Old Arabia'.[8] He now notes the principle, 'Do not reject the changing of rulings with the changing of the times', and continues:

> And since this court finds that, generally speaking, the primary reason of the later jurists of the school to differ from the saying of the imam was the corruption of the time, it is necessary to put that to work here and affirm the obligation to leave the daughter with her mother until [sexual] maturity [*bulugh*] [. . .] in our times. In a way different from that which has been the custom for centuries, in this era she is more secure in the care of her mother than her father, as the law obliges her to study in school, and fathers are generally busy [working] [. . .] As for the fear of sexual temptation [*fitna*], [. . .] that goes back to the customs of those times, which allowed for centuries the marriage of immature [*ghayr baligh*] girls [. . .][9] But in our present time and in this country of ours, [. . .] he who desires young girls [. . .] is classed as a pervert, not to mention the existence of laws that punish sexual contact with under-age [*ghayr baligh*] girls with no less than five years in prison with hard labour [. . .] [here he cites the relevant section of the penal code]. And since it seems that the reasons that the jurists relied on for disregarding the imam's position should not be taken into account today, it is therefore necessary to return to the authentic position within the school.

And so, arguing from what constitutes a young woman's interest (*maslaha*) today, he awards custody of the boy to his father, but the eldest daughter and the two younger girls to their mother, to be effected after the end of the school year to avoid disrupting their studies. The tone of the ruling seems confrontational: the standard line, that of the appeals court, is associated with conceptions of sexuality and sociality centuries out of date, indeed now considered criminal perversion; today's jurists, he notes, pin the responsibility for this sorry situation on the scholars of yesteryear instead of themselves. The ruling was indeed, as expected, appealed (although the appeal was in this case rejected on procedural grounds).

[8] According to the judge, the legal device thus being employed by the courts is that of 'blocking the path to harm' (*sadd al-dhara'i'*), where you forbid something permitted in order to stop something prohibited – totally over-used nowadays in his opinion. This is 'legal conservatism' (*al-tashaddud al-fiqhi*).

[9] Here the judge also adduces notions that the age of physical onset of sexual maturity may vary between different environments.

Shaykh D uses the principle that the interests (*maslaha*) of the child should be paramount more widely.[10] The father might be violent. Sometimes he sends them to the psychologist in order to decide which parent to give the child to. Or say there are, for example, five children, aged two, three, five, seven (a boy) and nine (a girl). The seven- and nine-year-olds should go to their father. But he can argue that it is in the interests of the children that they are kept together. Or say a daughter is rebellious, even striking her father, completely disobedient of him. How could he look after her then? This would be contrary to the aims (*maqasid*) of the sharia in this domain. As a sympathetic lawyer put it to me, 'The sharia has a spirit' (*ruh*), which should be honoured. 'Which is better, to keep the children with their mother? Or to send them to a father who's remarried and has other children?' The tradition contains the resources to provide: 'Islamic law is broad' (*al-fiqh al-islami wasi'*). But the appeals court would, according to Shaykh D, strike these arguments down. *Maslaha* and *maqasid* have become fashionable tools of modernist Sunni legal scholarship,[11] but the supreme court did not then find a clear basis for them in the relevant texts, to his frustration. 'Come on!'[12]

The Rebel

Shaykh D may be much appealed. But this is not because he does not know or apply the rules. His rulings are formally justified in terms far beyond the norm: to argue against the standard line requires one to be more explicit, more 'political' at times. These are arguments from within the tradition, for which there are plenty of resources. Nevertheless, the

[10] This is a move found elsewhere: see Welchman 2007: 133–142, 219–220n4. Of course just what a child's best interests are is open to debate. And, notwithstanding the 'contemporary' nature of this judge's positions, they do not always fall in the places a Western observer might expect. One case Shaykh D shared with me concerned a mother now living in France, where she divorced her husband and won custody rights to their child, challenged by the husband in the Lebanese courts. The wife's side, in their submission, invoked the child's interest (*maslaha*) in remaining in France. But the judge ruled against them, stating the contrary: 'entrusting the child [...] to his father the plaintiff falls within the interest of the child, due to the harm and danger of his remaining in the countries of the West without the guidance of his guardian ... as regards preserving his religion and morals, looking to the temptations [*fitan*] which present themselves to children in this age.'

[11] See e.g. Opwis 2005.

[12] The partial new code for the Sunni courts that came later, on the other hand, does make explicit use of the principle of the interests (*maslaha*) of the child, including their religious interests and noting the importance of not disrupting the school year, in addition to raising the standard period of custody by the mother (but not others taking her place in her absence) to twelve years of age for both boys and girls (sections 11, 15, 16, 21, resolution 46/2011).

limits of the conversation that this judge can have about the sharia within the courts are still real enough. The wider world of sharia discourse, however, offers tantalisingly more. Further, the impossibility of the establishment monopolising sharia discourse entails that the sharia also provides the resources for others to act independently. The challenge can come from outside of the establishment as well as from within it. This will be most readily demonstrated by returning to the issue of marriage.

As we saw in Chapter 6, for a marriage to be religiously legitimate it does not have to be contracted within the state-sponsored official framework; indeed such independent arrangements are pretty much the norm in the Shi'i system, although the contract needs then to be registered with the state courts. The Sunni system, on the other hand, officially rejects such 'external contracts' (sing. *'aqd khariji*), preferring to issue licences for its shaykhs to perform officially sanctioned ceremonies outside of the courts' physical environs, but inside its jurisdiction.

There are nevertheless reasons to take the unofficial route, as a shaykh explained to me at the Beirut offices of the Jama'a Islamiyya, or Lebanese Muslim Brotherhood, which is not part of the official Sunni community institutions.[13] (He was clear, however, that the Jama'a Islamiyya would never facilitate such unlicensed arrangements themselves: in Lebanon, he told me, they work 'with the courts and not against them'.) Some might want an informal but religiously sanctioned union between a couple, 'For the sake of the permitted and the prohibited' (*min ajl al-halal wa-l-haram*), so that they could get to know one another on a more intimate basis during what could be styled an 'engagement', given that for some people social and religious norms prohibit much but the most reserved interactions between the sexes. Should things go well, then a public, official marriage would be contracted through the courts. For others, the official court system is itself unattractive, due to its bureaucratic and overwhelming nature, or because of its slow, cumbersome and, for the poorest, expensive procedures. This is especially the case for Palestinian refugees – settled populations spanning generations now in Lebanon, but whose non-normalised status means that official marriages could take something of the order of six months. One judge thus talked of an extra-legal (*ghayr qanuni*) world, among Palestinians and the poor.

Or sometimes people need to get married in secret or in a hurry. An illicit relationship may suddenly need to be normalised – in the advent of pregnancy for example. Young people sometimes just can't wait.

[13] Interviews with Shaykh Husam al-Ghaly, Beirut, 2 July 2007, 13 March 2008.

Or, more likely, their choice of partner is unacceptable to their family. In the courts, the consent of the bride's guardian (*wali*), usually her father, is required, as we have seen. But here again, as we also noted, the sharia contains within itself the means to dispute that: not all authoritative opinion finds the approval of the *wali* a necessity. This then entails the possibility of a sharia-compliant marriage being contracted outside of the state sharia court system without the need for a guardian's permission. Our young Shaykh Muhammad told me that he received 'so many' offers for such secret contracts, outside the court. And they would be prepared to pay him handsomely too: $5000 even. He would never do such a thing. But there are shaykhs who do.[14]

I was interested to meet with such a figure. But this is sensitive business, and thus 'secret' in most cases. To have a public, or at least semi-public, reputation for such independence from and lack of deference to the state-sanctioned official community would speak to a very considerable social and political base, capable of sustaining such autonomy – not very common. Two names, however, were suggested to me. One, in Beirut, was reluctant to talk. The other, Shaykh Maher Hammoud, based in Saida, was happy to meet. Shaykh Hammoud is indeed a public figure (hence my naming him), notorious within the Sunni community for closely allying himself with Hizballah rather than the Sunni mainstream. On the one hand, this puts him on the right side (in local terms) of key issues like resistance to Israeli aggression and Western imperialism and support of the Palestinian cause, uncomplicated by the Lebanese Sunni mainstream's then closer ties to the West and its clients in the region. On the other, this makes him in turn a client of the Shi'a, now the Lebanese Sunni community's greatest rival. He maintains a high profile, a regular of programmes on *al-Jazeera* and other channels and with his own website advertising his prolific meetings, activities and pronouncements.[15]

Shaykh Hammoud's online biography tells us that he was born in 1953 and studied Islam first as a child in the mosques of Saida and then in the sharia college of the University of Damascus (1972–1977), where he also dabbled in the (civil) law and literature and frequented the study circles of various mosques. He was one of the founders of the Jama'a Islamiyya in Saida and active within it until 1979, the year when he was made an official mosque imam and Friday sermon preacher. His activism turned to work with the Islamic Front and the Association of Muslim

[14] Such unofficially sanctioned marriages have been the subject of much debate elsewhere, as in the 'customary' (*'urfi*) marriages of Egypt, for example. See Hasso 2011.

[15] www.maherhammoud.com, last accessed 28 June 2016.

Clerics in the 1980s, by his account playing a leading role in various events, uprisings and peace efforts during the years of civil war and Israeli occupation, in Saida and Beirut. A supporter of the Resistance, an ally of Hamas, Islamic Jihad and Palestinian resistance organisations more generally, he professes to have excellent French and some knowledge of English. A frequent attender of international Islamic conferences, he has written many articles but, he regrets, no published books as yet.[16]

When I went to Saida in 2008 to interview him in his offices near 'his' Jerusalem mosque (Masjid al-Quds),[17] he arrived from prayers striding briskly and surrounded by attendants, looking much like the officially credentialed Sunni shaykhs I knew, wearing a robe and white wrapped turban rather than the simple skull cap of many non-official Sunni Islamic specialists. (On closer inspection, I noted a subtle difference: the turban was just white wound cloth, shaped into the familiar 'Sunni' shape, but not wrapped round a tarbush, as the official ones are.) The offices bore some discrete markers of his current political affiliations – a small yellow Hizballah sticker and a picture of their recently assassinated military commander 'Imad Mughniyya in the reception area. Shaykh Hammoud's well-appointed office followed the familiar format, with a desk with a plaque bearing his name, some leatherette easy chairs and a well-stocked bookcase behind him, in this case featuring, among other things a large collection of the speeches of Sayyid Hasan Nasrallah, Hizballah's Secretary General.

While far from unfriendly (if busy), it was very apparent that Shaykh Hammoud was more politically involved than most of the figures I sat with. He questioned me carefully as to my provenance and project, and took my photo with his mobile phone and sent it off to some unknown recipient, later receiving a call during which he clearly discussed my presence. Rarely among the shaykhs I consulted, he insisted on having the interview taped (and I quote from that recording here, which he was very happy to stand by). Very soon into our conversation, one of the most important figures within the Sunni religious establishment of Saida arrived, robed splendidly, and rather taken aback to see me there. I had to turn off the recorder and wait outside while sensitive business was discussed. Shaykh Hammoud was clearly a figure of some weight.

Shaykh Hammoud told me that he provides a variety of services: 'Fatwas, or social assistance, or political or judicial assistance: because I have links with politicians and the judiciary and the army and the security services and others of course.' 'Thanks be to God, we have a

[16] www.maherhammoud.com/_CV.php, accessed 23 June 2014. [17] 4 April 2008.

firm relation with society helping their needs.' Remembering the gravity of the title of mufti, his explicit claim to offer fatwas is worth noting. Here he styles himself as progressive. 'I am for progress' (*tatawwur*), he said, 'I give legal opinions [*ufti*, 'I act as mufti'] . . . where developing the sharia [*tatwir al-shari'a*] is necessary, but within the text', citing as analogies the new Egyptian law for divorce at the wife's instance (*khul'*) or the mandatory bequest (*al-wasiyya al-wajiba*) to ensure that grandchildren inherit if their parent dies before the grandfather (not the case in the Lebanese courts).[18] He sees the opportunity and need for fresh argument (*ijtihad*) here, for 'piecing together' (*talfiq*) rulings from different schools, rather than sticking to just one as is nominally the case in Lebanon. 'The courts do not oppose Hanafi law. I can give an opinion according to any *madhhab* I want.' This, it is worth noting, is not a negligible claim.

The website reproduces some of these fatwas, many of which touch on the issues we discussed earlier. One (from 2014), 'Fatwa concerning a third divorce', is based upon a question (*istifta'*) concerning a husband's repudiation of his wife, 'the result of severe anger', which was the third after two previous divorces in court. Shaykh Hammoud, having been apprised of the facts of the incident in detail, and in particular of the intensity of the husband's anger (another, almost exactly similar fatwa talks of the husband banging his head against the wall and smashing up what was around him) and the lack of real intention (*irada haqiqiyya*), gives his opinion that the divorce does not stand.[19]

Another service demanded of him is 'a certain path in marriage or registering marriage or divorce. Here I have a problem with the courts. I do procedures the courts don't.' That includes performing a marriage without registering it with the state. Perhaps someone wants to emigrate. 'Sometimes, it depends on the laws', being married would make this more difficult. Or, 'Lebanese army members can't marry except after three years. So if they need to marry, they can't register it with the state, so I do that for them.' More than that, as some of his critics that I spoke with put it (a sharia court judge; a leading lawyer in the city), his popularity comes from being able to offer religious positions that are 'easy' (*mutasahila*). And he makes things easy (*tashil*) in other ways too: he does not charge very much; Palestinians go to him, again because of

[18] On the new Egyptian *khul'* law see Welchman 2007: 112–116. The 'mandatory bequest' is applied in Egypt and Syria. See Anderson 1955: 46–47.

[19] www.maherhammoud.com/_SubjectSearch.php?Action=Details&SubjectID=10... and www.maherhammoud.com/_SubjectSearch.php?Action=Details&SubjectID=13. . ., both accessed 23 June 2014. A judge who worked in Saida did report seeing in court such cases of divorce where the couple had had recourse to Shaykh Hammoud's opinions.

their difficult dealings with the Lebanese state. 'But no one respectable [*muhtaram*] would go there', the lawyer told me.

An important matter where Shaykh Hammoud's freedom counts is in the case of marriages where the father – the *wali*, or legal guardian – is against it.

This is a matter I was a specialist in, if that's the right expression, in the whole of Lebanon: if a person wanted to marry a girl and her father didn't want it. Sometimes I would write the contract without consulting the father, if I saw that the marriage was sincere [*muqni'*], as I heard it from the couple. But in truth this gave rise to problems, big problems – not due to my fault, but because it clashed with certain customs. So there was a big uproar against me in the courts, and cases. So eventually I changed, to telephoning the father of the girl and trying to convince him: new methods to allow this after big problems. Now I don't write the contract without the guardian except after consulting him, giving him the opportunity for that, knowing that sometimes he might have false suppositions – sometimes the *wali* is stormy [*muta'assif*]. But I go for agreement.

It is not that the courts do not have the power to overrule the *wali* if his opposition is unreasonable, as we have seen. 'But sometimes lads are in a hurry and want marriage directly. I say it needs at least 24 hours.' In any case, he told me, 'I'm relaxed, because I haven't done a contract, even contrary to the *wali*, where I have not seen that it has turned out for the best, over the years. Because I do this in pious fear [*taqwa*] of God and I consult [*astakhir*, i.e. perform *istikhara* of] God before doing it.' 'Yes, some people wrong me', by making allegations that he earns a great deal of money in the process. But, he told me, he mediates disputes involving millions of dollars, regarding real estate or inheritance, 'and I don't take a penny from anyone'.

What do the courts think? 'They changed all their rulings because of me', he chuckled. This was not the first time either, according to his account, which he was rather relishing. He referred to the institution of the arbitrator (*hakam*), resorted to in cases of judicial divorce in the Sunni courts as we have seen. Shaykh Hammoud served as a *hakam* for the courts for about ten years, he explained, and excelled in this quintessential shaykhly role. 'My office became the place for sorting out disputes, without them even going to the court. People would deal with me as though they didn't need the court – they have got Shaykh Maher.' The incoming president of the courts looked into the matter and decided to institute a new system for arbitration, whereby the *hakam* had to go to court and swear an oath before the judge, a clear expression of what he thought the proper hierarchy of authority was. 'It made it so [the *hakam*] was like an employee [*muwazzaf*] for the judge. So I wouldn't do that – and he knew that. The aim was to remove me from being a *hakam* – and he succeeded. But I was happy as it took a lot of my time.'

As for his activities assisting people get married, his problems began some years back because of one particular marriage he helped contract.

At 7 AM an officer, a major, above a sergeant, came with a girl – not nice-looking, sorry – he wanted to marry her. I knew that she was the daughter of the biggest grandee in Tripoli. This is an officer: he has a position in society. Her father was very angry – he is highly respected, and a good man, not just rich. Ten years afterwards, by chance I asked [someone], 'Do you know what happened about that marriage?' There was so much uproar [at the time], and, because of that marriage, Shaykh Nasr Salih – who was president of the courts then – made all the courts of Lebanon not accept the contract of Shaykh Maher. Shaykh Nasr was a very respected person, of course. And they said to me, 'That officer you married, it was famous – he was very bad, had lots of women, but after he married he became upstanding and has six boys by her.' God be magnified [*subhan Allah*]!

When the tide turned against him and the courts started to stop recognising marriage contracts that he had overseen, he went to the president of the courts and complained:

The marriage contract of Shaykh Maher, a man well-known [*ma'ruf*], has a weight in society, has political distinction [*haythiyya siyasiyya*], and thank God everybody knows our sincerity and steadfastness, but [the courts] don't accept it because, for you, Shaykh Maher doesn't have an official ascription [*sifa rasmiyya*] – and along comes someone who has married, in his hand he has a little piece of paper from a shaykh in a little village, unknown, we don't know his religion or his understanding of it, and they register it?!

So, according to Shaykh Hammoud at least, they changed the whole law on his account.[20] It became so that they would not register such a contract for anyone, except in desperate circumstances.

However, if these marriages are not registered with the state, I wondered, how could any subsequent disputes be adjudicated? Would he be prepared to rule with divorce, or custody of children, for instance? He reminded me that there was a woman waiting patiently for him today (still waiting, while we talked): she had come exactly for this (i.e. divorce), he told me. 'If I make a contract outside of the courts, I arrange this document', he continued, showing me a form. Headed 'Marriage contract' (*'aqd qiran*), with *basmala*, a suitable Quranic verse ('By another sign He created for you spouses from among yourselves, that you might live in peace with them, and planted love and kindness in your hearts. Surely there are signs for thinking men'; 30:21)[21] and then the *hamdala* ('Thanks be to God ...'), it sets out the names of the

[20] At the beginning of the 1990s, according to him.

[21] In Dawood's 1956 translation.

spouses, their dates of birth and mothers' names, the details of the bridal gift (*mahr*) and the time and date of the marriage, along with a line for 'observations'. There then follows a distinctive addition, a 'contract of arbitration' (*'aqd tahkimi*), stipulating that:

> The two contracting parties agree that Shaykh Maher Hammoud is a comprehensive arbitrator [*hakam mutlaq*], whose judgement is confirmed and effective in itself [*mubram nafidh 'ala asl-h*] in any dispute which may pertain between the spouses, and that he may rule as he sees fit, even were the matter to require that he rule with divorce between the spouses without recourse to the husband, if strife and discord [*al-shiqaq wa-l-niza'*] are apparent to him and the wife were to demand divorce, with what that entails with regard to legal and sharia responsibility. And this contract of arbitration is considered a binding condition of the contract in the event of its registration in the sharia court.

And below there are arranged places for the signatures of the spouses, the *wali* (note), two witnesses and the contractor (*al-'aqid*).

Shaykh Hammoud was proud of what he saw as his innovation, which he thought helped resolve some of the problems of 'external' contracts, namely that they left the wife in a weak position, and thought it clearly binding. 'Unfortunately the courts don't understand this. Where is the sharia proof [*dalil shar'i*] that this is wrong? None can answer.' Indeed he thought that if marriages contracted in court had a similar clause giving the judge such powers as a condition of the marriage, 'then if the judge sees that those conditions aren't applied, he can divorce her directly, and not spend years in court.' He is not, that is, an opponent of state involvement per se: 'There is a clear public interest [*maslaha*]. Without registration [i.e., of marriage] there would be chaos. I am not against registration. I am not against courts, no. We say that some details are not possible because the courts are tied by certain laws. We have more freedom in some matters.'

However, this kind of activity constitutes a profound challenge to the authority of the state, and Shaykh Hammoud has plenty of critics. As the lawyer quoted above put it, he profits from Lebanon's chaotic situation, and from its weak state. Such people are like 'mushrooms': when the state is weak up they come; when the state is strong it will cut them down. It was that same lawyer who apparently suggested to Shaykh Hammoud his new bureaucratic approach to his extra-legal activities, giving him a copy of the Beirut Chamber of Commerce and Industry's 'Rules of Conciliation and Arbitration' out of concern for his safety (the two are in fact kin by marriage, if very distant in outlook). If the Lebanese state ever becomes strong enough, the lawyer thought, Shaykh Hammoud could be prosecuted for all these 'crimes'.

Conclusion

In this chapter and the previous one, I have widened the perspective to include the world of sharia discourse and actors outside of the courts. Faced with a dilemma, people may well feel the need to seek the advice of a religious specialist on a more or less formal basis, and there is no shortage of them, within and outside the official community institutions. Such interactions may include discussions of what could be seen as legal issues (like divorce), as well as more strictly personal ethical ones, even if the official sharia courts alone have formal, state-recognised jurisdiction over family law. Where a shaykh serves as ethical or legal advisor, this is, potentially at least, a paradigmatically pedagogical moment. The frustrations of the judgeship in this regard can hopefully be avoided. (Although such interactions bring their own frustrations too, no doubt.)

As part and parcel of such attempts to help people with their problems, the plurality of the sharia becomes available in ways impossible within the courts. That is not to say that one cannot argue as a judge for different positions within the tradition – of course one can, as the example of our 'reformist' showed. But there are limits. In the courts, those limits can only really be transcended by a change to the institution itself. Against the inertia that such a complex institution of so many actors presents, such 'reform' can seem so daunting as to require someone of almost 'magical' powers to achieve it. An alternative path is independence from such institutions, setting oneself up as an authority, both pedagogical and – to a certain extent – judicial, outside of the official system altogether, as Shaykh Hammoud has. The sharia provides the resources to do so legitimately, although one needs more to carry it off in practice: a political and economic base upon which to work. Here, then, as in the example of our three judges, the tensions intrinsic to trying to 'apply' the sharia drive action, and thus also individual careers, and can do so in different directions.

Shaykh Hammoud's freedom to draw upon the breadth of the sharia tradition is important to the success of his project. Like the reformist judge Shaykh D, he invokes the classic modernist device of *talfiq*, the patching together of rulings from different *madhhab*s. He also invokes the talismanic notion of *ijtihad*, the scholar's 'effort' to derive the rulings of the sharia from its sources. For reformists, it is through *ijtihad* that new rulings can be developed to fit changing times. But such efforts have to be made by properly qualified scholars following the requisite methods. To claim such powers is to claim to be a scholar of some standing – and such claims can be contested. Similarly, although Islamic religious professionals constantly dispense advice as to the sharia as part of their pedagogical role, explicitly to term such advice a fatwa gives it a formality and weight that not every shaykh might want. In the final part of the book I turn to what is thus the ultimate form of such autonomy – and hence prestige – the capability not only to proffer guidance on, but even to determine the sharia, so far as humans can. I trace the path to becoming a *mujtahid*, an independent scholar of the law exercising his powers of *ijtihad*.

Part III

Sharia outside the State

12 Becoming an Ayatollah

One travels down the airport road from metropolitan Beirut to the Dahiya, the southern suburbs now the hub of Lebanon's Twelver Shiʿi community.[1] The big dual carriageway highway comes in from the centre of town, becoming – according to formal designation at least – Imam Khomeini Avenue. During my first fieldwork in 2003–2004 it passed over a mighty flyover, 'the airport bridge' (*Jisr al-matar*), to avoid the traffic of the suburbs. In 2007–2008, the bridge had gone, destroyed by Israeli bombardment in the 2006 war like much of the rest of the vicinity, reducing through traffic to a painfully slow crawl. Just past the bridge comes a road taking you into the municipality of Harat Hrayk, site of one of the Jaʿfari courts that I regularly attended. On the corner is the home of the Supreme Shiʿi Islamic Council, official centre of the Lebanese Twelver Shiʿi community, and its current chair and Shiʿi Mufti, Shaykh ʿAbd al-Amir Qabalan. Next door is what was then a brand new cultural centre, glittering with glass, the new Lebanese base for the offices of Iraq's Ayatollah ʿAli al-Sistani, widely talked of as 'the most learned' Shiʿi scholar of the age. Going down the side-road, one passes a seminary building on one side, on the other what had been an apartment block that housed the sharia affairs office of Ayatollah ʿAli al-Khamenei, Supreme Leader of the Islamic Republic of Iran and leading patron of the Lebanese Hizballah, but was in 2007–2008 just a hole in the ground. (The office moved to another apartment building nearby.) Portraits of Khamenei, his illustrious predecessor Imam Khomeini and Hizballah's charismatic secretary general Sayyid Hasan Nasrallah, are common across the area, reflecting Hizballah's dominance here.

Further down again, on a crossroads, sits the capacious al-Imamayn al-Hasanayn mosque. This was where my case study of a *mujtahid* preached, Ayatollah Muhammad Husayn Fadlallah (d. 2010), perhaps then Lebanon's most famous Shiʿi scholar. Like Sistani and Khamenei

[1] On life in the Dahiya see Deeb 2006 and Deeb and Harb 2013.

(but not Mufti Qabalan), Fadlallah was considered by his supporters a *marja'*, a 'source' of authoritative opinion as to the sharia, the highest form of religious authority in Shi'i Islam. As such he received religious tithes and donations – the mosque's construction was financed by one of his super-rich enthusiasts – and in turn maintained an expansive set of charitable institutions under his patronage.[2] Unlike the rival institutions of Hizballah, supported by the Islamic Republic of Iran, Fadlallah's income was independent of state subsidy.[3] Collections are taken within the mosque and outside it, through charity boxes, booths and offices where one can sponsor an orphan. One key staff member told me how he had announced a few days previous that new fans were needed for the mosque. Straight away one man had given him $300, a few others 100,000 Lebanese Lira. He opened up a wad of notes, and there they were. 'They trust the sayyid.'[4] On another level, an especially wealthy and generous benefactor might, hearing of a new project for a school for the blind for example, write out a cheque for a million dollars there and then.[5] Fadlallah's institutions had further been put on independent financial footing through investment in a chain of busy petrol stations ('The stations of the orphans' *Mahattat al-aytam*) and a now global restaurant enterprise ('The village', *al-Saha*), neo-traditional Lebanese consumer complexes with outlets in London and Doha, whose profits are ploughed back into the fund.[6]

I saw the mosque take shape over the years of my research, growing into a building capable of accommodating thousands, part of a complex that includes an impressive general public library and cultural centre

[2] The outlay was very considerable. In 2003, for instance, Fadlallah's charitable organisation al-Mabarrat alone spent some $7 million US on its then 3,500 orphans and 350 handicapped dependents (El-Ghoul 2004).

[3] But see Kramer's (1997: 105) comments on Fadlallah's nominal financial independence in his earlier years. The Lebanese state does provide part payment for some of these social services, let it be said (El-Ghoul 2004). Recently the charity complained of being unfairly damaged by the fall-out from US financial sanctions against Hizballah (Bassam 2016).

[4] A note on terms of address: a sayyid is a descendant of the Prophet Muhammad – as Fadlallah was – and accorded respect as such. Those shaykhs who are sayyids are generally addressed as 'sayyid' (roughly, 'Sir') rather than as 'shaykh'. 'Ayatollah' is a step up from that, indicating the highest levels of scholarship. In public contexts one might want to assert (or deny) such a status by using Ayatollah. But in general and informally, one referred to 'Sayyid Fadlallah' or just 'the sayyid'. I alternate between them. More grandly one might say 'His Eminence [*Samahat*] the Sayyid'; more affectionately, 'Sayyid Muhammad Husayn'.

[5] Sukkariyya 2007: 223. According to Deeb (2006: 89), the Bahman hospital was built with a donation of $60 million.

[6] On al-Saha see Deeb and Harb 2013.

extending several floors underground.[7] Beside the mosque is the sizeable Bahman Hospital, endowed by the same wealthy benefactor and an important part of the ayatollah's charitable network, *Jam'iyyat al-mabarrat al-khayriyya* ('The association of charitable organisations'), known as *al-Mabarrat* for short. According to Fadlallah's busy website, www.bayynat.org, as of 2012, al-Mabarrat ran nine orphanages across Lebanon supporting 4,000 orphans and fifteen schools educating 22,000 children, alongside numerous special needs schools, health centres and hospitals, and religious and cultural centres; a parallel office for social services provided assistance to 26,245 poor people, 7,640 orphans within foster families, 965 disabled persons and 817 elderly.[8]

Just across the road is a department for religious outreach (*al-tabligh al-dini*) in contact with outposts all over the world; turning right at the crossroads would take us down towards the site of Fadlallah's main offices and what used to be his house before it too was obliterated by Israeli bombing. And then there were his colleges of higher religious education, a media apparatus (with website, semi-operational television channel, radio station and weekly magazine), intellectual centres organising workshops, a publisher (Dar al-Malak) and an archive. And beyond, a whole set of institutions outside of Lebanon, including charitable foundations in Iraq, mosques and Islamic centres in Sydney, Abidjan, Berlin and Brazil, an Islamic school in Burkina Faso, and official offices in Syria and Iran, the latter not only distributing Fadlallah's books and raising awareness about him in Iran in Farsi, but also supervising the Farsi pages of the website and supporting activities in Pakistan, Afghanistan and Azerbaijan, not least through publishing the ayatollah's works in Urdu, Azeri and Turkish.[9]

I was a regular visitor here and elsewhere in the surrounding streets, going to court, visiting various parts of Fadlallah's organisation, buying books and meeting with other Shi'i religious personalities. And, whenever I could, I would attend the ayatollah's Friday sermon, the central moment in his weekly round of engagements and for me an iconic

[7] The library, opened to the public in 2004, claims a collection of 60,000 books, 'as a first step', including a section devoted to Fadlallah's works, and provides photocopying, computer and Internet facilities, as well as access to newspapers and magazines, dedicated study rooms and children's areas, and scientific and linguistic research resources provided, interestingly enough, by a gift from the (Saudi) Walid bin Talal Humanitarian Foundation. I draw here on a publicity leaflet from the centre.

[8] See arabic.bayynat.org.lb/tahkikat/tahkik_12062012.htm, accessed 13 June 2012; see also www.mabarrat.org.lb/profile/LOCATIONS, accessed 12 September 2013 and Deeb 2006: 88–90.

[9] See arabic.bayynat.org.lb/HtmalSecondary.aspx?id=2086, accessed 12 September 2013. See Clarke 2016 for further details.

representation of his work in the round. Fadlallah was known as a perspicacious and influential commentator on current affairs, and the sermon was a notable political event in its own right, its text circulated to Lebanon's major national and international news networks.[10] But it was not solely political, containing, as is conventional, a 'religious' section (*al-khutba al-diniyya*) of moral instruction as well as the 'political' sermon (*al-khutba al-siyasiyya*), the totality taking place, as it says at the top of the circulated version, 'in the presence of a number of clerical, political and social personalities and a gathering of the faithful', and broadcast on Fadlallah's radio station al-Basha'ir and his fledgling television channel al-Iman, posted on his website, and reproduced in the weekly youth newsletter *Bayyanat* distributed outside the mosque.

To enter one has to pass through a security check, filing through metal detectors and a pat-down search: Fadlallah was once the subject of an assassination attempt in the mosque itself.[11] The inner hall, entered through fine wooden doors, is gorgeously decorated as is the Shi'i (Iranian) norm, with glass, tiles, lights and a huge chandelier that dominates the dome above the richly carpeted floor. By and large, visiting dignitaries and those close to the sayyid would sit at the front, near the elaborate pulpit. One could imagine, if not quite map out, concentric circles of closeness to the personality at their centre. There is a gallery on the floor above for women, who enter by a separate entrance. Worshippers spill over into the outer ring, on carpets besides the extensive shelving for shoes, following the sermon through television relays. If this does not suffice for the overflow, mats can be laid down outside the mosque, weather permitting. This was a crowd of thousands, with people coming from across Beirut, as I could see afterwards as I rode the minibus back to the centre of town, along with groups of young men clutching the reading materials distributed. Not all would have been 'followers' of Fadlallah in the strict sense of religious dependency. The mosque is a congenial place for worship, and Fadlallah a more widely respected figure than that.

A key member of the sayyid's staff serves as compère, walking up and down the rows with a microphone and an assistant with the collection box, inviting the congregation to chant, 'God bless Muhammad and the family of Muhammad' (*Allahumma salli 'ala Muhammad wa-al Muhammad*), and distributing literature for the edification and education of the

[10] In 2007, I attended the Friday sermon seven times, in 2008 eight times; the wider corpus is readily available through other media: the weekly newsletter *Bayyanat*, cassette recordings and the website.

[11] Rosiny 2001: 219 and Sankari 2005: 265–266.

faithful – very often a slim volume of one hundred Islamic legal questions to and answers from the ayatollah, selected from the archives. I overheard a father and young son examining one together: 'It's about impurity [*najs*]', the father explained. The boy was fidgety during the sermon, but when the famous Quranic passage on the oneness of God (112:1–4) was recited ('He is God, one, God the eternal; He does not beget and was not begotten, and He has no equivalent'), his father turned to him to note, 'That's the most important thing.' This is an occasion for instruction and moral development: notice boards at the entrance announce various courses of religious education; and the compère would tell the congregation to keep quiet as a portion of the Quran was recited in beautiful tones over the PA. 'This is an opportunity for you to listen. The mosque is a place for devotion,' he would urge, sometimes even feeling the need to remind them that it is obligatory to listen to the sermon too. Such a large crowd needs marshalling.

And then the ayatollah himself would appear on the pulpit, flanked by two bodyguards cum helpers, and greeted by the congregation standing and chanting 'God bless Muhammad', the effect of thousands of voices impressive, and repeated whenever the names of the Prophet and Imams are mentioned during the hour-long sermon. The 'religious' section would proffer moral instruction, on the cultivation of a God-fearing attitude (*taqwa*), or sincerity (*sidq*) and faith (*iman*), for instance, or the proper attitude to anger or brotherly care and compassion; the examples of the Prophet and the Imams might be deployed; Fadlallah's characteristic emphasis on the centrality of reason (*'aql*) in understanding and exercising one's faith often developed. Then came the political section, usually somewhat longer, an incisive and well-informed analysis of the week's events, generally starting with the latest news concerning the Palestinian situation, before turning to the ongoing machinations of Zionist, American and European imperialism, developments in the region and Lebanese affairs. Fadlallah's style, at this point in his life at any rate, was not that of the haranguing demagogue: rather it was calm and measured, intellectual and academic, with the occasional flash of righteous anger, the linguistic register correspondingly formal, but not obscurantist, the use of colloquial Arabic rationed.[12]

The sermon completed, there is an immediate transition into the prayers, a long and complex routine, the more so because the Shi'i tradition allows the joining of the noon and afternoon prayers consecutively in this one session. These are further punctuated with individual

12 See also Karanshawy 2013: 213ff. Cf. Kramer's description of the younger Fadlallah's style (1997: 92).

supererogatory prayers and the making up of ones previously missed, worshippers processing devotional movements at high pace. With such a large crowd, the effect is less regimented than stereotype might lead one to expect, but undeniably powerful. One leaves to the chanting of devotions over the loudspeakers, perhaps receiving some perfume daubed on one hand or a book thrust upon you as you grab your shoes. Outside, people tarry in the vicinity, mingling and greeting friends and colleagues. There is much activity: people begging, distributing copies of the newsletter, selling posters of the sayyid, taking donations for the resistance; there are vegetable sellers further down the road.

All in all, this is a total event to match the totality of its presiding authority: a religious, spiritual obligation and experience; moral edification but also political enlightenment. Its scale is impressive. It speaks to and brings together many elements of a larger organisation – charitable, educational and politically engaged – that is deeply embedded in local society and centred on one notable personality. That totality is, however, not quite complete, in at least one important respect. This authority does not extend to a monopoly over violence, legitimate or otherwise: it is not, in other words, totalitarian. Its security is guaranteed rather by its situation within the sphere of Hizballah's control, as discreet signs remind you.[13] Notwithstanding Fadlallah's reputation as the paramilitary movement's mentor, that speaks to a certain vulnerability, as we will see.

I started this book with an account of a shaykh at the beginning of his career: I now end it with one who was in its fullest flower, a towering figure on the Lebanese and indeed global stage, with, he estimated, more than a million followers across the world.[14] To be a *marja'* – or, in full, a *marja'* (pl. *maraji'*) *al-taqlid*, a 'source of emulation', or 'Grand Ayatollah' (*ayat allah al-'uzma*, 'Supreme Sign of God') – is to have reached the very heights of what is a relatively formal religious hierarchy within Shi'i Islam. But, stripped back, we can discern the same fundamental principles of the shaykhly vocation that I have stressed throughout: the prestige of learning of course, but also the obligation to share it through pedagogy; the openness to the problems of the community and intense commitment to addressing them; and the courage to speak truth to power, to be a 'real shaykh' and not merely one licensed through paper qualification. A *marja'* is, however, above all an authoritative scholar of the sharia. Every *marja'* is, necessarily, a *mujtahid*, qualified to perform *ijtihad* – that is, to derive the rulings of the sharia from its sources. But the

13 On Hizballah's provision of Fadlallah's security see Sankari 2005: 202.

14 For the claim as to the number of his 'followers' (*muqallidin*, see below), hard to verify, see Sukkariyya 2007: 73.

role, at least as incarnated by Fadlallah, is much broader than that. In this chapter, I want to begin by giving a further sense of that breadth, before going on to focus more narrowly on the sharia discursive aspects that are the particular concern of this book.

A Multi-Faceted Career

This phenomenon did not emerge spontaneously on such a scale. It took decades of work, even if Fadlallah started with many advantages.[15] He was born in 1935 in the prestigious shrine city of Najaf, Iraq, to a distinguished Lebanese scholarly family with roots in the Jabal ʻAmil in the south of Lebanon, which holds a special place in the Shiʻi imaginary.[16] Such origins remain highly prestigious within the Lebanese Shiʻi community, as does Fadlallah's claim to be related to the Prophet through his elder grandson Hasan, whence his title as '*sayyid*' – roughly, 'sir' – reflected in the black turban he wore. Fadlallah's father had, like so many before him, travelled from Lebanon to what was then the greatest centre of Shiʻi learning in the world to pursue his religious studies. Fadlallah remembered his childhood as a hard one, due to the severe poverty of the scholarly life, and Najaf as a 'suffocating' place in which to grow up. Then there was the political turmoil which Iraq endured during the 'chaos' of the monarchy and the revolution of 1958 when the country was 'plunged into a sea of blood'. And the young Fadlallah was also deeply affected by the wider plight of the world's Muslims, and most especially by the fate of Palestine. The sufferings broadcast by the media, he said, 'implant[ed] inside us a political pain [*alaman siyassiyan*]', that became 'a missionary pain [*alaman risaliyyan*]' that he would bear for his whole life.

As a young man, he attracted attention more through his literary endeavours – his poetry fills several volumes. But he also embarked on a classical *hawza* (seminary) education. Apparently an outstanding student, he began the highest level research classes at the age of sixteen, studying under such luminaries as Ayatollah Muhsin al-Hakim (d. 1970), then senior cleric of the Najaf colleges, and his successor

[15] Fadlallah's biography has been well treated elsewhere, and I thus only provide a sketch here. See Kramer (1997) and especially Sankari (2005) for fuller accounts. In addition to those, I also draw on the biographical data provided on Fadlallah's website (*al-Sira al-dhatiyya*, henceforth referred to here as '*al-Sira*', arabic.bayynat.org.lb/sira, accessed 4 July 2010) and a rich collection of wide-ranging and revealing interviews with him near the end of his life (Sukkariyya 2007).

[16] Scholars from there, so tradition has it, 'converted' Iran to Shiʻi Islam, summoned by its Safavid rulers to institute its scholarly tradition. See e.g. Abisaab 2004.

Ayatollah Abu l-Qasim al-Khu'i (d. 1992). But where Khu'i upheld the values and teachings of the traditional *hawza*, Fadlallah was also intimately involved in the radical intellectual currents of those turbulent times, a close collaborator with Ayatollah Muhammad Baqir al-Sadr (d. 1980), the brilliant reformist scholar commonly seen as the intellectual founder of the Islamist Iraqi Da'wa party, with which Fadlallah would retain enduring ties. Khu'i was pre-eminent in Najaf for decades, in Fadlallah's words, simply 'the seminary's teacher' (*ustadh al-hawza al-'ilmiyya*), standing 'at the summit of the education of thousands'. His scholarly pre-eminence made him also the favoured 'source of emulation' for millions of Shi'a worldwide and thus the channel for vast charitable resources. His financial support would be important for Fadlallah later. But the sheer numbers of Khu'i's students made his scholarly *imprimatur* hard to obtain. Fadlallah would leave Najaf in 1966 after twenty-two years of religious studies, fifteen at the highest level without having become one of the handful of his most favoured pupils.[17] Notwithstanding his years of study, the level which Fadlallah had reached within the traditional seminary framework by the time he left would later be the subject of debate.

While the reasons why Fadlallah left Najaf are not wholly clear, it was on the invitation of a Shi'i religious association in an impoverished suburb of East Beirut that proved an ideal location for Fadlallah's missionary zeal.[18] The subsequent move to the rapidly expanding southern suburbs came amidst the turmoil of the civil war. Fadlallah's enduring presence amongst his people during the war, sharing its terrors with them, was appreciated and remembered in my conversations with those around him (and later repeated during the war with Israel in 2006, when he remarked, 'I love to be with the people, and I do not like to be set apart from them, even in this way'[19]). Even in such circumstances he maintained an impressive intellectual output, authoring, among many other things, a pioneering work on *Islam and the Logic of Power*, as well as a treatise on Muslim-Christian dialogue.[20] In Shi'i scholarly terms, however, Beirut was then very much on the margins.

He had come to Lebanon at a particularly dynamic moment, its Shi'i community galvanised under the leadership of Sayyid Musa al-Sadr (see Chapter 1). While the two were no doubt on cordial terms, Fadlallah was

[17] Kramer 1997: 87–88; Sankari 2005: 47–49; Sukkariyya 2007: 115, 187 and Mottahedeh 2016: 344. On Khu'i, see e.g. Corboz 2015.

[18] On Fadlallah's reasons for leaving contrast Kramer 1997: 90 with Sankari 2005: 120–121.

[19] Sukkariyya 2007: 180, 251.

[20] Sankari 2005: 157–158.

an adamant supporter of the Palestinian cause, where Sadr had to manage the ravages of the PLO's war with Israel in the Shi'i south of Lebanon; and Fadlallah would have preferred an ecumenical Islamic council uniting Sunnis and Shi'a over Sadr's creation of a Supreme Shi'i Islamic Council as an equivalent to the Maronite Patriarchate and Sunni Dar al-Fatwa – the official seat of the community, recognised by the state. Fadlallah kept his distance, saying he would not stand for or vote in elections to the council. That was not his way: 'I work in the general Islamic public sphere [*al-saha al-islamiyya al-'amma*]. So when the Shi'i Council was founded, and people rushed to congratulate it, I did not.'[21]

After Sadr's disappearance on a trip to Libya in 1978, the council would be headed by his deputy, Fadlallah's childhood friend and fellow traveller in Najaf, Shaykh Muhammad Mahdi Shams al-Din, who also had southern Lebanese roots and had returned to the ancestral land to follow his own mission. Fadlallah and Shams al-Din had grown up together – 'brothers in all but name', had both been members of that emerging young Islamist coterie in Najaf, and were in many ways intellectually and jurisprudentially like-minded.[22] Their personal styles seem to have differed, however. According to the no doubt partisan account of one of Fadlallah's staff members, Shams al-Din was not one to accept discussion. 'He set himself above the people. The Sayyid [Fadlallah] was with the people.' But it was their institutional commitments that would divide them. Shams al-Din became part of the Lebanese Shi'i establishment in a way that Fadlallah did not. According to my source, that entailed having to make compromises, perhaps unfortunate alliances. Others would see this as the hard graft of ensuring integration into the knotty political fabric of Lebanon.[23] Whatever the case, while his admirers would reckon him a peerless intellect, Shams al-Din did not achieve the same renown (or academic interest) as his childhood friend.

The Iranian revolution and the institution of the Islamic Republic in 1979 brought great opportunities for Lebanon's Shi'a, but also risks, namely a tension between securing Iran's good will and not panicking other communities with fears of an Islamic state or Iranian puppet-masters. Those among Lebanon's Shi'i clerical elite who had secured posts in the newly constituted 'official' community bodies, such as the Supreme Shi'i Council and the Ja'fari courts, were conflicted in this

21 Sukkariyya 2007: 192. See also Sankari 2005: 144–147.

22 On the latter point see e.g. El-Husseini 2008. The quote is from Kramer 1997: 135. See also Sankari 2005: 91, 104, 179–180, 331–332n91 and Shams al-Din's official biography (Mu'assasat al-Imam Shams al-Din li-l-Hiwar 2004).

23 On Shams al-Din's politics see Kawtharani 2016.

regard in ways that Fadlallah, who had carefully eschewed such roles, was not.[24] Fadlallah embraced the revolution, as well as, initially at least, the Khomeinist doctrine of the 'guardianship of the jurisprudent' (*wilayat al-faqih*) over the state, although in qualified fashion: he argued for a plurality of elected such ruling clerics for different localities, rather than a single ruler over all.[25]

It was not, however, that Fadlallah was attempting to erect himself as the governing 'guardian jurist' for his locality. He stayed clear of party politics and direct action. His particular inflection of *wilayat al-faqih* was, it seems, more a way of maintaining his autonomy. While he was clear that, in good Islamist fashion, Islam was 'religion and state' (*din wa-dawla*) and that the ultimate struggle was for an Islamic state, he was also clear that that end goal was not one to be imposed on Lebanon through revolutionary overthrow of the current political system. He advocated a gradualist approach, based on reform of Muslim society and dialogue with other religious constituencies, and an interim stage of a 'humane state' (*dawlat al-insan*) that would guarantee individual rights regardless of religion.[26] He was known for his ecumenical stance, interested in both Sunni–Shi'i and Muslim–Christian rapprochement; and his vision of Lebanese civility was one that sought to transcend the sectarian accommodation. He had influential supporters beyond the Shi'i community, including sometime Prime Minister Salim al-Hoss and Ghassan Toueini, editor of the distinguished al-Nahar newspaper. One middle-aged Sunni woman even told me that she had had a dream about Sayyid Fadlallah when she was first pregnant, in which he told her the child would be a boy (and it was). She 'likes him a lot'.

But on the other hand, he also became closely associated with a new power on the Lebanese scene, the Iranian-backed Hizballah. This close association brought him enduring notoriety in Western policy and media circles, which dubbed him the movement's 'spiritual guide' and blamed him for the devastating suicide bomb attacks on the American marine compound and French paratrooper barracks in 1983, as well as harbouring suspicions over his role in the subsequent Lebanese hostage crisis.[27] Fadlallah was suddenly a globally recognised phenomenon. While he eschewed any formal role within the movement, as he had with al-Da'wa, he was certainly instrumental in the education and politicisation of a generation radicalised by the Israeli invasion and occupation of South

24 Kramer 1997: 102. 25 Aziz 2001: 212 and Sankari 2005: 176–177.
26 Sankari 2005: 176–181, 238–241.
27 Much ink has been spilled over this. See Kramer 1997: 109–114, 136–141; Sankari 2005: 205–210, 217–219 and Sukkariyya 2007: 199–201.

Lebanon in 1982. As he himself later acknowledged, 'In reality, every generation of Hizballah was brought up by my hand.'[28]

Fadlallah's increasingly high profile brought risks. He was the subject of a number of assassination attempts, including most notably a massive car bomb in 1985 that missed him but killed more than 80 people, injuring some 260 others and causing widespread destruction. Following the reports of *The Washington Post* and American journalist Bob Woodward, as well as a Hizballah-led investigation, Fadlallah attributed the genesis of the attack to the CIA, in revenge for the Marines' barracks bombing (which he denied having any part in) and fear of his growing influence, and pursued through a shadowy network of hostile local and regional actors and financiers.[29]

Such was the scale of the 'massacre' (*majzara*) and the narrowness of Fadlallah's escape, his survival was widely believed to imply special divine favour. The bomb had been placed on his habitual path from Friday prayers to his home; he was rescued only by being delayed by the persistent attempts of a woman to get him to answer some questions for her. According to the woman herself, she had had a dream prefiguring the event, but in which Fadlallah had been killed – rumours of his intended assassination were then rife. She had performed a divination (*istikhara*) to see whether she should go to the mosque to tell the sayyid about her dream. The response was positive, indeed insistent. But having gone, she found him surrounded by a dense crowd after prayers. She would never normally have had the courage to be so importunate, but it was, she said, as though an angel descended upon her from on high inspiring her to do so. The sayyid refused her requests to talk, pleading exhaustion, but she would not let him go, emboldened by some divine, spiritual power. It was 'a grace from God' (*fadl min allah*) that saved him, not her, she said.[30]

It has been claimed that it was from this date that his followers started calling him 'ayatollah'.[31] Certainly, the commemoration of the event that started the next year and its incorporation into the Fadlallah narrative

[28] Sukkariyya 2007: 167–168. On the wider activist society that he helped nurture see e.g. Deeb 2006.

[29] Woodward 1987: 396–398; Kramer 1997: 131–132; Sankari 2005: 209 and Markaz Bayyanat li-l-Internet wa-l-Dirasat 2008.

[30] Markaz Bayyanat 2008: 53–56.

[31] Kramer 1997: 131–132. For some corroborative evidence see the quotation of a relative of one of the victims of the explosion in a 1986 edition of the Hizballah periodical *al-'Ahd* and the opening address of the first annual commemoration of the event, both cited in a commemorative booklet circulated by Fadlallah's offices (Markaz Bayyanat 2008: 34, 35).

testify to its importance for the construction of his authority.[32] Although, as we will see, Fadlallah carved out a role as representative of a rationalist and modernist vision of Islam and the Shiʿi tradition, this miraculous escape from the aggression of the overwhelming power of the enemy played some part in the forging of his charisma. But it speaks too to the dedication of the 'real shaykh' to their flock. Fadlallah was saved by his loyal following, in the quintessential form of one woman's questions.

Fadlallah had thus by now built a multi-faceted reputation of the first order. And at the end of the civil war, there came a window of opportunity within the field of highest Shiʿi religious authority, with the deaths of the dominant figures of first Khomeini, in 1989, and then of Khu'i, in 1992. That window threatened immediately to close again, however, in new ways. Moves were made in the Islamic Republic to promote Khomeini's designated successor as Supreme Leader, ʿAli al-Khamenei, to the rank of *marjaʿ* in order to preserve the unity of religious and political authority that Khomeini had represented. To consider Khamenei, no great scholar, as 'the most learned' was inconceivable, and the move was controversial and contested. While Fadlallah had deemed Khomeini exemplary in his political consciousness and engagement with the global issues of the age, he was not, it seems, prepared to acknowledge Khamenei, obviously not his superior in learning, as heir to that mantle. Instead, in the mid-1990s, Fadlallah allowed his followers to put him forward as a *marjaʿ* himself.[33]

The *Marjaʿiyya*

Some further explanation is needed at this point of the role of *marjaʿ*, or the *marjaʿiyya*, as the institution is called.[34] Let me begin by quoting the opening words of the three volume comprehensive guide to the sharia authored by perhaps currently the most widely recognized such figure, Ayatollah Sistani, based in the famous seminary city of Najaf, but with admirers all over the world:

> It is obligatory for every person religiously liable [*mukallaf*, i.e., before God] who has not reached the level of *ijtihad* to be, in all his devotions and transactions, and

[32] Markaz Bayyanat 2008: 6, 25 and passim. This commemoration was used for such purposes after Fadlallah's death as well: see Clarke 2016.

[33] Hasani 1994: 80–81, 87–89, 122–123 and Khalaji 2006: 22–24, 27–31. One does not proclaim one's own ambition, let it be said – that would be to detract from the aura of piety the role requires. Fadlallah denied that he himself desired to become a *marjaʿ*, with all the pressures of its 'traditional aspects', occupied with other affairs as he was. That is why, he said, he initially backed Sistani. Sukkariyya 2007: 206 and Walbridge 2014: 25–26.

[34] See e.g. Walbridge 2001; Corboz 2015.

the rest of his deeds and his omissions, an emulator [*muqallid*, i.e., of someone who has reached that level, a *mujtahid*].[35]

Ijtihad is the effort of deriving the rulings of the sharia from its sources; a *mujtahid* is someone properly qualified to do so. This is, one might note, a rather shallow hierarchy of religious authority: one is either a *mujtahid*, capable of grasping the sharia properly oneself, or one is not. But to be a *mujtahid* is no small thing. It takes years, decades even, of dedicated study to master the sharia, in all its breadth and depth. Admittedly, in today's reformed seminaries, in Iran at least, one can now pursue degree-like courses that culminate in a certificate of *ijtihad*. But in the religious imagination, in Lebanon at least, the achievement remains something more rarefied. *Mujtahid*s are scholars of the most exceptional stature, formed in the greatest colleges of the Shi'i world.

When you reach the age of majority, you should – according to this, the 'textbook' model – choose a *mujtahid* to guide your religious observance, and ideally stick to them. This will then guarantee the soundness of your religious observance. Of course, far from everyone's religious practice follows the ideal version. Most religious duties are a matter of common knowledge rather than dilemma and many only turn to such an expert in rare cases of need. And when they do, they might turn to whichever source happens to be closest to hand. And while there may indeed be many contemporary committed Shi'i Muslims fully engaged with this dominant model of religious observance, there are many others, educated, confident or simply blasé, who feel they can do very well for themselves in religious terms. For them, 'emulation' (*taqlid*) may seem outdated. We must reckon then on a spectrum of loyalty ranging from formal adherence through to a more vaguely expressed enthusiasm: 'I like him.' And allegiances change.[36]

Those *mujtahid*s that allow and attract such 'emulation' of their opinions emerge as *marja'*s.[37] Becoming a *marja'* is thus not a matter of official appointment: one rises through popular demand rather than by *fiat*.[38] Not every *mujtahid* has such ambitions. Some fear the potentially polluting engagement with the world that it entails. And God will weigh the scholar's responsibility for the moral decisions of their adherents on Judgement Day. As Fadlallah's son Shaykh 'Ali put it to me in a neat, if conventional, play on words, their *taqlid* is like a necklace (*qilada*) upon

[35] Sistani 2002 vol. 1: 9. [36] See e.g. Clarke and Inhorn 2011.
[37] So all *marja'*s are *mujtahid*s – and I sometimes use the phrase *marja'-mujtahid*s to remind the reader of that point – but not all *mujtahid*s become *marja'*s.
[38] Amanat 1988. The case of Iran's Supreme Leader, Ayatollah Khamenei, effectively backed by the Iranian state apparatus, is arguably different. See Khalaji 2006.

the *marja*'s shoulders.[39] The predominant opinion, not shared by Fadlallah, due perhaps to his relatively marginal status, is that one should have recourse to 'the most learned' (*a'lam*) *mujtahid* of all. But who that might be is, in our era, far from clear. There are dozens of *marja*'s across the Shi'i world with more or less significant followings. As a mark of their status, it is expected that the *marja*' will produce a comprehensive guide to the demands of the sharia for their enthusiasts' benefit, the *risala 'amaliyya*, or 'practical treatise'.[40] I quoted above from that of Sistani, 'The Way of the Righteous' (*Minhaj al-salihin*). Such handbooks cover pretty much the full sweep of life, from religious observance to family relations to commercial transactions, in a clear representation of the 'totality' of the sharia's address. But they will not answer every question, and the *marja*' is thus also open to the queries of the faithful, nowadays very often received and answered via email and a website.

This is, it should be said, a distinctively Twelver Shi'i model of religious authority. Nonetheless, in terms of the schematic contrast I invoked earlier in the book between the judge and the mufti, the *marja*' clearly fulfils the latter function, albeit in the most prestigious and exclusive terms: it is the *mujtahid*s, and they alone within the Shi'i scholarly community, who have the right to issue fatwas, definitive opinions as to the sharia. Sunni Islam differs in having come to allow the possibility of lesser, non-*mujtahid* muftis, not licenced to derive such opinions themselves, but able to relay those of others.[41] 'Mufti' is, however, not a term I heard used much in Shi'i scholarly circles. In contemporary Lebanon at least, the title evokes more the cadre of administrative posts in the official religious community rather than any sense of scholarly prestige. In Sunni circles, on the other hand, while the role and title of mufti is a familiar one, that of *mujtahid*, by contrast, is not. It would seem too grand perhaps, evoking the greatest innovators of the founding era of the schools of Sunni law, even if there are many bold contemporary Sunni jurists and much talk of their practice of *ijtihad*.

More controversial is the extent of the Twelver Shi'i *mujtahid*'s right to judgement and rule (*qada'*, or *hukm*). The 'traditionalist' position sees the *mujtahid* as qualified to arbitrate over people's disputes, and as having *wilaya*, 'authority' or 'guardianship', over the financial affairs of minors, orphans and those otherwise legally incapable. A *mujtahid* could certainly

39 Interview, Beirut, 21 June 2008.
40 See Mottahedeh 2014.
41 Hallaq 1996. In Shi'i circles, scholars who are not yet *mujtahid*s can become 'agents' (*wukala'*, sing. *wakil*), or representatives, of the *marja*'s, licenced by them to communicate their opinions to the laity, among other things. But there remains a radical distinction between them and the *mujtahid*s proper.

serve as a judge then (here usually termed *hakim*, or *hakim shar'i*, the 'rightful judge'). But in the absence of the perfect justice of the Twelfth Hidden Imam, who will only return at the end of days, all human rule is perceived as fundamentally illegitimate. The question then becomes that of the legitimacy of working for such necessarily unjust government. We have already noted how this motif and the long history of the Shi'a's relative exclusion within the Ottoman Empire plays into the imaginaries of judges in the Ja'fari courts, who suppose that their Sunni colleagues are far better acquainted with the demands of working within the state. But this rather unworldly stance seems almost quaint in the contemporary setting, where, since the culmination of the Iranian Revolution in 1979, the notion of an 'Islamic state' has been exemplified by the Shi'i Islamic Republic, underpinned by Khomeini's famous extension of the authority or guardianship of the jurist (*wilayat al-faqih*) over executive government, and Hizballah has become the dominant force in Lebanese Shi'i and national politics.[42]

Highly controversial, Khomeini's position (which itself evolved over time) has now become an inescapable reference point in a wide-ranging debate in Shi'i scholarly circles.[43] As we have seen, Fadlallah saw himself – and was seen by others – as an 'Islamist', an 'activist' (*haraki*) rather than a 'traditionalist' (*taqlidi*). And his legal handbooks maintained a correspondingly expansive, if qualified, notion of the political authority of the jurist, who is to have 'authority and power over administering the general affairs of the people'.[44] Nevertheless, as we have already noted, his particular interpretation of *wilayat al-faqih* maintained the possibility of local independence, and thus resisted the subordination of all to the Supreme Leader of Iran, 'Ali al-Khamenei. And, over time, this independence was, it seems, accompanied by an increasing scepticism towards the Khomeinist model and appreciation of the positive aspects of Western liberal democracy. It was in this sense, I think, that some have seen Fadlallah as, by the end of his life, 'the most important jurisprudent

[42] On the judgeship in Shi'i thought see Calder 1979; Madelung 1980 and Gleave 2000, 2003, 2008; on Khomeini's notion of *wilayat al-faqih* Calder 1982 and Amanat 2007.

[43] See Aziz 1996; Gleave 2007 and Rizvi 2010.

[44] *Li-l-faqih al-wilaya wa-l-sulta 'ala idarat shu'un al-nas al-'amma* (Fadlallah 2002–2003 vol. 1: 17). And see ibid. 17–19 and Fadlallah 2005a vol.1: 26 and 2009: 31–37, where a potential plurality of guardian jurisprudents could hold general, if qualified power over political, economic, social, and security matters, subject to election by majority and in consultation with a panel of technical experts. See also Mottahedeh 2014: 17–18. I have to admit, however, that I have not found it easy to establish definitively where Fadlallah stood here. (Aziz 2001 finds such ambivalence typical of Fadlallah's stances more generally.) His position on *wilayat al-faqih* clearly evolved over time, and other commentators say otherwise.

standing against the idea of *wilayat al-faqih'* in Lebanon.[45] But we should still remember that there were and are very many in clerical circles in Lebanon, and especially within the state-sponsored Shiʿi religious establishment, much more deeply suspicious of political Islam in general, and Hizballah in particular, for reasons of both domestic politics and religious conviction. Given its formidable capabilities, Hizballah is spoken of by some, pejoratively, as a 'state within the state', although that also speaks to its anti-establishment positioning, even if it has chosen – against the wishes of some of its key figures – to enter the field of Lebanese parliamentary politics.[46] Fadlallah, on the other hand, remained aloof from all such involvements. In terms of the distinctions that I have drawn in this book, he firmly belonged to the world of independent authority beyond the state.

Keeping up with the Times

Fadlallah's political consciousness and engagement, his being 'with the people' throughout the war and Israeli occupation, the provision of social services, miraculously surviving attempted assassination by the CIA, his Arab, Lebanese and aristocratic identity, and above all his local presence, all gave him the base he needed to sustain his claim to the highest authority in Lebanon.[47] But his popularity also derived from the range of distinctive sharia-legal opinions that he held, which were in themselves essential to his emergence as a *marjaʿ*, a source of authoritative religious guidance. The publication in the mid-1990s of a collection of his responses to people's sharia-legal questions (*istiftaʾat*) was taken as a public statement of his claims to the *marjaʿiyya*. This would later – in the early 2000s – be sealed with the publication of his *risala ʿamaliyya*, the comprehensive, multi-volume legal handbook the *marjaʿ* provides for the guidance of his followers.[48] Becoming a *marjaʿ* is thus, one might note in passing, more a gradual process than a discrete event.

45 Deeb and Harb 2013: 244n44. See also Abisaab and Abisaab 2014: 185–186, 200, but cf. 198. Notwithstanding the published positions cited earlier, one very well-placed source told me in 2008 that Fadlallah had not held to the expansive notion of *wilayat al-faqih* for some years by that point. Rather he maintained the need to preserve public order for the Muslim *umma*, whether served by an Islamic jurist or not. Authority belongs to the law (*al-wilaya li-l-qawanin*), or to Islamic legal discourse rather than the jurist as individual (*wilayat al-fiqh* rather than *wilayat al-faqih*, a neat play on words).

46 Abisaab and Abisaab 2014: 144.

47 Regarding his nationalist credentials, he said that he was always Lebanese, even when he was in Iraq; he never held a passport other than a Lebanese one (Sukkariyya 2007: 234).

48 Fadlallah 2005a [1995?] and 2002–2003 respectively. On the former see Aziz 2001: 208, 213.

Just as, in his social and political activism, Fadlallah could be seen as engaged in 'solving our problems', so too did he address his community's 'religious problems', as a staff member put it. Religion came to serve people's needs, not vice versa, the ayatollah maintained: it should be easy, not a hardship.[49] So Fadlallah affirmed the intrinsic purity of the human being (*taharat al-insan*), as against those who thought contact with the religious other (Christian, atheist) religiously polluting. That was important in a plural context like Lebanon, or indeed the West or other sites of migration. Fadlallah was not the first or only to rule in this way: the great Lebanese scholar Sayyid Muhsin al-Amin (d. 1952), also from Jabal 'Amil, famously held that opinion. But it was important and symptomatic, part of his wider 'universalist' approach to religion, rather than the particularism of sectarian stances, that also led him to advocate a 'humanist state' (*dawlat al-insan*), albeit nominally as a stepping stone to an Islamic one.[50] And he 'made things easy' in other ways too. Shaving of the beard was allowed by him, thus allowing men to abide by office regulations. Playing cards and other games without gambling was permitted. He did not forbid music, nor even song, not even sung by a woman, so long as the words are not inappropriate. He did not forbid images of the person, nor even films depicting the Prophet and his companions, which could be so useful for 'calling' people to Islam (*da'wa*). He allowed the eating of certain types of seafood (lobster), unusually, but helpfully given that they were commonly fished in the south.[51]

His progressive attitude towards combating what one of his leading students calls the 'jurisprudential oppression of women' was especially renowned and appreciated.[52] Recall from Chapter 6 his allowing women to marry as they wish, without requiring the permission of their father. Women could also, according to him, but not all other Shi'i authorities, inherit land; they do not require their husbands' permission to leave the house; they can be divorced from their husbands if neglected. This latter was tied to Fadlallah's open and realistic attitude towards sexuality: women have sexual needs; controversially, he even deemed female masturbation possible if the woman would otherwise be dragged to sin. Abortion might be allowed if a woman's life was in danger from 'honour

49 Sukkariyya 2007: 29, 45. Remember one lawyer's invocation of this motif.

50 Kramer 1997: 128; Fadlallah 2002–2003 vol. 1: 46–47; 2009: 56 and Mervin 2000: 196. And see Sukkariyya 2007: 32 on 'the humanity of the person' (*insaniyyat al-insan*).

51 Shakhuri 1998: passim. See also Aziz 2001 and Deeb 2006: 71n12, 92–94 and Deeb and Harb 2013: 80–84, 87, 137–138.

52 Shakhuri 2002: 13. See also Sukkariyya 2007: 209–210.

crimes'. Women in the West can wear a wig instead of the veil if it spares them discrimination. Nail varnish is not an impediment to ritual purity. He even allowed the possibility of female *maraji'*, ruled out by most others.[53]

His 'keeping up' with scientific advance was exemplified by his advocacy of the use of astronomy to determine the onset of the new moon, and hence the beginning of the lunar month and thus the fasting month of Ramadan. He was well known for his opinions on medical ethical issues, and was a regular speaker to scientifically minded audiences, even at the prestigious American University of Beirut and Catholic St Joseph University, challenging venues for a Muslim clerical actor. The jurist should, he felt, never find themselves on the wrong side of 'scientific data'. That was what underpinned his position on female masturbation: where some legal traditions discussed women's vaginal excretions as analogous to male semen, modern medical science knows them to be lubricants without reproductive material. To think otherwise, comments one of his students, would be like sticking to the notion that 'the earth rests on the horns of a bull', also to be found in the traditional corpus. His positive – or at least not dismissive – reaction to the advent of research into cloning was heavily trailed in the media.[54]

This 'open-mindedness' was portrayed as a result of the Lebanese context in which Fadlallah found himself, plural, cosmopolitan and open to modernity and the West, as opposed to the cloistered environs of the shrine cities of Iran and Iraq, in which the majority of *maraji'* are situated. Being in Lebanon forces an engagement with the realities of global contemporary life rather than allowing a scholar to ignore them: 'I am a child of the times' (*ana ibn al-'asr*), he said. As Fadlallah's son Sayyid Ja'far put it to me, Lebanon has diversity (*tanawwu'*) – Christians, but also atheists and communists – and from diversity comes openness. He quoted his father: 'The truth is the daughter of dialogue'. Thus, as Fadlallah himself averred, in the 'traditionalist milieu' of Najaf and Qom (Najaf's great rival in Iran), 'It is very hard for these colleges [*hawzat*] to advocate the message of contemporaneity [*risalat al-mu'asara*], to push people towards the heart of the age to a degree where they will not fall before its challenges and aberrations.' Lebanon, however, with its unique freedoms, gave him 'an opening onto the global plane',

53 Hamiyya 2004: passim; Deeb 2006: 210, 215–216; Sukkariyya 2007: 68, 256–257; el-Hosseini 2008; Clarke 2009: 147n35 and Deeb and Harb 2013: 81–84.

54 Shakhuri 1998: 21 and Markaz al-Dirasat wa-l-Abhath al-Islamiyya – al-Masihiyya 1999: 289–292; Husayni 2007: 22–23; Qubaysi 2007: 14–15; Sukkariyya 2007: 28–29, 137ff. and Clarke 2009: 66, 85n21.

and encounters and conversations which naturally 'had a great share in the flowering of many of our thoughts'.[55] In an inversion of the traditional hierarchy, being at the margins of the Shi'i scholarly world was, in this reading, in fact an indispensable advantage.[56]

Justifying Authority

Perhaps unsurprisingly given his emphasis on standing apart from the establishment, Fadlallah's claim to the *marja'iyya* was bitterly contested. A Lebanese shaykh led in the late 1990s an intense assault backed by influential figures within the great seminaries. This focused on Fadlallah's doctrinal rectitude, in particular concerning traditional Shi'i accounts of the death and superhuman qualities of the Prophet's daughter Fatima, as well as the cursing of the Sunni caliphs. Fadlallah's characteristically ecumenical, rationalist and disenchanting positions were widely perceived as unacceptable. He was obliged to submit to an inquisition by a leading Iranian revolutionary figure who questioned him by telephone and in writing, and even travelled to Beirut to meet him and attend one of his sermons. He was absolved, although the accusations were reproduced on dedicated websites and reflected in Internet discussion forums up to and even beyond his death.[57] Despite earlier mutterings about the hand of the CIA, Fadlallah later attributed the controversy to the threat his independent *marja'iyya* posed to that of Khamenei and Iran. Poor relations had also ensued with Hizballah, who took Khamenei as *marja'* as well as *al-wali al-faqih*, only repaired by the solidarity enjoined by the cataclysmic Israeli assault of 2006. Fadlallah also blamed seminary politics: the advent of *marja*'s outside of the traditional centres might entail a diminishment of their income. And the onslaught had had local backers too, including, apparently, his old friend but now rival Shams al-Din, himself in bitter conflict with the polarizing force of Hizballah and a staunch opponent of Khomeinist notions of *wilayat al-faqih*. 'Sorry to say', one of Fadlallah's staff members told me, but Shams al-Din had 'a complex' about the sayyid.[58]

Popular support was invaluable then, but Fadlallah's claims needed legitimation in the terms of the establishment too. The attacks on his

55 Interview, Beirut, 21 June 2007; Sukkariyya 2007: 117–119, 201, 211.

56 See Clarke 2018 for a more extended version of this argument.

57 Shakhuri 1998: 279n, 282–283 and ff. and Rosiny 2001: 207–219.

58 Sukkariyya 2007: 69, 169, 172, 182, 197 and Mervin 2008a: 282–283 and Walbridge (2014: 131) reports that Shams al-Din severely criticised Fadlallah on a visit to the US in 1995, an intervention that was not well received, as being beyond the bounds of customary civility. See Kawtharani 2016 on the hostility between Hizballah and Shams al-Din.

credibility went to the very essence of his scholarly credentials.[59] His detractors challenged the status of a man who had left the Najaf *hawza* at a relatively young age, and without, it seemed, obtaining the customary written licence (*ijaza*) as a *mujtahid* from a great teacher. He announced his *marja'iyya* more than twenty-five years later, years spent in the scholarly wilderness of Beirut rather than in the great colleges with their towering scholar-teachers. The contrast with Khu'i's 'successor' as the leading scholar of Najaf, Ayatollah Sistani, could not be clearer. Khu'i did pen a *mujtahid*'s licence for the latter, his pupil, one of the very few formal endorsements he issued: 'May God prolong the days of his effusion of learning and excellence and multiply his like among the active scholars!', he wrote. 'For he has expended in this path a sizable portion of his noble life, devoting himself to living in the vicinity of 'Ali [i.e., the Imam's shrine] . . . at Noblest Najaf.'[60]

This line of argument would rule out the possibility of any *marja'* emerging outside of the established *hawza*s. How, then, to flourish and be recognised in the margins? Fadlallah argued that one could come to know a scholar's mettle 'from studying under him or teaching him, or through his conversation and discussion, or through examining his researches and writings'.[61] One's students are thus as important as one's teachers. Fadlallah had taught the seminary curriculum when in Najaf, and continued once in Beirut. He rapidly institutionalised his teaching circle as 'The Islamic Legal Institute' (al-Ma'had al-Shar'i al-Islami), one of what would become two seminaries sponsored by him[62]; and his leading students, many now substantial scholars in their own right, were crucial to the fabric of his legal authority. Even if Fadlallah's voluminous legal discourse was his responsibility and carried out in his name, its evolution was thus also in a sense a collaborative project.

Part of the contribution the students made was through editing an extensive series of handsome hardback volumes transcribing his lectures at the highest, research level classes (*dars al-kharij*), ranging widely over the legal terrain.[63] His offices specifically cited this mass production of fully elaborated researches (*abhath istidlaliyya*), which give profound insight into the ayatollah's legal thinking, as evidence of his powers.[64]

59 Here and below see further my discussion in Clarke 2018.
60 Mottahedeh 2016: 347. 61 Fadlallah 2002–2003 vol.1: 13.
62 *Al-Sira*, section *al-'Ita' al-'ilmi*. The other seminary was Hawzat al-Murtada in the Shi'i suburb that sprang up around the shrine of Sayyida Zaynab in Damascus.
63 For details see Clarke 2018.
64 Here I am citing a Q&A on Fadlallah's credentials from www.bayynat.org.lb, section '*Istifta'at*', sub-section '*al- marja'iyya*' (since lapsed), dated 16 June 2006, accessed 13–20 May 2009.

Such lecture notes (*taqrirat*) are historically conventional. Making them so freely available and in such volume to a wider public, however, is perhaps less so, and constitutes an openness to scholarly examination that was clearly felt to be unparalleled.

From the books, we learn that Fadlallah's teaching takes ostensibly traditional forms, frequently that of a commentary on another work, but as a way of 'orienting the research, and omitting now [merely] theoretical issues and applications and adding subjects and researches that are important for the present time', such as, for example, a discussion of the admissibility of DNA evidence in the course of a two-volume commentary on the sections on judgement in Kazim al-Yazdi's (d. 1918) *al-'Urwa al-wuthqa*, a seminary staple. And the editors sometimes add introductions expounding in more programmatic form Fadlallah's 'mode of derivation' (*minhaj istinbati*). There is a tension here between Fadlallah's status as a 'creative renewer' (*mujaddid mubaddi'*), and the concern that that not be misunderstood as in any sense implying a departure from the limits and rules of the established tradition. As he himself put it, 'we do not talk of a new method: the method is the method [*al-minhaj huwa-l-minhaj*]', even if he did have characteristic emphases in his approach.[65]

Fadlallah's concern for contextualised legal reasoning extended to his 'realism', and his appreciation of the 'social dimension', a holistic mentality, attendant to the fundamental aims (*maqasid*) of the law. In the thick of it in cosmopolitan Beirut, open to the concerns of his flock, he had, he claimed, a grasp on the real issues that he could never get from books alone, in contrast with the 'abstract', 'hypothetical' and fragmented approach of others, more isolated in the ivory towers of the seminary cities. A student reports that Fadlallah 'does not hide his anger' at this latter approach, 'sunk in a deep coma in this fog of expressions and a great deal of pretending to be clever and linguistic wrangling', turning some legal argumentation into 'what resembles mathematical equations'. He decried the ready, 'canned' answers of this 'engineering jurisprudence' (*al-fiqh al-handasi*), 'with no excuse for them except their being technically and artificially correct', 'attempts to pygmify the sharia according to the personal orientation of the jurist'.[66]

Fadlallah diagnosed this individualist approach as the source of a contemporary tendency for jurists to rule with caution (*ihtiyat*): that is, to enjoin their followers to avoid a course of action as a measure of prudence, due to their own lack of confidence in issuing a definitive

[65] Shakhuri 1996: 6; Husayni 2007: 9; Khishn 2007: 270–283 and Qubaysi 2007: 9–10.
[66] Husayni 2007: 13, 19, 23; interview with Shaykh Husayn al-Khishn, Beirut, 4 February 2008.

ruling of its permissibility. This is despite the potentially negative consequences 'on the social human level' for their lay followers, who actually have to live life according to these prescriptions. Again, this tendency is deemed to arise from most jurists' narrow range of experience. An eye to other contexts would allow them to see, for example, the damage that an insistence on the heaviest of veiling does to the wider reception of Islam, or that prudentially ruling out playing cards (without gambling) or the shaving of the beard on the basis that 'no religious person' does that, is to be ignorant of the millions driven to sin by this 'mentality of prohibition and caution'. Fadallah, by contrast, thought 'that when a jurist has reached a clear point of view then there is no excuse for him to rule with *ihtiyat*: caution must rest on a realistic study of the circumstances of the obligated [*mukallafin*, i.e. lay people] and not those of the *mujtahid*.' That is, 'he has intellectual courage about putting forth his legal ideas when he reaches a fixed conviction', not afraid of what one student calls 'the war of nerves' in legal circles, the jurists' 'reluctance to face fierce attacks from their peers' and tendency to let another scholar take that risk. So where Fadlallah held controversial opinions, this was not, his school argued, because he departed from the tradition. Rather, he fearlessly lived up to its demands. Merely differing from the majority view (*al-mashhur*) is not in itself to err. On the contrary, if a jurist has nothing new to say, then he can hardly be said to be a *mujtahid*.[67]

'Every *Marja'* Is a Rose, Each with Their Own Perfume'

Fadlallah's validation of his authority thus rested in large part on his prodigious intellectual production. He was a hugely prolific author, in a variety of genres. Writing in 2007, a journalist reported ninety books, many of many volumes. But in the same year, I went through a catalogue of his works with one of his staff and we estimated the number at 150. 'But this is an old list', he said. 'We'll get you a new one, inshallah.' That list includes volumes of his poetry, a huge collection of his lectures in Damascus running to twenty large hardback volumes (*al-Nadwa*), his twenty-five volume commentary on the Quran, books on pilgrimage, migration, 'Ashura, youth problems, women's issues, Muslim-Christian dialogue, and on and on. And then there were all the other lectures and articles, the sermons, the press statements, the interviews – in the papers and on television: this was an intellectual torrent. One staff member told me that, 'The sayyid needs forty people there to write down everything he

[67] Shakhuri 1998: 5–6, 13, 26, 27, 31, 48 and Husayni 2007: 24–25; *al-Sira*, section '*al-Minhaj al-fiqhi al-usuli*'.

says.' Not a moment could be wasted. 'The appointment is to the second, you can't be late', as a journalist remembers.[68]

That points again to this being a collaborative endeavour, even if centred on one personality. Although much of Fadlallah's appeal rested on his up to the minute, engaged persona – his immediacy – his message inevitably had to be mediated. At the most basic level, the ayatollah could be represented in person by others: by his students, including two of his sons, the eldest, Sayyid 'Ali, and a younger favourite, Sayyid Ja'far, and by other shaykhly members of his offices, at gradually further removes. Clearly such layers of mediation might occasionally rupture, if not so close to the centre, then in the wider hinterland of Fadlallah's organisation, his staff and representatives.[69]

Communications technologies allow more direct transmission of course. Fadlallah's own sermons and lectures were broadcast on the radio station (on which his son and foremost deputy Sayyid 'Ali had his own morning call-in show) and the fledgling television station, al-Iman, both linked in to YouTube, Facebook and the rest, as well as posted on the multilingual website. The website, a technology which Fadlallah took up relatively early,[70] enabled the collation and dissemination of a great deal of relevant information, from Fadlallah's biography and justification of his claims to the highest religious authority, through to a searchable online version of his Quran commentary, catalogues and later electronic versions of his books and then more general material, on the lives of the Prophet and his descendants, for example. It also included news, updated daily, of Fadlallah's meetings with politicians and other dignitaries, as well as copies of his press releases, circulated, along with the text of his Friday sermons. As one staff member put it to me, 'Some *marja*'s won't talk in front of the media. They have a certain *protocol* [using the English]. Sayyid Fadlallah's *marja'iyya* broke this barrier. Sayyid Fadlallah talks to the media, journalists, even has women journalists come to interview him. Many, many *marja*'s don't allow that.'

This torrent of open, engaged jurisprudence was deeply worrying to some within the Shi'i religious establishment: as a *marja'*, a source of authoritative opinion, what Sayyid Fadlallah said was 'law', as it were, or

68 Sukkariyya 2007: 18, 25. On his schedule see also Kramer 1997: 117–118 and Sankari 2005: 10–11.

69 Certainly in my earlier work on bioethics I found tying down the exact position of the school (on admittedly technical points), occasionally difficult. See Clarke 2009: 67–72. Deeb and Harb report similar problems over Fadlallah's position on the permissibility of using nail polish (2013: 83–84, 244n42, discussed further in Clarke 2015: 237–241). However, I would reckon Fadlallah's organisation to be far tighter than most.

70 In 1997. See arabic.bayynat.org.lb/, accessed 11 June 2011.

could at least be taken as a fatwa, an official statement of that authoritative opinion. For a public figure, informality becomes an impossibility. And he said a very great deal. Barely a day went by without a television interview or a press release. Such a prodigious output was a mighty achievement, and vital to the creation of Fadlallah's claim to authority, but it also rendered him vulnerable – it gave plenty of ammunition for his critics. It is said that first editions of his works fetched higher prices in the seminaries of Qom because one could thereby track how he had changed his mind over the years. He himself complained that the fuss over his discussion of various Shi'i partisan traditions had arisen over remarks taken out of context, like, for instance, when he had been replying to a question from some Sunnis in Damascus about the Shi'i claim that the Prophet appointed 'Ali as his successor, as part of his efforts at ecumenical engagement.[71]

Here a comparison was often drawn by my interlocutors with Ayatollah Sistani of Iraq, currently, so far as one can tell, the world's most widely recognized claimant to the title of 'the most learned' (*al-a'lam*) Shi'i scholar. This is a man of the traditional religious establishment who apparently commands the loyalty of millions and immense financial and institutional resources.[72] But by contrast, Sistani famously is known almost never to stir from his simple room in a small house in a side street in Najaf. His public statements are tightly rationed, he never gives interviews to the media, and save one or two official portraits he does not suffer to be photographed. That had been his understandable norm under the rule of Saddam Hussein, when the Shi'i clergy were frequently heavily persecuted, especially after the 1991 uprisings in the wake of the first Gulf War. Sistani had ceased appearing in his habitual mosque and had stopped convening his teaching circle, his published scholarly output correspondingly relatively modest in quantity.[73] His comparative obscurity did not, however, survive the American invasion of Iraq in 2003, when he was catapulted to global attention due to the extent of his potential influence over Iraq's Shi'i population. But his relative economy of pronouncement continued. As Sistani's only official media spokesman Hajj Hamid al-Khaffaf told me in the ayatollah's

[71] Sabrina Mervin, personal comment; Shakhuri 1998: 290–292 and Sukkariyya 2007: 70. Asked whether there was a fatwa that he had issued that he later regretted, Fadlallah denied it, although he did admit that there were some that he had moved on from (Sukkariyya 2007: 214).

[72] See e.g. Khalaji (2006: 9), who estimates his annual income at $500–700 million and his worldwide assets at over $3 billion.

[73] Khalaji 2006: 4, 8, 12.

Beirut offices, 'In today's media, the press wants statements all the time, every day. That's not the Sayyid's way.'[74]

There are, then, differences in style. Fadlallah, explicitly more activist, socially and politically, engaged with the press. Sistani, resolutely disengaged from mundane politicking and the Khomeinist school, seeks to preserve a certain distance. Of course, the conflict being played out here between the irreproachable piety and moral probity required of a *marja'* and the worldliness the role demands is an old one, one that leads some qualified candidates to eschew the role, and one that resonates with our previous discussion of the judge. How does one best preserve the respect, or awe (*hayba*), associated with one's office, given the engagement it can be seen to require? Distance and closeness, disengagement and engagement, require careful management. One can take different paths, and different *marja'*s, like different judges, have different styles. Or, as the saying goes, every *marja'* is a rose, each with their own perfume.

Unlike judges, however, such authorities are in direct competition. Fadlallah's path was in some ways thrust upon him, although no doubt also fitted his personality. Carving out a niche on the margins meant marking oneself as a man apart. But in Lebanon, Fadlallah had the advantage of local presence over an establishment figure like Sistani, as well as his chief rival, the Supreme Leader of the Iranian Islamic Republic, Ayatollah Khamenei, similarly 'activist' and with the resources of a nation state to back his claim.[75] And Beirut was a particularly congenial site for developing a cosmopolitan and contemporary jurisprudence, if one fraught with its own dangers. Fadlallah was a controversial figure. He had taken sides – as one had to – in the big debates within Shi'i Islam about the religious acceptability of Islamist politics. He had taken sides on other fronts too. His unrelenting hostility to Israel and solidarity with the Palestinian cause was attractive for many, locally, regionally and globally. But the armed resistance to Israeli occupation that he supported, even if vital for national pride, had fallout within Lebanon too. And earlier controversies over his support of suicide bombing tactics, or his later commending of the killer of Israeli seminary students in 2008 as a 'hero' for instance,[76] marked the gulf that separated him

[74] Beirut, 22 May 2007. For Sistani's public pronouncements on 'the Iraqi question' see Khaffaf 2007; for further academic comment, Visser 2006 and Clarke 2010.

[75] As for who had the upper hand – at least in terms of their number of 'followers' (not the only measure of influence of course) – that is not so easy to judge. See Clarke and Inhorn 2011.

[76] In his Friday sermon of 7 March 2008.

from acceptability to the West. Away from geopolitics, true scholarly flourishing and the more nuanced approach that plural Lebanon needed required intellectual autonomy. But hard-won independence from Iranian patronage entailed jeopardising the security that Iran's allies in Lebanon provided. Prominent careers in difficult times demand hard choices and make enemies.

13 Making Law from the Bottom Up

The previous chapter introduced the figure of the *mujtahid*, the scholar capable of defining the religious law through their own efforts, independent of the state, in this case within the Twelver Shi'i tradition. We gained a sense of the potential breadth of the role. In this chapter I now focus on the paradigmatic task of such a figure, the defining of the religious law. On one level that might be through the publication of definitive works, legal handbooks and treatises; on another, it could be in response to the particular queries of the laity. As we noted before, in this latter role, even if the title has little resonance for today's Shi'a in Lebanon, the scholar can be said to serve as a mufti, issuing formal opinions, or fatwas. And of course those opinions, which may themselves be disseminated to a wider audience, should be reflected in the *mujtahid*'s other, more substantial publications.

The fatwa has become something of an icon of Islamic authority for Muslims and non-Muslims, and consequently, as I have already noted, now has a rather grand ring to it. Much recent academic literature sees it as the primary mechanism for dynamism and change in the Islamic legal tradition.[1] But answers to questions about the sharia can take very different forms (as can the questions which provoke them), from a bare 'yes' or 'no', to a much more fully elaborated response. The English pages of Fadlallah's website translate *istifta'at* – requests for opinions – as 'Q&A', which perhaps gives a better flavour of what is involved.[2] Not all such 'Q&A' is of momentous importance, nor indeed does it all break new ground. As in the parallel world of the courts, the vast bulk of such work is routine rather than scholarly fireworks; most such 'fatwas' are ephemeral rather than historic, although no less interesting for that.[3] And, again, it has thus been argued that to view the fatwa as simply a

[1] See e.g. Hallaq 1994 and Masud et al. 1996.

[2] The Arabic pages also avoid referring to the responses as 'fatwas': the 'answer' (*jawab*) is rather filed under the section, 'consultations' (*istifta'at*).

[3] Messick 1996: 312, 319.

mode of legal utterance is to obscure the wider implications of seeking and obtaining such opinion. The fatwa should also be seen as a situated, ethical process, one of the techniques within the Islamic tradition for the formation of virtuous selves, the mufti acting to help the morally needy along the path of righteousness by responding to their religious dilemmas.[4] That resonates with my treatment throughout this book of the engaged, pedagogical stance central to the shaykhly vocation.

In the previous chapter, I discussed Ayatollah Fadlallah's research-led teaching in the context of the seminary. But his pedagogical efforts were certainly not just directed at religious students. In terms of publication, at the most modest level, there were the '100 questions and answers' volumes distributed in the mosque. The weekly newsletter *Bayyanat*, also distributed at the mosque, covers a mixture of current affairs, sports coverage and news of the Fadlallah organisation's activities. But it features as well a regular section on 'the jurisprudence of life' (*fiqh al-hayat*), with topical issues addressed from the Islamic legal perspective. And then there were more substantial, but still highly approachable texts addressing new themes and audiences: 'The world of children' (*Dunya al-tifl*); 'The world of women' (*Dunya al-mar'a*); 'The world of the youth' (*Dunya al-shabab*). 'Which other *marja'* would write a book about children?', one of his staff asked me. Another staff member told me that he had known how special the sayyid was since he was ten years old, when he saw his book, 'Islamic law made easy' (*al-Fiqh al-muyassar*, actually a digest of the positions of Ayatollah Khu'i, but brought out under the name of Fadlallah as Khu'i's representative at that time). Alone in his family in being interested in religion, he had taught himself Islam from it. Another of Fadlallah's most popular earlier Islamic legal works was his annotated edition of Muhammad Baqir al-Sadr's 'Clear fatwas' (*al-Fatawa al-wadiha*), intentionally more accessible than the seminary standard, as the title suggests: the rulings of the sharia are presented in a conversational, question and response format, and key technical terms explained.[5]

And Fadlallah's own *risala 'amaliyya*, or comprehensive handbook of legal guidance, while a three-volume work, 'The jurisprudence of the sharia' (*Fiqh al-shari'a*) in the classic style, is rendered more accessible for its lay audience, again through explanations of the specialised vocabulary employed and also the addition of material indicating the reasoning behind some of the rulings given. Thus, as was pointed out to me by a member of his staff, it is considerably larger than the norm. (A one-volume,

4 Agrama 2010a. 5 Fadlallah 1998, 2004, 2005b; Qadi 1998 and 'Atwi 2004a.

pocket paperback summary edition is also available.[6]) A comparison with the more traditional Sistani's handbook, whose opening section I quoted in the previous chapter, is instructive. Where Sistani goes straight into the list of obligations required of a Muslim, Fadlallah opens with an 'Entry into the science of Islamic law' explaining some important technical terms.[7]

> S1. The sharia is: every ruling taken from the noble Quran or from the traditions of the Prophet and his family, God almighty's blessings on him and on them...
>
> S2. Every one of a Muslim's actions must, in the sharia, be either:
>
> Obligatory: and that is that whose performance is obligatory and whose omission has sanctions against it.
>
> Or forbidden: and that is that which must be avoided and whose commission by the religiously liable adult is punished.
>
> Or commendable...

And on it continues in straight-forward fashion.

Such pedagogy, addressing a lay audience as well as a scholarly one, was thus vital to Fadlallah's vision of the proper work of the *mujtahid*. And it extended to direct interaction, including 'Q&A'. Fadlallah had, from his earliest days in Beirut, held open lectures for youth clubs and groups to bridge a perceived gap between the younger generation and their religion, allowing questions from the floor. No question was, he said, forbidden. And he remained available to his popular base, even when he had reached the clerical and media heights, holding weekly sessions where people could come and put their queries to him.[8] This work was crucial to shaping a committed Shi'i public. But the traffic was not merely one-way. It took the form of a mutual relationship. As Fadlallah himself put it,

> Perhaps I try to play the role of psychiatrist [*tabib nafsi*] for many of the people who come to me, women and men ... I want to get to know the problems which they face ... And so, I consider that ... I am not a teacher [*mu'allim*] but a pupil [*muta'allim*] ... I study society face-to-face, and in the public sphere, which gives

[6] Fadlallah 2003. [7] Fadlallah 2002–2003 vol. 1: 7–8.

[8] Kramer 1997: 92–93; Sankari 2005: 136; Sukkariyya 2007: 18, 25; Clarke and Inhorn 2011 and Deeb and Harb 2013: 78–84.

me a culture deeper than that I get from the books I read ... I do not live abstraction in my life. Rather, I always try to live the reality.[9]

This close engagement with people's real-life problems was in fact essential to the project of a creating a 'contemporary' jurisprudence, in touch with the needs of today's Muslims. By learning from ordinary folk as well as informing them, Fadlallah could ensure that his vision of the sharia could 'keep up with the times', a common demand of public discourse in the activist Shi'i society that Fadlallah had helped build.[10] I frequently heard it remarked that Twelver Shi'ism is particular well equipped in this regard, with its insistence on the authority of a living *mujtahid*, capable of interpreting the sources afresh.[11] But we also encountered this modernist concern that the sharia not be perceived as 'backward' in my description of a reformist judge in the Sunni courts in Chapter 11. And it is further shared by the post-Orientalist academic literature on the sharia, which has a strong interest in the fatwa as the prime mechanism for dynamism and change, and a fascination with the 'bottom-up' nature of historic Islamic legal discourse.[12] In this chapter I show in some detail how exactly such a bottom-up process of legal innovation worked in the contemporary case of Fadlallah's offices, starting from the most routine personal interactions, moving up to the public circulation of responses to individual queries and ending with the crafting of definitive legal treatises.

Istifta'at: Answering People's Needs

The Islamic legal office (*al-maktab al-shar'i*), or 'Q&A office' (*maktab al-istifta'*), which responds to requests for religious-legal opinions, formed part of what Fadlallah's institutions referred to as 'the apparatus of the *marja'iyya*' (*jihaz al-marja'iyya*), alongside a judicial office (*maktab al-qada'*) providing arbitration services. The legal office is also responsible for determining the lunar date and thus the onset of important religious occasions such as Ramadan, and supervises the editing and publishing of Fadlallah's authoritative legal handbooks.

The legal office was, at the time of my research, headed up by one of my most generous collaborators, Shaykh Muhsin 'Atwi. His core concern in his work in the office is relaying, in one form or another, the legal opinion of the ayatollah. But, like most of the other figures we have considered, in his wider activities and mission he lives the vocation of

[9] Sukkariyya 2007: 220–221. [10] See Deeb 2006.
[11] On the requirement to follow a living authority, see Clarke 2016.
[12] In paradigmatic form, Hallaq 1994, 2009: 364ff., 543ff.

the shaykh in the round. It is as though a series of Russian dolls lie embedded within the larger frame of the *marja'iyya*, each reproducing its functions of engagement and pedagogy, nominally according to the same design, but on a greater or lesser scale.

If I saw Shaykh Muhsin in the mosque, abstracted, muttering prayers, I would also see people around him with questions as to the law, or seeking a divination (*istikhara*) told out on his prayer beads. He told me that people even come up to him and give him the obligatory alms (*zakat*) just like that, on the street, without wanting a receipt. His reputation as a reliable diviner was unparalleled amongst all the shaykhs I knew: in the office his telephone would always ring several times with such requests during our meetings, and he would break off to open the Quran or flick through his prayer beads, after a prayer. 'No problem' (*mish mushkila*), he might then say, or, conversely, 'Not nice at all' (*mish mnih abadan*), perhaps quoting them the verse that had come to light. Many people ring, I noted. He chuckled: if he let anyone who wanted to ring him then he would never have any time for anything else, he thought.

And he is a published author himself, of pedagogical works such as a series of 'Simple researches in legal guidance' – little booklets on choosing the right spouse for instance, or on commerce or temporary marriage – and a large volume of missionary guidance, with a preface by Sayyid Fadlallah and appendices giving descriptions of different countries, dates of Islamic and national festivals and international prayer times, to accompany the missionary (*muballigh*) on their travels.[13] All his books are distributed free of charge: some note that 'you can ring the author on this number before noon'. Shaykh Muhsin's work, then, is that of the shaykh more generally – an open source of guidance, moral and spiritual, for the people of his community and beyond (including me). He is also a legal expert. But, as a non-*mujtahid*, he works for another and transmits the ayatollah's opinion rather than his own. Modest, absent-minded and kindly in demeanour, he is the object of affection rather than reverence from those around him – jokingly putting upon him in the office, feeling free to argue points with him – even if his real stature was reflected after Fadlallah's death by his acting as the preacher of the Friday

[13] 'Atwi 2002. The 'simple researches' (*buhuth tawjihiyya fiqhiyya muyassira*) I have, or know of, from the series include: vol. 1, 'How we bring up our children' (*Kayf nurabbi abna'-na*); 2, 'Choosing one's partner: between the heart and the mind' (*Ikhtiyar al-sharik: bayna al-'aql wa-l-'atifa*); 3, 'The law of commerce and its ethics' (*Fiqh al-tijara wa-adab-ha*); 4, 'Healing and its rulings' (*al-'Ilaj wa-ahkam-hu*); 5, 'The fifth [i.e., the religious tax]: divine obligation' (*al-Khums: farida ilhiyya*); 6, 'Thought as worship' (*'Ibadat al-tafkir*); 7, 'Temporary marriage: its legitimacy and its rulings' (*al-Zawaj al-mu'aqqat: mashru'iyyat-hu wa-ahkam-hu*).

sermon in the sayyid's great mosque on occasion. Beyond his personal qualities, we see something of the fulfilment of the shaykhly role that work as a judge, say, can render problematic. He is free to engage with those who have recourse to him, to help them. And they in turn appreciate him, as I did.

I first met him on my very first visit to Fadlallah's offices in 2004, introduced over the photocopier amidst pandemonium in the offices in the run up to the annual Hajj pilgrimage. A bank of phones was continuously ringing, a stream of people coming and going, needing detailed information as to the various duties required and drafting and certifying their wills before they left on what has historically been a hazardous journey. The wills are recorded on a paper form provided ('a gift of the offices of His Excellency the Religious Authority Sayyid Muhammad Husayn Fadlallah'), including details as to prayers and fasts missed and alms unpaid for a nominated person to make up for them, to ease their path on the day of judgement. Outside of such busy periods, Shaykh Muhsin's work usually takes a more relaxed form: sitting in his office writing the replies to the queries people send in by email, and answering some such questions by telephone and occasionally in person. He is also involved in the compiling and editing of some of the ayatollah's legal works, as we will see.

When I first would go to visit him in 2004, the offices were then by the sayyid's house, near the mosque in Harat Hrayk, off a little side street near the municipality. Shaykh Muhsin had a spartan little room there. In the 2006 war the offices were destroyed, so my visits in 2007 were to a temporary home in an apartment building some distance away. Shaykh Muhsin's room had a desk and chairs, but no book shelves at this point, the books piled on the floor in great stacks. But the ascetic style suited him. He dresses in shaykhly robes and turban of course, but he would often have taken them off to work in the office, revealing an old jumper and trousers in the winter. Come 2009, a brand new building had been erected on the original site, very clean and contemporary, and Shaykh Muhsin had a good-sized ground floor office with new furniture and shelves for his books. He has a computer, although I have never seen him use it. He works together with at least one other, more junior shaykh, as well as a number of 'lay' assistants.

Some people come to visit in person, and I might be asked to leave if it were a sensitive matter, although others did not mind my sitting in. Take two brothers, for instance, come to discuss the case of one of them, just returned to Lebanon from years in Canada, where he had married but also divorced – in the courts. Now he wanted to remarry, and they wanted to ask about the religious, or *sharʿi*, position. Shaykh Muhsin ran through the essentials of how a religious divorce might be effected and secured them an appointment with the judicial office down the corridor. Questions come by telephone too, concerning the rules for a woman who has just given birth, or the legality of certain foods or working for a certain company. Some required more prolonged pedagogical engagement: one about a Christian man converting to Islam and marrying a Shiʿi Muslim woman, for instance, the worry being the genuineness of the conversion; another from a lady in London worried about the effect of this non-Muslim environment on her children's morals. She should try to keep an eye on their activities, Shaykh Muhsin advised, go with her daughter to the swimming pool, get to know her friends, invite them to the house so they understand their culture. She can contact the office for advice whenever she needs to – 'ring, ask for me'. They have experience with this.

But the bulk of Shaykh Muhsin's work is textual. At the beginning of the day he will be brought a large sheaf of papers by one of the staff. These are printouts of questions sent in to the website. The pile was usually a large one, largest on Mondays given the traffic over the weekend – maybe 100–150 submissions, but normally 50–70, he thought. There would be more at certain times of year, such as the pilgrimage season or Ramadan – pregnant women asking about fasting and the health of their baby, for example; or if there was some especially pressing political question or an issue in the news, or if the sayyid had had an interview on television, then they would get an especially heavy load.[14]

The traffic is very considerable. Having been given a portion of this correspondence from the archives, I could see from their identification numbers that the number of non-identical questions and answers goes beyond 100,000 (where a new topic or answer has been broached, rather than simply a duplicate of a commonly encountered scenario, then they are entered into the archives).[15] The introduction to a 2009 revised edition of the office's compilation of questions and answers, *al-Masa'il*

[14] So, for instance, Shaykh Muhsin put into context a request he had just received from a woman in the US asking if it is allowed to build Churches in Muslim lands. This question had been discussed in the media recently, because the first church in Qatar's history had just been opened.

[15] As of 2001, Lara Deeb (2006: 126–127) was told, the website was receiving one and a half to two million hits a month. Between mid-1997 and the first four months of 2001, Fadlallah received 2118 questions via email, 421 via fax and 424 by mail. An exponential increase over time was at this time apparent, as the questions from the second half of 1997 filled one binder, those from 1998 filled three, those from 1999 filled four, and those from 2000 filled eight. This traffic clearly increased even more dramatically after that, if Shaykh 'Atwi's and my own estimates are correct.

al-fiqhiyya, talks of 'hundreds of thousands' of such requests.[16] Shaykh Muhsin, while acknowledging that he had no exact information in this regard, guessed that this is more than most *marja*'s. Here he wanted to point out something he felt to be important: 'Sayyid Fadlallah [at this point still alive] accepts any question.' He had 'an open door' policy. Other *marja*'s might stipulate that they accept only legal (*fiqhi*) questions. Fadlallah, on the other hand, accepted questions about politics, history and religious doctrine (*'aqida*). Others limit it to, say, not more than three questions. They do not. One time, I arrived to find him writing a letter to the imam of a mosque in the Emirates answering some thirty-five questions about Fadlallah's opinions on matters ranging from politics, to doctrine, to jurisprudence. Sometimes, he told me, they would receive letters of twenty pages, with fifty or hundred questions.

This openness extends to correspondence with non-Muslims, even hostile ones. They sometimes get questions from the West, the United States for instance, which display confusions about Islam or take a very critical, not to say insulting, stance, on issues such as *jihad*, for example. They feel they must answer, to correct these misapprehensions.

Response number 71,720 from the database (dated November 2007 and quoted in its original English):

> My Mom says that God loves me and wants all people to go to heaven. Your Religeon says that Im a Infidel that should die [*sic*]. Why do you want to kill people for Allah?

(The reply patiently explains that Islam holds that it is wrong to kill people and that Christians and Jews go to heaven too.)

Conversely, they also receive many questions betraying misconceptions about Christianity: 'Are they infidels [*kuffar*]?' Yes, they are not Muslims. 'Are they polytheists [*mushrikin*]?' No. Or they receive questions from Sunnis, because they have heard of the sayyid's ecumenical stance, or have confused notions about the Shi'a. To call all this correspondence 'fatwas' would, again, in some ways be to over-crystallise what is in fact a more fluid set of genres, much routine, pedagogical engagement, rarely announcements of ground-breaking positions.

Most of the correspondence is in Arabic, but much thus also comes in English, French and other languages and will have to be translated – raising further issues of mediation. That does not necessarily imply non-Arab followers: of one written in bad French and requesting a reply in Arabic, Shaykh Muhsin commented that this was probably an Arab living

[16] Fadlallah 2009: 7.

in France and without an Arabic keyboard. But the internationalism is striking; one obtains a sense of the extent of this global community of the legal imagination, stretching from Brazil to Azerbaijan, from Canada to Afghanistan. Shaykh Muhsin told me of one letter from a woman in Indonesia who had become Shi'i, requesting someone to come from Fadlallah's offices to provide them guidance and teaching. She had claimed that the sayyid had a million followers in Indonesia. Incredible, they had had no such idea – 'More than here!'[17]

People contact them in a simple way, just like that, in their dialect (*'amiyya*). (He gave me an impression of a woman writing in Gulf dialect.) A woman will be in her kitchen... Or a man may be in his bathroom, washing himself after having had sex. Have I done it right, he suddenly wonders? Sexual matters make up a large proportion of the questions. Can I have sex with the lights on, or must they be off? They cannot help but laugh about it in the office sometimes: every day they have at least one question about masturbation, he thought. A selection of issues from one visit, just the ones in French and English that he showed me, ranged from one letter from a woman whose husband had taken a new wife – he will not divorce her; she has children, no home and has received no money for two years. What is their ruling? – to another asking how to perform a religious divination (*istikhara*), another on the reliability of certain transmitters of hadiths, another wanting to know why Imam 'Ali let his daughter marry (the second caliph) 'Umar if we Shi'a say that 'Umar was no good, and one enquiring after the proper form of a marriage contract.

Over the course of the morning, Shaykh Muhsin and his colleague will work their way through the pile of questions. Shaykh Muhsin answers off the top of his head or, if in doubt, consults the ayatollah's published works. If it was a really tricky or unprecedented matter then he might consult the sayyid himself. (One time I heard him on the telephone with someone who had a question to which he did not know the answer; but, he said, the sayyid was asleep. So the office would pass on the question in writing, the sayyid himself would answer it, and they could come and get it the next day.) Shaykh Muhsin writes the answer on the sheet below the query and then they are taken away as a bundle towards the end of the morning by one of the lay assistants to be typed up, translated if need be,

[17] According to Deeb (2006: 127), as of 2001, the largest part of the emails had been received from Bahrain, followed closely by the United States, with Lebanon coming in third. Others had been received from almost every other Arab and European country as well as Iran, India, Malaysia, Pakistan, Canada, Nigeria, Australia, New Zealand, the Philippines and Brazil, among others. The internationalism was remarked upon by Shaykh 'Atwi as well, who further mentioned Azerbaijan and Bosnia.

and sent off, after having been reviewed by the ayatollah himself. The authenticity of authority must be preserved, something of a concern for Muslims familiar with the vagaries of the Internet age. 'Of course we help the sayyid. We look up the answers, write it – but he reads the responses', Shaykh Muhsin told me.[18] In contrast with the similar web-based provision of some ayatollahs, Fadlallah's offices would appear to have offered a reliable and routinised service that ostensibly guaranteed the attention of the *mujtahid* himself, as well as one that is comparatively efficient, providing a reply in days rather than months, as with some.[19] Fadlallah's avowed policy of up-to-the-minute, genuine engagement was thus borne out in the operations of this core part of his enterprise.

Making Law from the Bottom Up

Such 'Q&A' could simply be a private end in itself of course, a one-off individual exchange. But some opinions get out into the wider world, as I saw in my earlier research on medical ethics, concerning infertility treatment in particular. In response to such individual questions, Fadlallah came to allow the use of donor egg IVF procedures, which he, like many others, had previously ruled out, but subject to a temporary marriage contract between the egg donor and the husband of the recipient. Patients started telling doctors this in IVF clinics; the doctors confirmed it with the ayatollah's offices; printed statements to the effect started circulating. Donor egg procedures for Shi'i clients became a phenomenon, picked up by medical anthropologist Marcia Inhorn, as well as by me. So too Lara Deeb and Mona Harb describe how Fadlallah's position on the legitimacy of the use of nail polish evolved during their researches in 2008–2009 in response to young women's questions, and itself became something of a cause celebre.[20]

[18] In an interview with Fadlallah's son Najib, Deeb (2006: 127) was told that the shaykh's handwritten answer was first passed to Fadlallah who read and revised the answer and then sent it back to the programmer. He would then type it up and send the final typed version back to Fadlallah, who would look it over and, if he approved, stamp the paper. The answer would then be emailed to the petitioner and the stamped paper filed.

[19] According to Deeb (2006: 127), as of 2001, this process had initially taken an average of seventeen days, but then took an average of four; by 2010, the turnaround for standard question was 24 to 36 hours (Deeb 2010: 411). This would tally with the sort of interval suggested by my sources. The website itself, after stressing the importance of sending the email to the right address, notes that if a reply has not been received within two weeks then the petitioner should consider the possibility of a technical problem and try again: arabic.bayynat.org.lb/ahdathwakadaya, accessed 11 June 2011.

[20] Clarke and Inhorn 2011: 422–423; Deeb and Harb 2013: 83–84 (and see my discussion in Clarke 2015).

Individual responses might become more widely known by word of mouth. But the offices themselves might publish them, not least on the website, with its extensive Q&A pages,[21] but also in other ephemera like the *Bayynat* newsletter, or the series of booklets of one hundred questions and answers often distributed in the mosque before the Friday sermon. Compiled from the office's records, these show little systematic organisation – more a collection of what seemed interesting that time around. At another level, however, stands the substantial, two-volume compilation of responses, *al-Masa'il al-fiqhiyya* ('Legal questions'), which long stood as Fadlallah's *risala*, or definitive treatise for the guidance of his followers. This was first published in the mid-1990s, before the advent of his website, and the introduction talks of gathering what was scattered across written responses to questions from various quarters (and countries) and social classes, and also recorded oral responses during the ayatollah's lessons and lectures. There is no reason to think that the more recent, web-based correspondence did not feed into the later revised and updated editions. Across the two volumes there are well over 2,000 such questions and answers, but here arranged (sometimes artificially, as they admit) under the standard headings of the legal handbooks: the broad division (in each volume) between the obligations of worship (*'ibadat*) and social transactions (*mu'amalat*), further divided into the standard sub-sections of chapters on prayer, religious purity and so on. (A later, revised version takes the systemisation further, with a separate volume for worship and for transactions, and is far expanded, with some 5,500 entries altogether.[22]) The introduction (to the earlier edition) notes that some chapters are disproportionately large – prayer, the Shi'i religious tithe *khums* ('the fifth'), commerce and marriage – reflecting their predominance in people's questions. And they have left the questions as they were, 'in their spontaneity', with only minor modifications for the sake of clarity or to avoid redundancy.[23]

Some example questions, taken almost at random from the section on prayer:

Q: Sometimes it's written on clothes for sale that they are 100% silk [not allowed for men to wear and not for prayer, the heading under which this query is placed]. But if they really were, their price would be ten times the asking price. So can we say that the item is not made of pure

[21] See Messick 1996 on such public fatwas (in his case disseminated on the radio) and their consequences, and my comments at Clarke 2010: 364.
[22] Fadlallah 2009 and 2010. [23] Fadlallah 2005a vol.1: 5–6.

silk? [The answer, in summary: if there is doubt that it is pure silk then it can be worn.]

Q: I have a friend who is travelling to a country very far away, which means there is a time difference between the two countries. And the problem is that he is travelling from his country in the morning and arrives at his destination in the afternoon, when the time in his country is sunset. Must he complete the prayers which he missed, or must he follow the time zone he is in? [The answer, in summary: he should pray in the aeroplane following the time there.][24]

In Fadlallah's legal treatise proper, on the other hand, the three volume *Fiqh al-shari'a* ('Jurisprudence of the sharia'), which was published subsequently and stands as the definitive guide to the ayatollah's positions, the presentation is wholly systematic and generalised, without reference to the particular questions of the needy:

Book 1 (Worship), Chapter 2 (Prayer), Section 1 (Preliminaries to prayer), Topic 2 (Dress for prayer), Matter no. 7: The robe of the man should not be of pure silk.[25]

This is of course a stock topic, the law here well established. But in other cases it cannot but be the case that changing circumstances require deliberations that feed into the evolving body of systematised law.

From the earlier Q&A compilation: If we suppose that someone undertakes a surrogacy procedure [*tajribat al-umm al-badila*], who is the true mother of the child in this case, the woman who is the source of the egg or the one who bears the foetus? [A: the former]

From the legal handbook, the chapter on marriage and the family, sub-section the effects of marriage, sub-sub-section kinship and within it the paragraphs on filiation (*nasab*): The foundational principle in the relation of the child to their father is their being from his sperm, just as the foundational principle – for us – in the relation of the child to their mother is their being from her egg ... So if an infertile couple were to resort, in search of a child, to the procedure known as surrogacy [*al-rahm al-musta'ara*, 'hired womb'] ... [the child's] mother would clearly be the woman who is the source of the egg, not the one who bore them in her womb and delivered them.[26]

Shaykh Muhsin assumes an important role in editing these works. One time sitting in his office I saw a man come asking in person, most

[24] Fadlallah 2005a vol. 1: 63, 68–69. [25] Fadlallah 2002–2003 vol. 1: 268.

[26] Fadlallah 2002–2003 vol. 3: 523, 2005a vol. 1: 274. See Clarke 2009: 125ff. for a more nuanced discussion. Fadlallah is, I would say, unusual in incorporating such cutting-edge issues into the main body of the conventional treatise form. Others might put them instead in an appendix on 'Recent issues' (*Mustahdithat al-masa'il*). See e.g. Sistani 2002 vol. 1: 425ff.

concerned, about ritual pollution and its transmissibility: if, for instance, a book has something polluting on it, blood say, and you wipe it without using (ritually cleansing) water and then touch it, are you polluted? Yes (in the opinion of the Sayyid), came the response. 'What about if I then shake your hand? Am I polluted?' No! The man was citing Fadlallah's early work *al-Fatawa al-wadiha*; Shaykh Muhsin explained that this has been superseded: the sayyid has since changed his mind. After the man had left, Shaykh Muhsin felt impelled to ring the publishers to tell them that a new edition of this popular book might be required. Direct experience of the modes of popular religious practice thus drives the production of published legal work.

The Age of Religious Majority

A fuller example, one that was presented to me as a paradigmatic instance of Fadlallah's responsiveness to popular need, should demonstrate in more detail this process whereby the questions of ordinary people drove the ayatollah's legal thought, the latter gradually being released in published form. The issue at hand is that of the age of religious majority for girls (*sinn taklif al-bint*). When do they have to take responsibility for religious duties such as prayer, veiling, fasting and pilgrimage? The standard answer is nine (lunar) years, which now seems very young to many. As Fadlallah's son Sayyid Ja'far told me,

> For years, it has been apparent from people's questions that there are difficulties here. For instance, girls were fasting before they were physically capable. Or with prayers, girls aren't actually conscious of what they mean: they just want to play with their friends. So many fathers and mothers were seeing issues here and there were always questions about this. So Sayyid Fadlallah knew there is a problem.[27]

And so, he continued, 'The *mujtahid* asks, is it possible to solve this problem, with some flexibility [*muruna*], open-mindedness [*infitah*], in understanding the texts? The *mujtahid* has to have courage here', a courage that, as we have seen, Fadlallah's school would see their master as exemplifying. Sayyid Ja'far himself edited his father's lectures on the topic to his students, before whom he tried out new ideas. The book, *al-Bulugh* ('Maturity'), is relatively brief (180 pages) and compact (a small paperback) in comparison with some of the others in what is a series of such volumes, as previously discussed. That perhaps reflects the potential non-specialist audience for this particular topic. But like the

[27] Interview 21 June 2007.

other volumes it gives us a good idea as to his characteristic legal method, which I can now present in a little more detail.

Fadlallah's arguments here turn on privileging the Quran over other relevant sources. This emphasis on the 'authority [*marja'iyya*] of the Quran' is portrayed by the school as characteristic of his method, and Sayyid Ja'far says as much in his editor's introduction.[28] Of course, the same holds for all Muslims, but, his students explain, Fadlallah insisted on taking the whole Quran as setting the legislative context, and not just the five hundred so-called 'verses of judgement' containing explicit legal instructions.[29] His massive commentary, 'From the Revelation of the Quran' (*Min wahy al-Qur'an*), written and intermittently published in pamphlet form during the civil war years, and subsequently collected and edited by his students, now in a new twenty-five volume edition, testified to his expertise. In this effort Fadlallah, as a poet and litterateur, was, they claimed, aided by his mastery of the Arabic language and keen awareness of the idiom in which scripture was delivered, as well as his appreciation of the context in which it was revealed, what one student calls 'the historical tendency' in Fadlallah's thought.[30]

The emphasis on the authority of the Quran comes at the expense of the hadith, or 'narratives' (*riwayat*) literature relaying the words and deeds of the Prophet and, for the Shi'a, the Imams, the other great scriptural source of the law. This vast body of often contradictory material is, according to Fadlallah's school, the principal source of disagreement between jurists.[31] While of course wholly committed to the corpus as a source of law, Fadlallah held that it must be seen as largely oriented towards the practical application of the principles put forward in the Quran and as answering questions that arose about those principles. Thus *riwayat* can never be used as stand-alone legislative sources and certainly not to overrule the primary Quranic directives.[32]

The volume on majority thus starts with a summary of the references to the issue in the Quran, before moving on to discuss those in the hadith literature and then their uses in the jurisprudential tradition. If we focus on the age of majority for females as the issue in question, we find,

[28] J. Fadlallah 2006: 30ff.

[29] See also e.g. Shakhuri 1998: 303; Khishn 2004: 23; Farhat 2007: 8; Husayni 2007: 10–11, 16–19 and Qubaysi 2007: 10–12.

[30] Husayni 2007: 13, 21.

[31] Not least because of the problems of establishing when a report should or should not be discounted as an instance of dissimulation (*taqiyya*) in the context of oppression of the Shi'i faith. Shakhuri 1998: 50, 77–78.

[32] Farhat 2007: 11 and Husayni 2007: 10–11; interview with Shaykh Husayn al-Khishn, 4 February 2008.

according to the volume, that the best-known opinion (*al-mashhur*) is that their age of maturity is at nine years of age. Fadlallah quotes a series of authorities, from classical jurists such as Tusi (d. 1067) and al-Muhaqqiq al-Hilli (d. 1277), through authorities of the modern era such as Muhsin al-Hakim (d. 1970) and Khu'i, as well as noting the opinion of the Sunni schools. He then discusses the pertinent hadiths before presenting his own opinion, starting with the position of the Quran. Where the Quran mentions the onset of maturity, it does so in connection with sexual maturity, either in connection with marriage, that is, sexual intercourse (*nikah*; as in the verse at Quran 4:6, '... *hata idha balaghu al-nikah* ...') or sexual dreams as evidenced by nocturnal emissions (as in the verse at 24:59, '*wa-idha balagha al-atfal min-kum al-hulum* ...'). Following his view on the authority of the Quran then, this must be taken as the authoritative, defining principle – that majority comes with the onset of sexual maturity – around which turn the secondary, contextualising statements of the hadiths.[33]

Now, the hadith literature does in some instances give a definite age for the majority of females: nine years, in some cases, but also thirteen, in others. Where such an age for female majority is mentioned, however, Fadlallah notes, it is frequently with reference to the onset of menstruation, as in the *riwaya* that states that 'girls reach majority at nine ... and that is because they have their periods at nine', or indeed another which has it that it applies 'if she has reached thirteen years or has started her periods before then'.[34] This confirms, for Fadlallah, that it is sexual maturity that is the principle at stake, that has 'objectivity' (*mawdu'iyya*) in this domain. Stipulated ages should be taken as conventional assessments of when that happens, which is itself a contingent phenomenon to be observed in particular places and times. According to his sources (not stated, although Sayyid Ja'far told me that, 'he asks doctors'[35]), expert opinion now holds that the average age for menstruation is thirteen, although its onset varies with respect to diet and genetic factors. Peoples and places thus differ in this regard, and ages of first menstruation can vary between nine and seventeen years. Thirteen is the average for average climates. (And thus if one did want to come down on the side of one or other of these secondary qualifications of the hadith literature, then he would do so on the side of those that stipulate thirteen as the age of female majority.)[36]

Fadlallah concedes that it could be said that if one took the onset of menstruation as one's principle for determining maturity then that would

[33] J. Fadlallah 2006: 137ff., 174ff. [34] J. Fadlallah 2006: 150, 164.
[35] See also Clarke and Inhorn 2011: 422. [36] J. Fadlallah 2006: 175, 178 and its note.

preclude there being one fixed age as one's standard, even though such fixed standards are frequently employed by legislators as a basis for effective law (such as speed limits, for instance – my example, not his). That could be the case for the application of the Islamic sharia too, especially in the context of establishing an Islamic state, as in states more generally. This is not, Fadlallah thinks, a binding concern, but it does bring us back to the issue of what is usual in a given society. One could then, if it was felt necessary, erect such a standard based on the average age of the onset of menstruation in that society.[37]

Overall, the preponderant position is thus, in his view, that maturity comes with menstruation. Those hadiths that stipulate an age are compatible with that position, and if a fixed age is needed it should be the average age of menstruation in that society. However, at the last, Fadlallah hedges: caution may still enjoin a girl starting to undertake some religious obligations such as prayer, fasting and veiling at the age of nine, in case this more established opinion is in fact the right one.[38] At this point, in 2006, it seems that he was not quite yet fully confident in his views.

One sees this line of thought already present in earlier statements of his position for popular circulation. In the collection of responses to people's questions, *al-Masa'il al-fiqhiyya*, first published in the mid-1990s, one petitioner asks, 'When do girls become religiously responsible such that they are obliged to perform the totality of religious obligations like prayers and fasting and veiling and otherwise?' Fadlallah's response is that:

> The well-known opinion [*al-mashhur*] is that she reaches the stage of responsibility according to age, and that is 'completion of nine [years]'. But it is clear from many indications that she reaches majority through menstruation, so that there are some *riwayat* that speak of [the age of] nine in which comes [the phrase], 'and that is because she starts menstruating at nine' . . . But the position of precaution is that one should not abandon it [i.e., ruling with nine years for the age of majority].[39]

Another questioner asks whether it is correct that Fadlallah holds a distinctive opinion on the matter. He replies, 'The age of responsibility for girls is their reaching nine lunar years based on obligatory precaution, and until now a different opinion has not reached maturity for us.'[40] When we turn to the later systematic and definitive handbook *Fiqh al-shar'ia*, published in 2002–2003, we find the same position, indeed

[37] J. Fadlallah 2006: 178–180. [38] J. Fadlallah 2006: 180.
[39] M.H. Fadlallah 2005a vol. 2: 16.
[40] M.H. Fadlallah 2005a vol. 2: 16, and see also ibid.: 17.

almost word for word the same as the first response above. Opinion, formulated in response to question, in some sense becomes sedimented into other genres, here that of the legal handbook.

Fadlallah later became more confident of his own distinctive opinion, issuing at some point in 2007, I think, an announcement of his new ruling: that the age for girls should be the same as that of boys, coming at puberty, which is thirteen years, or earlier if the physical signs are present. Well-informed journalist Mona Sukkariyya, editor of an important series of interviews with Fadlallah towards the end of his life, told me in 2007 that she had asked him about his 'new fatwas', and he had cited this.[41] So too Shaykh Muhsin 'Atwi told me in 2007 that, after being Fadlallah's opinion for some time, it was now 'a fatwa', disseminated in the usual ways (the mosque, the newsletters, the website). Fadlallah's eldest son Sayyid 'Ali said that generally when his father talked about an opinion he was already sure of it, but wanted to try it out. He estimated that it usually took about five years of consideration before such an opinion could be publicly announced (although the process would seem to have taken longer in this instance).[42] Fadlallah's ideas would also be scrutinised by a 'judicial council' made up of his leading students amongst others, before reaching final, publishable form.[43]

Come 2009 and the publication of a new, revised edition of the 'Q&A' compilation *al-Masa'il al-fiqhiyya*, things had changed. The issue is given new prominence, now the very first encountered in the volume. Question number 1 of 2899 asks, 'What is the age of responsibility for boys and girls, when acts of worship such as prayer, fasting and others become obligatory for them?' And, after a statement of the position for boys, the answer given for girls is:

> As for girls, they become responsible if they have reached thirteen lunar years, which corresponds to twelve solar years, seven months and twenty days, or upon the observation of menstrual bleeding before then. Commendable precaution would be to arrange the effects of responsibility at nine lunar years, especially for prayer and veiling.[44]

His own position is thus now stated with more confidence, although the note of caution is still sounded. Now, however, the precaution of

[41] Interview 22 May 2007. See also Sukkariyya 2007: 213–214 for Fadlallah's discussion of this and also his emergent opinions on divorce (see below).
[42] Interview 21 June 2008.
[43] See http://arabic/bayynat.org.lb/ArticlePage.aspx?id=3447, accessed 12 September 2013, for its fifteen members (also listed in Clarke 2016). The page maintains that this council is a relatively unusual resource for such a figure.
[44] Fadlallah 2009: 11.

following the mainstream opinion of nine years is merely 'recommended' (*mustahabb*) rather than obligatory. It would seem that Fadlallah was not yet confident enough to dispense with this qualification altogether. But, in the highly legalistic terms of Shi'i discourse, this was now a relatively bold statement of his stance.

Conclusion

We have seen how Fadlallah's openness to the issues of his community led to his rethinking of a legal question, within the paradigm of his overall legal approach, tested before his students and other legal audiences, hinted at in rulings for his followers which gradually peeled away layers of precaution before resulting in a clearly stated position, disseminated through various outlets. That process took time – years – and great care. And it was just one element of a far larger project, developing such nuanced positions across the breadth of sharia discourse, as compiled in comprehensive handbooks and a range of popular works.

This looks the very image of the sort of dynamism and progression in the Islamic legal tradition that academic scholars, and many Muslims, wish to emphasise. Even its mechanisms are reminiscent of those that Wael Hallaq, for instance, has influentially celebrated as the means for change within the classical sharia tradition. The personal details and particular circumstances of fatwas, responses to individual questions, are stripped out. And then, in their barebones, generalised forms, these are incorporated into the legal handbooks of the author jurist.[45] Fadlallah's school would, however, see themselves as exceptional in this regard. Not all scholars are so open to the needs of the people or so responsive to the demands of the age. Others can be branded 'traditionalists', stuck in the past.

Here we must note again that what made Fadlallah's 'flexible' attitude possible was in large part the ecological setting within which it was situated. Of course, the particular location where Fadlallah found himself, relatively cosmopolitan Lebanon, lent an especial momentum to the project of 'contemporaneity'. But far from all Lebanese scholars were or are so celebrated. It was away from the constraints of state bureaucracy that a truly conversational stance towards the sharia could be adopted (even if an organisation as large as Fadlallah's still needs its own modes of administration). The independent jurist is not subject to a superior, or even the need to forge a consensus with his peers, in the way that a

[45] Hallaq 1994, 2001.

scholar working within the courts or establishment might be. One does of course need a base on which to stand, and in Chapter 12 we saw the enormous amount of work that went into establishing that base in Fadlallah's case. In this respect, being distant from the scholarly centre, as Fadlallah was, cut both ways: it entailed vulnerability, but also freedom. Flexibility is thus not a quality necessarily intrinsic to sharia discourse (let alone alien to it), but one dependent on a multiplicity of structural factors.

14 The Limits of Authority

In Chapter 13, we saw how a comprehensive and progressive vision of the sharia could be built from the bottom up. Questions remain, however, as to the status of this independent vision in the wider world. In particular, what relation, if any, might it have to the domain of legal dispute and the state that we explored earlier in this book?

As we noted in Chapter 12, the formal vision of the *mujtahid*'s powers does not restrict him to discoursing authoritatively on the sharia. It also considers the extent to which the *mujtahid* has the right to put his legal vision into action. The maximalist interpretation, a relatively recent innovation, is represented by Khomeini's notion of 'the authority of the [Islamic legal] jurist' over affairs of state. The 'traditionalist' stance, by contrast, limits this authority to religious affairs more strictly defined: charitable endowments; the financial affairs of those legally incapable of administering them themselves. Both camps, however, give the *mujtahid* the power to act as judge over people's disputes. The classical debates on this point were more over whether this could be done in the service of what is, in the absence of the perfect justice of the Hidden Imam, a necessarily illegitimate state. By agreement, the *mujtahid* has the right to act as judge. Or, as one judge put it to me, 'Every *mujtahid* is a court in himself.' Indeed, more than that, the preponderant opinion is that only a *mujtahid* has that right; further, his verdict is final and cannot be overturned by another.[1]

Restricting adjudication to the *mujtahid* class would, however, have dramatic consequences for judicial practice, not least in a country like Lebanon, at the relative margins of the Shiʿi scholarly world and thus without the concentrations of very high-level scholars that would be required. Indeed, perhaps as an effect of that distance from the imagined centre, in Lebanon the figure of the *mujtahid* sometimes seems to take on

[1] See e.g. Khishn 2004: 135 (an edition of Fadlallah's research lectures on judgement and the judiciary); Gleave 2008.

an exaggerated, almost mythical stature, as the summit of the religious hierarchy.[2] Some feel there are none such locally. Some even find the generally accepted leading figures of today, in storied Najaf and Qom, no match for the giants of yesteryear. The lawyer who we met in Chapter 8, for instance, who preferred to cite the greats of a past generation like Khu'i, could dismiss even his successor as the pre-eminent figure of Najaf, Ayatollah Sistani, then in his late seventies, with the comment, 'He's new.' Whatever the case, it is hard to imagine scholars of such magnitude being content with the sort of everyday bureaucratic grind that I described in earlier chapters. The actual functioning of the contemporary Lebanese Ja'fari courts thus depends on non-*mujtahid*s being able to serve as judges; and, while not the majority position, there are formal opinions that facilitate this, as I will explain further.[3]

Looked at the other way around, however, what about the possibility of a *mujtahid* who is not a state-appointed judge arbitrating in people's disputes regardless? If one agreed that he was entitled to be considered a *mujtahid* (remembering that his status as such was controversial), Sayyid Fadlallah ought in formal terms to be entitled to act in this way. And, in a limited fashion, he did, through his 'judicial office' (*maktab al-qada'*), also part of the 'apparatus of the *marja'iyya*', alongside the Islamic legal office that we examined in the previous chapter.

Fadlallah's Judicial Office

Like the Islamic legal office, Fadlallah's judicial office was headed up by one of his shaykhly staff, the incumbent at the time of my research being Shaykh 'Ali Mir'i. Shaykh Mir'i told me that the office had then (in 2008) been open for twenty-three years and that he had worked there for seven

[2] In Iran, on the other hand, not only are there a multiplicity of prestigious centres of religious learning, but subsequent to extensive reform of the seminary system, one can also now obtain degree-like certifications of *ijtihad* in relatively short time. Further, many state-appointed positions in the Islamic Republic require *mujtahid* status. One can thus imagine a greater routinisation in this regard, in comparison with Lebanon at least. On the transformation of the judiciary after the Revolution, see Arjomand 1988: 184–188 and Zubaida 2003: 197–217.

[3] See Khishn 2004: 163ff. on such 'conditions of necessity' (*halat al-darura*). This was obviously also the case in previous generations and elsewhere in the Shi'i world. See e.g. Mervin 2000 and Weiss 2010 on the Ottoman and early Lebanese precedents and Floor 1983 on nineteenth century Iran. Article 162 of the Constitution of the Islamic Republic of Iran stipulated that judges should be *mutjahid*s. But Khomeini allowed non-*mujtahid* judges to serve because of the lack of suitably qualified candidates. Where a judge did not himself exercise *ijtihad*, he was to follow a recognised authority (Article 167), in practice most often Khomeini apparently (Schirazi 1997: 65–68, 82n27; see also Arjomand 1988: 188 and Zubaida 2003: 199–200).

of them, his predecessor, Shaykh Hasan ‘Abdallah, having served for eleven years before that.[4] In 2007–2008, this office was in the same building as the legal office, just across the landing, and somewhat more comfortably furnished although cosy in size. As in the state courts, though on a more modest scale, a few black leather-look easy chairs sat by the shaykh’s desk, and a calligraphic wall hanging appropriately cited a Quranic verse on the right treatment of wives. Unlike the state religious courts, a small portrait of Sayyid Fadlallah hung on the wall, reminding one of the personalized authority on which the office depends. The bookshelves in Shaykh Mir‘i’s office were, I could not help noticing, also much more fully stocked (with Fadlallah’s works but also those of others): Shaykh Mir‘i possesses the space in a different way from judges in the courts.

In keeping with this more ‘personal’ setting, the proceedings of the office were unfortunately markedly less accessible to me than those of the state sharia courts, whose publicity constitutes part of their ‘civility’, as I have discussed. When I asked if I could attend the office’s sessions, I was refused, because of ‘people’s secrets’. Going to the office for answering individual questions about the sharia, the *maktab al-istifta’at*, as I did regularly as Shaykh Mir‘i knew, was no problem, he said; but sitting in with him would be. Issuing fatwas in response to people’s queries and making judgements over their lives are not of the same order. Not only were the sessions private, so were the documents, and I did not have access to any case files either. They don’t let anybody see them, including even the parties involved, Shaykh Mir‘i told me. People might want a copy, but they don’t let them have one. Only the ayatollah would see the papers.

I wanted to clarify the standing of the office and his work in it. First of all, is it a court (*mahkama*)? Shaykh Mir‘i here invoked a distinction with which we are by now very familiar. From a religious legal (*shar‘i*) point of view, it is, he told me. But as far as the law (*qanun*) is concerned, it is not. It has no executive powers, unless – reminiscent of our discussion of Shaykh Hammoud’s offices in Chapter 11 – the parties to a case were to

[4] Interview 21 June 2008. I also draw on an earlier interview on 4 July 2007. Fadlallah’s website stated that the ayatollah had performed the role of ‘judicial recourse’ (*marja‘iyya qada’iyya*), especially in marital matters, for longer than that – more than forty years, and only began to delegate such obligations to his representatives in the early 1980s, presumably because of the increasing density of these and his other commitments: http://arabic.bayynat.org.lb/sira/moassasat.htm, accessed 13 October 2009. That would imply that his activities in this field dated back to before his *marja‘iyya* had ‘emerged’. According to Shaykh Mir‘i, this is to be explained by that fact that Fadallah was a *mujtahid* long before he became a *marja‘*.

draw up an agreement at a public notary. Then they could take the office's ruling to a court of execution, in cases of financial disputes at least – for the business of the office falls into two broad parts, financial and marital. And so, as in the case of Shaykh Hammoud, one might better see the work of the office as one of arbitration (*tahkim*).[5] For those who acknowledged his authority, Fadlallah's verdict would be binding in God's eyes (where that of the civil courts might not be). But he had no executive apparatus beyond people's proper sense of religious obligation. Of course, 'If there were an Islamic state . . .', comes the familiar refrain.

During Fadlallah's lifetime, while statements and evidence would be taken and compiled by Shaykh Mir'i, the files would be sent to the ayatollah himself, who might even meet with the parties concerned or listen to a witness afresh, something he apparently used to do more frequently in earlier years. Shaykh Mir'i is happy to help mediate, or supervise a mutually agreed divorce, or witness a divorce at the husband's instance. But he could not impose a decision. 'I said to him [i.e., Fadlallah] at the beginning, if you want me to do this I won't judge, this is a very great responsibility.'

As far as matters of family law are concerned, why would people have recourse to Fadlallah's office instead of the state courts? Echoing themes we have also met before, the most important reason, in Shaykh Mir'i's opinion, was time. Where in the state courts, just to get the first appointment would take three to four months, with them it would be a week to ten days. He estimated in 2008 that each day they had four appointments, so twenty cases a week. Allowing for a month's holiday in August, one could say they practice for forty weeks a year. Not all those appointments would represent different cases of course. I thus suggested a rough estimate of about 200 different files a year, and Shaykh Mir'i did not disagree.

Sayyid Fadlallah's judicial office was not the only one: other *marja*'s have offices in Lebanon and Hizballah provide their own judicial and arbitration services as well.[6] I thus wondered if one had to be a *muqallid*, or follower, of Fadlallah to use his services in particular. This was not so.

[5] See also Khishn 2004: 164. This way of framing the *mujtahid*'s judicial authority has historical depth. See e.g. Bhalloo 2015 on Iran.

[6] On the latter see Hamzeh 1997. Hamzeh draws on interviews with Shaykh Naim Qassim, Deputy General Secretary of Hizballah, who makes some striking assertions about the scope and reach of these services, which include courts proper – that is, that assume executive power, although, since the end of the 1975–1990 civil war, this has generally been restricted to cases between party members. They do not charge for their services, which presumably adds considerably to their attraction (ibid.: 102–105). For my own part, I interviewed (5 April 2008) the sharia legal representative of Ayatollah Khamenei in Lebanon, Shaykh Muhammad Tawfiq Muqdad, who acknowledged the work of his own

In cases of financial arbitration, for example, it was enough that the parties trusted the sayyid as an arbitrator: as a *marja'*, he could be considered of irreproachable probity. Of course other *marja'*s could be equally trusted. But whichever *marja'* one might choose to arbitrate, they would need to have all the relevant documentation to hand. That was much easier in the case of Fadlallah's locally based operation than it might be for others, based in Iraq and Iran, and they thus had a corresponding competitive advantage.

But what of the other potentially distinctive and attractive characteristic of their office, Fadlallah's notably 'open-minded' and 'contemporary' rulings, famously progressive in matters of women's rights, and thus family law? Supervising marriage contracts, for which Fadlallah notoriously did not require the permission of a bride's guardian as we have seen, was something that happened elsewhere and not one of the judicial office's concerns, focused more on disputes after marriage. (As Shaykh Mir'i joked, 'The Sayyid marries people, I divorce them.') Regarding maintenance and the provision of a sharia compliant marital home, issues which Shaykh Miri'i did have to deal with, there is little legal debate. Regarding 'obedience' (*ta'a*), however, there is a point of difference as to whether a wife can leave the house without her husband's permission: where the various *marja'*s mostly agree that she cannot, Fadlallah said she can.[7] Cases of custody (*hadana*), where Fadlallah also had his own relatively progressive opinion, were rare.[8] Most important, however, was Fadlallah's position on those forms of divorce that require the intervention of *al-hakim al-shar'i*, 'the rightful judge', generally taken as synonymous with the *mujtahid*. Not least of those is *talaq al-hakim*, 'divorce by the judge', where a judicial divorce is imposed against the husband's will; but they also include an annulment (*faskh*) for reason of physical or mental impairment or its concealment before the marriage.[9]

office in mediation, and indeed in ruling on some disputes, awarding maintenance for instance. But, he noted, 'we don't divorce'.

7 Sukkariyya 2007: 214.

8 Fadlallah (2002–2003 vol. 3: 545) ruled that the right to custody remains with the mother until seven (lunar) years of age for both boys and girls, where the best-known opinion, applied in the courts, was two years (the period of breastfeeding) for boys and seven for girls (Ni'ma 1996: 119).

9 On the latter point, one important area of debate is over sexual incapacity. Many other authorities find that if the husband were capable of consummating the marriage but then became incapable this does not constitute grounds for annulment. But Fadlallah thought it did (2002–2003 vol. 3: 466; cf. Khu'i 1975 vol. 2: 380; Ni'ma 1996: 55 and Mir'i 2003: 205–206 and Sistani 2003 vol. 3: 84).

Talaq al-Hakim

As we noted earlier, such a judicial divorce is notoriously difficult to achieve in the Ja'fari courts, in contrast with the equivalent procedure in Lebanon's Sunni courts (*tafriq*). While the latter were amongst the most common cases that I encountered, I never saw one of *talaq al-hakim*. Indeed, one of my best lawyer contacts was still boasting of one he had managed to get through the courts in 1996. This was the case that had 'made him famous'. A ruling of *talaq al-hakim* in the courts requires proof of desertion (my terms), defined as a lack of maintenance. That is, the husband must choose between either maintaining his wife or divorcing her: if he refuses both, then the judge may impose divorce. *Infaq* (maintenance) or *talaq*, as the saying goes.[10] Most disputes thus start with a suit for maintenance, and it is not hard for a husband, or someone acting on his behalf, to avert the issue by paying it. Even this rather modest infringement of the husband's sovereignty over his marriage seems controversial.[11] Still more so is the possibility of taking other forms of maltreatment of the wife by her husband as grounds for judicial divorce, which can in any case be hard to prove. Someone could be gentle in public, but beat his wife in private, as one judge put it. A contrast can be drawn with the more accommodating procedures that are in place in the Sunni courts considered earlier, and the greater willingness on the part of those judges to accept a range of evidence as proof.

That brings us to the crux of the problem. The root of the difference between the two court systems, as it was put to me, is in the quality of the judge who can institute such a divorce, against the husband's will. For the Sunnis, as the Shi'a would see it, 'any judge in a court' can perform such a divorce; for the Shi'a, only the '*hakim shar'i*', the 'rightful judge', can do so. This is because of the gravity accorded such a procedure, given that the Islamic tradition has made divorce a core

[10] See e.g. Khu'i 1975 vol. 2: 413.

[11] I find the jurisprudence here difficult, but sense that this represents an extension of the discussions over the permissibility of divorce in the case of a missing husband, on which see e.g. Khu'i 1975 vol. 2: 411–413; Ni'ma 1996: 168ff. and Fadlallah 2002–2003 vol. 3: 607ff. Mughniyya (1979: 452–454) says as much, and notes the general conservatism of Twelver Shi'i scholars on this point, while also citing a number of leading authorities of an older generation (Yazdi, Isfahani, Hakim and others) who backed more accommodating positions (from the wife's perspective). He comments that those who radically restrict the possibilities of judicial divorce do so 'on account of caution and the fear that this power should be misused by persons devoid of the necessary learning and commitment to the faith ... This is the sole reason which has caused me to refrain.' See also Mughniyya 2003: part 6, pp. 61–65, where he says he knows of no more pressing a legal issue.

right of the husband. It thus requires great exactness, one judge insisted. Here, unlike in other cases, only a real *mujtahid* will do it seems.[12] This strengthening of the requirements, as one lawyer had it, is 'because the regular judge [*al-qadi al-'adi*] is nearer to the regular man', whereas 'You don't get to be *al-hakim al-shar'i* [i.e., a *mujtahid*] unless you do not share the characteristics of a normal person.' Otherwise divorce could be imposed for the wrong, possibly corrupt, reasons: 'Maybe the woman says to the judge, "Divorce me now and I'll sleep with you tomorrow."' The scenario seems fantastic, but one gets a sense of the logic.

As a *mujtahid*, then, according to his own school at least, Sayyid Fadlallah should have been so qualified. And, as ever, he had his own, more helpful (for women) positions on the matter. As per his usual method, here he argued from the Quran, taking the Quranic verse (2:229) discussing divorce, 'Keep [your wife] married with the conventional kindness or release [her] in the good and right way' (*fa-imsak bi-ma'ruf aw tasrih bi-ihsan*), as 'the general principle which governs the relation between spouses'. Where the husband is not treating his wife well, as when he does not maintain her or beats her, he should thus then change his ways or else he must divorce her.[13] If we add to this the verse (4:19), 'And live with them [wives] as it is known you should' (*wa-'ashiru-hunna bi-l-ma'ruf*), we must know that right marriage entails not denying sexual relations to one's wife.[14]

This is important because the conditions for *talaq al-hakim* are commonly defined in part by the following tradition concerning the sixth Shi'i Imam and great legal authority Ja'far al-Sadiq (d. 765). The Imam was reportedly asked about,

> A woman whose husband was away for four years and did not maintain her, and she did not know if he were alive or dead. Is his guardian compelled to divorce her?
>
> THE IMAM: Yes. And if he did not have a guardian then the ruler divorces her.
> THE QUESTIONER: And if the guardian said, 'I shall maintain her'?
> THE IMAM: Then he is not compelled to divorce her.

[12] See e.g. Mughniyya 2003: part 6, p. 65.

[13] At Fadlallah 2010: 527, he finds that physical maltreatment must be of a level to constitute a danger to her life.

[14] As Sayyid 'Ali Fadlallah explained (interview, 21 June 2008), much turns on what one makes of 'the known' (*al-ma'ruf*) way of treating one's wife. The mainstream of the tradition concentrates on the provision of maintenance; Fadlallah's reading was wider, including a woman's sexual needs, about which there is also a difference between the *marja*'s. See the very full discussion in Shakhuri 2002: 25ff.

THE QUESTIONER: What if she said, 'I want what women want [i.e. sex], and I cannot forbear and I cannot stay as I am'?
THE IMAM: She cannot, and receives no favour, if he were to maintain her.

Fadlallah was wary of using this tradition as a basis for restricting the wife's possibilities for divorce, as others do, as it seems to contravene the fundamental principles laid down in the Quran and may lead to her falling into the terrible sin of adultery (*zina*). He thus came to argue that in such a situation the rightful judge could divorce her without her husband's consent, a controversial position, and one contested in Lebanon.[15]

Given Fadlallah's relatively progressive opinion on the matter and the difficulty of making such a case in the courts, women did, it seems, come to the office for this purpose. Here, Shaykh Mir'i told me, they should be an adherent (*muqallida*) of his teachings more generally and they do check if they are. In keeping with the restriction of this power to *al-hakim al-shar'i*, as Shaykh Mir'i told me, 'Only the Sayyid can do this.' Of course, first of all Shaykh Mir'i recommended and attempted reconciliation. But then he collected all the evidence and handed it on to the ayatollah, while continuing to follow the case from beginning to end. And if it came to it, Fadlallah would then give Shaykh 'Ali permission to divorce the couple on his behalf.

The Ayatollah Spurned

I could not see examples of such cases myself. For reasons of privacy, they had to remain occluded. But they do leave their traces, albeit dim ones, in the rulings of the state sharia courts that I did have access to. One published ruling from the Ja'fari court of Saida in 2001 concerns a case to establish a woman's divorce, 'a *talaq al-hakim* from her husband ... at the office of Sayyid Muhammad Husayn Fadlallah'. The woman produced the document (*waraqa*) from the office, which stated that the divorce had been made on the basis of the husband neither maintaining nor divorcing her. It emerges from the ruling that the

[15] Qubaysi 1995: 30–31. For a more straightforward statement of Fadlallah's position see Fadlallah 2010: 526–527. Towards the end of his life he had reportedly been working on another opinion, that where a wife hated her husband, the judge could also divorce her. This would be a form of *khul'*, divorce at the wife's instance in return for a consideration, but judicially imposed. It seems, however, that he never finalised his thinking and was not confident enough at that point to publish it. Interviews with Sayyid 'Ali Fadlallah, 12 June 2008, and Shaykh Muhsin 'Atwi, 13 June 2008; Sukkariyya 2007: 213–214.

respondent, her husband, was in prison. He – or his lawyer – argued for rejection of the case on a procedural technicality, on the grounds of jurisdiction, that is, her having raised the case before the wrong court (in terms of location). And the court found in his favour on just those grounds, obviating the need for a potentially fraught discussion of the validity of Fadlallah's divorce.[16]

For such pronouncements from a non-state authority are clearly a challenge to the courts' jurisdiction. Fadlallah's offices were sensitive to that. A notice in the waiting room of the judicial office read, 'Please, no cases to be raised that are the subject of cases at other courts'. Nominally, their office was for people who were convinced of the ayatollah's probity as arbitrator and happy to abide by his decisions. As one judge had it, thinking of a *mujtahid*'s authority more generally, if he were given a ruling against his interests by the *mujtahid* judge he would think, 'Oh is that the right thing to do? Oh good.' Or as Shaykh Mir'i put it, you either believe in the sharia or you don't.

But of course the reality of conflict is otherwise. If one party does not receive the ruling they were hoping for then they may well pursue the matter at a different venue, most notably the courts. A *mujtahid*'s ruling is, however, supposed to be unchallengeable, even by another *mujtahid*. That is the formal model at least.[17] In theory, then, from the perspective of Fadlallah's offices, the rulings of their authority ought to be respected by their fellow religious professionals working in the official courts. But in practice they were not. While there were rumours of individual judges who were sympathetic towards Fadlallah and his opinions, I could never track one down. It was difficult, a matter of 'politics'. Fadlallah's organisation stood apart from the networks of patronage to which the official Shi'i community is tied, the latter more closely affiliated to Amal than its rival Hizballah, from which Fadlallah had in any case become somewhat estranged. And the shaykhs manning the official community, and especially its previous leader Muhammad Mahdi Shams al-Din, were not well disposed towards the Shi'i Islamist current generally. It would seem that in many, if not most cases, Fadlallah's rulings were actively spurned. According to Shaykh Mir'i, some judges would not even respect a marriage contract supervised by him. If someone came with a contract written by Fadlallah then they would make the couple repeat the marriage in court. This was confirmed by others. I asked an experienced lawyer whether there were judges that followed Fadlallah or employed his opinions. 'No!', he scoffed. He suspected that this hostility stemmed

[16] Barakat 2005: 149–150. [17] See e.g. Sistani 2002 vol. 1: 15 and Khishn 2004: 221ff.

from envy. 'The courts don't like him, because he knows more than them.' He mentioned one judge, who, he thought, if he was presented with a ruling from Fadlallah, would 'throw it in the bin'.

While I did not see anything so dramatic, the judge he mentioned certainly was not well disposed. I saw a woman come before him trying to establish a marriage contract her sister had performed through Fadlallah's offices. She had come to the judge with a document she wanted him to authorise. But he was having none of it. 'But this is from Sayyid Muhammad Husayn!', she said (note the affectionate tone). No problem with Fadlallah performing a *katab al-kitab*, the judge said, he is a 'man of religion' after all (*rajul al-din*, hardly magnificent recognition). But he does not have an administrative role; this is not one of his competencies. Another time I saw this judge performing a *katab al-kitab* himself. Afterwards the bride's father was joking, 'Doesn't the Sayyid say' that you do not have to have the father's permission to get married. 'Which sayyid?', asked the judge sharply. The father was rather nonplussed. 'Well ...' 'No, don't worry, which sayyid?' 'Sayyid Muhammad Husayn ...' 'Fadlallah you mean.' 'No no, it's ...' The man's awareness of having spoken out of turn was tangible.

It is not, then, that one does not see the signs of the activities of Fadlallah's organisation and others in the court system. I saw one couple come before another judge with a problem: the husband had wanted to divorce his wife and marry someone else, but there had been a question as to the way he had gone about it, some issue as to its validity. So they had asked about it at Fadlallah's office and been told to wait three months before doing anything, 'according to the opinion of the *marja'*'. 'All the opinions are the same here', the judge commented.[18] One woman complained to another judge that, her husband was threatening 'to take me to Hizballah', that is, to the similar services offered by Hizballah, so she would be judged 'by the sharia' (*shar'an*): 'But I want the path of the court, I don't want the path of the sharia' (*bas ana biddi tariq al-mahkama, ma biddi tariq al-shar'*). 'Look', the judge said, 'it's *shar'* here and *shar'* there. Do you think he will apply something different?' The court had no relation to such things, she was told.[19] The recorder of an initial court judge was asked about the consequences of

[18] In another such incident before the same judge, a couple reported seeing the same shaykh at Fadlallah's offices, as a result of which the husband had given the wife $15,000 as a present (*hadiya*), which surely speaks to the authority such offices can exert. But, 'Two days later she brought a case against me!' (i.e. in the courts), he complained.

[19] Conversely, I saw a case of visitation (*ru'ya*) of children, where the judge asked the father why he was not letting the mother see her child, and the man produced the original of an

taking a dispute to such an out of court authority. It has no effect in court, he replied. You could bring a *marja‘* and it would have no effect.

The Intimacy of Authority

Notwithstanding Fadlallah's controversial reputation, the ease with which he, and indeed the notion of any *marja‘* intervening, could be dismissed within the court system seemed striking. That was not only due to the intense impression of Fadlallah's prestige and scholarly acumen that I had gained from my research in his organisation, but also because of the clarity of what I had taken to be the formal model of Shi‘i religio-legal authority. Again, in that model, which is of course that of the *mujtahid* class itself, a radical difference is drawn between the expert *mujtahid*s on the one hand (from whose ranks the even higher status *marja‘*s emerge) and non-*mujtahid*s on the other, who should follow a *mujtahid*'s guidance in matters of religious conscience. *Mujtahid*s are clearly qualified to arbitrate over people's disputes; more than that, they alone are so qualified according to the majority scholarly position. But this personal and ultimate authority of the *marja‘-mujtahid* seemed largely effaced in the Lebanese Ja‘fari courts.

The view that a judge has to be a *mujtahid* is, however, let it be said, not the only one.[20] President of the Ja‘fari courts, Shaykh Hasan ‘Awwad, while reluctant in a brief interview to elaborate there and then upon what he clearly thought a complex and important topic (one which we unfortunately never got to discuss in more detail), sketched out a broad opposition between the opinion that the judge does have to be a *mujtahid*, and one that he could be given the deputed authority (*wikala*) to act as such by a *mujtahid*, or even that he could judge without such licence, in as much as he knows the relevant rulings and applies them. He himself allowed both the latter possibilities, without which – remembering the rarefied status the title of *mujtahid* implies – a viable court system in Lebanon would not be a realistic prospect. Or as one of the judges I sat with put it, while it might be true that Ayatollah Sistani, for example,

agreement (*ittifaq*) from 2007 signed by a shaykh at Hizballah's judicial office in Beirut (*Qada' hizb allah fi bayrut*). This judge was, I knew, not an enthusiast of Hizballah. He admitted as such, but he said, he knew the shaykh in question. And he entered a note for the file that the defendant had produced a binding document of agreed settlement (*sulh*). See also Hamzeh 1997: 102.

20 See Khishn 2004: 133–163 for a review of the arguments. According to Deputy Secretary General Na‘im Qassim, the judges in Hizballah's non-state courts must be *mujtahids*, with at least fifteen years of sharia studies behind them. (Here one imagines the routinised, rather than mythologised, *mujtahid*.) But, where there is no *mujtahid*, ‘a *muqallid* may preside’ (Hamzeh 1997: 101, 104).

holds that the judge has to be a *mujtahid*, in Lebanon they thought 'it is enough that he knows what he is doing'. There are different sorts of judging (*qada'*) at issue: for what you get in the Lebanese family law courts, there is no problem with a judge applying the generally agreed rulings. By and large, the legal questions that come before the courts would indeed seem hardly to require the pondering of God's law afresh. Does a husband have to pay his wife maintenance? Yes. To bring a *mujtahid* to bear would be like the proverbial sledgehammer and nut.

I also discussed the matter with two of Shaykh 'Awwad's most prominent consultant judges, Sayyid Muhammad Hasan al-Amin[21] and Shaykh 'Abd al-Halim Sharara. Sayyid al-Amin thought the judge must be a *mujtahid* (and openly said that he considered himself one), without commenting on whether all the judges practicing in Lebanon were such, but also thought that there was little need for *ijtihad* in the context of the law applied in the courts, given that it was mostly settled. Shaykh Sharara also privileged the notion that the judge should be a *mujtahid*, but said that in practice, some judges are *mujtahid*s and others are not, but have a licence (*ijaza*) to practice from one. Where there are differences of opinion, which is not often in matters of family law, then there are well-known opinions (*ara' mashhura*), and there is a third school of opinion that says the judge should rule with that. A highly competent scholar not involved with the courts told me that, struck by the same issue, he had asked judges the same question, and they had told him that they go by the best-known or preponderant opinion within the school (*al-mashhur*) as to a given legal issue.[22]

These are the opinions of those at the top of the courts' hierarchy. As for the initial court judges that I spent most of my time with, one explained that, 'In every court the judge applies either his own opinion – if he is a *mujtahid* – or he applies that of the *mujtahid* he sees as the most learned.' I wondered whether many of the judges in the courts were

[21] A public figure in his own right as a leading liberal and critic of the Shi'i Islamist movement. See Abisaab 2009: 237; Abisaab and Abisaab 2014: xxii.

[22] I could add another possibility, which is that one could be a 'partial' (*mutajazzi'*) *mujtahid*, able to interpret the sharia in some issues but not all, as opposed to the comprehensive competence of an 'absolute' (*mutlaq*) *mujtahid*. Fadlallah, for instance, asserted this (2002–2003 vol. 1: 17; indeed he went further, seeing no barrier to any person of quality [*insan fadil*] undertaking the judgeship, and, characteristically, wondering whether they might not be better at administration than some *mujtahids*, 'who live with books more than they live with reality' [Khishn 2004: 163]). But it is not the preponderant position (see Khishn 2004: 139–140), nor was it one I heard aired in the courts. I tried out the idea with one of my judges and he dismissed it out of hand: 'Either you've got it [total mastery], or you haven't.' On the other hand, if I read things right, Sistani, generally more conservative, does allow the partial *mujtahid* to judge on issues in which he is competent (2002: 14–15).

*mujtahid*s. 'Look', he told me, 'you don't see someone who is forty who is a *mujtahid*. It takes years and years and years. And people have to judge you a *mujtahid* – they look to his writings, but also to his works.' Or, as another judge suggested, we would know them from their pupils, who should themselves be great scholars (*'ulama' kibar*). Hence, 'There aren't very many.' That would clearly imply that there are not many, if any judges in Lebanon who are *mujtahid*s, and also, one might assume, that neither of these two are putting themselves forward as such: both are in their fifties at the most, rather than the seventies that might be the norm; and while both impressively scholarly, neither, to my knowledge, is yet the author of substantial works of their own or commands any disciples. The judge must have a license (*wikala*) from the *marja'*, the first noted. 'This is important: I have to know if God is content for me to judge.' But when I asked him directly whether he was himself a *mujtahid* and if not, which one he depended upon, he evaded the question.[23] On another occasion I tried another tack, asking him how many *mujtahid*s there were in all Lebanon. He told me that he had a position on this, but he was not going to tell me what it was.

It was not so much that the model of sharia-legal authority that I was used to did not apply then, as that establishing where people placed themselves with reference to it was problematic. However, even if much of the legal business of the courts is relatively uncontroversial, some issues are less settled and thus, I thought, might have some further diagnostic potential. I was sitting with my first judge one time, when a lawyer asked about a sensitive and contested point, the ages at which boys and girls are normally considered to have left the custody of their mother and to be transferred to that of their father. The preponderant opinion (*al-mashhur*) within the school is that this is at two years for a boy and seven for a girl, a position itself heavily critiqued by the women's reform movements that we mentioned earlier in the book (in Chapter 2).[24] A yet more conservative opinion, favoured by such distinguished figures as Sistani and, more important still perhaps, his great teacher and predecessor as leading scholar of the seminaries of Najaf, Ayatollah Khu'i, is

[23] I missed what seems in retrospect an important distinction here. To have a licence of delegated authority (*wikala*) from a *marja'* does not, I think, necessarily imply 'emulation' (*taqlid*) of them.

[24] Again, this movement did win change for the Sunni courts in 2011, but not for the Ja'fari ones. There are, however, individual judges in the Ja'fari courts reportedly prepared to award mothers custody until greater ages, but those rulings can then still be overturned on appeal. See Hamdan 2017.

two years for both (which is the one this judge in fact usually employed).[25] As to what is actually ruled, it depends on the judge, he told her. 'What, which *marja'* they follow?', she asked (admittedly perhaps inspired by the conversation I had just been having with him). 'No, how they read the texts.' This seemed at odds with his previous position that, unless the judge were himself a *mujtahid*, he applied the opinion of the scholar he thought the most learned. I tried picking up the same point another way on another occasion, saying that I had found that the authoritative *marja'*s Khu'i and Sistani ruled with two years for both sexes but the courts did not, rather following the preponderant view of two and seven for boys and girls respectively. No, he corrected me. Rather, each judge rules according to his opinion. And if it goes to appeal then the appeals court panel will rule with theirs.

My second judge also favoured two years as the age of paternal custody for both boys and girls. I asked him straight out if this indicated that he was practising *taqlid* of Khu'i or Sistani. As was his wont, but also perhaps indicating the indelicate nature of the question, he did not answer directly. Rather he began by discussing the notion of 'the most learned' (*al-a'lam*), and noting that Khu'i definitely was such. So, regarding custody, many scholars follow his opinion. Or they go with the preponderant opinion (*al-mashhur*); or they follow their *ijtihad*, according to strict conditions of course. I pressed him as to his own case. Was ruling with two years for both girls and boys an instance of him following Khu'i or his own *ijtihad*? 'A bit of both perhaps.' My line of questioning was clearly awkward, perhaps even misguided.

One might nevertheless assume that, however discreet a judge might be in conversation, in their written rulings they would have to be more explicit about the basis for their decisions. But in keeping with the broader lack of Islamic legal discussion in the courts' rulings discussed in Chapter 8, references to such scholarly authority are also absent from their recorded verdicts. Again, in these rulings, there is almost no citation at all of sharia discourse per se, except in the vaguest terms: 'the sharia' (*al-shar'*); 'Ja'fari law' (*al-shar' al-Ja'fari*); 'as is written in Islamic

[25] See Khu'i 1975 vol. 2: 391; www.sistani.org/arabic/qa/0450, accessed 8 September 2017; this is also the implication of Mir'i 2003: 202. Khu'i remains the definitive *marja'* for many of the older generation, including, one would hazard, many judges. Sistani has only gradually and more recently emerged as his 'successor'. It is Khu'i's long pre-eminence rather than any 'official' status that explains why 'Arif al-Zayn (2003a: 6) cites passages from his legal handbooks in a compilation of legislation relevant to Lebanon's sharia courts. I have seen copies of both Khu'i's and Sistani's books on judges' desks.

jurisprudence' (*ka-ma muharrar fi-fiqh*).[26] We have already met the lawyer who prided himself on being 'the only lawyer who also writes *shar*'', his epic submissions rich in references to the legal giants of the past. But the rulings show that the judges de-particularise such discussions. In a complex divorce case involving a highly mobile couple, both working for the United Nations, one resident in Croatia, the other in Georgia, where the wife was suing for divorce based on ill-treatment and a long-standing lack of maintenance, the two teams of lawyers brought to bear arguments drawing on sayings of the Prophet and Imam 'Ali, as well as distinguished authorities such as Lebanon's Shaykh Muhammad Jawad Mughniyya (d. 1979) and Ayatollah Khu'i, and a compendium of personal status law by previous president of the Ja'fari courts Shaykh 'Abdallah Ni'ma (1996). After pages recounting these arguments, the ruling swiftly dismisses the case with no discussion of these sharia-legal justifications. In a case I have already cited, where a divorced wife asked that the bridal gift (*mahr*) she was owed be recalculated in order to mitigate its radical diminishment due to inflation since their marriage, and her ex-husband argued that this was inadmissible, citing in support a fatwa from Ayatollah Sistani, the ruling found in his favour, but referenced only the less specific support of 'the opinions of the jurists' (*ara' al-fuqaha'*).[27]

Although there are a number of ways in which one could explicitly and specifically justify the authority of the Ja'fari court judge in terms of the *marja'–mujtahid–muqallid* model then, much remained unsaid. In pragmatic terms, and certainly as far as the Lebanese state is concerned, however, this hardly seems to matter. The courts function regardless. By not depending on the opinions of an external master jurist, they also thereby preserve their autonomy within the wider field of Shi'i religious authority. Nevertheless, the awkwardness that my line of questioning provoked seemed to me significant, symptomatic of a certain intimacy to the topic. *Taqlid* – that is, which *mujtahid* one 'emulates' – is, I should say, more generally portrayed as a 'private' (*khass*) or 'personal' (*shakhsi*) matter.[28] In the case of these Islamic legal specialists in particular, it is still less surprising that a relationship that could be seen to imply scholarly dependency might not be a subject for casual public discussion. One does not surrender one's autonomy and authority so lightly. But the stark

[26] Barakat 2005: 40, 74, 204. One could multiply the examples.

[27] Barakat 2005: 165–172, 189–191.

[28] As I noted earlier, the same is also said of Sufi commitments and allegiances, which also speak to relationships of religious dependency. See Clarke 2014 for a discussion there of authority's intimacy and vulnerability.

formal opposition between *mujtahid* and non-*mujtahid* also seems radically reductive of a much richer gradation of knowledge and self-esteem.[29] These judges' learning clearly cannot be equated with that of the non-specialist, even if some are more scholarly than others. That is not to say that they are beyond challenge, especially on the part of a sharp lawyer. Far from it. Intimacy also speaks to a certain vulnerability, a vulnerability that extends even to the claims of someone of Fadlallah's stature, as we have seen. To talk of oneself as a *mujtahid* is to invite critical comment, or even ridicule. The formal binary model of *mujtahid* versus *muqallid* does not cover all of what one might want to say about the landscape of authority in the courts, or indeed outside of them. It does, however, provide the dominant discourse for discussing it.[30]

Talaq al-Hakim Revisited

There is one exception, however, to this effacing of personal religious authority within the court system, an exception that does indeed seem to prove the rule. That is those rare cases of judicial divorce (*talaq al-hakim*), which cannot do without the weight of a *mujtahid* as we have seen. Although I have no field evidence, fitting the reported rarity of such cases, I do have a handful of published cases. Ironically, given the rivalry between him and Fadlallah, it would seem that before his death in 2001 Shaykh Muhammad Mahdi Shams al-Din, then chairman of the Supreme Shiʿi Islamic Council, the community's officially recognised administrative institution, was the one acting as 'the rightful judge', *al-hakim al-sharʿi*.[31] The words of a lawyer with a deep memory say it

[29] So too, *taqlid* – adopting the opinion of an acknowledged authority – presumably means something different for the layman and for a professional jurist. In the latter case, I could be over-reading the significance in terms of scholarly prestige of an admission of *taqlid*, 'hardly seen as "blind" or mindless acquiescence to the opinion of others, but rather as the reasoned and highly calculated insistence on abiding by a particular authoritative legal doctrine', as Hallaq puts it (2001: ix; see also Reinhart 1994: 20). The Sunni tradition, which is what Hallaq has foremost in mind, has a more developed structure of gradated authority, perhaps due to its historically closer involvement in the practice of the state: see e.g. Hallaq 2001; Burak 2015; Al-Azem 2017. But note also my discussion of the 'partial [*mutajazzi'*] *mujtahid*'.

[30] See Bhallo 2015 on nineteenth century Iran, where judges' claims to *mujtahid* status were rubbished as a way of challenging their verdicts.

[31] Going further back, I have a published ruling from 1931 of a *talaq al-hakim* on the grounds of desertion and lack of maintenance (Ayyub 2008: 379–382). The judge is stated as Sayyid Muhammad Ibrahim al-Husayni, who writes that although such a ruling is a difficult one for the *hakim* (using that term) to bring, he finds her case made and 'decides with her divorce from him according to our sharia-legal guardianship [*wilaya sharʿiyya*]'. Mughniyya (2003: part 6, p. 65) cites distinguished Lebanese scholars Muhsin al-Amin (d.1952) and ʿAbd al-Husayn Sharaf al-Din (d.1957) as having

all: in his day, Shams al-Din was 'a *marja'*, a *faqih*, he divorced people'. In the context of wider understandings of the global and Lebanese landscape of the upper echelons of Shi'i religious authority this might seem surprising. Shams al-Din was certainly a highly respected scholar, but not generally spoken of as a *marja'*. Indeed he had rather dismissive comments on the very institution. But here, despite his never having gained – or even sought – the popular following that Fadlallah had, he could enjoy what perhaps he and his rather less numerous supporters nevertheless thought his due.[32]

In one ruling, a wife brought a case of establishing divorce (*ithbat al-talaq*) before the initial court judge of Tyre at the end of 1999, two days after receiving a ruling of divorce from 'His Excellency Ayatollah [the title implies *mujtahid* status] Shaykh Muhammad Mahdi Shams al-Din' for lack of maintenance and impossibility of marital relations. A signed copy of his ruling was included in the file. The defendant, the husband, had argued that he was going to bring an objection before Shams al-Din, but nothing subsequently emerged and the judge went ahead and ruled in the wife's favour.

Since divorce at the hand of the husband is among the foundations of the sharia.

And since also established in the principles of the sharia is the permissibility of divorce by the legitimate judge [*talaq al-hakim al-shar'i*] for she whose husband denies her maintenance.

And since the divorce of the plaintiff from her husband was effected as an irrevocable divorce by *al-hakim al-shar'i* for the stated reason and for ill treatment in marriage, relying on the certificate of *talaq al-hakim*.

Therefore: based on sections 17, 91, 242 and 116 of the Law of Sharia Courts, it is resolved to rule with the establishment of the divorce of X from Y, an irrevocable divorce, *talaq al-hakim*.[33]

Another comes in the form of a supreme court ruling of 2000. This arose as an appeal of an initial court ruling in 1999 nullifying the wife's marriage (*ibtal al-zawaj*), subsequently referred to as a ruling of *talaq al-hakim*, issued by 'the *marja' shar'i* [note the explicit status attribution] His Excellency Imam [a strikingly grand honorific[34]] Shaykh Muhammad

performed such divorces, and claims that dozens were effected with the license of the leading *marja'* of an earlier era, Abu-l-Hasan al-Isfahani (d.1946).

[32] See e.g. Abisaab 2009: 236–237 and Karanshawy 2015: 197–198.

[33] Barakat 2005: 157–159.

[34] The use of the term 'Imam' for the very most prestigious Shi'i religious leaders seems recent, most associated with Khomeini, but also, in the context of Lebanon, used of Musa al-Sadr.

Mahdi Shams al-Din', and ratified by the initial court judge.[35] The appellant, the husband, is thus in the difficult position of having to challenge the nominally very highest religious authority, evoked in the most grandiloquent terms. He (or rather, his lawyer) argues that Shams al-Din's ruling does not satisfy the conditions of a ruling in law (*qanun*) and does not bind the sharia courts even if it is issued by an acknowledged scholar (*faqih*), while simultaneously avowing that 'he respects and honours and bows before the *talaq al-hakim* arising from Imam Shaykh Muhammad Mahdi Shams al-Din.' One senses the awkwardness that such a stark affirmation of Shams al-Din's prestige entails in the context of adversarial litigation. And the case clearly posed problems for the judges as well: three in turn recused themselves and had to be replaced; the final decision (in favour of the wife and maintaining the application of Shams al-Din's ruling) was by majority rather than unanimous.[36]

A copy of a lawyer's submission in another appeals case (representing the appealed against, the wife who had obtained a ruling of *talaq al-hakim*, again from Shams al-Din) further testifies to the problems.[37] Shams al-Din is eulogised, as to his credentials and proper discharge of his role as *hakim*: he is, 'the president of the Higher Shi'i Islamic Council, His Excellency the Learned Muhammad Mahdi Shams al-Din, well-known for taking his time and his pronounced caution and scrutiny in every matter before producing the fruit of his labour.' His verdict is unassailable: 'the ruling of the *hakim* is not allowed to be contradicted, even by another *mujtahid* ... [H]e who rejects the ruling of the *faqih* is rejecting the ruling of the Imam [here the divinely inspired Hidden Imam, I assume] and the one rejecting the ruling of the Imam is rejecting the ruling of God, and any polytheism is mightier than that.' The explicit invocation of *mujtahid* status thus entails a massive inflation in the stakes in play. Challenging the ruling becomes an almost unmanageable dance around being forced into a naked challenge of the religiously supercharged status of the scholar who issued it.

[35] Barakat 2005: 113–121. The arguments do not touch on the substance of the case made before the *hakim*, but rather on the admissibility of his ruling as the basis for a sharia court judgement, on the procedure he followed (not hearing the husband's objection and witnesses), and on whether or not the wife in fact had shown her consent to the continuing marriage. It is thus not easy to discern the actual workings of the *talaq al-hakim* procedure itself.

[36] Again, appeals cases are tried by a panel of three senior judges.

[37] The (unpublished) submission is not dated, but it is apparent from the content that the dispute dates back to 1991.

After Shams al-Din's death it would seem that his successor as head of the Supreme Shi'i Council, Shaykh 'Abd al-Amir Qabalan, relied instead on a learned council to decide such cases.[38] Such a clear instance of routinisation and bureaucratisation reduces the stakes in terms of personal self-esteem and public standing, and fits Shaykh Qabalan's less imposing reputation for scholarship. Should the council divorce a couple, they do so, I was told, relying on Shaykh Qabalan's licence (*wikala*) from Iraq's Ayatollah Sistani, as was confirmed by Sistani's offices in Beirut.[39] That represents an interesting move under the aegis of the *marja'* system, albeit a strictly limited one, so far as I know. Reliance by Qabalan (not a judge himself) on Sistani in this matter did not mark a new, overall dependence by the Shi'i institutions on one particular authority over others. On the contrary, it seems to have coincided with a relaxation of the competitive tensions locally. Shaykh Mir'i, for instance, in charge of Fadlallah's independent judicial office, noted an easing of the situation with regard to the status of Fadlallah's rulings: taken to this council, they were meeting with a more sympathetic reception.[40]

Conclusion

In the earlier chapters on the sharia courts, we saw their frustrations: bound to a certain vision of the law and a necessarily tight bureaucratic procedure, they can seem irritatingly rigid to many litigants, lawyers and indeed judges. The possibilities available beyond the courts afforded by the vast plurality of sharia discourse appear more attractive. In this last part of the book, we thus turned to considering the work of a scholar and authority who struggled for and achieved autonomy, independent of such official institutions. In the previous chapter we focused on Fadlallah's efforts to create law from the bottom up, in response to people's needs and in harmony with the demands of the age. The profusion of religious legal discourse that resulted seems almost the ideal of 'flexible' Islam so attractive to academic observers, progressive with regard to gender and women's rights and open to the advances of modern science and medicine, even if politically the ayatollah and the liberal West were in many respects poles apart.

[38] I rely on interviews with lawyers and a lawyer's submission I have had access to. I have no official confirmation from the council or the courts.
[39] Interview with Hamid al-Khaffaf, 18 April 2008.
[40] Aside from the passing of Shams al-Din, this could also have been tied to a rapprochement between the competing blocs of the Shi'i community, notably Amal – again, the dominant patrons of the official institutions – and Hizballah.

In this final chapter we have considered the relationship between this vision and the practice of the state, in the form of the state-sponsored Ja'fari courts. As we saw, that relationship is a difficult one – hostile even, when not simply non-existent. What, then, is the ultimate status of such an independent vision of the sharia, whose authority rests on that of an autonomous individual scholar? In Fadlallah's case, like many others, it was nominally to culminate in an authentically 'Islamic state', although what that would entail remained elusive, gradually attenuated and indefinitely deferred. In the meantime, however, the pious could shape their own lives in accordance with this reformed vision of religious law regardless, just as the enthusiasts of other such authorities could.

The demands of a committed religious life could, however, then seem out of step with the rest of the world. As Zouhair Ghazzal has put it, in a review of one of Fadlallah's earlier legal handbooks, Islamic legal discourse (*fiqh*) is generally 'not concerned with its own historicity'. For example, a Shi'i believer should pay the *khums*, 20 per cent of their income, to their *marja'*. But how does this relate to the additional demands of the Lebanese state and its taxes? 'What type of "consciousness" will this believer end up with', faced with such competing and radically different demands? Ghazzal likens the result to Sartre's famous image of radical inauthenticity, or 'bad faith', the waiter who, as a waiter, is necessarily performing a role rather than expressing their essential being.[41] It was, however, of the essence of Fadlallah's particular programme that he tried to minimise such inauthenticity, so that followers of his 'contemporary' positions would be able to satisfy the demands of a religious life without a sense of being out of joint with the rest of the world. In him they would find, as his son Sayyid Ja'far has put it, 'a *marja'* that provides, relative to others, a high level of conformity with their ... needs and the requirements of life'.[42] Under his guidance, they could also shape a more pious public culture that would in itself help to minimise such disjuncture. But Fadlallah maintained that in any case the believer should not act in such a way as to undermine the public order of the society they found themselves in. They should follow the law and pay their taxes, except where it was unconscionable not to, even if they should still struggle for justice in the ways available to them: by boycotting American goods and supporting the Resistance for example.[43] Good conscience and good citizenship should coincide.

41 Ghazzal 1998: 455, the allusion being to Sartre's *Being and Nothingness*.

42 In an interview with Lara Deeb and Mona Harb (2013: 81), referring to the youth in particular.

43 See e.g. Fadlallah 2010: 9–14, 217–220.

Nevertheless, unless this model for good living became general, and further, recognised by state law, some such tensions must surely inevitably continue. At the beginning of this book, our young Sunni shaykh talked of how one might nevertheless at least turn the television off and create an Islamic state in one's own home. But even that is to assume unchallenged patriarchal authority. Within the home there are differences, too, between the sexes and the generations: because, for instance, Fadlallah thought the onset of the lunar month, and thus Ramadan and its end, should be determined by astronomical means where other authorities did not, families might find themselves fasting and feasting on different days. And some differences become conflicts, perhaps even between those who acknowledge the same authority. Some become so serious as to require arbitration, a service which Fadlallah provided.

Faced with a verdict against them, however, people might balk. This refusal could itself be viewed in terms of the logic of conscience, as an act of 'bad faith', of being inauthentic to oneself. As Fadlallah's son Sayyid Ja'far put it to me, 'You can choose or choose not to follow Islam. If you choose to, then it is binding [*mulzim*]. It's like marriage – choose it and you accept your life will change . . . you can't do what you did before.'[44] Or as Shaykh Mir'i had it, either you believe in the sharia or you don't. But marriages, even those with one's conscience, break down. In the case of a judicially imposed divorce, say, it is of the essence that the two parties do not agree as to what the right of the matter is. If a husband accepted the authority of the scholar presiding, then he would accept the need to divorce if that is what the scholar advised. And then there would be no need for it to be judicially imposed. But this is not the course of all disputes in reality, hence the sharia's recognition of the necessity for legal judgement as well as ethical guidance and agreed settlement.

Ultimately, if justice is to be done in this world, we cannot escape the need for an executive branch to ensure that judgement is carried out. Here the independent scholar's autonomy defeats him at the last.[45] Whatever his stature in the wider community, within the state-backed sharia legal system Fadlallah was almost as nothing – faced with his verdict, a judge might 'throw it in the bin'. In this respect his imagined legal world remained apart, a matter of conscience rather than law in effect. The domains of state law and non-state religious conscience

[44] Interview, 21 June 2007. Cf. Deeb and Harb 2013: 82–83.

[45] While that was the case for Fadlallah, as we have seen, the same is not necessarily true of Hizballah. Nor has it always been the case for the *marja'-mutjahid*s historically, who have had their own means of enforcement. See e.g. Algar (1969: 19) and Floor (1981: 89–90) on Iran and Litvak (1998: 124) on Iraq.

remain independent, but not, it seems, self-sufficient, each in a sense generating the need for the other: the bureaucratic courts found wanting because they stifle the sharia's plurality and flexibility; autonomous authority left impotent in the face of bad faith.

In formal terms, however, as I have tried to describe throughout the book, sharia discourse does not make this state/non-state, or legal/extra-legal distinction, at least not in the same way. Indeed, the dominant formal model within Twelver Shi'i Islam collapses the distinction by giving the verdict of a *mujtahid* such as Fadlallah claimed to be (unlike most judges in the courts it would seem) an absolute pre-eminence. That allows the independent scholar to appear – in 'religious', sharia-legal terms – as in competition with the courts. However, in practice, the courts can easily resist the personal authority of the independent *mujtahid* class. Where the question of the latter's right to rule is not merely politely ignored, it can be answered through an *ad hominem* dismissal of individual claims to such status, as in the case of Fadlallah. That turns the matter into one of 'politics'. The exaggerated nature of *mujtahid* status in Lebanon and its corresponding vulnerability to such radical criticism makes it harder to imagine the courts justifying their own authority locally in such personalised form, too easily contested. If Fadlallah's claims could be rubbished, then how much more easily could those of the sharia court judges? They could nevertheless put themselves publicly under the aegis of a great *mujtahid* elsewhere, as does seem to happen in some very restricted circumstances. But in practice, generally speaking, the question as to what the courts' authority depends on (in sharia, but not state legal terms) is left more open than that, and a clear answer is consequently harder to pin down. Rather than collapsing the authority of the initial court judge into a matter of stated dependency on a named member of the learned elite, their autonomy and dignity is preserved, even if their rulings may be appealed. And rather than the particularity and competition of the world of the *mujtahid–marja*'s, in the courts 'all the opinions are the same', the legal differences minimised (even if still present), the preponderant position within the school the assumed default. The authority of the sharia court judge is thus, I would argue, less a matter of individual scholarly achievement and trust – although some judges are more respected than others for sure – than a more general respect for the shaykhly class, and thus also for the sharia in general rather than a particular version of it. And beyond that, the judge's authority also of course derives from the official, state-backed institution within which they work. Where *mujtahid* status is a highly contestable achievement, being a judge is a clear matter of appointment.

The structural constraints and possibilities of these different ecological niches – that of the independent scholar and that of the state-sponsored courts – thus lead to different expressions of authority as well as different degrees of flexibility and responsiveness, even if, in formal terms, 'it's *shar'* here and *shar'* there'. While I spent much of the earlier sections of the book pointing out the frustrations of working in the courts, here, looking from the other direction, we can be reminded of the solidity of status that work as a judge offers, underpinned by the weight of authority that the state lends. And that weight of the state exercises a certain gravitational pull too, which draws disputes, as well as contracts and agreements, into its orbit, even if it is counter-balanced by the centrifugal force of the repellently 'wooden' nature of its bureaucracy. In contemporary Lebanon, state and non-state sharia authority are thus disjoined, subject to different forces and tendencies, but not completely isolated.[46] Their relationship is 'political'. But rather than being pitted against one another in a zero-sum game, they can also be seen as in some senses complementary. I asked one judge if he felt a rivalry between the courts and the judicial services of Fadlallah and others. No, he replied, because they have nothing to do with each other. But maybe it is nice for him if those outside of the courts share some of the load, in trying to reconcile people's differences.

[46] The courts are clearly aware and subject to the pressures of the wider intellectual currents, for instance, even if they also seem to have considerable capacity to resist them.

Conclusion

This book has addressed the relationship between Islam and law in Lebanon. Lebanon's distinctive confessional legal and political system shows respect for religious identities by giving legal autonomy and privileges to a limited number of official religious communities. The paradigmatic expression of this recognition is the granting to them of legal jurisdiction over family law. Not everyone is happy with this arrangement and there have been many attempts to change it, or to resist it on an individual level. But Lebanon remains an example of what some people have called a 'dual' legal system, in that it incorporates both civil and, to this limited extent, religious law. This duality in abstract terms takes the form of a much wider plurality in practice, given the number of officially recognised religious communities with their own court systems. The Sunni and Shi'i Muslim communities that are my especial focus both have their own 'sharia courts', which are, for historical reasons, part of the state legal apparatus. A portal into the life of the state is thereby opened for the religious professionals of those communities, some of whom are employed by the state as judges and functionaries in these courts. Both communities also have their own official self-governing institutions, which are not formally located within the state in the same way, but are part of the established elements of its broader legal and political structure and are also staffed by religious professionals trained in their respective traditions. Beyond these official religious establishments there is a wider and varied world of independent religious actors and institutions, many of whom are also specialists in sharia discourse, who collaborate, compete and sometimes conflict with the establishment. The sharia provides an idiom for the discussion and enactment of proper Islamic practice far beyond the scope of family law. It is in this sense that one can talk of the social life of the sharia in Lebanon, within and outside of the state and the official religious community institutions.

Given the central importance in those institutions of Islamic religious professionals, or shaykhs, I examined in some detail at the outset the expectations of the role. I noted a distinction between the authentic practitioner, for whom this is a vocation, and the inauthentic one, for whom it is merely a job. The authentic practitioner displays commitment to their role, which entails both learning and exemplary moral behaviour, but also engagement with the spiritual needs of others and their religious education. To be so taken over by Islam in the setting of contemporary Beirut is not easy: the committed Muslim inevitably remains as a 'stranger' to what is in many ways a less pious – in parts even irreligious – surrounding society.

Turning to the sharia courts, I showed how, in keeping with the dual nature of the legal system, these are frequently portrayed as in themselves something of a hybrid institution, both 'religious' and 'civil', or 'political', in ways that are not always comfortable for the shaykhs who work in them. The most common idiom in which this rhetorical division is discussed is in terms of a distinction between the sharia (*al-shar'*) and *qanun*, or 'law'. This division can be aesthetic, as between the religious dress adopted by the shaykhs who work in the courts as opposed to the non-religious dress of the lawyers who also do so and are seen as representing the civil legal tradition by contrast. It is also portrayed (by the shaykhs) as a difference in ethos, between the ethic of the Islamic religious professional, committed to justice and engagement with the problems of others and their religious education, and the 'wooden' proceduralism of the civil law and the lawyers who pursue it. And it further speaks to an ultimate, ontological distinction, between what matters to the omniscient God and what matters to the Lebanese state. Those concerns need not coincide (although they can). To be married in God's eyes does not require the approval of the Lebanese state. Nevertheless, the very existence of the sharia courts speaks to some sort of compulsion to enact a union between the two.

A great deal of time is necessarily devoted to the legal procedures and processes that a bureaucratic court system requires. These efforts seem overly laborious to many, including those working within the court system, perhaps even harmful to the enactment of proper justice. Given the symbolic weight attached to the sharia, these pernicious aspects of court procedure are rhetorically assigned to human 'law' instead. The sharia is more commonly invoked in a vaguer sense of ideal justice. Even in the rulings with which many disputes end, sharia discourse seems muted in comparison with the careful citation of the procedural laws that govern the courts. More highly valorised is the path of mutually agreed settlement (*sulh*). Despite the importance of religious-legal learning for the aura of the Islamic professional, it is in this domain, rather than in the writing of legal judgements, that sharia court judges can more often show their craft, guiding people towards a resolution of their differences in ways that resonate with the pedagogical, pastoral aspects of the shaykh's expected role.

Nevertheless, the sharia court judges find themselves necessarily implicated on both sides of the divide between 'sharia' and 'law'. Fulfilling the bureaucratic requirements of their role is compromising for their realisation of their broader shaykhly vocation, and different judges are pulled in different directions by this tension. Their somewhat conflicted position is exacerbated, in my reading, by the frequent invocation of sharia norms outside of the courts. Lay people have recourse to shaykhs as experts on the sharia in a variety of other contexts. In formal terms, one may speak of the institution of *ifta'*, giving an opinion as to where the right path lies in a given situation, although most interactions are not so formal. Here one is thinking more in terms of conscience, what matters in God's eyes, than law, what is sanctioned by the state. In practice, however, such guidance can provide, if not legal, then social sanction; and shaykhs outside of the court system are often resorted to as arbitrators and mediators – again, a highly valorised role. The sharia's ultimate grounding in God's will rather than that of the state means that such non-state jurists exercise such functions with full religious legitimacy. The sharia's vast scope as a plural discursive tradition means they can offer a more 'flexible', more pedagogically engaged and thus potentially more attractive vision of the sharia than can be practiced in the courts, which must maintain certain agreed legal and bureaucratic standards and have an inevitable institutional inertia. I refer to this as the plasticity of the sharia, at some points flexible and at others inflexible, depending on the different ecological circumstances within which it is taken up.

Having examined the social life of the sharia from the perspective of the courts, I thus next looked at the ways in which the sharia is discussed and employed by a major (Shi'i) jurist working independently of the state and the official religious establishment, Ayatollah Muhammad Husayn Fadlallah. His independence in itself lent a certain prestige, but also increased the scope of what was possible in terms of interpreting God's will. Fadlallah developed a vision of the sharia directly and explicitly in conversation with people's contemporary needs, one that could reduce the potential tension between being a committed Muslim and living in the modern, cosmopolitan world, in ways that helped create a new, pious public sphere in parts of Beirut.

In addition to providing moral and religious guidance attuned to the concerns of his enthusiasts, Fadlallah also practiced arbitration, and his offices helped mediate family disputes in line with his relatively progressive legal positions. However, if we look back to the official court system that has an effective, if not total monopoly on executive action, these opinions and verdicts were largely dismissed. Although the dominant model of learned Shi'i discourse grants personal moral and legal authority to individual qualified members of the scholarly elite, the court system functions almost completely independent of such considerations and the contested hierarchy that they imply. Rather than the particularity and competition of the world of independent actors, in the courts such differences are minimised in favour of a more general authority, whose underpinning by the weight of the state exercises a certain gravitational pull of its own.

One is thus faced with a plurality of values, institutions and processes, which often seem in tension, or even conflict, with one another. The relationship, for instance, between a thoroughgoing commitment to Islam and the demands of everyday life and civility in plural and divided Lebanon is not always a comfortable one. There seems a fundamental difference in kind between the sharia and civil law. The demands of bureaucratic procedure can contradict those of manifest justice. Autonomy is attractive, but so is the power to make things happen. Sometimes this is a matter of conflicting interests, between institutions or individuals.[1] At other points one is thinking more of opposed values.[2] In these Lebanese contexts, 'sharia' gains much of its meaning through its opposition to 'law', for example; being a 'real shaykh' can be measured by its difference from being a mere functionary. Such value oppositions are most often ranked: sharia is, in Islamic terms, superior to positive law.[3] Value judgements motivate action, and I have examined the ways in which these tensions create the impetus for different judges to manifest their own different styles, or lead scholars to take up different paths in life, to quit the life of the establishment, or attempt to reform the system, or shape society. Such conflicts are thus not solely destructive or paralysing (although they certainly can be, as we have also seen); they can also be generative.

Nevertheless, for the sharia-minded actors I worked with, the tensions they experience do appear pathological, symptomatic of Lebanon's particular legal system, whereby religious law is granted a limited place within a civil republic. This negative assessment would be true of secularists and civil society activists too, albeit from a different direction. For them the solution would be, I presume, a more secular arrangement. For

[1] Ido Shahar (2015) frames his account of sharia courts in Jerusalem in terms of institutional pluralism and competition, for instance.

[2] For a differently oriented discussion of Islam and value pluralism see e.g. Bowen 2003 on Indonesia.

[3] 'Hierarchical opposition' in the terms of Louis Dumont (1982), now enjoying something of a return to fashion (see e.g. Robbins 2013).

the Islamic religious professionals, on the other hand, colonial and post-colonial secular modernity is seen as the problem more generally. The remedy that, for their part, I heard some of them air, even if in the vaguest of terms, was that of an 'Islamic state' (*dawla islamiyya*). While a highly alarming prospect for secularists, Christians and indeed many Muslims, this was not, I felt, invoked as a realistic and immediate project for Lebanon. Even Hizballah seems to have deferred the idea indefinitely.[4] Of course, many of those I talked with might well have had clear and detailed ideas as to the form an Islamic state should take, even if we did not discuss them. But my general sense was of something more utopian than that, an 'Islamic state idea' that can be appealed to in the same way as the idea of the state itself, whose powerful mythical aspects social scientists have sought to distinguish from the concrete institutions of government.[5] This seemed to me analogous to the way in which I found the sharia invoked in the courts: more as a symbol of ideal legal practice in the round, than just the correct set of precepts for application.

The fear – and perhaps the attraction – of the contemporary Islamic state is no doubt of something more monist than pluralist, that would transcend the secular state's enfolding of religion within private life and in its turn encompass the public life of the state as well as the private life of religious conscience.[6] Islam is both 'religion and state' (*din wa-dawla*), as the slogan goes. Claims for Islam's 'totality' ('a comprehensive system embracing all aspects of life'[7]) could, in the form of an Islamic state, seem potentially totalitarian. One can point in response to numerous alternative models and historical instances of Islamic states with constitutionally and effectively limited powers.[8] The modern 'state effect' is such, however, that it intrinsically raises the question as to where the boundary lies between the state and society, and a corresponding fear that the state will encroach too far. So too, it has been argued, the effect of modern secularism is essentially to raise continuously, and

4 See e.g. Abisaab and Abisaab 2014: 145, 182–188.

5 See Abrams 1988, Mitchell 2006, and, for an exploration of 'fantasies' of the secular state in a Middle Eastern case (Turkey), Navaro-Yashin 2002.

6 The notion of encompassment is also owed to Dumont.

7 These being the influential terms of the Egyptian Muslim Brotherhood's founding leader Hasan al-Banna (d. 1949), who continued: 'it [Islam] is a state and a country, a government and a nation: it is morality, power, mercy and justice; it is culture, law, knowledge and legislation' (cited by Jadaane 1990: 255–256). In this form, claims as to the sharia's totality might look distinctly modern. On the notion of Islam as system (and its modernity) see also e.g. Eickelman 1992.

8 See e.g. Jackson 1996; Arjomand 2007 and Hallaq 2013. For a very effective analysis – and ultimately refutation – of the notion that the Islamic Republic of Iran, for instance, could be seen as a totalitarian project see Chehabi 2001.

unanswerably, the question of the proper boundaries of religion within political life.[9] One cannot help but suspect that one aspect of the 'Islamic state effect' might be, in addition to worrying about its proper boundaries of rule, the continual and inevitable questioning of just how Islamic such a state actually is. It is not so much that an Islamic state is an impossibility then: there are plenty of attempted examples. Rather, any such attempt will inevitably be subject to criticism – more or less widespread and publicly expressed – for not being properly Islamic.

On the one hand, then, the sharia's legalistic form and historical resonance as a source of law make it an enormously potent and readily available icon of what authentically Islamic state life might look like. In Lebanon – decidedly not an Islamic state – 'sharia courts' are thus a, perhaps *the*, key way in which the state shows respect for Islam (and, by extension, *mutatis mutandis*, Christianity too). On the other hand, the sharia's transcendental source and object (divine salvation) gives it a powerful 'anti-state effect'. The sharia's comprehensive scope makes it a powerful icon of totality; but the openness to interpretation that its divine source inevitably entails means that no human attempt to map out God's law totally can be definitive.[10] Critical perspectives are always available. In this aspect, to adopt the distinction made by Emmanuel Levinas, the sharia might be better conceived of as an 'infinite discourse' rather than a total one, continuously overflowing any attempt to limit its definition.[11] And the sharia's ideal status means that any of the inevitably problematic aspects that bureaucratic state legal practice entails have to be blamed on something else: broadly, in Lebanon, civil law. While an 'Islamic state' thus becomes the utopian solution, the obverse, and here more salient, implication is that the lack of one provides a ready way of parsing dissatisfaction.

Overall, I would thus argue that my ethnography of Lebanese Muslim religious professionals and the institutions they work in has something to say not only about family law in Lebanon, but also about larger historical processes and broader analytical concerns. The frustrations for Islamic religious professionals of state legal practice in Lebanon no doubt have historical parallels; they also shed light on the utopian desire for an 'Islamic state' and its potential paradoxes. The sharia's transcendental source and consequent openness to interpretation, combined with its

[9] Mitchell 2006 and Agrama 2010b.

[10] *Pace* Messick 1993 then, not only could ideas of sharia discourse as 'total' look distinctively modern, but the open texture of sharia discourse continues under modernity (see also Clarke 2010).

[11] Levinas 1969.

legalism and comprehensive address, pose still more general questions about normative ordering in distinctive and thought-provoking ways. Sharia discourse brings together domains that the ideology of modernity tends to separate, in ways that continue to be relevant today. We should therefore resituate studies of the sharia in wider comparative frames, not merely to debate its relationship to modernity, but in order to provide alternative vantage points on shared questions of the relationship between state law, personal ethics and good conscience.

Bibliography

ARABIC SOURCES

'Amili, Muhammad 'Ali al-Hajj al- (ed.) 2007. *Al-zawaj al-madani: bayna al-Islam wa-l-masihiyya*. Beirut: Markaz al-Dirasat wa-l-Abhath al-Islamiyya-al-Masihiyya.

'Atwi, Muhsin. 2002. *Zad al-muballighin* (2nd printing). Beirut: Dar al-Mahajjat al-Bayda'.

2004a (ed.). *Al-fiqh al-muyassar: tibqan li-fatawa al-marja'al-dini al-Sayyid Muhammad Husayn Fadlallah*. Beirut: Dar al-Malak.

2004b. *Ikhtiyar al-sharik: bayna al-'aql wa-l-'atifa*. Beirut.

Ayyub, 'Ali Murhij. 2008. *Al-qada' al-shar'i (wufqa al-madhhabayn al-sinni wa-l-ja'fari)*. Beirut: Manshurat al-Halabi al-Huquqiyya.

Barakat, Salman. 2005. *Al-qada' al-shar'i al-Ja'fari: ijtihadat, nusus*. Beirut: Manshurat Zayn al-Huquqiyya.

Fadlallah, Ja'far (ed.) 2006. *Al-bulugh: bahth 'ilmi fiqhi li-Samahat Ayat Allah al-'Uzma al-Sayyid Muhammad Husayn Fadlallah*. Beirut: Dar al-Malak.

Fadlallah, Muhammad Husayn. 1998. *Al-fatawa al-wadiha* (2nd edn). Beirut: Dar al-Malak.

2002–2003. *Fiqh al-shari'a* (3 vols.) (6th edn). Beirut: Dar al-Malak.

2003. *Ahkam al-shari'a* (2nd printing). Beirut: Dar al-Malak.

2004. *Dunya al-tifl* (3rd printing). Beirut: Dar al-Malak.

2005a. *Al-masa'il al-fiqhiyya* (2 vols.) (10th edn). Beirut: Dar al-Malak.

2005b. *Dunya al-mar'a* (6th edn). Beirut: Dar al-Malak.

2009. *Al-masa'il al-fiqhiyya: al-'ibadat* (new edn). Beirut: Dar al-Malak.

2010. *Al-masa'il al-fiqhiyya tibqan li-fatawa al-marja' al-dini Samahat Ayat Allah al-'Uzma al-Sayyid Muhammad Husayn Fadl Allah: al-mu'amalat* (new edn). Beirut: Dar al-Malak.

Farhat, Jihad (ed.) 2007. *Fiqh al-hajj: taqriran li-abhath sayyid-na al-ustadh Samahat Ayat Allah al-'Uzma al-Sayyid Muhammad Husayn Fadl Allah* (vol. 1). Beirut: Dar al-Malak.

Hamiyya, Siham. 2004. *Al-mar'a fi-l-fikr al-falsafi al-ijtima'i al-islami: dirasa fi fikr al-Sayyid Muhammad Husayn Fadl Allah*. Beirut: Dar al-Malak.

Hana, Badawi. 1995. *Al-ahwal al-shakhsiyya: ijtihadat, nusus, dirasat* (part 1). Tripoli: al-Mu'assasa al-Haditha li-l-Kitab.

Hasani, Salim al-. 1994. *Al-ma'alim al-jadida li-l-marja'iyya al-shi'iyya: dirasa wa-hiwar ma' Ayat Allah al-Sayyid Muhammad Husayn Fadl Allah.* Beirut: Dar al-Malak.

Homsi, 'Ali Nadim al-. 2003. *Majmu'at al-mabadi' wa-l-qawa'id al-shar'iyya wa-l-qanuniyya allati tabbaqat-ha al-mahakim al-shar'iyya al-sunniyya.* Beirut: Manshurat al-Halabi al-Huquqiyya.

Husayni, Muhammad al-. 2007. Murtakizat asasiyya fi al-minhaj al-fiqhi 'ind al-Sayyid Fadl Allah. In Muhammad al-Husayni, (ed.), *Al-ithbat al-qada'i – al-shahada: taqriran li-abhath al-marja' al-dini Samahat Ayat Allah al-'Uzma al-Sayyid Muhammad Husayn Fadl Allah*, 9–25. Beirut: Dar al-Malak.

Jalal al-Din, Salim. 2002. *Mudhakkirat Samahat al-Mufti al-Qadi al-Shaykh Salim Jalal al-Din.* Sidon (privately published).

Khaffaf, Hamid, ed. 2007. *Al-nusus al-sadira 'an Samahat al-Sayyid al-Sistani fi-l-mas'ala al-'iraqiyya.* Beirut: Dar al-Mu'arrikh al-'Arabi.

Khishn, Husayn al-. 2004. *Fiqh al-qada': taqriran li-bahth Samahat Ayat Allah al-'Uzma al-Sayyid Muhammad Husayn Fadl Allah* (vol. 1). Beirut: Dar al-Malak.

2007. *Fiqh al-qada': taqriran li-bahth Samahat Ayat Allah al-'Uzma al-Sayyid Muhammad Husayn Fadl Allah* (vol. 2). Beirut: Dar al-Malak.

Khomeini, Ruhollah. 1989. *Tahrir al-wasila* (2 vols). Beirut: Embassy of the Iranian Islamic Republic.

Khu'i, Abu-l-Qasim al-. 1975. *Minhaj al-salihin* (2 vols). Qom: al-Matba'a al-'Ilmiyya.

Markaz al-Dirasat wa-l-Abhath al-Islamiyya – al-Masihiyya. 1999. *Al-istinsakh bayna al-islam wa-l-masihiyya: maqalat wa-abhath wa-muqabilat li-kibar rijal al-din wa-mufakkirin wa-l-bahithin min mukhtalif al-adyan wa-l-madhahib.* Beirut: Dar al-Fikr al-Lubnani.

Markaz Bayyanat li-l-Internet wa-l-Dirasat. Circa 2008 (no date given). *Kay la nansa. Majzarat Bi'r al-'Abd: dhakirat al-irhab al-amriki.* Beirut (privately published).

Mawlawi, Faysal al-. 1996. *Nubuwwat Adam (al-salam 'alay-h) fi ijtihadat al-mahakim al-shar'iyya al-'ulya fi bayrut.* Beirut: al-Mu'assasa al-Islamiyya li-l-Taba'a wa-l-Sahafa wa-l-Nashr.

Mir'i, Husayn. 2003. *Jami' al-ahkam fi-l-halal wa-l-haram (al-mu'amalat) tibqan li-ara' al-maraji' al-'izam.* Beirut: Dar al-Mahajja al-Bayda'.

Mu'assasat al-Imam Shams al-Din li-l-Hiwar 2004. *Al-Imam al-Shaykh Muhammad Mahdi Shams al-Din (1936–2001), al-'alim al-mujahid wa-l-faqih al-mujaddid: sira wa-mu'allafat.* Beirut: Mu'assasat al-Imam Shams al-Din li-l-Hiwar.

Mughniyya, Muhammad Jawad. 1979 [1960]. *Fiqh al-madhahib al-khamsa (al-Ja'fari, al-Hanafi, al-Maliki, al-Hanbali).* Beirut: Dar al-'Ilm al-Malayin.

2003. *Fiqh al-Imam Ja'far al-Sadiq* (6 parts, here collected in 3 volumes). Qom: Sibtayn International Foundation.

2007. *Tajarib Muhammad Jawad Mughniyya* (ed.) 'Abd al-Husayn Mughniyya. Qom: Anwar al-Huda.

Musawi, Ahmad Husayn al-. 2007. *Qanun usul al-muhakamat al-madaniyya al-lubnani.* Beirut: Manshurat al-Halabi al-Huquqiyya.

Ni'ma, 'Abdallah. 1996. *Dalil al-qada' al-ja'fari*. Beirut: Dar al-Balagha.
Qadi, Ahmad Ahmad 'Adil al-. 1998. *Dunya al-shabab: hiwar ma' Samahat Ayat Allah al-'Uzma al-Sayyid Muhammad Husayn Fadl Allah*. Beirut: Mu'assasat al-'Arif li-l-Matbu'at.
Qazzi, Jean al-. 2007. *Al-zawaj al-madani: al-qadi al-lubnani fi muwajihat qawanin al-'alam*. Beirut (privately published).
Qubaysi, Muhammad al- (ed.). 1995. *Risala fi-l-rida': taqriran li-bahth Samahat Ayat Allah al-'Uzma al-Sayyid Muhammad Husayn Fadlallah*. Beirut: Dar al-Malak.
2007. *Fiqh al-at'ima wa-l-ashriba: taqriran li-abhath sayyid-na al-ustadh Ayat Allah al-'Uzma al-Sayyid Muhammad Husayn Fadlallah*. Beirut: Dar al-Malak.
Shakhuri, Ja'far al- (al-Bahrani). 1996 (vol. 1) and 2002 (vol. 2). *Kitab al-nikah: taqriran li-bahth Samahat Ayat Allah al-'Uzma al-Sayyid Muhammad Husayn Fadl Allah*. Beirut: Dar al-Malak.
1998. *Ayat Allah al-'Uzma al-Sayyid Muhammad Husayn Fadl Allah wa-harakiyyat al-'aql al-ijtima'i lada fuqaha' al-shi'a al-imamiyya*. Beirut: Dar al-Malak.
Sistani, 'Ali al-. 2002. *Minhaj al-salihin* (3 vols.). Qom: Maktabat Fadak.
Sukkariyya, Muna. 2007. *'An sanawat wa-mawaqif wa-shakhsiyyat: hakadha tahaddath... hakadha qal* (interviews with Ayatollah Muhammad Husayn Fadlallah). Beirut: Dar al-Nahar.
Traboulsi, Ibrahim. 2000. *Al-zawaj wa-mafa'ilahu lada-l-tawa'if al-mashmula fi qanun 2 nisan 1951*. Beirut: Al-Manshurat al-Huquqiyya.
No date. *Ishkaliyyat al-tabanni fi-l-qawanin al-ta'ifiyya wa-l-madaniyya: dirasa wa-ta'liq 'ala al-qirar al-sadir 'an mahkamat al-daraja al-ula fi-l-Matn*. Unpublished manuscript.
Zayn, 'Arif Zayd al-. 2003a. *Qawanin wa-nusus wa-ahkam al-ahwal al-shakhsiyya wa-tanzim al-tawa'if al-islamiyya fi lubnan*. Beirut: Manshurat al-Halabi al-Huquqiyya.
2003b. *Qawanin wa-qirarat al-ahwal al-shakhsiyya li-l-tawa'if al-masihiyya fi lubnan*. Beirut: Manshurat al-Halabi al-Huquqiyya.
Zuhayli, Wahba al-. 2006 [1984]. *Al-fiqh al-islami wa-adillat-hu* (11 volumes). Damascus: Dar al-Fikr.

EUROPEAN LANGUAGE SOURCES

Abisaab, Rula. 2004. *Converting Persia: religion and power in the Safavid empire*. London: I.B. Tauris.
2006. The cleric as organic intellectual: revolutionary Shi'ism in the Lebanese *hawzas*. In Houchang Chehabi (ed.), *Distant relations: Iran and Lebanon in the last 500 years*, 231–258. London: Centre for Lebanese Studies and I.B. Tauris.
2009. Lebanese Shi'ites and the *marja'iyya*: polemic in the late twentieth century. *British Journal of Middle Eastern Studies* 36(2): 215–239.
Abisaab, Rula and Malek Abisaab. 2014. *The Shi'ites of Lebanon: modernism, communism, and Hizbullah's Islamists*. Syracuse, NY: Syracuse University Press.
Abou El Fadl, Khaled. 2002. Islamic law and ambivalent scholarship (review of L. Rosen, *The justice of Islam*). *Michigan Law Review* 100(6): 1421–1443.

Abou Ramadan, Moussa. 2015. Islamic legal hybridity and patriarchal liberalism in the shari'a courts in Israel. *Journal of Levantine Studies* 4(2): 39–67.

Abrams, Philip. 1988. Notes on the difficulty of studying the state (1977). *Journal of Historical Sociology* 1(1): 58–89.

Agmon, Iris and Ido Shahar. 2008. Introduction (to the theme issue, *Shifting perspectives in the study of shari'a courts: methodologies and paradigms*). *Islamic Law and Society* 15: 1–19.

Agrama, Hussein. 2010a. Ethics, tradition, authority: toward an anthropology of the fatwa. *American Ethnologist* 37(1): 2–18.

2010b. Secularism, sovereignty, indeterminacy: is Egypt a secular or a religious state? *Comparative Studies in Society and History* 52(3): 495–523.

2012. *Questioning secularism: Islam, sovereignty, and the rule of law in modern Egypt*. Chicago, IL: Chicago University Press.

Ahmed, Shahab. 2015. *What is Islam? The importance of being Islamic*. Princeton, NJ: Princeton University Press.

Ajami, Fuad. 1986. *The vanished Imam: Musa al-Sadr and the Shia of Lebanon*. London: I.B. Tauris.

Akarli, Engin. 1993. *The long peace: Ottoman Lebanon, 1861–1920*. London: Centre for Lebanese Studies and I.B. Tauris.

Al-Azem, Talal. 2017. *Rule-formulation and binding precedent in the madhhab-law tradition: Ibn Qutlubugha's commentary on The Compendium of Quduri*. Leiden: Brill.

Al-Azm, Sadiq. 1981. Orientalism and Orientalism in reverse. *Khamsin* 8: 5–26.

Alghar, Hamid. 1969. *Religion and state in Iran, 1785–1906: the role of the ulama in the Qajar period*. Berkeley, CA: University of California Press.

Ali, Kecia. 2008. Marriage in classical Islamic jurisprudence: a survey of doctrines. In Asifa Quraishi and Frank E. Vogel (eds.), *The Islamic marriage contract: case studies in Islamic family law*, 1–45. Cambridge, MA: Islamic Studies Program, Harvard Law School (Distributed by Harvard University Press).

Amanat, Abbas. 1988. In between the *madrasa* and the marketplace: the designation of clerical leadership in modern Shi'ism. In Said Arjomand (ed.), *Authority and political culture in Shi'ism*, 98–132. Albany, NY: State University of New York Press.

2007. From *ijtihad* to *wilayat-i faqih*: the evolution of the Shiite legal authority to political power. In Abbas Amanat and Frank Griffel (eds.), *Shari'a: Islamic law in the contemporary context*, 120–136. Stanford, CA: Stanford University Press.

Anderson, Benedict. 1983. *Imagined communities: reflections on the origin and spread of nationalism*. London: Verso.

Anderson, J.N.D. 1951a. Recent developments in Shari'a law III: the contract of marriage. *The Muslim World* 41(2): 113–126.

1951b. Recent developments in Shari'a law V: the dissolution of marriage. *The Muslim World* 41(4): 271–288.

1955. The Syrian law of personal status. *Bulletin of the School of Oriental and African Studies* 17(1): 34–49.

Anderson, Jon. 2003. The Internet and Islam's new interpreters. In Jon Anderson and Dale Eickelman (eds.), *New media in the Muslim world: the emerging public sphere*, 45–60. Bloomington, IN: Indiana University Press.

An-Na'im, Abdullahi. 2002. *Islamic family law in a changing world: a global resource book*. London: Zed Books.

Antoun, Richard. 1980. The Islamic court, the Islamic judge, and the accommodation of traditions: a Jordanian case study. *International Journal of Middle East Studies* 12(4): 455–467.

1989. *Muslim preacher in the modern world: a Jordanian case study in comparative perspective*. Princeton, NJ: Princeton University Press.

2000. Civil society, tribal process, and change in Jordan: an anthropological view. *International Journal of Middle East Studies* 32(4): 441–463.

Arjomand, Saïd. 1988. *The turban for the crown: the Islamic Revolution in Iran*. Oxford: Oxford University Press.

2007. Islamic constitutionalism. *Annual Review of Law and Social Science* 3: 115–140.

Armbrust, Walter. 1996. *Mass culture and modernism in Egypt*. Cambridge: Cambridge University Press.

Asad, Talal. 1986. The idea of an anthropology of Islam. *Occasional Papers Series*. Washington, DC: Center for Contemporary Arab Studies, Georgetown University.

1993. *Genealogies of religion: discipline and reasons of power in Christianity and Islam*. Baltimore, MD: John Hopkins University Press.

2003. *Formations of the secular: Christianity, Islam, modernity*. Stanford, CA: Stanford University Press.

Aydar, Hidayet. 2009. *Istikhara* and dreams: learning about the future through dreaming. In Kelly Bulkeley, Kate Adams and Patricia Davis (eds.), *Dreaming in Christianity and Islam: culture, conflict and creativity*, 123–136. New Brunswick, NJ: Rutgers University Press.

Aziz, Talib. 1996. Popular sovereignty in contemporary Shi'i political thought. *The Muslim World* 86(3–4): 273–293.

2001. Fadlallah and the remaking of the marja'iya. In Linda Walbridge (ed.), *The most learned of the Shi'a: the institution of the marja'i taqlid*, 205–215. Oxford: Oxford University Press.

Baldwin, James. 2017. *Islamic law and empire in Ottoman Cairo*. Edinburgh: Edinburgh University Press.

Bassam, Laila. 2016. Lebanese charity says unfairly hit by U.S. anti-Hezbollah law. *Reuters News*. 21 May.

Berkes, Niyazi. 1964. *The development of secularism in Turkey*. Montreal: McGill University Press.

Berkey, Jonathan. 2001. *Popular preaching and religious authority in the medieval Islamic Near East*. Seattle, WA: University of Washington Press.

Bernal, Victoria. 1994. Gender, culture, and capitalism: women and the remaking of Islamic 'tradition' in a Sudanese village. *Comparative Studies in Society and History* 36(1): 36–67.

Bhalloo, Zahir. 2015. Judging the judge: judicial competence in 19th century Iran. *Bulletin d'études orientales* 63: 275–293.

Bilani, Bachir, Ibrahim Najjar, and Antoine El-Gemayel. 1985. Personal status. In Antoine El-Gemayel (ed.), *The Lebanese legal system* (vol. 1), 267–390. Washington, DC: International Law Institute.

Blanford, Nicholas. 2006. *Killing Mr Lebanon: the assassination of Rafik Hariri and its impact on the Middle East*. London: I.B. Tauris.

Bowen, John. 2003. *Islam, law and equality in Indonesia: an anthropology of public reasoning*. Cambridge: Cambridge University Press.

2012. *A new anthropology of Islam*. Cambridge: Cambridge University Press.

Brenner, Suzanne. 1996. Reconstructing self and society: Javanese Muslim women and 'the veil'. *American Ethnologist* 23(4): 673–697.

Burak, Guy. 2015. *The second formation of Islamic law: the Hanafi school in the early modern Ottoman Empire*. Cambridge: Cambridge University Press.

Calder, Norman. 1979. Judicial authority in Imami Shi'i jurisprudence. *British Journal of Middle Eastern Studies* 6(2): 104–108.

1982. Accommodation and revolution in Imami Shi'i jurisprudence: Khumayni and the classical tradition. *Middle Eastern Studies* 18(1): 3–20.

2010. *Islamic jurisprudence in the classical era*, Colin Imber ed. Cambridge: Cambridge University Press.

Calhoun, Cheshire. 2000. The virtue of civility. *Philosophy and Public Affairs* 29(3): 251–275.

Chamas, Sophie. 2015. When weddings become protests: the debate over civil marriage in Lebanon. *Deseret News*, March 18. Online source: www.deseretnews.com/article/865624471/When-weddings-become-protests-the-debate-over-civil-marriage-in-Lebanon.html?pg=all; accessed 10 November 2016.

Chehabi, Houchang. 2001. The political regime of the Islamic Republic of Iran in comparative perspective. *Government and Opposition* 36(1): 48–70.

Clarke, Morgan. 2009. *Islam and new kinship: reproductive technology and the shari'ah in Lebanon*. Oxford: Berghahn.

2010. Neo-calligraphy: religious authority and media technology in contemporary Shiite Islam. *Comparative Studies in Society and History* 52(2): 351–383.

2012. The judge as tragic hero: judicial ethics in Lebanon's shari'a courts. *American Ethnologist* 39(1): 106–121.

2013. Integrity and commitment in the anthropology of Islam. In Magnus Marsden and Kostas Retsikas (eds.), *Articulating Islam: anthropological approaches to Muslim worlds*, 209–227. New York, NY: Springer.

2014. Cough sweets and angels: the ordinary ethics of the extraordinary in Sufi practice in Lebanon. *Journal of the Royal Anthropological Institute* 20(3): 407–425.

2015. Legalism and the care of the self: *shari'ah* discourse in contemporary Lebanon. In Paul Dresch and Judith Scheele (eds.), *Legalism: rules and categories*, 231–257. Oxford: Oxford University Press.

2016. After the Ayatollah: institutionalisation and succession in the *marja'iyya* of Sayyid Muhammad Husayn Fadlallah. *Die Welt des Islams* 56(2): 153–186.

2018. Making a centre in the periphery: the legitimation of Muhammad Husayn Fadlallah's Beirut *marja'iyya*. *British Journal of Middle Eastern Studies* 45(1): 39–57.

Clarke, Morgan and Marcia Inhorn. 2011. Mutuality and immediacy between *marja'* and *muqallid*: evidence from male IVF patients in Shi'i Lebanon. *International Journal of Middle East Studies* 43(3): 409–427.

Commins, David. 1990. *Islamic reform: political and social change in late Ottoman Syria*. Oxford: Oxford University Press.
Corboz, Elvire. 2015. *Guardians of Shi'ism: sacred authority and transnational family networks*. Edinburgh: Edinburgh University Press.
Coulson, Noel. 1956. Doctrine and practice in Islamic law: one aspect of the problem. *Bulletin of the School of Oriental and African Studies* 18(2): 211–226.
Courbage, Youssef and Emmanuel Todd. 2011. *A convergence of civilizations: the transformation of Muslim societies around the world*. New York, NY: Columbia University Press.
Crone, Patricia. 1999. Weber, Islamic law, and the rise of capitalism. In Toby Huff and Wolfgang Schluchter (eds.), *Max Weber and Islam*, 247–272. New Brunswick, NJ: Transaction Publishers.
Dawood, N.J. (trans.) 1956. *The Koran*. London: Penguin Books.
Deeb, Lara. 2006. *An enchanted modern: gender and public piety in Shi'i Lebanon*. Princeton, NJ: Princeton University Press.
2010. Sayyid Muhammad Husayn Fadlallah and Shi'a youth in Lebanon. *Journal of Shi'a Islamic Studies* 3(4): 405–426.
Deeb, Lara and Mona Harb. 2013. *Leisurely Islam: negotiating geography and morality in Shi'ite South Beirut*. Princeton, NJ: Princeton University Press.
Devlin, Patrick. 1981. *The judge*. Oxford: Oxford University Press.
Donahue, Charles, Jr. 2008. The Western canon law of marriage: a doctrinal introduction. In Asifa Quraishi and Frank E. Vogel (eds.), *The Islamic marriage contract: case studies in Islamic family law*, 46–56. Cambridge, MA: Islamic Studies Program, Harvard Law School (Distributed by Harvard University Press).
Dresch, Paul. 2000. Wilderness of mirrors: truth and vulnerability in Middle Eastern fieldwork. In Paul Dresch, Wendy James and David Parkin (eds.), *Anthropologists in a wider world*, 109–128. Oxford: Berghahn Books.
2006. *The rules of Barat: tribal documents from Yemen*. Sanaa: Centre français d'archéologie et des sciences sociales.
2012. Legalism, anthropology, and history: the view from part of anthropology. In Paul Dresch and Hannah Skoda (eds.), *Legalism: anthropology and history*, 1–37. Oxford: Oxford University Press.
Dumont, Louis. 1982 [1980]. On value, modern and nonmodern. In his, *Essays on individualism*, 234–268. Chicago, IL: Chicago University Press.
Dupret, Baudouin. 2000. *Au nom de quel droit: Répertoires juridiques et référence religieuse dans la société égyptienne musulmane contemporaine*. Paris: Maison de sciences de l'homme.
2006. The practice of judging: the Egyptian judiciary at work in a personal status case. In M.K. Masud, Rudolph Peters and David Powers (eds.), *Dispensing justice in Islam: qadis and their judgements*, 143–168. Leiden: Brill.
2007. What is Islamic law? A praxiological answer and an Egyptian case study. *Theory, Culture and Society* 24(2): 79–100.
Dupret, Baudouin, Maurits Berger and Laila Al-Zwaini (eds.) 1999. *Legal pluralism in the Arab world*. The Hague: Kluwer Law International.
Dworkin, Ronald. 1975. Hard cases. *Harvard Law Review* 88(6): 1057–1109.

Eickelman, Dale. 1992. Mass higher education and the religious imagination in contemporary Arab societies. *American Ethnologist* 19(4): 643–655.

El Alami, Dawoud and Doreen Hinchcliffe. 1996. *Islamic marriage and divorce laws of the Arab world*. London: Kluwer Law International.

El-Cheikh, Nadia. 2000. The 1998 proposed civil marriage law in Lebanon: the reaction of the Muslim communities. In Eugene Cotran (ed.), *Yearbook of Islamic and Middle Eastern Law, volume 5 (1998–1999)*, 147–161. London: Kluwer Law International.

El-Ghoul, Adnan. 2004. Delivering in the toughest of times. *Daily Star*, Beirut. 25 October.

El-Husseini, Rola. 2008. Women, work, and political participation in Lebanese Shia contemporary thought: the writings of Ayatollahs Fadlallah and Shams al-Din. *Comparative Studies of South Asia, Africa and the Middle East* 28(2): 273–282.

Ergene, Boğaç. 2003. *Local court, provincial society and justice in the Ottoman Empire: legal practice and dispute resolution in Çankırı and Kastamonu (1652–1744)*. Leiden: Brill.

2014. Qanun and sharia. In Rudolph Peters and Peri Bearman (eds.), *The Ashgate research companion to Islamic law*, 109–120. Farnham: Ashgate.

Fahmy, Khaled. 1999a. The anatomy of justice: forensic medicine and criminal law in nineteenth-century Egypt. *Islamic Law and Society* 6(2): 224–271.

1999b. The police and the people in nineteenth-century Egypt. *Die Welt des Islams* 39(3): 340–377.

Faour, Muhammad. 2007. Religion, politics and demography in Lebanon. *Middle Eastern Studies* 43(6): 909–921.

Farha, Mark. 2015. Stumbling blocks to the secularization of personal status laws in the Lebanese Republic (1926–2013). *Arab Law Quarterly* 29: 31–55.

Fischer, Michael. 1980. *Iran: from religious dispute to revolution*. Madison, WI: University of Wisconsin Press.

Fitzgerald, Timothy. 2007. *Discourses on civility and barbarity: a critical history of religion and related categories*. Oxford: Oxford University Press.

Fitzpatrick, Peter. 1984. Law and societies. *Osgoode Hall Law Journal* 22(1): 115–138.

Floor, Willem. 1981. The political role of the lutis in Iran. In Michael Bonine and Nikki Keddie (eds.), *Modern Iran: the dialectics of continuity and change*, 83–98. Albany, NY: State University of New York Press.

1983. Change and development in the judicial system of Qajar Iran (1800–1925). In Edmund Bosworth and Carole Hillenbrand (eds.), *Qajar Iran*, 113–147. Edinburgh: Edinburgh University Press.

Freeland, Richard and Martin Lau. 2008. The shari'a and English law: identity and justice for British Muslims. In Asifa Quraishi and Frank E. Vogel (eds.), *The Islamic marriage contract: case studies in Islamic family law*, 331–347. Cambridge, MA: Islamic Studies Program, Harvard Law School (Distributed by Harvard University Press).

Gaffney, Patrick. 1994. *The Prophet's pulpit: Islamic preaching in contemporary Egypt*. Berkeley, CA: University of California Press.

Gellner, Ernest. 1981. *Muslim society*. Cambridge: Cambridge University Press.
1991. Civil society in historical context. *International Social Science Journal* 43: 495–510.
1994. *Conditions of liberty: civil society and its rivals*. London: Penguin.
Gerber, Haim. 1994. *State, society, and law in Islam: Ottoman law in comparative perspective*. Albany, NY: State University of New York Press.
1998. Rigidity versus openness in late classical Islamic law: the case of the seventeenth-century Palestinian mufti Khayr al-Din al-Rumli. *Islamic Law and Society* 5(2): 165–195.
Ghamroun, Samer. 2013. La communauté sunnite libanaise saisie par les femmes. In Florence Rochefort and Maria Sanna (eds.) *Normes religieuses et genre*, 203–215. Paris: Armand Colin.
2014. Effets d'état: mobilisations et action publique au Liban à l'épreuve du pluralisme juridique. *Gouvernement et action publique* 4: 57–82.
Ghazzal, Zouhair. 1998. Review of Waddah Sharara, *al-Umma al-qaliqa*, and Muhammad Husayn Fadlallah, *al-Masa'il al-fiqhiyya*. *Islamic Law and Society* 5(3): 448–456.
2007. *The grammars of adjudication: the economics of judicial decision making in fin-de-siècle Ottoman Beirut and Damascus*. Beirut: Institut Français de Proche-Orient.
Gleave, Robert. 2000. Two classical Shiʿi theories of qada'. In Gerald Hawting, Jawid Ahmad Mojaddedi and Alexander Samely (eds.), *Studies in Islamic Middle Eastern texts and traditions in memory of Norman Calder*, 105–121. Oxford: Oxford University Press.
2003. Political aspects of modern Shiʿi legal discussions: Khumayni and Khu'i on *ijtihad* and *qada'*. In Barbara Roberson (ed.), *Shaping the current Islamic reformation*, 95–113. London: Frank Cass.
2007. Conceptions of authority in Iraqi Shi'ism: Baqir al-Hakim, Ha'iri and Sistani on ijtihad, taqlid and marja'iyya. *Theory, Culture and Society* 24(2): 59–78.
2008. The qadi and the mufti in Akhbari Shiʿi jurisprudence. In Peri Bearman, Wolfhart Heinrichs and Bernard Weiss (eds.), *The law applied: contextualizing the Islamic shariʿa*, 235–258. London: I.B. Tauris.
2010. Introduction. In Noel Calder, *Islamic jurisprudence in the classical era*, Colin Imber (ed.) 1–21. Cambridge: Cambridge University Press.
Goldman, Harvey. 1988. *Max Weber and Thomas Mann: calling and the shaping of the self*. Berkeley, CA: University of California Press.
Gräf, Bettina and Jakob Skovgaard-Petersen. 2009. *Global mufti: the phenomenon of Yusuf al-Qaradawi*. London: Hurst.
Haeri, Niloofar. 1997. The reproduction of symbolic capital: language, state, and class in Egypt. *Current Anthropology* 38(5): 795–816.
Hallaq, Wael. 1994. From *fatwa*s to *furu*ʿ: growth and change in Islamic substantive law. *Islamic Law and Society* 1(1): 29–65.
1996. Ifta' and ijtihad in Sunni legal theory: a developmental account. In M.K. Masud, Brinkley Messick and David Powers (eds.), *Islamic legal interpretation: muftis and their fatwas*, 33–43. Cambridge, MA: Harvard University Press.

2001. *Authority, continuity and change in Islamic law*. Cambridge: Cambridge University Press.

2004. Can the shari'a be restored? In Yvonne Haddad and Barbara Stowasser (eds.), *Islamic law and the challenges of modernity*, 21–53. Walnut Creek, CA: AltaMira Press.

2009. *Shari'a: theory, practice, transformations*. Cambridge: Cambridge University Press.

2013. *The impossible state: Islam, politics, and modernity's moral predicament*. New York, NY: Columbia University Press.

Hamdan, Hanan. 2017. Lebanon's mothers see glint of hope in custody ruling. *Al-Monitor*, 27 December. Online source: www.al-monitor.com/pulse/originals/2017/12/lebanon-shiite-mothers-children-custody-laws.html, accessed 16 February 2018.

Hamzeh, Nizar. 1997. The role of Hizbullah in conflict management in Lebanon's Shia community. In Paul Salem (ed.), *Conflict resolution in the Arab world*, 93–121. Beirut: American University of Beirut.

Hamzeh, Nizar, and Hrair Dekmejian. 1996. A Sufi response to political Islamism: al-Ahbash of Lebanon. *International Journal of Middle East Studies* 28(2): 217–229.

Hann, Chris and Elizabeth Dunn (eds.) 1996. *Civil society: challenging Western models*. London: Routledge.

Hanssen, Jens. 2005. *Fin de siècle Beirut: the making of an Ottoman provincial capital*. Oxford: Clarendon Press.

Harik, Iliya. 1968. *Politics and change in a traditional society: Lebanon, 1711–1845*. Princeton, NJ: Princeton University Press.

Harik, Judith. 2006. Hizballah's public and social services and Iran. In Houchang Chehabi (ed.), *Distant relations: Iran and Lebanon in the last 500 years*, 259–286. London: Centre for Lebanese Studies and I.B. Tauris.

Hasso, Frances. 2011. *Consuming desires: family crisis and the state in the Middle East*. Stanford, CA: Stanford University Press.

Haykel, Bernard. 2009. On the nature of Salafi thought and action. In Roel Meijer (ed.), *Global Salafism: Islam's new religious movement*, 33–57. London: Hurst.

Henley, Alexander. 2013. *The politics of religious leadership in modern Lebanon*. PhD dissertation, University of Manchester.

Hermez, Sami. 2012. 'The war is going to ignite': on the anticipation of violence in Lebanon. *Political and Legal Anthropology Review* 35: 327–44.

Herzfeld, Michael. 1997. *Cultural intimacy: social poetics in the nation-state*. New York, NY: Routledge.

Hill, Enid. 1979. *Mahkama! Studies in the Egyptian legal system: courts and crimes, law and society*. London: Ithaca Press.

Hirsch, Susan. 1998. *Pronouncing and persevering: gender and the discourses of disputing in an African Islamic court*. Chicago, IL: University of Chicago Press.

2006. Islamic law and society post-9/11. *Annual Review of Law and Social Science* 2: 165–186.

Hirschkind, Charles. 2006. *The ethical soundscape: cassette sermons and Islamic counterpublics*. New York, NY: Columbia University Press.

Hodgson, Marshall. 1974. *The venture of Islam: conscience and history in a world civilization. Vol. 1 The classical age of Islam*. Chicago, IL: Chicago University Press.

Hoodfar, Homa. 1997. *Between marriage and the market: intimate politics and survival in Cairo*. Berkeley, CA: University of California Press.

Hourani, Albert and Nadim Shehadi. 1992. *The Lebanese in the world: a century of emigration*. Oxford: Centre for Lebanese Studies.

Huff, Toby and Wolfgang Schluchter (eds.) 1999. *Max Weber and Islam*. New Brunswick, NJ: Transaction Publishers.

Hull, Matthew. 2012. *Government of paper: the materiality of bureaucracy in urban Pakistan*. Berkeley, CA: University of California Press.

Human Rights Watch. 2015. *Unequal and unprotected: women's rights under Lebanon's religious personal status laws*. Online publication: www.hrw.org/sites/default/files/reports/lebanon0115_ForUpload.pdf, accessed 10 November 2016.

Ibrahim, Ahmed. 2015. *Pragmatism in Islamic law: a social and intellectual history*. Syracuse, NY: Syracuse University Press.

Imber, Colin. 2002. *The Ottoman Empire, 1300–1650: the structure of power*. Basingstoke: Palgrave Macmillan.

Jackson, Sherman. 1996. *Islamic law and the state: the constitutional jurisprudence of Shihab al-Din al-Qarafi*. Leiden: Brill.

Jadaane, Fahmi. 1990. Notions of the state in contemporary Arab-Islamic writings. In Giacomo Luciani (ed.), *The Arab state*, 247–283. London: Routledge.

Johansen, Baber. 1997. Truth and validity of the qadi's judgment. *Recht van de Islam* 14: 1–26.

1999. *Contingency in a sacred law: legal and ethical norms in the Muslim fiqh*. Leiden: Brill.

Johnson, Michael. 1986. *Class and client in Beirut: the Sunni Muslim community and the Lebanese state, 1840–1985*. London: Ithaca Press.

Jones, Linda. 2012. *The power of oratory in the medieval Muslim world*. Cambridge: Cambridge University Press.

Jones-Pauly, Christina. 2008. Marriage contracts of Muslims in the diaspora: problems in the recognition of *mahr* contracts in German law. In Asifa Quraishi and Frank E. Vogel (eds.), *The Islamic marriage contract: case studies in Islamic family law*, 299–330. Cambridge, MA: Islamic Studies Program, Harvard Law School (Distributed by Harvard University Press).

Kabha, Mustafa and Haggai Erlich. 2006. Al-Ahbash and Wahhabiyya: interpretations of Islam. *International Journal of Middle East Studies* 38(4): 519–538.

Kanafani-Zahar, Aïda. 2006. Les tentatives d'instaurer le mariage civil au Liban: l'impact des *Tanzîmât* et des réformes mandataires. In Pierre-Jean Luizard (ed.), *Le choc colonial et l'islam: les politiques religieuses des puissances coloniales en terres d'islam*, 427–448. Paris: La découverte.

Karanshawy, Samer El-. 2013. *The day the Imam was killed: mourning sermons, politics, history and the struggle for Lebanese Shi'ism*. DPhil dissertation, University of Oxford.

2015. The scholar's turban versus the warrior's: the shifting basis of religious and political authority in Lebanese Shi'ism. *Journal of Shi'a Islamic Studies* 8(2): 193–207.

Katz, Marion. 2002. *Body of text: the emergence of the Sunni law of ritual purity*. Albany, NY: State University of New York Press.

Kawtharani, Farah. 2016. Integrating Shiʿa in the modern nation-state: Shaykh Muhammad Mahdi Shams al-Din, Hizbullah, and engagement in Lebanese politics. *Middle East Journal* 70(3): 419–438.

Khalaf, Samir. 2002. *Civil and uncivil violence in Lebanon: a history of the internationalization of communal conflict*. New York, NY: Columbia University Press.

Khalaji, Mehdi. 2006. *The last marjaʿ: Sistani and the end of traditional religious authority in Shiism. Policy Focus* (59, Sept.). Washington, DC: Washington Institute for Near East Policy.

Khater, Akram. 2001. *Inventing home: emigration, gender, and the middle class in Lebanon, 1870–1920*. Berkeley, CA: University of California Press.

Khuri, Fuad. 1987. The ulama: a comparative study of Sunni and Shiʿa religious officials. *Middle Eastern Studies* 23(3): 291–312.

Kramer, Martin. 1987. Syria's Alawis and Shiʿism. In Martin Kramer (ed.), *Shiʿism, resistance and revolution*. London: Mansell.

1997. The oracle of Hizbullah: Muhammad Husayn Fadlallah. In R. Appleby (ed.), *Spokesmen for the despised*, 83–181. Chicago, IL: University of Chicago Press.

Laidlaw, James. 2014. *The subject of virtue: an anthropology of ethics and freedom*. Cambridge: Cambridge University Press.

Layish, Aharon. 1982. *Marriage, divorce and succession in the Druze family: a study based on decisions of Druze arbitrators and religious courts in Israel and the Golan Heights*. Leiden: Brill.

Leichtman, Mara. 2013. Migration, war, and the making of a transnational Lebanese Shiʿi community in Senegal. *International Journal of Middle East Studies* 42(2): 269–290.

Levinas, Emmanuel. 1969 [1961]. *Totality and infinity: an essay on exteriority*, Alphonso Lingis trans. Pittsburgh, PA: Duquesne University Press.

Litvak, Meir. 1998. *Shiʿi scholars of nineteenth century Iraq: the 'ulama' of Najaf and Karbala'*. Cambridge: Cambridge University Press.

Lombardi, Clark. 2006. *State law as Islamic law in modern Egypt: the incorporation of the shariʿa into Egyptian constitutional law*. Leiden: Brill.

Longrigg, Stephen. 1958. *Syria and Lebanon under French Mandate*. Oxford: Oxford University Press.

MacIntyre, Alasdair. 1981. *After virtue: a study in moral theory*. London: Duckworth.

Madelung, Wilferd. 1980 A Treatise of the Sharif al-Murtada on the legality of working for the government. *Bulletin of the School of Oriental and African Studies* 43(1): 18–31.

Mahmood, Saba. 2005. *Politics of piety: the Islamic revival and the feminist subject*. Princeton, NJ: Princeton University Press.

2016. *Religious difference in a secular age: a minority report*. Princeton, NJ: Princeton University Press.

Mahmood, Tahir. 1972. *Family law reform in the Muslim world*. Bombay: Indian Law Institute.

1987. *Personal law in Islamic countries: history, text and comparative analysis*. New Delhi: Academy of Law and Religion.

Makdisi, Ussama. 2000. *The culture of sectarianism: community, history, and violence in nineteenth-century Ottoman Lebanon*. Berkeley, CA: University of California Press.

Maktabi, Rania. 2013. Female citizenship in the Middle East: comparing family law reform in Morocco, Egypt, Syria and Lebanon. *Middle East Law and Governance* 5: 280–307.

Mallat, Chibli. 1988. *Shi'i thought from the South of Lebanon*. Oxford: Centre for Lebanese Studies.

2007. *Introduction to Middle Eastern law*. Oxford: Oxford University Press.

Mallat, Tamer and Samar Howayek. 2013. Lebanon. *Yearbook of Islamic and Middle Eastern Law* 17: 271–288.

Ma'oz, Moshe. 1968. *Ottoman reform in Syria and Palestine, 1840–1861: the impact of the Tanzimat on politics and society*. Oxford: Clarendon Press.

March, Andrew. 2015. What can the Islamic past teach us about secular modernity? *Political Theory* 43(6): 838–849.

Masters, Bruce. 2001. *Christians and Jews in the Ottoman Arab world: the roots of sectarianism*. Cambridge: Cambridge University Press.

Masud, M.K., Brinkley Messick and David Powers (eds.) 1996. *Islamic legal interpretation: muftis and their fatwas*. Cambridge, MA: Harvard University Press.

Masud M.K., Rudolph Peters and David Powers (eds.) 2006. *Dispensing justice in Islam: qadis and their judgements*. Leiden: Brill.

Méouchy, Nadine. 2006. La réforme des juridictions religieuses en Syrie et au Liban (1921–1939): raisons de la puissance mandataire et raisons des communautés. In Pierre-Jean Luizard (ed.), *Le choc colonial et l'islam: les politiques religieuses des puissances coloniales en terres d'islam*, 359–382. Paris: La découverte.

Mermier, Franck and Elizabeth Picard (eds.) 2007. *Liban, une guerre de 33 jours*. Paris: La découverte.

Mervin, Sabrina. 2000. *Un réformisme chiite: Ulémas et letters du Gabal 'Âmil (actuel Liban-Sud) de la fin de l'Empire ottoman à l'indépendence du Liban*. Paris: Karthala.

2008a. Muhammad Husayn Fadlallah, du 'guide spirituel' au *marja'* moderniste. In Sabrina Mervin (ed.), *Le Hezbollah: état des lieux*, 277–285. Paris: Sindbad.

2008b. Normes religieuses et loi du silence: le mariage temporaire chez les chiites du Liban. In Barbara Drieskens (ed.), *Les metamorphoses du mariage au moyen-orient*, 47–58. Beirut: Presses de l'IFPO.

Messick, Brinkley. 1983. Prosecution in Yemen: the introduction of the *niyaba*. *International Journal of Middle East Studies* 15(4): 507–518.

1989. Just writing: paradox and political economy in Yemeni legal documents. *Cultural Anthropology* 4(1):26–50.

1993. *The calligraphic state: textual domination and history in a Muslim society*. Berkeley, CA: University of California Press.

1996. Media muftis: radio fatwas in Yemen. In M.K. Masud, Brinkley Messick and David Powers (eds.), *Islamic legal interpretation: muftis and their fatwas*, 310–320. Cambridge, MA: Harvard University Press.

2001. Indexing the self: intent and expression in Islamic legal acts. *Islamic Law and Society* 8(2): 151–178.
2005. Madhhabs and modernities. In Peri Bearman, Rudolph Peters and Frank Vogel (eds.), *The Islamic school of law: evolution, devolution, and progress*, 159–174. Cambridge, MA: Islamic Legal Studies Program, Harvard Law School.
2008. Shari'a ethnography. In Peri Bearman, Wolfhart Heinrichs and Bernard Weiss (eds.), *The law applied: contextualizing the Islamic Shari'a* (eds.), 173–193. London: I.B. Tauris.
2014. The judge and the mufti. In Rudolph Peters and Peri Bearman (eds.), *The Ashgate research companion to Islamic law*, 73–91. Farnham: Ashgate.
2017. *Shari'a scripts: a historical anthropology*. New York, NY: Columbia University Press.
Mikdashi, Maya. 2014. Sex and sectarianism: the legal architecture of Lebanese citizenship. *Comparative Studies of South Asia and the Middle East* 34(2): 279–293.
Mir-Hosseini, Ziba. 1993. *Marriage on trial: a study of Islamic family law*. London: I.B. Tauris.
2000. *Islam and gender: the religious debate in contemporary Iran*. London: I.B. Tauris.
2008. A woman's right to terminate the marriage contract: the case of Iran. In Asifa Quraishi and Frank E. Vogel (eds.), *The Islamic marriage contract: case studies in Islamic family law*, 215–230. Cambridge, MA: Islamic Studies Program, Harvard Law School (Distributed by Harvard University Press).
Mitchell, Timothy. 2006 [1999]. Society, economy, and the state effect. In Aradhana Sharma and Akhil Gupta (eds.), *The anthropology of the state: a reader*, 169–186. Oxford: Blackwell.
Mittermaier, Amira. 2011. *Dreams that matter: Egyptian landscapes of the imagination*. Berkeley, CA: University of California Press.
2012. Dreams from elsewhere: Muslim subjectivities beyond the trope of self-cultivation. *Journal of the Royal Anthropological Institute* 18(2): 247–265.
Moors, Annelies. 1995. *Women, property and Islam: Palestinian experiences 1920–1990*. Cambridge: Cambridge University Press.
Mottahedeh, Roy. 2014. The quandaries of emulation: the theory and politics of Shi'i manuals of practice. (The ninth [2011] Farhat J. Ziadeh distinguished lecture in Arab and Islamic Studies.) Seattle, WA: University of Washington.
2016. The Najaf hawzah curriculum. *Journal of the Royal Asiatic Society* 26(1–2): 341–351.
Moussavi, Ahmad Kazemi. 1996. *Religious authority in Shi'ite Islam: from the office of mufti to the institution of marja'*. Kuala Lumpur: International Institute of Islamic Thought and Civilization.
Muhanna, Elias. 2013a. Will civil marriage end Lebanon's confessional system? *Jadaliyya*, January 26. Online source: www.jadaliyya.com/pages/index/9796/will-civil-marriage-end-lebanon%E2%80%99s-confessional-sys, accessed 11 February 2013.

2013b. Highly unorthodox: the week Lebanon went secular (and ended up more sectarian than ever...). *Jadaliyya*, February 21. Online source: www.jadaliyya.com/pages/index/10291/highly-unorthodox_the-week-lebanon-went-secular-(a, accessed 13 January 2016.

Mundy, Martha. 1991. Between the oral and the written (review of L. Rosen, *The anthropology of justice*). *History Workshop* 32: 184–192.

1995. *Domestic government: kinship, community and polity in North Yemen*. London: I.B. Tauris.

Nasir, Jamal. 2002[1986]. *The Islamic law of personal status*. The Hague; London: Kluwer Law International.

Navaro-Yashin, Yael. 2002. *Faces of the state: secularism and public life in Turkey*. Princeton, NJ: Princeton University Press.

Norton, Augustus. 1987. *Amal and the Shi'a: struggle for the soul of Lebanon*. Austin, TX: University of Texas Press.

(ed.) 1995. *Civil society in the Middle East*, vol. 1. Leiden: Brill.

(ed.) 1996. *Civil society in the Middle East*, vol. 2. Leiden: Brill.

2007. *Hezbollah: a short history*. Princeton, NJ: Princeton University Press.

Opwis, Felicitas. 2005. *Maslaha* in contemporary Islamic legal theory. *Islamic Law and Society* 12(2): 182–223.

Orsanloo, Arzoo. 2006. Islamic-civil 'rights talk': women, subjectivity, and law in Iranian family court. *American Ethnologist* 33(2): 191–209.

Othman, Aida. 2007. 'And amicable settlement is best': *sulh* and dispute resolution in Islamic law. *Arab Law Quarterly* 21: 64–90.

Owen, David and Tracy Strong. 2004. Introduction. In Max Weber, *The vocation lectures*, David Owen and Tracy Strong (eds.), Rodney Livingstone (trans.), ix–lxxv. Indianapolis, IN: Hackett Publishing Company.

Pandian, Anand. 2008. Tradition in fragments: inherited forms and fractures in the ethics of South India. *American Ethnologist* 35(3): 466–480.

Peletz, Michael. 2002. *Islamic modern*: religious courts and cultural politics in Malaysia. Princeton, NJ: Princeton University Press.

2013. Malaysia's Syariah judiciary as global assemblage: Islamization, corporatization, and other transformations in context. *Comparative Studies in Society and History* 55(3): 603–633.

Peters, Rudolph. 1997. Islamic and secular criminal law in nineteenth century Egypt: the role and function of the qadi. *Islamic Law and Society* 4(1): 70–90.

1999. Paradise or hell? The religious doctrine of election in eighteenth and nineteenth century Islamic fundamentalism and Protestant Calvinism. In Toby Huff and Wolfgang Schluchter (eds.), *Max Weber and Islam*, 205–216. New Brunswick, NJ: Transaction Publishers.

2005. *Crime and punishment in Islamic law: theory and practice from the sixteenth to the twenty-first century*. Cambridge: Cambridge University Press.

Peters, Rudolph and Peri Bearman. 2014. Introduction: the nature of the sharia. In Rudolph Peters and Peri Bearman (eds.), *The Ashgate research companion to Islamic law*, 1–10. Farnham: Ashgate.

Powers, David. 1990 *Fatwa*s as sources for legal and social history: a dispute over endowment revenues from fourteenth-century Fez. *Al-Qantara* 11: 295–341.

1992. On judicial review in Islamic law. *Law and Society Review* 26(2): 315–342.

1994. *Kadijustiz* or *qadi*-justice? A paternity dispute from fourteenth-century Morocco. *Islamic Law and Society* 1(3): 332–366.

2002. *Law, society, and culture in the Maghrib, 1300–1500*. Cambridge: Cambridge University Press.

Priest, George and William Klein. 1984. The selection of disputes for litigation. *Journal of Legal Studies* 13(1): 1–55.

Pye, Lucian. 1999. Civility, social capital, and civil society: three powerful concepts for explaining Asia. *Journal of Interdisciplinary History* 29(4): 763–782.

Rabb, Intisar. 2015. Against *Kadijustiz*: on the negative citation of foreign law. *Suffolk University Law Review* 48: 343–377.

Rabbath, Edmond. 1982. *La constitution libanaise: origines, textes et commentaires*. Beirut: Publications de l'Université Libanaise.

1986 [1973]. *La formation historique du Liban politique et constitutionnel: essai de synthèse*. Beirut: Publications de l'Université Libanaise.

Reinhart, Kevin. 1990. Impurity/no danger. *History of Religions* 30(1): 1–24.

1994. Transcendence and social practice: *muftis* and *qadis* as religious interpreters. *Annales Islamologiques* 27: 5–28.

Rheinstein, Max. 1954 Introduction. In Max Rheinstein (ed.), *Max Weber on law in Economy and Society*, xxv–lxxii. Cambridge, MA: Harvard University Press.

Rizvi, Sajjad. 2010. Political mobilization and the Shi'i religious establishment (*marja'iyya*). *International Affairs* 86(6): 1299–1313.

Robbins, Joel. 2013. Monism, pluralism and the structure of value relations: a Dumontian contribution to the contemporary study of value. *HAU: Journal of Ethnographic Theory* 8(1): 99–115.

Roberts, Simon. 1998. Against legal pluralism: some reflections on the contemporary enlargement of the legal domain. *Journal of Legal Pluralism and Unofficial Law* 30(42): 95–106.

Rondot, Pierre. 1947. *Les institutions politiques du Liban: des communautés traditionnelles à l'état moderne*. Paris: Institut d'études de l'Orient contemporain.

Rosen, Lawrence. 1980–1981. Equity and discretion in a modern Islamic legal system. *Law and Society Review* 15(2): 217–246.

1989. *The anthropology of justice: law as culture in Islamic society*. New York, NY: Cambridge University Press.

2000. *The justice of Islam: comparative perspectives on Islamic law and society*. Oxford: Oxford University Press.

Rosiny, Stephan. 2001. The tragedy of Fatima al-Zahra in the debate of two Shiite theologians in Lebanon. In Reiner Brunner and Werner Ende (eds.), *The Twelver Shia in modern times: religious culture and political history*, 207–219. Leiden: Brill.

Rougier, Bernard. 2007. *Everyday jihad: the rise of militant Islam among Palestinians in Lebanon*. Cambridge, MA: Harvard University Press.

2015. *The Sunni tragedy in the Middle East: Northern Lebanon from al-Qaeda to ISIS*. Princeton, NJ: Princeton University Press.

Rubin, Avi. 2011. *Ottoman Nizamiye courts: law and modernity*. New York, NY: Palgrave Macmillan.

Saadawi, Ghalya. 2013. Civil marriage fatwas, the Lebanese state, and renegade bacteria. *Jadaliyya*, February 20. Online source: www.jadaliyya.com/pages/index/10278/civil-marriage-fatwas-the-lebanese-state-and-reneg; accessed 13 January 2016.

Salloukh, Bassel, Rabie Barakat, Jinan Al-Habbal, Lara Khattab and Shoghig Mikaelian. 2015. *The politics of sectarianism in postwar Lebanon*. London: Pluto Press.

Sankari, Jamal. 2005. *Fadlallah: the making of a radical Shi'ite leader*. London: Saqi.

Schauer, Frederick. 1985. Easy cases. *Southern California Law Review* 58: 399–440.

1991. *Playing by the rules: a philosophical examination of rule-based decision making in law and in life*. Oxford: Oxford University Press.

2009. *Thinking like a lawyer: a new introduction to legal reasoning*. Cambridge, MA: Harvard University Press.

Schielke, Samuli. 2009. Being good in Ramadan: ambivalence, fragmentation, and the moral self in the lives of young Egyptians. *Journal of the Royal Anthropological Institute* 15(S1): S24-S40.

2010. Second thoughts about the anthropology of Islam, or how to make sense of grand schemes in everyday life. *Working Papers* (no. 2). Berlin: Zentrum Moderner Orient.

Schirazi, Asghar. 1997. *The constitution of Iran: politics and the state in the Islamic Republic*, John O'Kane trans. London: I.B. Tauris.

Schluchter, Wolfgang. 1999. Hindrances to modernity: Max Weber on Islam. In Toby Huff and Wolfgang Schluchter (eds.), *Max Weber and Islam*, 53–138. New Brunswick, NJ: Transaction Publishers.

Shaery-Eisenlohr, Roschanack. 2008. *Shi'ite Lebanon: transnational religion and the making of national identities*. New York, NY: Columbia University Press.

Shahar, Ido. 2008. Legal pluralism and the study of shari'a courts. *Islamic Law and Society* 15: 112–141.

2015. *Legal pluralism in the Holy City: competing courts, forum shopping, and institutional dynamics in Jerusalem*. Farnham: Ashgate.

Shalakany, Amr. 2008. Islamic legal histories. *Berkeley Journal of Middle Eastern and Islamic Law* 1(1): 1–82.

Shehadeh, Lamia. 1998. The legal status of married women in Lebanon. *International Journal of Middle East Studies* 30: 501–19.

Shils, Edward. 1966. The prospect for Lebanese civility. In Leonard Binder (ed.), *Politics in Lebanon*, 1–11. New York, NY: John Wiley and Sons.

Singerman, Diane. 1995. *Avenues of participation*. Princeton, NJ: Princeton University Press.

Skovgaard-Petersen, Jakob. 1996. Religious heads or civil servants? Druze and Sunni religious leadership in post-war Lebanon. *Mediterranean Politics* 1(3): 337–352.

1998. The Sunni religious scene in Beirut. *Mediterranean Politics* 3(1): 69–80.

2004. A typology of state muftis. In Yyonne Haddad and Barbara Stowasser (eds), *Islamic law and the challenges of modernity*, 81–97. Walnut Creek, CA: AltaMira Press.

2005. Levantine state muftis: an Ottoman legacy? In Elisabeth Özdalga (ed.), *Late Ottoman society: the intellectual legacy*, 274–288. London: RoutledgeCurzon.

Sonbol, Amira. 2008. A history of marriage contracts in Egypt. In Asifa Quraishi and Frank E. Vogel (eds.), *The Islamic marriage contract: case studies in Islamic family law*, 87–122. Cambridge, MA: Islamic Studies Program, Harvard Law School (Distributed by Harvard University Press).

Starrett, Gregory. 1998. *Putting Islam to work: education, politics, and religious transformation in Egypt*. Berkeley, CA: University of California Press.

Stiles, Erin. 2009. *An Islamic court in context: an ethnographic study of judicial reasoning*. New York, NY: Palgrave Macmillan.

Strathern, Marilyn. 1985. Discovering social control. *Journal of Law and Society* 12(2): 111–134.

Tamdoğan, Işık. 2008. *Sulh* and the 18th century Ottoman courts of Üsküdar and Adana. *Islamic Law and Society* 15(1): 55–83.

Tarabey, Loubna. 2013. *Family law in Lebanon: marriage and divorce among the Druze*. London: I.B. Tauris.

Thompson, Elizabeth. 2000. *Colonial citizens: republican rights, paternal privilege, and gender in French Syria and Lebanon*. New York, NY: Columbia University Press.

Tillier, Mathieu. 2015. Le pluralisme judiciaire en Islam, ses dynamiques et ses enjeux. *Bulletin d'études orientales* 63: 23–40.

Tucker, Judith. 1988. Marriage and family in Nablus, 1720–1856: toward a history of Arab marriage. *Journal of Family History* 13(2): 165–179.

1996. Revisiting reform: women and the Ottoman law of family rights, 1917. *Arab Studies Journal* 4: 4–17.

1998. *In the house of the law: gender and Islamic law in Ottoman Syria and Palestine*. Berkeley, CA: University of California Press.

2008a. Questions of consent: contracting a marriage in Ottoman Syria and Palestine. In Asifa Quraishi and Frank E. Vogel (eds.), *The Islamic marriage contract: case studies in Islamic family law*, 123–135. Cambridge, MA: Islamic Studies Program, Harvard Law School (Distributed by Harvard University Press).

2008b. *Women, family, and gender in Islamic law*. Cambridge: Cambridge University Press.

Turner, Bryan. 1974. *Weber and Islam: a critical study*. London: Routledge and Kegan Paul.

Van Velsen, Jaap. 1969. Procedural informality, reconciliation, and false comparisons. In Max Gluckman (ed.), *Ideas and procedures in African customary law*, 137–152. London: Published for the International African Institute by the Oxford University Press.

Vikør, Knut. 2005. *Between God and the sultan: a history of Islamic law*. London: Hurst and Co.

Visser, Reidar. 2006. *Sistani, the United States and politics in Iraq: from quietism to Macchiavellianism?* NUPI paper 700. Oslo: Norwegian Institute of International Affairs.

Vogel, Frank. 2000. *Islamic law and legal system: studies of Saudi Arabia*. Leiden: Brill.

Wadud-Muhsin, Amina. 1998. Qur'an and woman. In Charles Kurzman (ed.), *Liberal Islam: a sourcebook*, 127–138. New York, NY: Oxford University Press.

Wagemakers, Joas. 2009. The transformation of a radical concept: *al-wala' wa-l-bara'* in the ideology of Abu Muhammad al-Maqdisi. In Roel Meijer (ed.), *Global Salafism: Islam's new religious movement*, 81–106. London: Hurst.

Walbridge, Linda (ed.) 2001. *The most learned of the Shi'a: the institution of the marja'i taqlid*. Oxford: Oxford University Press.

2014. *The thread of Mu'awiya: the making of a* marja' al-taqlid, John Walbridge (ed.) Bloomington, IN: The Ramsay Press.

Weber, Anne Françoise. 2008. Briser et suivre les normes: les couples islamo-chrétiens au Liban. In Barbara Drieskens (ed.), *Les metamorphoses du marriage au moyen-orient*, 13–31. Beirut: Presses de l'IFPO.

Weber, Max. 1978. *Economy and society* (2 vols.), Guenther Roth and Claus Wittich eds. Berkeley, CA: University of California Press.

2001. *The Protestant ethic and the spirit of capitalism*, T. Parsons trans. London: Routledge.

2004. *The vocation lectures*, David Owen and Tracy Strong eds., Rodney Livingstone trans. Indianapolis, IN: Hackett Publishing Company.

Weiss, Max. 2010. *In the shadow of sectarianism: law, Shi'ism, and the making of modern Lebanon*. Cambridge, MA: Harvard University Press.

Welchman, Lynn. 2007. *Women and Muslim family laws in Arab states: a comparative overview of textual development and advocacy*. Amsterdam: Amsterdam University Press.

White, Benjamin. 2011. *The emergence of minorities in the Middle East: the politics of community in French Mandate Syria*. Edinburgh: Edinburgh University Press.

Winter, Stefan. 2010. *The Shiites of Lebanon under Ottoman rule, 1516–1788*. Cambridge: Cambridge University Press.

Woodward, Bob. 1987. *Veil: the secret wars of the CIA 1981–1987*. New York, NY: Simon and Schuster.

Wynn, Lisa. 2008. Marriage contracts and women's rights in Saudi Arabia: *mahr, shurut*, and knowledge distribution. In Asifa Quraishi and Frank E. Vogel (eds.), *The Islamic marriage contract: case studies in Islamic family law*, 200–214. Cambridge, MA: Islamic Studies Program, Harvard Law School (Distributed by Harvard University Press).

Yilmaz, Ihsan. 2005. Inter-madhhab surfing, neo-ijtihad, and faith-based movement leaders. In Peri Bearman, Rudolph Peters and Frank Vogel (eds.), *The Islamic school of law: evolution, devolution, and progress*, 191–206. Cambridge, MA: Islamic Legal Studies Program, Harvard Law School.

Young, Michael. 2010. *The ghosts of martyrs square: an eyewitness account of Lebanon's life struggle*. New York, NY: Simon and Schuster.

Zahraa, Mahdi and Nora Hak. 2006. *Tahkim* (arbitration) in Islamic law within the context of family disputes. *Arab Law Quarterly* 20(1): 2–42.

Zalzal, Marie Rose. 1997. Secularism and personal status codes in Lebanon. *Middle East Report* 203: 37–39.

Zamir, Meir. 1985. *The formation of modern Lebanon*. Ithaca, NY: Cornell University Press.

Zubaida, Sami. 1993 [1989]. The ideological preconditions for Khomeini's doctrine of government. In his, *Islam, the people and the state*, 1–37. London: I.B. Tauris.

2003. *Law and power in the Islamic world*. London: I.B. Tauris.

Zuhur, Sherifa. 2002. Empowering women or dislodging sectarianism? Civil marriage in Lebanon. *Yale Journal of Law and Feminism* 14: 177–208.

Zulficar, Mona. 2008. The Islamic marriage contract in Egypt. In Asifa Quraishi and Frank E. Vogel (eds.), *The Islamic marriage contract: case studies in Islamic family law*, 231–274. Cambridge, MA: Islamic Studies Program, Harvard Law School (Distributed by Harvard University Press).

Index